MW00980328

High-Resolution Graphics Display Systems

Jon Peddie

Windcrest®/McGraw-Hill

New York   San Francisco   Washington, D.C.   Auckland   Bogotá
Caracas   Lisbon   London   Madrid   Mexico City   Milan
Montreal   New Delhi   San Juan   Singapore
Sydney   Tokyo   Toronto

FIRST EDITION
SECOND PRINTING

© 1994 by **Windcrest**.
Published by Windcrest, an imprint of McGraw-Hill, Inc.
The name "Windcrest" is a registered trademark of McGraw-Hill, Inc.

Library of Congress Cataloging-in-Publication Data

Peddie, Jon.
    High-resolution graphics display systems / by Jon Peddie.
        p.   cm.
    Includes index.
    ISBN 0-8306-4292-7   ISBN 0-8306-4291-9 (pbk.)
    1. Information display systems.   2. Computer graphics.   3. Video
display terminals.   I. Title.
TK7882.I6P43   1993
006.6'2—dc20   92-21418
                                             CIP

Editorial team: Jennifer Holt DiGiovanna, Acquisitions Editor
                Kellie Hagan, Book Editor
Production team: Katherine G. Brown, Director
                Tina M. Sourbier, Coding
                Rose McFarland, Layout
                Wendy L. Small, Layout
                Linda L. King, Proofreading
                Jodi L. Tyler, Indexing
Design team: Jaclyn J. Boone, Designer
                Brian Allison, Associate Designer   WC1
Cover design and illustration: Sandra Blair, Harrisburg, Pa.   4320

Acknowledgments

It took me literally years to research and write this book. I spoke with every monitor and flat-panel manufacturer, every color-system producer, hundreds of users and integrators, and dozens of application suppliers. It was amazing to see how many experts in the field didn't agree on basic terms like *dot pitch* or *multimedia*. It was also amazing how cooperative and helpful everyone was. As you'll see, there are some interesting illustrations and photographs in the book. Most of them are from manufacturers and researchers, presenting the latest products and projects that will soon become products.

Contents

Foreword

As the Information Age matures, displays have an ever-increasing significance in our daily lives. The need to understand display systems is no longer limited to those who specialize in the field as technologists. I am pleased to introduce this book by Jon Peddie, who has compiled a complete compendium of information particularly suitable for the users and selectors of display systems.

In the past few years, the growth of interactive displays has been phenomenal. For 1993, the sale of computer displays in the U.S. is expected to surpass that of color TVs, which are selling at approximately 21 million sets per year. Our lives are filled with interactive displays: automatic teller machines, public phones, even terminals for purchasing gasoline. Yet there is very little information available on how display systems work and how to select an appropriate product for a specific application.

Jon has taken this into consideration and covered display technologies from various aspects: computer graphics, color perception, and display systems. There are many comments aimed particularly at system users, where the performance and economics of display systems is discussed. This book presents the information necessary to select an optimum display for a given application.

As someone who is engaged in display hardware manufacturing, I found that this book enhanced my understanding of display system issues. I trust that others will find the book very useful.

Dr. Tei Iki, Senior Vice President
Display Systems
Sony Engineering and Manufacturing of America

Preface

It used to be that only technicians and engineers had to be concerned with and understand display systems. They were esoteric and complex, and only a few scientists and engineers had them. Today, we all have a display system—be it a large 21-inch computer display, a 9-inch color flat panel in a laptop, or a 15-inch desktop unit. We use them for everything from spreadsheets and word processing to full-color, prepress, image enhancement, and computer-aided design. We use them every day, all day.

All displays are not the same, however, and one size does *not* fit all. A small 9-inch black-and-white (or orange or green) monitor was good enough for simple data entry and early word processing, but today we live in a world of graphics. We use graphical user interfaces on our PCs, Macintoshes, and UNIX workstations. We deal with scalable fonts, TV images, complex 2-D and 3-D drawings, medical images, and various graphic-art images and photographs. We've gone graphical and in the process put new demands on our displays and ourselves.

This book should help you make sense of all this new and potentially confusing technology, and provide you with answers to the following questions:

Why is a monitor important?   Knowing how to judge displays, both ones you own and units you're contemplating buying, is extremely valuable and important. Displays radiate, change color depending where they're placed, have various resolution parameters, and could flicker, just to name a few issues.

How does the display system affect color?   Getting good color from a display isn't trivial. The term *good* here doesn't mean good enough; it means correct. If you want to see a red apple on your screen, and if you want the same color printed, you have to know how color works in the monitor and various parts of a system.

Do different applications require different monitors?   Users who are concerned only with multimedia can probably be satisfied with a 15- to 17-inch display. Users who want to do computer-aided design or prepress color layouts will need a 21-inch display. But the physical size of the tube is just one of a half-dozen parameters used in selecting the proper display.

Should I consider a flat-panel display?   Are flat panels going to replace the trusty old CRT? Will we ever have TV on a wall? And what about HDTV? These are current and ongoing questions that users, managers, and people who integrate systems have. They're typically answered by consultants, salespeople, trade magazines, other users (usually those who've learned things the hard way), and, of course, books. The problem for the person asking the questions is how to resolve the different answers he gets for the same question. In this book, I'll give you not only the different ways these questions can be answered, but also the reasons for the answers.

I wrote this book because I couldn't conveniently find all the things I wanted to know, at one time or another, about displays. Also, I found that my need for information varied from one week to the next, which caused me to go looking through dozens of sources and question dozens of people. Furthermore, I often found that the answers I got were conflicting, and I had to do even more research to get the truth. I reasoned that if I had this need and was having problems (and mind you, I'm supposed to be an expert in the field), then others must be having the same problem. I bet people who haven't been trained as engineers must have fits trying to make sense out of all the information on displays.

Introduction

The most expensive part of a computer is its display system. It wasn't always that way. In the early days of minicomputers, monitors were small (9 or 11 inches in diameter) ASCII-based monochrome displays. High-resolution, color display systems with 19-inch monitors were just for computer-aided design and image processing—expensive top-end devices. Well, that was then and this is now. Today, every form of available information can appear on your screen, as illustrated by FIG. I-1.

Today, the computer world has gone graphical. Although Apple computer can't take credit for inventing it, the company certainly popularized graphics and created a general awareness of the benefits of a graphical environment. Computers with an ability to communicate using graphics have been with us since the early 1960s. The problem in providing a graphical display, as opposed to the 80×25 character display that computers have had since the 1960s, has been the cost of memory, processor speed, and the monitor. With today's advancements in large-scale integrated circuitry and the subsequent lowering of costs, powerful computers with multimegabytes of memory are within the budget of home-entertainment centers. However, the cost of display systems isn't dropping as quickly as the computers. Therefore, it behooves the user and system builders to know as much as possible about this most expensive part of a graphics-oriented computer system.

Graphics are everywhere

That doesn't mean that everyone has to become a computer technologist, any more than everyone had to become a telephone operator to be able to make a long-distance call. However, to use our phones we did have to learn about country codes, area codes (with and without a leading zero), time zones, and the difference between rotary and touch-tone dialing. Along the way, we also learned about answering machines, cordless phones, cellular phones, and (*where would we be without them?*) faxes.

The argument or criticism about the complexities of using a computer have been, ``When a computer truly becomes an appliance, then people will really use it.'' This is a silly position to take—one that denies the truth and places obstacles in front of the timid. Computers will never become an appliance any more than a fax, cellular phone, or a VCR is. Appliances, like toasters or refrigerators, aren't things you sit in front of all day and work with. If they were, there would be more controls on them and more features, or you'd get pretty bored after the first half hour.

Appliances are designed to perform one simple operation. Is a dishwasher an appliance? Of course, but take a look at the control panel of one of the new ones. No more rotary dial with only five settings; now there are either a couple of rows of buttons or a keypad, and often an LCD display the casual user can't operate (although most kids under 15 can). Like it or not, you live in a technology-based world and have to deal with machines, be they the in-dash CD player in your car, the VCR in your home, the video kiosk in your shopping center, or the computer you make your living with.

GRAPHIC DISPLAY SYSTEMS

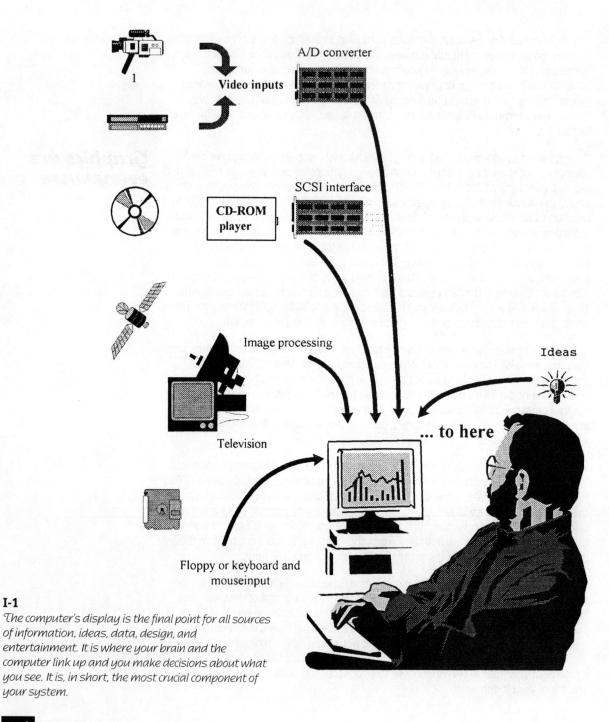

From here...

A/D converter

Video inputs

SCSI interface

CD-ROM player

Image processing

Ideas

Television

... to here

Floppy or keyboard and mouseinput

I-1

The computer's display is the final point for all sources of information, ideas, data, design, and entertainment. It is where your brain and the computer link up and you make decisions about what you see. It is, in short, the most crucial component of your system.

It's not really that difficult. Start by expanding your vocabulary and learning a few relationships and principles. There's really no memorization necessary; you'll remember what you need to do the job. The reason your VCR blinks 12:00 at you is because you can't remember how to set it. If you do set it, it's only after a power failure or because you changed over to daylight savings time. If you had to change it two or three times a week, it would be as natural to you as using the microwave. You don't have to learn new math, old math, or even fractions in order to use this book. Just as you learned that the VCR has to have its tape rewound before you can play it, you can learn the principles of your computer's display system.

And why should you, you ask? Because as cars, microwaves, ovens, telephones, TVs, and computers get more powerful and more useful, you have to make more choices about what you buy and how you're going to use them. If all you want to do is heat water quickly for a cup of tea, you don't need a 1,500-watt multifunctional microwave oven with four preset timers and 128 levels of power, plus a rotisserie and browning element.

And with prices steadily declining, you don't have to buy features you won't need for the next one or two years. In one or two years, you'll be able to throw away your current system and get a much better one for the same or less money.

What's in it for me?

This book is going to be your guide and reference source for all the questions you've had about display systems. You don't have to memorize it—just read it and remember you have it. Then when you encounter a question, refer to the book. And you'll likely encounter questions during a variety of procedures: installing new software, upgrading your computer or buying a new one, changing jobs and inheriting a computer, or making recommendations for a computer system.

Remember—if you're like most workers today, whether in a small or large company, government, university, factory, or distribution organization, you probably spend four to eight hours a day looking at a computer display. Is your productivity being improved or hampered by it? How could it be improved? What more could it provide? Ask yourself these questions and, better still, answer them.

The trend in modern offices and factories is to give workers as much responsibility as they can handle. Then they can provide recommendations and sometimes demands. The net result is a more efficient operation, happier, more fulfilled employees, and an environment people want to be in. If you're going to take your rightful place in that scenario, you have to be prepared to bring something to the party.

There's also the issue of health and safety. Display systems radiate all types of emissions. Some, like x-rays, are known to be harmful and are attenuated and deflected. Others, like low-frequency electromagnetic radiation, might not be harmful, but we're still collecting data. In the meantime, some standards and laws have been suggested or imposed. Do you know what they are? Does your display system comply? There's also the issue of eyestrain—again, how does your display measure up? Hopefully, this book will help you with those issues as well.

So here's what you'll get in this book. It will explain the hardware, and explain software only when it's necessary to describe a relationship. *There's no code, nor any software examples in this book*, so you don't have to be an engineer to read it. I'll discuss hardware in terms of operation, not theory—so there's no math (well, there's one place where math is necessary, but I promise it'll be easy). If you've gotten this far, you have a pretty good idea of what the writing will be like—informal, direct, and hopefully informative. I'll present things in a step-by-step manner, and the more advanced of you can jump ahead until you're challenged.

History of display

I've designed this book to be a major reference source for you. With such a goal, it's necessary to provide a little history so you'll know how we got where we are. With that introduction, let's take a look at where these graphical display systems came from.

Graphic display systems were independently developed in three industry application areas: image processing (IP), computer graphics (GC), and television (TV). There are good reasons why they were developed independently and why they'll eventually merge. Let's look briefly at each one.

Image processing

Image processing was begun with the goal of using electronics as an augmentation (and hopefully someday as a replacement) for silver-halide image film capture and analysis. It was started by the newspapers of the 1890s as a way to send images or pictures great distances faster than the mail could provide. In the 1950s and 1960s, image processing was used to capture and analyze military intelligence. Also in the 1960s, it was used for remote sensing of geological, geographical, and agricultural effects. Then it was applied to medical diagnosis and machine vision applications (production-line inspection and robotics). In the 1980s, it was adopted by the graphic arts industry and used to create special effects in still photographs and advertising.

Computer graphics

Computer graphics was begun to provide a means to visualize data and concepts. The old saying "a picture is worth a thousand words" has been the motto of computer graphics for decades. Probably the first use of computer graphics was the SAGE air-defense system developed in the mid 1950s. It was used to convert radar information into computer images. In 1962 at MIT's Lincoln Labs, with a garage-sized computer called TX-2, Ivan Sutherland demonstrated his now famous Sketchpad, considered by many to be the birth of the computer graphics era. Early experiments with visualization were conducted at RAND Corporation in 1968, and again at Xerox PARC.

These early demonstrations sparked the imagination of developers and users. Companies and governments were using miles of paper to print out tabular columns or data. Often, that data could be summarized and demonstrated with a pie or bar chart. That was the beginning of data presentation and visualization.

At the same time, following a more obvious track from Sutherland's experiment, developers worked with computer-aided engineering systems. The early ones used a display technology known as *vector refresh* or *vector stroke*. They were later replaced by raster displays, similar in construction to a TV. The early displays were line drawings. Later developers filled in the boxes and added color. That led to photorealism, the ultimate in visualization—a simulation of something that never materially existed.

Television

Television was the logical follow-up from radio—moving images in your home. It has been largely responsible for the availability of most of the technology used in computer displays. With TV also came certain limitations, due to the time period in which it was developed and the need to keep costs down.

The concept of an interlaced display and the use of power lines for synchronization were very clever ideas that helped put TV within the price range of millions of families. Television hasn't changed much since AT&T, RCA, and Westinghouse first demonstrated it in 1927. The last major change was the adoption of a color standard, NTSC, by the U.S. in 1953. Today, major changes are being introduced in the form of HDTV. *I Love Lucy* will never be the same.

Image processing has been described as the use of a computer to manipulate real images, computer graphics uses a computer to create simulated images from data, and television has been an adjunct to both types of computer-based display systems. Each display system—image processing, computer graphics, and television—initially used a different technology to create and display its images. Today, elements of all three are finding their way into each other's domain. The net result is a richness in presentation, imagery, visualization, information content, and entertainment.

As these technologies merge and integrate, visualization, virtual reality, and multimedia (the merging of television and computer graphics) will become the same. HDTV will stimulate system designers and help lower the cost of computer graphics. Flat-panel displays will continue to get larger and have higher resolutions. Eventually, we'll have large, thin, full-color, high-resolution screens on our walls where we communicate with friends, peers, and relatives, create new forms or presentations and ideas, and play games of unimaginable realism and complexity.

This book contains four chapters on display-system components and a glossary. Each chapter is designed to be self-contained and complete; therefore, you can go directly to the topic or chapter in which you're most interested. When appropriate, I'll make references to other chapters.

How this book is organized

Applications are described in chapter 1. As mentioned earlier, this isn't a programmer's book, so don't expect any code examples. However, there are issues concerning applications' display system needs and how the application software affects performance.

Display systems are components of, or *peripheral* to, a computer. There are dozens of types of computers, also known as *platforms*. Users, publicists, and manufacturers define them in various ways: minicomputers, supercomputers, workstations, PCs, etc. They're also defined by their location or size: remote servers, mainframes, desktops, laptops, desksides. This book focuses on the desktop and deskside computer, with a few references to laptops. These platforms are based on a few popular bus types: ISA, Microchannel, NuBus, and VME.

The elements of display controllers and different types of display controllers are not covered in this book. (For an explanation of controllers (adapters) and their components, refer to *Multimedia and Graphics Controllers*.) However, it's interesting to note that most people are surprised to learn that a VGA controller is a dumb frame buffer, and not (originally) a very sophisticated device.

Chapter 2 deals with color, and there are plenty of issues involved. Color generation in a display controller isn't trivial. Color WYSIWYG ("what you see is what you get") is a complex topic, and one that could fill a book of its own. Therefore, chapter 2 won't teach you how to do color reproduction, but it will show you what the "gotchas" are.

The monitor is, in most cases, the most expensive component in a display system. They're complex devices based on technology that was developed in the early

1920s. Monitors have continued to evolve with the demands of the market and the technology that drives them. Reports of their demise are greatly exaggerated. Chapter 3 explains how they work and provides clear-cut, unambiguous definitions of the most often misused terms and specifications.

In chapter 4 I'll describe and discuss flat panels. Flat-panel displays are the wave of the future. To date, they've seen their greatest usage in laptops, some military systems, a few process-control systems, and in some offices where radiation is a concern. New flat-panel technologies are being developed that will accelerate their use. Those technologies are explored in the chapter.

There is also a glossary and a list of acronyms in this book. The glossary is a comprehensive list of terms and definitions used with display-system technology. One of the most difficult parts of doing research on a topic, whether you're trying to make a purchase decision or write a book, is understanding the jargon. The problem is compounded when various manufacturers and users can't agree on the same names. Therefore, one of my goals was to establish a consistent and logical lexicon of terms.

Conventions

Wherever possible, I've used industry-standard terms and definitions. Although I use acronyms and abbreviations in speech and in several informal articles I've written, I won't do so here. The reason isn't to be pedantic; it's so you won't need a decoder to understand or use this book. Although terms like *blt'ing* might be common to controller designers and even the folks who sell them, it's a confusing term for mere mortals.

Having said that, I must also explain that there are some terms that are considered generic and common in the computer industry: for example, the letters *K* (kilo) and *M* (mega) denoting thousand and million, respectively, the term *byte* for 8 bits, the letter *S* for seconds, and the term *Hz* for Hertz (cycles/second). Therefore, if a monitor uses a signal that has a speed of 5 million cycles per second, I'll refer to it as 5MHz signal. If a controller uses 2 million bytes of memory, I'll describe it as 2Mb. Such memory is known as random-access memory and is commonly referred to as *RAM*. If it's a special type of RAM used for video applications, it's referred to as VRAM. Therefore, a controller could be described as having 2Mb of 100MHz VRAM—two million bytes of 100-million-cycles-per-second video random-access memory. Other common terms I've used in this book are *CRT* for cathode-ray tube, and *RAMDAC* for the combination of RAM and digital-to-analog converters integrated into one chip.

In some cases, I'll introduce or use a term in lieu of a common term or expression. For example, the term *dot pitch* is used extensively in the industry. As it turns out, the word *pitch* is misused, as is explained in chapter 4. So I use the term *dot triad* to describe the three-color phosphor dots in a CRT.

Finally, at the risk of explaining the obvious, references throughout the book to FIG. C-1, FIG. C-2, etc. are telling you to look at the appropriate color illustration in the color section, located near the middle of the book.

Summary

I've written this book for users, system builders, and designers of display systems, and designed it to bring together all the issues concerning modern display systems. I created it to provide a single source of explanation for the elements of a display system, and also as a reference source. Although not as riveting perhaps as *Gone with the Wind* or *War and Peace*, it's written to be easy, friendly, interesting reading. I hope you find this book useful and engaging, and the topic to be as interesting as I do.

1 *Applications*

As outlined in the Introduction of this book, graphic display systems were begun independently in three industry application areas: image processing, computer graphics, and television. There are good reasons why they were developed independently and why they will and should merge. Let's look briefly at each one:

❑ Image processing was begun with the goal of using electronics as an augmentation (and hopefully someday a replacement) for silver-halide image film capture and analysis.

❑ Computer graphics was created to provide a means of visualizing data and concepts.

❑ Television has become the ultimate source of information, a training vehicle, an entertainment source, and the most ubiquitous, pervasive communication of mankind.

You've already seen some of the effects of merging these segments in creating the new application area called *multimedia*. Visualization and multimedia will merge into a new ultra-realistic simulation vehicle, and HDTV will contribute to reducing the cost of computer graphics.

This chapter is designed to give you an overview of the major applications that use graphic display systems. It will introduce you to the commonly used terms and hopefully provide some clarification of those terms. It isn't a tutorial on the applications or the theories behind them, although I'll be discussing some of the mechanisms and processes. Figure 1-1 shows some of the most common applications in use today.

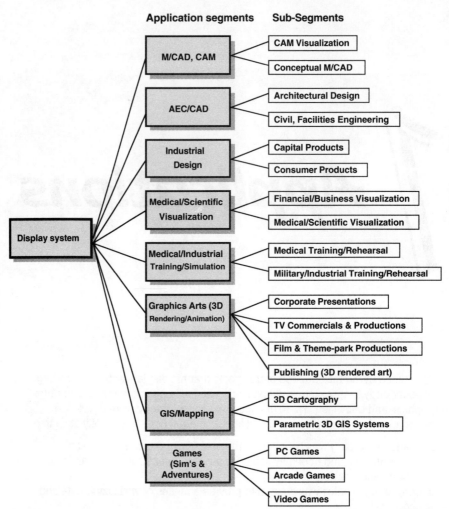

Application segments **Sub-Segments**

M/CAD, CAM
- CAM Visualization
- Conceptual M/CAD

AEC/CAD
- Architectural Design
- Civil, Facilities Engineering

Industrial Design
- Capital Products
- Consumer Products

Medical/Scientific Visualization
- Financial/Business Visualization
- Medical/Scientific Visualization

Medical/Industrial Training/Simulation
- Medical Training/Rehearsal
- Military/Industrial Training/Rehearsal

Graphics Arts (3D Rendering/Animation)
- Corporate Presentations
- TV Commercials & Productions
- Film & Theme-park Productions
- Publishing (3D rendered art)

GIS/Mapping
- 3D Cartography
- Parametric 3D GIS Systems

Games (Sim's & Adventures)
- PC Games
- Arcade Games
- Video Games

Display system

1-1
There are several major computer graphics applications, each having two or more subcategories. Although there is some overlap in these applications, several of them make specific demands on a display system.

There are many applications that use or require specific graphics capabilities and supports to function. Although these applications are similar and are in several cases merging, there are still some specific distinctions between them. These differences place sufficiently different demands on the display controller so it can be maximized for one application over another. This, in turn, reduces the cost of the display system. This usually results in one of two types of controllers:

❑ Great at application A, average to poor on B
❑ Average on A and B

Knowing which type of application you're using, or plan to use, will allow you to select the best, most cost-effective display system. The second choice (average on A and B) isn't a bad choice if you're using several types of applications on a regular basis.

The major types of applications are either vector or bit-map based. In this chapter, I'll explain the difference between the two for future discussion. I'll also discuss the classification of user types. Users and system builders of graphic display systems vary in experience, usage of applications, and price range of their displays. In this chapter, like the rest of the book, I'll use a few popular or illustrative examples to make a point or provide a foundation for future discussion. This doesn't mean that the chapter is a comprehensive list of all applications, or even a recommendation.

Vision contributes more to our understanding of the world than all other forms of sensory stimulation combined. The rich visual environment offered by most computers today will elevate the appeal of modern desktop systems from enjoyable to irresistible.

Humans assimilate information through their visual sense more readily than through any other means. Imaging, TV, and graphics technology is being integrated into virtually every computer application. As it is, this technology will follow the introduction of low-cost, visual or graphical user interfaces and applications, and easy-to-use visual data-display products. These applications and products will provide access to visual data in a way that emphasizes the strengths of computer systems and, in doing so, provide the foundation for an emerging mass market of integrated applications.

Applications are already appearing or are under development that will take you beyond what-you-see-is-what-you-get to a world of what-you-see-is-what-you-think, or what-you-want. Visualizing the richness of the imagination will allow you to examine and explore real data, fantasy, and what-if scenarios.

Such visualizations, virtual or real, will propel humankind ahead in understanding not only the physical world but also a new age of enlightenment, as cause-and-effect situations are simulated. The merging of these powerful presentation technologies, combined with creative and analytical tools, will create a new global awareness, and as some philosophers predict, a new global consciousness. To appreciate how these developments will take place, however, you must first understand some of the concepts of the technology, appreciate the historical developments that have got us to this point, and know a little bit about the characteristics of today's users.

People who use graphic display systems can be segmented by type or class of user. Look at these classifications and determine which one you and your organization fits in. Users often migrate from one to another as job requirements change. Migration is also stimulated by a better awareness of the possibilities and potential of other systems.

While user categorization is described in many ways by various market research and social scientists, for the purpose of this book users are segmented in two ways: by experience and buying habits or preference. There's a third segmentation that can also be used: the cost of a display controller.

There are four levels of experience: the novice or casual user, the professional, the power user, and the second-time buyer.

Casual & novice users   A casual or novice user is one who spends less than 50% of his time on any single application. Such a person might have a desktop computer (PC, workstation, etc.) that might be high performance (i.e., a SPARC or

The visual sense

Graphic display users

Experience

Pentium), with more than one application (word processing, spreadsheet, computer-aided design or desktop publishing, etc.).

It's possible for a casual user in one application (e.g., computer-aided design) to be a professional user of another application (e.g., word processing). People who use word-processing software comprise the largest group of users, and most of them are satisfied with a medium-resolution display and a 14- or 16-inch monitor. Casual users will be interested in a high-resolution display if they're involved with any GUI-based applications. An extended VGA display will suffice for the PC user and the built-in display that comes with a workstation or Macintosh will satisfy those casual users.

A casual user might spend most of his day in front of a computer working back and forth between one application (i.e., a word processor) and another (i.e., a database). Or a casual user might use one application for an hour or less, leave the program, and not come back to it for several hours or several days. A novice might use a program for several hours during the day but, due to either lack of interest or computerphobia, never understand its rules of operation.

These users don't place much demand on a computer or its display system, and usually get hand-me-down systems as the more aggressive users move on to more powerful systems.

Professional users   The professional user spends a significant percentage (more than 30%) of time performing graphics and graphics-related tasks on a high-performance computer. The professional user employs a desktop-publishing, computer-aided design, or image-processing package at least four and typically up to six or more hours a day. He or she is often a technical writer, graphic artist, drafter, mechanical engineer, business or financial analyst, or scientist.

The professional user often has a Pentium or 486, 68040 Macintosh, or RISC-based workstation and requires at least a high- or very high-resolution display. Most professional users prefer a 19-inch or larger monitor but, due to budget limitations, will get by with a 17-inch display.

A professional user doesn't have any problem demonstrating the return on investment (ROI) that can be obtained with a high- or very high-resolution display. The ROI is realized through the increase in productivity due to higher throughput, and can be obtained by employing more powerful, albeit more expensive, equipment.

Power or crucial users   The power user is a special case and can be either a casual or a professional user. The difference is that power users feel they must have the fastest, largest (memory, screen, etc.), most powerful system possible. They usually also have the budget or backing of management to support these desires. This is the smallest segment and the users in it require at least a high- and usually a very high-resolution display. A 17-inch monitor is often acceptable, but a 19-inch is preferred by the power user.

The power user is often derided as a prima donna or over-patronized darling of some senior manager. However, these power users are really the vanguard of our organizations. They try the latest hardware and software and are usually the ones to go when there is a particularly difficult problem.

Second-time buyers   This is typically a person who started out as a novice or casual user with a low- to medium-resolution display (e.g., Macintosh Classic, 640×480 workstation, or standard VGA). Such users will add high- and very high-resolution displays to their systems as their experience level, work level, and frustration with slow, low-resolution displays increases. This is a component of normal experiential growth and can also be thought of as a lateral move from casual to professional.

These users approach the market with different expectations, needs, budgets, and experience. They also seek products through different sales channels.

The buyers of display controllers and monitors fall into four categories: price, standard brands, discriminating, and specialist.

Price   Price-sensitive users will buy only the least expensive item available. They have no preference for brand names and view all computers and add-ons as generic; therefore, price is the only logical discrimination. The price-motivated buyer will mix and match components from different manufacturers and suppliers.

Standard brands   Some buyers are influenced by advertising and wants to make what is considered a "safe buy." This buyer holds similar views about products being generic, but believes there is either better quality or support from a brand-name company. The standard-brands buyer will try to buy a complete system from one company or supplier.

Buyers in general want to buy a standard name-brand product. They identify with it (and the alleged prestige it imports) and from an imagined union with other buyers of the brand. This is an important aspect to marketing, one often missed by manufacturers. Typically, a company will sense a user commitment to their brand or company name, and use that as a justification to charge more for its product. Except in the case of luxury automobiles, ladies' shoes and men's watches, this doesn't work for long. In the computer industry, with dozens of similar products, it works only for the first-time buyer.

Discriminatory   A buyer becomes discriminatory due to experience, education, and sometimes by forming opinions from reading articles or advertisements. The discriminatory buyer might buy a computer from one company, the graphics board from someone else, and the monitor from still another company. He will typically choose brand-name products, for the same reasons as stated in the previous paragraph.

Specialist   The specialist has technical experience (usually hard-won), knows how computer systems work, and isn't afraid to tackle its integration and setup. The specialist will buy from various vendors, and choose products for their price and performance and almost never by brand name alone.

The relative ratio of these types of buyers is roughly 27% for the price buyer, 27% for the brand-name buyer, 32% for the discriminatory buyer, and 14% for the specialist. These ratios change as users become more sophisticated and products more generic. TABLE 1-1 shows the relative relationship between experience and buying habits. In addition to experience and buying habits, users have also come to segregate products by price ranges.

Table 1-1
Users can be assigned to four categories, each
approaching product selection from a different angle.

	Price	Standard brand	Discriminatory	Specialist
Casual	◆	◆		
Professional		◆	◆	
Power			◆	◆
Second-time user	◆		◆	

Price range   In the early 1990s, a new market definition based on a combination of price and performance was introduced for add-in boards and monitors. Three segments, loosely defined as low end, mid range, and high end, were defined.

The separation point on these ranges varies over time as products drop in price and newer technologies are introduced. However, the notion will always be with us because there are so many analogs in the consumer and retail markets.

Low end   This segment is primarily for the PC because Macintosh and UNIX workstations came with built-in medium-resolution displays. VGA and SuperVGA boards are the least expensive, and millions of buyers have purchased them. Although most of the new-generation PCs have built-in graphics with VGA or better resolution, there are still many low-cost boards and monitors sold for retrofit, and new systems without built-in graphics. These products are labeled as entry-level products.

Mid range   The products in this segment are add-in boards and monitors for all platforms and upgrade options. They typically cost between two and four times as much as an entry-level product, and provide at least high resolution (1024×768) with 256 colors. They will have a controller or accelerator capability.

High end   At this point, the cost of specialized silicon on the add-in board starts to take effect. Boards costing two to five times more than mid-range products with various controllers and megabytes of RAM are in this category. High-quality 19-inch monitors costing as much or more than the computer are also in this range.

Now you know who you are, why you are, why you buy what you do, and possibly what you might become. The remainder of this chapter will focus on applications: their needs, characteristics, and results.

Applications & resolution   As you'll discover throughout this book, one of my goals in writing it is to stabilize terminology. Because computer graphics and display systems have evolved from three separate application areas, with influences from other areas (such as printing and photography), several terms are often found for the same thing. Similarly, one term might be used to describe multiple items.

It might be too ambitious to hope that my definitions in such areas of ambiguity will be universally accepted, but at least I can impose them here. I do so more for efficiency than posterity. Therefore, even if you don't fully agree with my definitions, please accept and apply them while using this book.

The following then is a discussion of one of the most-often-used terms in computer graphics—*resolution*. Throughout this book, I'll be providing you with definitions. At the end of the book is a glossary, which will be a bit redundant considering the definitions within the text, but easier to access. Included in the glossary is also an acronym list to help protect you from (to quote Randy Stickrod, founder of the magazine *Computer Graphics World*), "the tyranny of technobabble."

Resolution is defined in several ways, depending upon application, industry, and history.

Resolution

Photographic & image processing   In the photographic and image-processing industry, resolution is measured by the number of shades (of gray) that can be discerned with the naked eye. This is also known as interference cycles.

Desktop publishing   In the area of desktop publishing, resolution is measured in terms of dots per inch (dpi), also called *dot density*. A laser printer can print at between 300 and 1200 dpi. Most high-resolution displays can reach a maximum of 120 dpi.

Graphic arts   In the graphic arts and retouching industry, resolution is measured in dots per mm, and is referred to with a *Res* number. For example, Res 40 is 40 dots/mm or approximately 1000 dots (or pixels) per inch.

Prepress, halftones, & screens   Word-processing programs have gained so much functionality that they now compete with desktop publishing (DTP) and page-layout programs. However, one area where they do not compete with high-end layout programs is in preparing documents for reproduction at a printer, especially if the layout contains color, halftone screens, or grayscale photographs. Preparing documents with photographs, multicolor graphics, and screens (which represent percentages of solid colors) all require special treatment.

Hardcopy output devices, printers, imagesetters, slide recorders, and plotters print at various dpi values. Most laser printers print at 300 dpi, but some more expensive models can print at 600 or even 1200 dpi. Imagesetters print from 900 to 3000 dpi and beyond. The higher the resolution, the smaller the dots, which means more detail and subtleties, sharper lines and curves, and cleaner halftone screens and photographs. A combination of screen frequency and resolution affects image quality; resolution determines the printer's ability to print higher screen frequencies.

Halftones or screens (the terms are used interchangeably) are expressed as a percentage of a solid color. Grayscale photographs, in which shades of gray are made up of percentages of black, are basically screens, as are the percentages of colors that make up a four-color drawing or photograph.

Halftones

Grayscale, also known as halftone, is measured in terms of the wire mesh or screen used to give discrete points (which could be considered pixels) to the image. The screens are quantified by the lines per inch of the screen, and is expressed as *lpi*. Grayscale printing is affected by both the lpi of the screen and the dpi of the printer. Just because a scanner can pick up 256 shades of gray doesn't mean that's how many shades the printer can accommodate. Printers with 300-dpi resolution can achieve only about 25 shades of gray because of their resolution and screen-frequency restraints. The highest screen-frequency setting that 300-dpi laser printers have (before quality degradation) is about 60 lpi. Based on the following equation, the calculated grayscale level for an image printed with a laser is 25 shades of gray. Sixty lines per inch on a 300-dpi printer will give you 25 levels of gray. Here's the equation:

$$\text{graylevels} = \frac{\text{resprinter}}{\text{screenfreq}^2}$$

There are various reasons for adjusting shades of gray, the most important being continuous-tone quality. Other reasons include file size and printing time. The higher the resolution and lpi, the bigger the file and the longer it takes to print.

Another important issue, but beyond the scope of this book, is the ink spread on different paper types. The differences in how soft newsprint and coated glossy (magazine-quality) paper accept ink is crucial.

Color   Color resolution refers to the total number of colors displayable by each pixel. The number of colors that can be shown on the screen at one time is a function of the number of memory planes (or bits/pixel) and shouldn't be confused with the palette or potential number of colors. True color refers to 24-bit pixels, which yields over 16 million colors per pixel. Refer to TABLE 1-2 for a list of the various color resolutions used in graphic display systems.

Table 1-2
The names used for various color ranges vary from one manufacturer to another. This table lists the most commonly used terms.

Name	Bit range	Nominal bits per pixel	Colors
Low color	2 – 7	4	16
Pseudo color	8 – 14	8	256
High color	15 – 23	15	32,768
		16	65,536
True color	24 – 32	24	16,777,216
Real or ultimate color	33 – 36	36	68,719,476,736

Since the introduction of high-color capability on the PC (due to the XGA controller and popular Sierra HiColor LUT-DAC), and also the emergence of multimedia, there has been a great deal of confusion over terms. High color can be 15-bits per primary (RGB) for a total of 32,768 colors or 16 bits, for a total of 65,536 colors. However, aggressive and perhaps unaware marketers have referred to this color-resolution range as *true* or *full color*. To compound the confusion, when a TV signal is digitized, it's in the YUV color space. There, 15 bits can represent the equivalent of 24-bit RGB color.

So if you aren't sure what a specification means when stating that a system has true, full, or high color, you should ask how many bits represent the color and in what color space.

Color ranges are just that—a range. Therefore, low color is from 2 bits to 7 bits, pseudocolor is from 8 bits to 14 bits (which includes the once-popular 12-bit 4096), high color is from 15 bits to 23 bits, and true color is 24 bits and above. There are some systems that offer 36-bit color (12 bits per primary) that are used in the movie and prepress industry. These systems have occasionally been described as *ultimate* or *real color*. Additional discussion on color can be found in chapter 2, *Color*.

Spatial   Spatial resolution defines the total number of displayable or viewable pixels. Spatial resolution determines the amount of detail you can see or create on a graphics screen. When spatial resolution is used, the positioning accuracy of a monitor's deflection amplifiers is involved.

Spatial resolution is a function of how many pixels can be directly addressed—which is determined by the frame buffer's organization and memory-management capabilities of the graphics controller. It also involves the monitor's spot size—the diameter of the smallest illuminated spot on the screen. Spatial resolution is influenced by the focusing electronics, tirade size, shadow-mask pitch size, and type of phosphor used in the monitor. These features and functions are discussed in more detail in chapter 3, *Monitors*.

Spatial resolution is measured in various ways (e.g., dot pitch, X-Y pixels, screen dpi) and isn't commonly used.

Addressable   Addressable resolution is measured in the number of pixels per line and the number of lines of the display memory. The total number of pixels in a display is the number of pixels per line multiplied by the number of lines. A system might have a much larger addressable display memory than that which can be displayed. For example, a displayable 1280×1024 screen probably has a 2048×1024 addressable display memory.

Maximum resolvable frequency   Analogous somewhat to sound perception, the eye has a resolvable frequency range. The frequencies in this case are alternating lines of black and white bands, or stripes. This resolvable frequency is often confused with the modulation-transfer function (MTF), which is a measure of the contrast ratio distortion between the input and output of elements in the display system. (Refer to chapter 3, *Monitors*.)

Displayable   In the general desktop-graphics industry, resolution is typically measured by the number of displayable pixels of the controller, and commonly referred to as *displayable resolution*. In this book, I'll use *displayable pixels* as the definition for resolution. TABLE 1-3 lists some of the most popular display resolutions for graphics controllers.

Table 1-3
A few of the most common resolutions.
There are over 15 "standard" resolutions available.

Name or category	Pixels	Lines	Resolution
Color graphics adapter (CGA)	340	200	Low
Original Macintosh	512	384	Low
Enhanced graphics adapter (EGA)	640	350	Medium
Hercules (Herc)	720	348	Medium
Video graphics adapter (VGA)	640	480	Medium
SuperVGA	800	600	Medium
High-resolution (HR) or extended VGA (EVGA)	1024	768	High
Super high resolution (SHR)	1152	864	High
Very high resolution	1280	1024	Very high

A VGA display has 307,200 displayable pixels; a SuperVGA display has 480,000 pixels. A 1024×768 display has 786,432 displayable pixels, 2.56 times as much resolution as a VGA display. That means that 2.5 times as much detail or information can be displayed and, with the right monitor, actually seen.

Evolution of displayable resolutions The first bit-mapped board for the PC was the Hercules, with 720×348 resolution. It was monochrome but it opened users' eyes to the benefits and possibilities of higher resolution. IBM introduced the 648×350 EGA, which was extended to 852×350 by various clone manufacturers. EGA became very popular in 1985–86 because of its color and higher (than CGA) resolution. However, due to its digital output, it had a limited color range. The need, interest, and demand for higher resolution in the PC was obvious.

The Macintosh was introduced with a monochrome bit-mapped display and a low resolution of 512×384. Subsequent models and equipment from third-party vendors increased that to 832×640 and then to 1152×900. The Macintosh is typically measured in dots per inch (dpi) on the screen.

Workstations started out with 640×480 and quickly moved to 1152×900 and 1280×1024. Those resolutions have become the de-facto standards for the workstation market.

Resolution is an often misused and misunderstood term in computer graphics, TV, and image processing. As has been illustrated, no single definition will suffice. Therefore, I advise you to take care when evaluating display systems and applications. As will be explained in subsequent sections, even in the various application categories, *resolution* might have different meanings.

Application categories

As mentioned earlier, different applications have different needs for a display system. While the differences between applications blur, their individual needs don't. A few years back, the segmentation was TV and computer graphics. Computer graphics was then segmented into line drawing and bit-mapping. Line drawing was considered to be a computer-aided design requirement, and bit-mapping was thought to be important for image processing.

Image processing included scientific and industrial applications, as well as graphic arts. Graphic arts then expanded to include photorealism. Graphic arts also spread over into CAD for rendering applications. It gave industry analysts, like yours truly, and journalists fits trying to come up with a tidy set of definitions. As soon as one or the other of us thought we had it figured out, some smart aleck would come along and say, "Yeah, but what about . . ." We finally realized that it was almost impossible to draw functional lines between applications. That was when I began to see the ultimate finality of graphic display controllers and got the inspiration for this book.

CAD systems need good line-drawing capabilities, however, and graphic arts and image-processing applications don't. And window-based and desktop-publishing applications need good bitBLT capabilities, but CAD doesn't. Yet, in some cases a user might need both line drawing and bitBLT in either CAD or graphic arts. That is an example of needing a graphics controller that's good at one thing, but just fair at another.

In the beginning, all applications were custom-designed for a particular company and machine. Eventually, certain "standard" applications, such as those controlling payroll, general ledger, and inventory, were developed, but only for certain machines—mainframes in the beginning, minicomputers later. That was followed by the development of languages, utilities, and then the first general-purpose programs, like database programs, which weren't applications but could be used to build them.

Killer applications

When the first microcomputers were introduced, they generally had a primitive word processor and the BASIC language. Users were encouraged to write their own applications and many did. Then VisiCalc was introduced first on the Apple and then with the Radio Shack TRS80, Commodore PET, and CP/M machines. It started the revolution, which was further fueled by the subsequent introduction of WordStar, one of the first really useful word-processing packages.

When IBM introduced the PC, a new company called Lotus came out with a VisiCalc-like program called 1-2-3, and the market exploded. Then the Macintosh was introduced and the growth of desktop machines began. Many people referred to Lotus 1-2-3 as a "killer application" because of the impact it had on PCs. It has been said that Lotus sold more PCs than IBM ever dreamed possible.

The growth of word-processing programs like WordPerfect also helped. WordPerfect's rapid growth greatly influenced the growth of the PC, and was considered to be another killer application. Ever since those days, developers have been looking for the next killer application. Workstation manufacturers have also been looking for a killer application for their platforms.

Killer applications have long been heralded as the vehicle through which the scientific and engineering workstation will achieve commercial market acceptance commensurate with its capabilities. However, that view overlooks the historical perspective of the development of PC markets, and doesn't consider the inherent strengths of modern RISC-based systems.

IBM and Apple Computer didn't truly create the PC market, but their entry gave it the spark needed to propel it from a hobbyist enclave to a mainstream business solution. The Macintosh is almost single-handedly responsible for the proliferation of graphical user interface applications.

However, workstation manufacturers can't simply replay the IBM or Macintosh strategy. Application portability and hardware independence are facts in high-performance computing. And the continuity of the Macintosh human/machine interface and, more recently, the Windows interface has broadened the acceptance of new applications beyond the PC-compatible "killers" of the past.

Apple opened up the desktop market, first by providing continuity in the human/machine interface and second by recognizing that simply being tolerable wasn't a good enough standard. The Macintosh made personal computing easy and, more importantly, enjoyable. It delivered basic functionality in a familiar format, and seduced the lay user into exploring the power of computers in nonessential applications.

The trade press abounds with editorial prophecies of killer applications that will deliver the mass market and enable workstations to assume their rightful and lofty place in the information revolution. If such a forecast is to come true, manufacturers need to move these systems out of the lab and onto the street, identify their strengths, and focus on how those strengths translate to more mundane problem-solving.

Workstations were developed with UNIX, and today the many varieties of UNIX represents the main if not the only operating system for workstations. UNIX became popular first in universities where a computer-literate generation was unwilling to be held captive by the proprietary operating systems of mainframe and minicomputer manufacturers. Today, the many UNIX-based workstation suppliers are scrambling to figure out how to keep 'em down on the farm—whether the issue is proprietary graphics and imaging libraries, machine-specific development tools and interfaces, or the ongoing struggle between OSF/Motif and Open Look.

Although a commitment to standards and open systems is crucial to the development of a mass market, so far it has been a lot of words and little action by the workstation suppliers. You still can't take an application running on one brand or workstation with its version of UNIX and go to another brand and run it—application portability hasn't made it beyond the PC and Macintosh environment. And without portability there can be no killer applications. The other problem in UNIX land is the cost of ownership. The same word-processing program that sells for a few hundred dollars for a PC or Macintosh costs a thousand dollars or more for a UNIX-based workstation—who needs that?

There are rays of hope, however. In the high-science UNIX community, where pride of ownership of complex nonportable programs is common, there have been some exceptions. Low-level image processing is selling in the document and publishing markets. There are other examples, as well. Some geographic information system (GIS) vendors (e.g., ESRI, TYDAC, and Genasys) have introduced relatively low-cost products designed to provide access to GIS data files, minus costly and cumbersome full-blown GIS application packages.

These programs are data viewers and little more than user interfaces for visual data display. Nonetheless, they're responsive to user needs and promise to expand the UNIX-workstation user base significantly. XV, public-domain, image-display software lowers the ante further, even though it does little more than display image data.

Such products will hasten the proliferation of UNIX systems in graphic arts, desktop publishing, and geographic information systems. The key to the development of a mass market for workstations is the exploitation of their unique facility with visual data across the broadest spectrum of applications. This defines the need for hardware-independent visual data display and manipulation of software platforms. Such systems should serve as stand-alone generic image and graphic display applications, but must also accommodate application-specific customization.

The advantage of multitasking operating systems and high-MIPS processors enjoyed by the UNIX workstation suppliers, however, might soon be history. With the advent of equally fast processors and multiple operating-system choices (OS/2, Open Desktop UNIX, NT, "Pink," and others) for the PC and Macintosh, plus their inherent portability and huge installed base of users, the workstation suppliers might have missed the boat.

One thing is for sure—it's the availability of useful, portable, low-cost applications that will decide which platform is the one of choice. It's not likely we'll see a killer application again because there's little pent-up demand for basic computing functionality. However, we *will* see applications that are so inviting and compelling that they'll take on the aura of a killer. These are great times and you couldn't have picked a better moment in history to participate in the computer revolution.

Although it's difficult if not impossible to segment by function alone, you can segment by general application classes, which is what I'm going to do. In the process, however, it will be unavoidable to refer to or use other applications and functions as examples.

Application functions

The main functions in the graphic display system used by various applications are vector or line-drawing operations and bit-mapped or raster operations. The following sections will discuss the important aspects of those functions as they relate to applications, and hopefully prepare you for the rest of this book.

Although this isn't meant to be a general-purpose book on computer graphics, it's almost impossible to write a book like this without setting some foundations. It has been my experience that there are more confused and curious users than there are graduate students, so that's who this book is aimed at.

In examining applications, you'll see how the industry segments are merging. In the beginning of this chapter, I mentioned the three major segments: image processing, computer graphics, and TV. CAD is a computer-graphics application based on line-drawing techniques, and is used as a means of visualizing ideas and data. However, to obtain more realism in the visualization, image-processing techniques have been employed to render and in some cases distort the views. Mapping applications make heavy use of image-processing techniques, but few maps exist that weren't created with line-drawing equipment. TV images are found in both segments, as backgrounds for architectural designs and as special enlargements of selected locations in mapping applications.

Therefore, although I'll make every attempt to neatly define and segment concepts, applications, and functions, you'll also be constantly reminded of their integration.

Line-drawing applications

Line-drawing or vector-based applications include mapping and the many variants of computer-aided design. This section will briefly cover those major application segments. I won't discuss the relative merits of one application or product over another, nor explain how to use the features or operations of specific applications. (There are literally hundreds of books available for that purpose.) This chapter and section are designed to simply explain the basic elements of line-drawing graphics applications and hopefully clear up any ambiguities or confusion about them.

Computer graphics traces its roots back to the early 1960s when Ivan Sutherland was at MIT. Sutherland developed interactive graphics programs on a computer that had a vector-drawing CRT display connected to it. His thesis, called Sketchpad, developed a wide variety of concepts, including object-oriented programming, constraint-based visual computing, and real-time interactive programming. But Sketchpad was a 2-D system; 3-D required too many calculations for the computers of the day.

Computer-aided design (CAD)

Computer-aided design, commonly referred to as CAD, has become a catch-all for many line-drawing application segments. CAD applications are highly dependent on line-drawing vector operations as well as clipping and other functions. Initially, I'll explain some of the most common CAD applications, and then the functions necessary to implement such applications. There are several varieties of applications in the CAD segment, including computer-aided engineering (CAE), computer-aided design and drafting (CAD or CADD), and computer-aided manufacturing (CAM). Uses for the different segments of computer-aided design include the following:

2-D   Mechanical, architectural, clothing, and printed-circuit layout design

3-D   Mechanical and architectural design

FEA   Wire-frame solid modeling and finite element analysis

CAE   Integrated-circuit design and logic design

CAM   NC pathing and printed-circuit photo plotting

The term *computer-aided design* has been applied to all manner of applications. Literally anything that involves design, from airplanes to xylophones, has probably had a computer aid in its design. Therefore, although 2-D drafting is the most common and popular CAD application, and the one usually referred to or thought of when CAD is mentioned, it's far from the only CAD application.

It's way beyond the scope of this book to list all or even most of the varieties of CAD applications. The purpose of this chapter, and this section in particular, is to give you a general acquaintance with the most common CAD applications, and illustrate the importance of the display-controller design and capabilities in supporting such applications.

Basic drafting, 2-D CAD

Automation is defined in the dictionary as "the use of a machine or electronic device to replace the use of human labor in routine or repetitive tasks." CAD programs are designed to this in order to automate the drafting process. Drafting is a demanding, labor-intensive task that has had little automation since it was begun several hundred years ago. And if there was ever a task that needed automation, it was drafting. With a manual system, there are several details that must be attended to before you can even draw a single straight line: the paper must be firmly and properly attached to the drafting table, the scale of the drawing has to be calculated or selected, the drafting machine (T-square) must be located at the correct point on the drawing, and the correct diameter pencil must be selected. Finally, you can draw a line to connect the points of the desired line.

Compare this process with drawing the same line using a CAD program (see FIG. C-1). The program has to be installed only once (the equivalent of setting up the drafting table, paper, pencil, drafting machine, etc.). Line color, type, and width are already set, although they can be changed. All you have to do is move the cursor to the point where you want the line to start and press the mouse button. Then move to where you want the line to end and press the button again. Bam, the line is drawn—at the exact width and correct length, in the right style and color. And what's most important is that it's in electronic form. That means it won't shrink, fade, or smudge. It can also be easily changed, and that's the real benefit of CAD. Changes cost less—a lot less.

Every CAD package performs four essential functions: drawing, data import/export, editing, and plotting or printing. All packages have basic 2-D tools for creating lines, circles, curves, complex lines (commonly referred to as polylines), areas, and text.

Once the lines have been drawn, they need to be edited. Most CAD packages allow you to copy, move, and rotate objects, and fill areas with patterns. They usually offer a snap-to function that aligns lines to preset grid points. And almost all programs have a dimensioning feature, which automatically computes the distance of lines and writes the dimensions on the drawing. You can specify the dimensions in any units, and automatically insert leaders and arrowheads.

Drafting programs let you create, store, and reproduce 2-D engineering drawings. The majority of CAD programs for the PC are of a 2-D nature. They all offer pretty much the same functionality by providing menus of commands for basic drawing operations (lines, circles, polygons, etc.). Most of the programs have the ability to replicate drawing details (like a window or a chair), and rotate or create a mirror image of a selected detail. Most programs have a set of libraries of predefined shapes and symbols, as well as a long list of third-party library products. Most of the systems allow multiple-layer-drawing capabilities (first used in the drawing of printed-circuit boards).

Editing functions allow you to move a point from one location to another, remove a line, erase or move a block, and change the line type (say from solid to dashed). A feature called *rubberbanding* stretches or contracts a line automatically when you change the position of its end points. And with *dragging* (dynamic tracking), you can use the cursor to move objects around on the screen until you find the desired placement.

2-D drafting or CAD programs have become so powerful and affordable that it's rare to see a more expensive workstation being used for such tasks.

Basic three-view drafting (top, front, side) is a 2-D representation of a 3-D object. Most CAD programs support some form of 3-D. Besides basic drafting operations (as discussed in the previous section on 2-D CAD), 3-D programs furnish other

3-D CAD

functions, such as isometric lettering, viewing features that let you examine a model from any angle, simultaneous displays of multiple orthographics views, and linkage between such views (so when a change is made in one view or window it's also made in all others). There are four popular methods of representing a 3-D drawing or model:

- Extrusion (2½-D)
- Wire-frame
- Surface modeling
- Solid modeling

Extrusion techniques make a simulated form of 3-D. An outline of an object—the profile of the molding of a picture frame, for example—is used as the raw data. It's then extended in the z axis to form an image and model of a section of the frame. There have been some very clever representations done with 2½-D techniques.

Wire-frames are the easiest true 3-D models to create and display. Almost identical to drawing in 2-D, the difference is that you can draw in any plane (x-y, x-z, or y-z). However, a wire-frame model can get confusing because it lacks depth cues; it's like the classic eye-trick image—is this box pointing in or out? Hidden-line removal is an important part of wire-frame construction and helps overcome some of the confusion in viewing a model.

Surface modeling is useful for creating objects for visualization. It basically fills in the polygons formed by a wire-frame model, while automatically performing hidden-line removal.

Solid modeling uses elementary 3-D objects such as blocks, cones, and spheres. Solid objects (usually stored in a library) are used in lieu of traditional 2-D elements such as lines, arcs, and circles. There's further discussion on surface and solid modeling later in this chapter, in the section on bit-mapped applications.

In the coming decade, many new 3-D applications will be developed for graphics, and by the year 2000 consumer devices should routinely have a realistic 3-D graphics capability.

Import/export As more users of all types get involved with CAD, file compatibility will become an issue. The two main formats for file transfer are Autodesk's AutoCAD DXF, and the industry standard IGES or PDES. These file formats are considered by some to be too low-level to be of major help. However, work continues on extensions in order to include 3-D and rendering functions.

Architectural CAD The architectural profession's initial use of computers had a relatively slow beginning, and was limited to digital replications of manual drafting. The use of wire-frame models, while familiar to mechanical CAD engineers and designers, represented a new type of abstraction for architects. Architects were used to dealing transparently and exclusively with lines and edges, which allowed the designer to study abstract compositional issues, such as relationships between edges and across space.

Throughout history, architectural design has used graphics to convey the meaning and character of buildings. Architects used renderings of proposed designs to illustrate the intent of the designer before the building was constructed.

The quality of our buildings and environment is often a discovery made by architects through sketching, drawing, and model-building (see FIG. C-2). However, unlike graphic arts or the entertainment industry, the electronic simulations used in architectural design, interior design, and landscape architecture aren't end products, although some do end up as sought-after illustrations. Rather, they're a means to anticipate proposed physical environments.

CAD affects the decisions made during the process of design in a number of ways: The methods and order of design activity are changed, new types of simulations are added to the modeling vocabulary, and the range of imagery is expanded. Of greatest significance are the new graphics techniques and modeling methods being offered every year that provide new insights and information during the process of design.

Wire-frame models (also called *edge-vertex* or *stick-figure* models) represent an object's bounding edges with interconnected lines. Introduced on CAD systems in the late 1960s, they're the predominant modeling method in use today (when you hear of a program as having a *modeler,* that means it can generate 3-D wire-frame models). Modelers are popular because wire frames consume relatively little processing time and memory. Moreover, users can construct the models with ease.

Wire-frame models & animation

Most wire-frame modelers have hidden-line routines. This operation erases edge lines that would normally be hidden from view if the model were solid in order to give the model a quasi-solid rather than transparent appearance. It also makes the geometry easier to interpret because the background lines are eliminated on the screen.

Developed as a means to gain insight and perspective about proposed designs of airplanes, cars, houses, space stations, and even bicycle helmets without the computational burden of a fully rendered image, wire frames brought a new visualization tool to designers (see FIG. C-3). Wire-frame designs, 3-D in nature, also provided the basis for the form to be later rendered. They let you look inside a wing, walk through a building, or check the wire routings of a drill handle. You can also string together different views to form an animation, a technique that proved very helpful in designing satellites that had expanding solar panels and antennas once they were in space.

Walk-throughs and simplified animation sequences through a proposed design often address questions discussed during the design process but rarely experienced or carefully studied. It's in one sense a simulation. Showing a path through a design, with specific vantage points, focal points of interest, and associated attributes presents a proposed design in a way unachievable before computers and CAD systems.

A designer, especially one inexperienced in the process of visualizing space based on the two-dimensional abstract conventions used by mechanical designers, drafters, and the architectural profession, can see how his proposed designs will be experienced. As a result, discussions about designs can be focused on what they *are* like rather than what they *might* be like.

With careful selection of the viewpoint (or "camera location"), you can get a good sense of how large an automobile's interior, a hand tool, or a building is. These are the concepts that have led to virtual reality (discussed in a later section in this chapter). By creating an animation of existing conditions, you can create a sense of scale on the computer screen that can then be transferred to the design of new projects.

Finally, animation permits a designer to meet the challenges of designing with shapes and physical constraints that are unique or unusual. Simplified animation takes architectural design into a more understandable and predictable world.

Finite element analysis

Finite element analysis (FEA) is a method for determining the effects of stress, temperature, and other forces on a structure. It's a mathematical analysis technique and not a design technique per se, but it uses graphic display systems and wire-frame-like images to reveal the findings, and so has been associated with CAD.

FEA represents a structure with a model consisting of a grid-like network of interconnected elements, each having characteristics determined by classical laws of physics and mechanics. Typically, such a model is given some type of a stress or distortion to see how it behaves. This is done to predict the behavior of a system, airplane, building, etc. before it's built. The results are displayed on a computer screen and usually color-coded to represent either stress or temperature change.

Mapping & GIS

Mapping applications involve extensive use of line drawing on a computer. Although a lot of designs such as new roads, housing developments, airports, and malls are created in the application segment of mapping, the majority of the activity is in illustrating existing land forms, subterranean structures, and demographic models.

In the late 1970s, the segment was renamed to reflect the broader scope of the activity. The term *mapping* wasn't a broad enough description of how computers were used to develop plats, plans, and underground speculations. The more descriptive term, *geographical information systems* (GIS) was adopted and the term stuck. The GIS segment includes a variety of geo-based applications, such as (but not limited to):

❑ Cartography
❑ Demographics
❑ Mapping
❑ Geopolitical
❑ Seismic
❑ Geophysical

One of the main differences between GIS applications and CAD applications is the source material. Generally speaking, GIS data comes from sensors in satellites, SONAR, hydraphone sensors, seismometers, aerial photography, and surveyor's measurements. Overlay data provided by census tabulations, various market survey demographics, forecasts, and historical data is also a major source of input for GIS applications.

The range of uses for GIS data is as diverse as CAD. Intelligence gathering, oil prospecting, emergency vehicle routing, market planning, geopolitical and historical evaluation, utility locating, and every other function that has some connection with the earth fits into GIS (see FIG. C-4).

There are two basic forms of GIS systems: grid-based and polygonal. Grid-based systems take an area and subdivide it into small square segments. Multiple planes of data are then overlaid to form a model. For example, a topographical map or street plan is often the base plane. Then overlays of vegetation, underground utilities, rivers and lakes, and animal migrations, etc. are added. Each plane is stored separately and referenced to other planes by the coordinates of the girds. Grid-based systems have proven to be very cost-effective, easy to manage with a computer, and easy to modify or update. The main criticism of them is the resolution of the grid. There's a point of diminishing returns when reducing the grid size.

Polygonal, or polygon-based, systems are more traditional and used by cartographers and developers. They too are used in planes with overlays. Capable of providing a more realistic look and feel, polygonal GIS can offer a finer degree of accuracy. However, as polygons are overlayed, they can create an artifact of new unwanted polygons if the overlays aren't perfect superimpositions.

Neither approach is the best, although advocates of each will bore you to death explaining why theirs is better and the other is full of error. The main point of interest for this book is that both approaches use graphics in their representations, and in general they make extensive use of the line-drawing capabilities of graphic display controllers.

As a result of the development of different types of systems, the Spatial Data Transfer Standard (SDTS) has been approved as Federal Information Processing Standard (FIPS) #173. It provides an exchange mechanism for the transfer of spatial data between dissimilar computer systems. The SDTS specifies exchange constructs, addressing formats, structure, and content for spatially referenced vector and raster (including gridded) data.

Advantages of the SDTS include data and cost sharing, flexibility, improved quality, and less duplication of effort, all with no loss of information. SDTS components are: a conceptual model, specifications for a quality report, transfer-module specifications, and definitions of spatial features and attributes.

One of the main parts of the standard is its profile development. A *profile* is a clearly defined and limited subset of FIPS 173, designed for use with a specific type of data. The most effective way to use FIPS 173 is to first define a profile; the encoding and decoding of software can then be designed to handle only the options in that profile. The USGS coordinates the development of FIPS 173 profiles to ensure maximum commonality and consistency. A profile for topological vector data is being tested and a profile for raster data developed.

The USGS coordinates the development of a suite of public-domain software tools, including a package designed to support the encoding and decoding of logically compliant SDTS data into and out of the required ISO 8211-FIPS file implementation. (ISO- 8211 is a general-information interchange standard.)

Vector operations

This section examines the specifications most important to line-drawing applications such as CAD and GIS. I won't examine bit-mapped specifications for solid modeling or image-processing applications because they are more rendering and raster-operation oriented (and covered later in the chapter). However, keep in mind that line-drawing and bit-mapped functions don't exist in a vacuum, and will coexist in most applications.

Line drawing & vectors

All vector-based applications use line-drawing capabilities. As stated previously, the major applications are in CAD and GIS. There's also a special class of animation and presentation graphics programs based on vector techniques.

Vector manipulation and treatment is a major area of interest in display systems. A vector is represented by two coordinate pairs: x1, y1 and x2, y2. Such a representation makes storage simple, dimensioning easy (which includes enlargement or shrinking), and rotation and clipping very manageable. The speed at which vectors can be drawn and the smoothness of the line are areas of regular improvement for vector drawing systems.

Resolution & productivity

Ever since CAD was introduced and designers gave up their drafting tables for a CRT, they've wanted to be able to see the whole drawing at one time. Not being able to do that, drafters and designers using CAD systems have had to rely on zooming, panning, and higher resolution in order to quickly get to various parts of a drawing. *Zooming* involves magnifying the image or drawing on the screen. *Panning* is moving the image to reveal parts that are off screen.

When CAD was first introduced on a PC, the displays were very limited in resolution. The first monochrome medium-resolution (MR) 720×348 controller was from Hercules. It used existing monitors, was reasonably priced, and was quite successful. In the early '80s, companies introduced the first generation of high-resolution (HR) 1024×768 controllers. It used monitors that were available from the minicomputer market that were more expensive but satisfied a need and therefore became a quasi-standard. Soon, many other companies entered the field.

The workstation market moved very quickly from the 640×480 range to 1152×800 and 1280×1024 resolution. Still, for most 2-D and 3-D CAD and complex GIS applications, that isn't enough resolution. The problem is that the user just can't see enough detail without using the zoom function of a display.

Various studies have measured the number of times a CAD operator performs a zoom operation. On average (the average depends on many variables), it's one to three times a minute. The primary reason for zooming is the need to see more detail in a drawing. Therefore, the more you can see, the less you need to zoom—right? Not really, but there *is* a relationship.

A user benefits in two ways from a high-resolution display: less confusion about lines that are in close proximity, and the ability to see more of the drawing. Both of these reasons reduce the number of times a zoom is needed. However, a zoom operation will always be needed to get to certain points within a drawing, so even having 10K×10K resolution would still not completely eliminate the need to zoom.

It has been estimated that an operator can eliminate about 10% to 20% of the number of zooms needed for each 100% of improvement in resolution (it's difficult to quantify this because it's a function of the operator's skill, the drawing size and complexity, and the activity required for the drawing). Therefore, if an operator using a medium-resolution 640×480 display makes 100 zooms per hour, with a high-resolution display (which has 150% more resolution) it would be reduced to 84 zooms per hour. With a very high-resolution display (which has 520% more resolution) it would be reduced to 58 zooms per hour, as shown in FIG. 1-2.

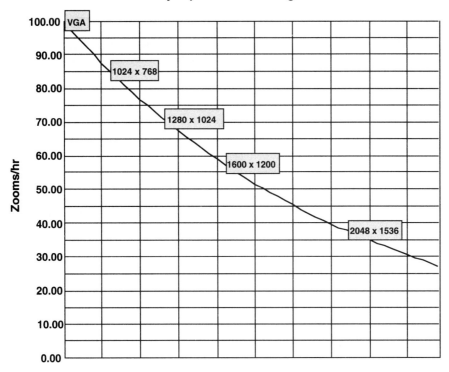

Productivity improvement with higher resolution

1-2 *As display resolution increases, a CAD user can see more of the drawing and therefore has to make fewer zooms, which are distracting. As a result, the user's productivity will increase with increasing resolution.*

Various attempts have been made to develop an analytical measurement of an operator's confusion factor. Although none have been universally satisfactory (several have been developed for very specific situations) it's well known that the problem exists. Therefore, no quantitative analysis of how much improvement can be realized from higher resolution; it just is.

The benefits of CAD are well understood and appreciated. Nonetheless, designers and drafters would prefer to have their drawing table back so they could see all the drawing at once, with detail. CAD displays require the operator to make several compromises. These compromises are a function of cost, i.e., the more you can afford to pay for a display, the better a display you'll get. A "better" display is one that has the highest resolution.

There are upper limits, however, both physically and economically, on how far resolution can be increased. Studies have shown that systems with 1600×1200 resolution offer the most cost-effective and user-comfortable displays and will hold that market position for several years, yet very few users seem to have 1600×1200 display systems.

When a CAD program sends a drawing to a display board, the data consists of a string of numbers that represents the coordinates of the end points of each line (refer to FIG. 1-3). The display board then converts those numbers into lines by calculating all the pixel points that fall on the line between the two end points. The process that does this calculation is the display board's *vector generator*.

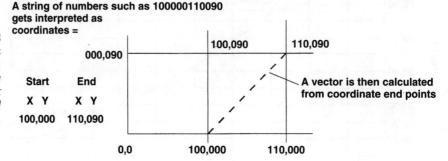

1-3

When a CAD program sends a drawing to a display board, the data consists of a string of numbers that represent the coordinates of the end points of each line.

Unless a board has a specific hardware vector generator (a few do), the vector speed is strictly a function of the type of graphics controller used. Therefore, if you find a board that uses a popular controller and if its vector drawing speed is significantly better than other boards using the same controller, you should find out why. Vector drawing speeds vary from as low as 30,000 per second to over 2 million per second.

There are two techniques offered by board manufacturers to provide a picture zooming capability: pixel replication and display-list management.

Pixel replication   As mentioned previously, CAD programs are widely used, and their most time-consuming function is picture regeneration or zooming. It's highly influenced by the bus and host-processor speed. One way to get around the bus speed is to capture the display list and then operate on it in the board's environment with greater speed. To do this, the board needs to be an on-board coprocessor or a dedicated processor. Such boards are sometimes called *zoom engines*. Another approach is to capture the drawing in a much larger frame area (e.g., 4096×4096 or 6400×6400), assign a window to any portion of the drawing, and then map the window to the entire screen, thus providing a zoomed view.

All CAD software programs have a zoom function that allows the user to enlarge the viewing area for more detailed work. However, the software operation is typically slow. That factor has led manufacturers to add hardware zoom to their boards.

Hardware zoom is accomplished by multiplying the number of pixels used, and is therefore also known as *pixel replication*. For example, if a single pixel dot is zoomed by a factor of two, four pixels will be used to display it (2×2), as illustrated in FIG. 1-4. Hardware zooming allows examination and correction of single-pixel

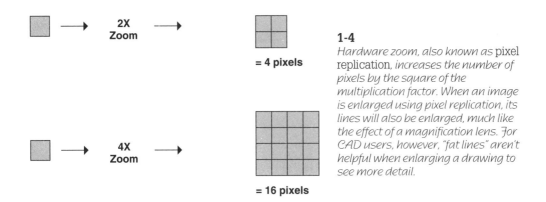

1-4

Hardware zoom, also known as pixel replication, *increases the number of pixels by the square of the multiplication factor. When an image is enlarged using pixel replication, its lines will also be enlarged, much like the effect of a magnification lens. For CAD users, however, "fat lines" aren't helpful when enlarging a drawing to see more detail.*

elements in a drawing or image. When a picture is zoomed, it will be larger than the display area. Therefore, to see all of the picture, you must be able to pan or move around in it.

A zoom function is specified in terms of its range. Some boards have a zoom range from 1:1 to 1:4. Other boards have a range from 1:1 to 1:16. For most CAD operations, a range greater than 1:4 isn't of much use—multiplying the size of the pixels makes a zoomed picture difficult to recognize.

Pixel replication makes the pixels larger. It basically blows up the picture, similar to enlarging a photograph. That means that *everything* in the picture gets enlarged, including the size of the lines. Some users object to the fat lines created with this method. The grid on the left side of FIG. 1-5 shows a normal view of a rhomboid; the one on the right shows the same rhomboid at a 2× enlargement. Notice that the pixels are fatter.

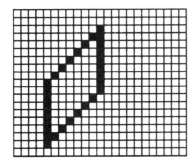 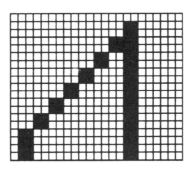

1-5
The grid on the left shows a normal view of a rhomboid. The one on the left shows the same rhomboid at a 2× enlargement. Notice that the lines are fatter.

A zoom function is usually dependent on the application software's ability to take advantage of it. If a board has hardware zoom, it might not work with all software. Most of the controllers that have a hardware-zoom feature are Macintosh boards and not used in CAD applications.

Hardware zoom is more often used in bit-mapped applications for pixel tweaking. Most Macintosh display boards offer this feature.

Display-list processing

A display list is a database generated by the application program when the user creates a drawing. It consists of the coordinates of the end points of each line, which are used to make the vectors in a drawing, as shown in FIG. 1-6.

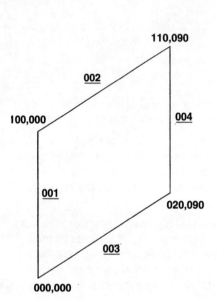

1-6
The series of end points that make up a line or vector form a display list. Display-list management and acceleration is a key feature in a display system's performance.

Display - List

Vector	Start	End
001	000,000	100,000
002	100,000	110,090
003	110,090	020,090
004	020,090	000,000

Zooming using a display-list manager requires recalculating and redrawing the picture every time the user wants to see an enlarged view or a different part of an enlarged drawing. Zooming uses all or part of the display list so a new (zoomed) picture can be displayed. Unlike pixel replication, when a board uses display-list management the enlarged drawing has the same line weight as the original, as is illustrated in FIG. 1-7. The diagram on the left is normal; the one on the right has been enlarged with a 2× zoom.

A board with display-list management recalculates the data in the display list, and then redraws the enlarged picture. Clipping vectors that extend beyond the screen or the viewing window is an important part of display-list management and can be very time-consuming. Most of the high-resolution and VHR boards have added display-list management. Several companies have come up with clever techniques to do on-board display-list management using a fast coprocessor (e.g., 34020, i860, or MIPS) or a custom processor.

A display list contains the starting and ending x,y coordinates of the lines used to create objects within a drawing. Most CAD programs maintain an internal display list of the vectors (lines) that define the objects in a drawing.

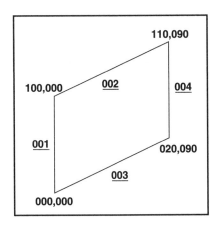
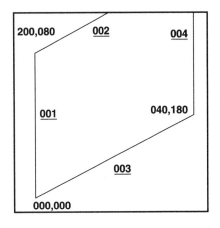

In most 2-D and 3-D programs, the display list is maintained within the application program and uses the host processor. However, if there's a coprocessor on the board, it might be able to do the display-list management. If so, the board should be able to make very fast screen drawings and zooms.

Some of the newer boards and accelerator boards are able to extract the display list from the application program and manage it. One of the slowest parts of generating a drawing is having the host processor send the display points to the graphic display board across the computer's bus. If the graphic display board has an on-board processor that can manage the display list, you can end up with a very tight coupling between the coprocessor and the display. This will speed up zooming and redrawing the image considerably.

If a board has an on-board coprocessor that does display-list management, it will require some memory in which to store the display list. The size of the memory (or its ability to be expanded) is important in evaluating a board's ability to handle large drawing files.

A few companies have also developed improved techniques using expanded memory with the host processor to obtain display-list management. Using the host eliminates the cost of a coprocessor. The results of either technique provide amazingly fast picture zooming and panning capabilities.

Anti-aliasing

In the early 1980s, edge-filtering techniques were developed that made vectors look smooth. This was done by making the intensity of the pixels next to vectors gradually darker the further away they got from the vector (the technique, developed by Akira Fujimoto and Kansei Iwata, was first discussed in the IEEE CG&A in December 1983). Figure 1-8 shows an anti-aliased line, which has less intense pixels placed next to it. This illustrates the general idea of how anti-aliasing works. It's also the technique used in high-dpi laser printers.

Anti-aliasing techniques are common on high-end workstations, and have begun to appear in the newer versions of PC-based display systems. The main reason they haven't been used very often in PC-based systems in the past is because of their cost and speed. It takes typically two to three times as long to draw an anti-aliased vector as it does an ordinary vector.

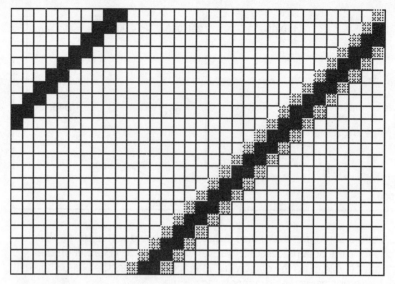

1-8
Anti-aliasing is used to trick the viewer's eyes into seeing a smooth line by adjusting the shade of adjoining pixels from the color of the line to the color of the background. The line on the left is a typical, jagged line. The one on the right is anti-aliased.

Companies that supply high-resolution graphics terminals for minicomputers have offered anti-aliasing capabilities for years.

Vector rate   In the early days of computer graphics, display systems were measured and compared by the number of vectors that could be drawn per second. It's an interesting number—one that suggests the raw speed of a system. The problem is that it doesn't mean very much. The limitations in drawing speed are usually due to the application program and the host CPU. Also, no one runs the test the same way: the setup time (i.e., loading in the data) is never included in the vector-speed specification, and that's usually the largest time-consumer, vector size isn't agreed upon (some use 10 pixels, some use one inch), and organization of the vectors is different from one manufacturer to another (some use continuous, some random, some use only horizontal).

For boards that take control of the application program's display list, the vector rate becomes a function of the graphics controller chip and, in addition, some boards have an additional hardware vector generator.

Panning   When the picture is enlarged, the user can see only the portion that fits in the display—like looking through a magnifying glass. The magnifying glass can be moved around the picture, changing the screen's view, by what's called a *panning operation*. There are two panning techniques: view-port and object.

View-port panning   Think of view-port panning as having a large picture (the zoomed drawing or image) and a movable window (your monitor). To see the left side of the picture, you would move your window to the left. View-port panning is called *free panning* in the Macintosh.

Object panning   In object panning, the window is stationary while the image is moved. To see the right side, you would move the image to the right. Object panning is known as *edge panning* in the Macintosh.

There are two types of panning control: hardware and software.

Hardware control   Hardware techniques usually offer two ways of panning in a picture: automatic and command.

Automatic panning moves the object or the window to the edge of the displayed image when you move the pointing device that controls the cursor. Then, if you continue to move the pointer, the cursor stays at the edge of the display and the image moves. Automatic panning is usually handled in the device driver.

Command panning requires you to give coordinates to the system to get to another viewing area. Command panning is commonly called *hand panning* in the Macintosh.

Software control   In software, the panning operation is a function of the application program. In those circumstances, the board's hardware panning functions aren't involved. Moving a scroll bar at the bottom or side of the screen or window is an example of software or application-oriented panning.

Some applications generate images that have dimensions or coordinates outside the display area. Clipping is the technique used to remove the unwanted portion of such images. It's most important in an application that uses windows. In addition to recognizing where to clip a line segment, the clipping function must know where to clip a block that contains a character. This is to ensure that no partial characters are left in the clipped area.

The clipping function is usually performed by the application software. However, it can be a significant calculation and keep the computer's processor busy. Therefore, some boards offer a clipping function either as part of their graphics library or as part of their coprocessor support.

Some boards have on-board 2-D or 3-D transformation functions. However, unless the application program takes advantage of it, it's of value or interest to only a potential applications developer. Some manufacturers provide software that performs the transformations in software on the PC's processor. This gives you the advantage of the functions, but their speed might not be fast enough for practical use. Check with manufacturers to learn which method they use.

The ability to rotate a drawing and manipulate the viewing angle or size of the drawing is called *transform*. It's most useful when a 3-D drawing needs to be examined. With either a wire-frame drawing or a drawing with hidden-line removal, being able to quickly look at another view of the drawing can be most beneficial. Some boards have a software, firmware, or hardware X-Y-Z coordinate transform capability. How fast a coordinate can be transformed from one position to another is a measure of the board's power.

If a given application program doesn't take advantage of the feature, it's wasted. Therefore, paying more for a board with such a feature wouldn't be advisable unless you intend to obtain an application program to use it. Transform rates are often given in vectors per second.

The area fill speed is how quickly each pixel within a polygon can be filled, and is measured in pixels per second. The speed specification might not take into consideration the time needed to select the function and set up the conditions needed to fill; therefore, raw pixel-per-second speed could be misleading.

Z-buffer operation

A Z buffer is a duplicate frame buffer used to store depth and hidden surface information about an image. Z buffers are usually at least 12 bits deep and can be as large as 24 bits. By using a Z buffer, hidden surfaces such as the far side of a mountain can be revealed to the graphics system operator just by pulling the data from the Z buffer.

Traditionally, a real-time graphics simulator is built with a Z buffer. A computational engine calculates all hidden surfaces for objects on a screen and stores these coordinates for future use.

There are several problems with Z-buffer architecture, however: They're expensive and often slower than they should be for a simulator that must compute and render more than a million 3-D pixels per second. Many Z buffers are constructed with 20ns static RAMs and, because the graphics engine must invariably calculate the coordinates for something that might never be shown, it wastes valuable clock cycles.

Software removal of hidden surfaces

The key to fast hidden-surface removal is identifying all visible elements of a picture just before it's portrayed on a screen. A pixel-processing algorithm that takes out hidden-surface coordinates on the fly without using a Z buffer was developed (and patented) by Megatek in 1988. Named the Xpan algorithm, it can, depending upon the host processor speed, provide a 5× speedup over systems using a Z buffer. Using the Xpan algorithm, the displayed polygons are first scan-converted vertically into horizontal segments, called *spans*. In the second step, the horizontal scan conversion transforms the spans into pixels.

This two-step process depends on the use of a span processor and a linked-list buffer. For each polygon portrayed on the screen, the span processor extracts span information from each polygon within the scan lines of the raster display device. The span information includes the horizontal location of the scan line, its color, and the intensity (or Z depth)—not for the whole span, just the left and right end points of the span. A multiple linked-list buffer stores the span information, ordering it according to the vertical screen location.

While the Xpan algorithm requires a span processor and linked-list buffer, besides normal frame buffers, it uses less hardware and software than traditional frame-buffer architecture. Each scan-line buffer is cleared as the data is transferred to the frame buffer. Thus, there's none of the overhead of a traditional full-sized Z buffer. On a 1280×1024-pixel screen, a Z buffer could take a full eight ms—25% of the frame time at 30Hz refresh rates—just to clear the screen.

Bit-mapped & raster-operation applications

Applications using bit-mapped and raster-operation functions are traditionally and broadly defined as *imaging*, and are categorized into the following general areas:

❑ Solid modeling
❑ Scientific imaging processing
❑ Document processing
❑ Graphic arts and multimedia animation
❑ Image editing and photorealism
❑ Industrial imaging processing
❑ Simulation

These applications, which used to be fairly separate, have become more and more overlayed with functions found traditionally in CAD and video applications. The result has been two additional application segments, simulation and multimedia, which don't fit nicely in just video, vector, or bit-mapped areas.

Some of the more popular bit-mapped and raster-operation applications in these areas are described in the following sections. Following them are descriptions of simulation and multimedia-application issues.

Solid models

As mentioned in the earlier section on vector operations, wire frames lend themselves well to 2-D applications, such as engineering drafting, NC programming of flat parts, and computation of areas, perimeters, diameters, and other simple geometric properties. However, they have severe limitations. Wire frames are incomplete and can therefore often be interpreted to represent more than one object. Because surfaces and solid and void spaces aren't represented in the computer, they can't be depicted on the screen. Moreover, wire-frame models of complex 3-D objects can often become a jumble of criss-crossing and overlapping lines that confuse the viewer.

Most solid modelers have automatic hidden-line routines. This operation erases edge lines that would normally be hidden from view, to give the model a solid rather than transparent appearance. It also makes the geometry more readily interpreted because the background lines are eliminated on the screen.

Surface models   Surface models overcome many of these limitations of wire frames by completely defining an object's surface. Solid-modeling applications provide extensive menus of surfaces from which to build models. These include flat planes between parallel straight lines (known as *flat shading*), tabulated cylinders between parallel curves, ruled surfaces between nonparallel curves, surfaces of revolution, sweep surfaces, and fillets. Sculptured surfaces can also be modeled by such means as B splines and cubic patches. Complex surfaces can also be shaded using techniques known as Phong and Gouraud shading.

The ability to define contoured surfaces makes surface modelers extremely useful where complex 3-D geometrics must be designed, especially when the primary concern is with the exterior shell of objects made of sheet metal, thin-walled plastics, or other thin material. Also, surface models can be used to create color-shaded images on the CRT screen with photograph-like realism. This allows the user to visualize the appearance of an object and check for any surface design flaws.

The primary disadvantage of surface models is that they don't convey information about an object's interior. The model doesn't specify where a surface is solid and where it's void. As a result, the user must personally keep track of a model's structure when performing cross-sectioning, interference checking, or other engineering applications. This might be obvious for many objects, but complex objects with cutouts and intricate details are often difficult to interpret.

Solid modelers   Solid models overcome the limitations of wire frames and surface models by defining an object's solid and void parts. For example, a solid model distinguishes between a brick and an empty box, while wire frames and surface models don't.

A solid model contains enough information for a computer to decide whether a point lies inside, outside, or on the surface of an object. Other modelers require the user to perform this task. In fact, this capability is a hallmark of solid modelers.

Solid models have many advantages. Like surface models, solid models can be used to produce color-shaded images of objects. Also, line drawings can be readily produced from the model, similar to wire-frame models. Unlike these models, however, solid models can be used to compute mass properties, study internal details, and serve as a starting point in structural analysis. Moreover, the solid model always represents a valid, realizable object. In contrast, wire frames and surface models can represent physically impossible objects.

Solid modeling has a drawback: Model construction requires massive amounts of computer processing power and memory capacity. In past years, this made the technique prohibitively expensive and slow for all but a few users. New advances in hardware have reduced computing costs significantly, but solid modeling still requires more operator time and expertise, and is still very expensive, relative to wire frames and surface models. Figure C-5 shows a representation of the Boeing 777 airplane, the first to be completely designed using solid-modeling technology.

Most PC-based modelers represent objects by boundary-edge definitions. Most packages give a user the option of defining models in either a text or graphics interactive mode. Graphics input can be entered via the keyboard, a data tablet, or a mouse.

PC-based systems can rotate, translate, scale, and otherwise manipulate the display on the screen. Users might have to wait a considerable period of time as the computer generates the new image. Nevertheless, this capability is useful in applications such as architecture, where both the exterior and interior of an object must be viewed.

Until about 1982, most solid modelers fell neatly into two groups: those that used constructive solid geometry to build and represent models in the computer, and those that used boundary representation.

Constructive solid geometry   Constructive solid geometry (CSG) programs (also called *combinational, building-block, volumetric, implicit,* or *unevaluated*) construct models by combining simple 3-D shapes, known as *primitives.* A CSG system stores a model in memory as a list of these primitives and the operations that combine them. This data list has a tree-like structure, with the primitives represented by branches connected at node points, which represent the operations. The computer analyzes the model by tracing through the list.

The block, cylinder, sphere, and cone, known as *natural quadrics,* are the primitives most commonly used in CSG model-building. To speed modeling, most CSG programs also supply so-called "convenience" primitives, such as fillets, wedges, and truncated cones. They save time in model-building because the user can select them from a menu rather than constructing each from scratch.

The user combines primitives with a set of three Boolean logic operations—union, difference, and intersection. These operations enable the user to make complex shapes from primitives. For example, you can create a pencil shape by using the union operation to add a cone to the end of a cylinder.

You can produce a hole by using the difference operation to subtract a cylinder from a solid block, and an octagonal bolt head by intersecting one cube with another superimposed over it and rotated 45 degrees.

Boundary representations   Boundary representation (B-rep) programs, also referred to as *explicit* or *evaluated systems*, build models by defining the surface envelope of the solid object. A B-rep system stores a solid model as a list of faces, edges, and vertices of the object, linked together via pointers to form a graph-like data structure. An entry defining a face, for example, contains pointers linking it to all edges bounding the face. Likewise, entries for edges have pointers identifying all faces whose intersections form the edges. Each vertex entry is linked to all edges for which it's a meeting point.

Typically, the model is created with conventional automated drafting techniques. In some systems, the user creates a wire-frame model and uses this geometry to define the various surface patches in a so-called fleshing-out operation. In this process, the geometric model is used as a framework on which the various surfaces are pieced together. This specifies enough data about the surface geometry parts for the computer to fill in the solid geometry.

The topological integrity of the model is guaranteed in B-rep systems because all surfaces are properly defined and connected. Faces can't be missing and edges must be attached. This automatically prohibits the construction of nonsense objects that are physically impossible to build.

2½-D & extrusions   You can also define models by sweeping a 2-D form, outline, or surface through space to trace out a volume. Several types of sweeps are available, depending on the type of geometry required. These sweeping operations are often analogous to the manufacturing steps used to fabricate actual parts.

❏ A linear sweep translates a section along a straight line to produce an *extruded* part of constant thickness.
❏ A rotational sweep revolves a section around an axis to make a *turned* part with axial symmetry.
❏ A compound sweep is a variation of these basic techniques, where a surface is moved along a specified curve (called a *spline*) to generate a more complex solid.

Objects modeled with sweeping operations can have a variety of face types, including planar, cylindrical, conical, spherical, and toroidal. The most general sweeping capabilities can produce even the complex contours of sculptured surfaces.

Scientific image processing

Within the area of scientific image processing (which some hard-liners refer to as "*real* image processing") there's a broad range of applications that require highly iterative pixel-array processing. The most common examples of image processing, or scientific image processing (to differentiate it from document image processing), are:

❏ Image analysis
❏ Medical image processing
❏ Remote sensing

Probably the first application of image processing was the transmission of digitized images for newspapers between London and New York (by Bartlans Cable Picture system). The next area to use image processing was the geophysical industry in the early 1960s, who used (at the time) large CDC computers for data reductions and analysis of seismic data. At the same time, in the early 1960s, image-analysis work using remote sensing and high-altitude aerial photography was employed by the military and a new agency in Virginia called the CIA. Later in 1964 at JPL, pictures from space probes were enhanced. Also, the Department of Agriculture began their remote-sensing image-processing program. It was this early work that got the industry started and established many of the algorithms and concepts widely used today.

In 1991, an international committee of 13 companies and organizations developed a plan for a consortium, which would be responsible for developing and promoting an image-processing standard for the ISO (International Standards Organization). The standard, called the Image Processing and Interchange (IPI) standard, is designed to facilitate application portability and file interchange across hardware platforms.

Image analysis   *Image analysis* is a technology used to extract quantitative information for the description of the structure or composition of objects in an image. Life-science and material-science researchers are the primary users of image analysis; other users can be found in medical fields, including forensics, genetics, modular biology, neurology, and pathology.

Initially a curiosity in the medical field, image analysis was quickly accepted in physics, chemistry, and medical research. Today, it has an increased acceptance in clinical applications, especially those requiring high throughput, accuracy, and repeatability.

Image-analysis programs typically offer a set of fundamental image-processing functions that are typically implemented as a library of subroutines, such as the following:

Affine transformation	Image arithmetic
Classification	Image warping
Color space conversions	Labeling
Convolutions	Logical operations
Edge detection	LUT manipulation
Enhancement and feature extraction	Morphology
	Optical character recognition
Fast Fourier transforms (FFT)	Pattern recognition
Filtering	Statistical operations
Gamma correction	Thresholding and halftoning
Histogram and dynamic threshold calculating	Transformation

Medical imaging   Medical imaging is the display of real-time images of medical data for the purpose of diagnosis. Traditionally, the medical-imaging industry has been the most common user of image technology, for such applications as body scanning and medical diagnostics.

Although medical-image processing is one of the most often mentioned image-processing application, it's difficult to determine what is and what isn't medical-image processing. It has to do with your definition and who is and who isn't a user. Medical-image processing (MIP) can be anything from a microscope to a huge CAT scanner. There are major systems that use MIP to capture live data from sensors (magnetic resonance interferometers MRI, nuclear, ultrasound, and thermography). All use some form of computer tomography (CT) or image processing, and they represent a major use of MIP. The largest MIP application involves putting a sensor (a CCD or photomultiplier) on a microscope and digitizing its output. These images are then manipulated, stored, and often transmitted.

In medical imaging, there has been a slow transition to filmless processes. In the past, the barrier to acceptance was the cost for the very high-resolution systems needed to provide an adequate picture. The ideal system for a radiologist would be four displays right next to each other or four views on one very large monitor, with 500 foot lamberts (fL) of lumination, and a resolution (in each monitor or panel) of 4300×3500. This, however, isn't possible with current technology and won't be for quite some time. Therefore, the requirements have been relaxed a little to be more in line with what's possible (and hopefully practical): a flat, monochrome display with 17×17-inch viewing area, a 500:1 dynamic range, 400 fL, and a minimum resolution of 2540×2540.

Satellite & remote sensing   The earth-science applications analyze data collected from earth resource work such as seismic analysis, oil services, atmospheric modeling, geosignal analysis, and various applications within the geophysics, geology, and meterology industries. These applications are used both in institutional research and commercial enterprises. Traditionally, the earth-science industry (remote sensing) has been the second most common user of imaging technology, for such applications as remote-sensed (LANDSAT or satellite-derived) data analysis.

The use of remote sensors (in balloons, airplanes, satellites, and other devices) with image-processing systems, or at least sensors, has been around since the early '60s. The most popular examples have been for military and agricultural data reduction and analysis, and weather-measuring systems. LANDSAT (originally named *Earth Resources Technology Satellite I*, or ERTS I) systems were introduced in 1972 and caught the imagination of the world. Many edge-enhancement algorithms and color techniques commonly used today came out of this area. A remote-sensing image-processing system will receive data usually via tape or radio link. It will have an image processor and a color display system.

The world view of remote sensing was begun with president Eisenhower when he developed the Open Skies policy and his 1960 proposals to the UN for international cooperation in outer space. That initiative was stated as (and has led to what we now take for granted): *better weather forecasting, improved worldwide communications, and more effective exploration not only of outer space but of our own earth.*

As a result of the Open Skies initiative, we in the industrialized nations have developed an awareness of global-change issues. This is turn has stimulated us to think in terms of the planetary view of earth now available in space images we regularly view on TV and PCs alike.

In 1992, a world conference was set up in Rio to discuss and hopefully mandate actions to protect the world's environment. Agenda 21, the 500-page framework for action that governments approved in Rio, calls for new efforts to increase human understanding of how the planet's life-support system operates and to translate this into action on the ground. Agenda 21 has a political status never before achieved at the global level. On the basis of institutional and other decisions governments have made and continue to make at the UN in New York, a process has started that will expand the need for remote sensing and GIS systems and expertise.

Document processing

Document processing is a very broad application of image processing. It doesn't include classic character-based word processing, but does include bit-mapped, raster-operation word processing and desktop publishing. It also includes complex prepress, document image-processing systems, and overlaps into the graphic-arts area. The most common major applications are:

❑ Desktop publishing
❑ Document imaging processing
❑ Prepress

Desktop publishing   The definition of desktop publishing has expanded in the last few years. Originally it described programs that enabled a user to manipulate text with selectable fonts. With PostScript, it became a true image-processing system. As nontext images were added to documents, it expanded still further. Today it overlaps in many areas with graphic arts. The major applications that fit this category are:

❑ Electronic publishing (text only)
❑ Technical manuals (text and graphics)
❑ Document image processing (DIP)
❑ Engineering drawing management (EDM)
❑ Prepress

Figure 1-9 shows the relative relationships of the steps and functions associated with the various applications and technologies of document processing.

Preparing documents with photographs, multicolor graphics, and screens (percentages of solid colors) requires special treatment. Page-layout programs (such as Aldus PageMaker, Ventura Publisher, FrameMaker, and QuarkXpress) have features specially suited to preparing the output needed for high-quality, high-resolution reproduction systems. The top word processors (such as Word, Ami Pro, and WordPerfect) don't.

Preparing a document for reproduction on a printing press is called *prepress*, or *making a document camera-ready*. Desktop-publishing software has prepress features that are lacking in word processors, although the two are getting closer every day.

Almost any application that has print controls can create a document at different dpi. However, desktop-publishing software with prepress features make maximum use of high-resolution commercial printers and typesetters. Resolution depends on the printer that's being used, not the software. By itself, dpi isn't important, but a combination of resolution and (printer) screen frequency can make or break a layout that has a combination of halftone screens and grayscale photographs.

Halftones, or screens (the terms are used interchangeably) are expressed as a percentage of a solid color. Grayscale photographs, in which shades of gray are made up of percentages of black, are basically screens, as are the percentages of colors that make up a four-color drawing or photograph. Four-color images are

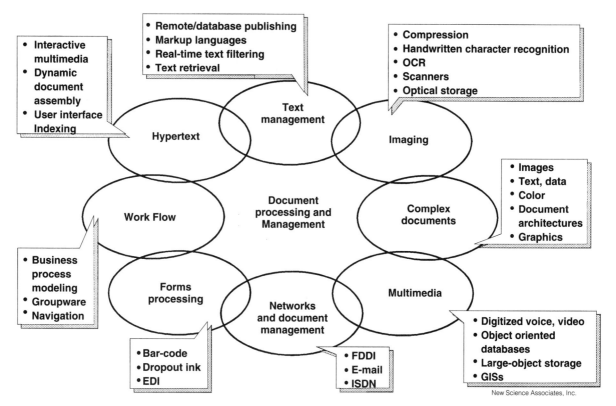

1-9 *Document processing and management has several applications, technologies, and steps associated with it.*

created on a printing press by mixing different percentages of cyan, magenta, yellow, and black (CMYK).

Conventionally, halftones are created with a camera. Fine mesh screens (measured in lines per inch, or lpi) are laid over the image or photograph to be screened. The mesh separates the image into lines of tiny dots, and the size and frequency of the dots determine where the printing press puts ink on paper, thus creating halftones. Computers and scanners have all but eliminated the need for the fine mesh screens, although printing presses still work primarily the same way.

Document imaging processing   Document image processing (DIP) is the capturing, processing, compressing, storing, and displaying of images. Image capturing is typically done by a scanner, but can also come from a data-communications port for EDI and e-mail. The captured data is compressed and then stored. Even after compression, image files can take up a lot of storage space so, in the case of DIP (which is often involved with archiving), the images are stored on an optical disk. Retrieving the images involves decompressing the images and displaying them at a viewing station on a high-resolution (greater than 1024×768) display system. The image processing, if there is any, is done at the creation or capture time. It usually involves the blending of photographs, text (often with scalable fonts), and handwritten images. Some systems use character recognition. Typically little or no image manipulation is provided at the viewing station.

While banks, insurance companies, and other commercial imaging sites have some need for graphics, notably for signature display and verification, a significantly larger percent of the paperwork at a manufacturing company is devoted to technical drawings and schematics. The government is also a big user of DIP.

Engineering drawing management The pressure of speed-to-market combined with the need for fewer mistakes and the ability to adapt products quickly are some of the reasons a handful of manufacturers have begun installing electronic document management systems (EDM).

Like imaging users in commercial settings such as banking and insurance, manufacturers are looking to imaging as a way to control, streamline, and automate the flow of records. In addition to conventional applications of imaging in their clerical departments, manufacturers are using imaging as a tool for routing drawings and technical documentation among designers, engineers, and the factory floor. For one aircraft maker, this has reduced the time needed to process drawings from as much as eight days to only 12 hours.

At Boeing's Commercial Airplane Group, for instance, an imaging subsystem known as the Reference Engineering Data Automated Retrieval System (REDARS) reduced the flow time of engineering changes by up to 90%, and cut by 80% the amount of time engineers and others waited to see data.

Combined with a high-speed fiber-distributed data-interface backbone network that connects 200 Sun Microsystems workstations, Boeing's system has more than 1 terabyte of information on 140 optical discs. The database includes more than three million graphics images created by Boeing's CAD system. (Refer to FIG. C-5 for an example of the type of drawings and images that Boeing deals with.)

In the past, these CAD images would have been output to microfilm and pasted onto aperture cards. This required a staff of 100 people to sort, file, and fetch the cards. Between 10 and 12 million obsolete aperture cards are stored in paper files.

Boeing also reduced the amount of time it takes to get a drawing released from engineering and sent to the factory floor—from six to eight days down to 12 hours. Along with engineering diagrams, REDARS contains all of Boeing's technical documentation and parts lists. REDARS also highlights two of the unique requirements of imaging in manufacturing: graphics and interfaces to CAD systems. It not only imports and exports data to a parts and document "accountability" system, but it also works with Boeing's CAD system. According to some analysts, creating these CAD-to-imaging interfaces can be tricky because the imaging system becomes a kind of common denominator for incompatible CAD systems.

EDM and DIP have been one of the benefits of the Apple Document Management and Control System (ADMACS), Apple Computer's global-imaging system. ADMACS provides on-line access to more than 120,000 pages of drawings and product documentation.

Aside from substantial productivity gains, Apple has used ADMACS as a common window onto its diverse CAD systems. Instead of giving each employee a $40,000 to $50,000 workstation, each loaded with $20,000 to $30,000 worth of CAD software for access to the on-line drawings, Apple is using its own Macintosh as the client for the imaging system.

About 600 employees have access to ADMACS today. The ADMACS host is a Digital Equipment Corp. VAX in Napa, California. Because Apple elected to use the Macintosh and send the images across the corporate Transmission Control Protocol/Internet Protocol (TCP/IP) network, access to engineering documents is theoretically available from every employee's desktop. Before ADMACS, turnaround time for design changes could be as much as 25 days, with diagrams on microfilm frequently shipped back and forth to Apple's manufacturing sites worldwide. Today, turnaround is 3 days and dropping. Some changes are down to one day.

A final application of imaging in manufacturing relates to customer support. Whirlpool Corp. installed an imaging system that provides customer-service agents with access to two decades worth of service and product manuals.

In a recent member survey by the Association for Information and Image Management, 56% of the manufacturers who responded said they were using imaging today; another 29% said they were investigating imaging.

A large proportion of DIP and most of EDM still use monochrome displays. As color is introduced to these areas, they'll benefit from the work being done in the graphic-arts area of image processing. Seeing the correct colors in documents on a screen involves having a proper color calibration scheme.

Color calibration in graphic arts & prepress   Various products influence how color calibration in graphic-arts programs is handled. Such products can offer an important capability of platform-independent color calibration. Most systems employ the same concept, but use different methods to attain the same final goal—consistent color manipulation.

The process starts at the scanner. Typically, a user will view a chrome or reflective artwork and make adjustments at the scanner to make it look right. At the separation station, the next operator will again view the piece. This time it's a TIFF file being viewed on the monitor, perhaps using a commercial application (e.g., Adobe Photoshop or QuarkXpress). Finally, at the page-layout station someone else views the file as it's being dropped into the page geometry for printing by the imagesetter. At no two points on the path, between the scanner and the imagesetter, is the color looked at as the same type of media. As such, there's no consistency in the way each is viewed.

This is where integrated programs (e.g., Cacher and ColorSense) can be of use. Using their own forms of methodology, each station is adjusted so that the output from that device is no longer unique. Documents that are scanned and then viewed on the monitor in Photoshop, on the page layout, and on the output from the imagesetter will all be consistent.

If a correction is made anywhere along the path, that correction will always be viewed the same as the file moves to its final format—separated film. These systems permit you to make a change, and then allows everyone in the process to view that color the same way. However, you still need the foundation of color experience to get good results.

Graphic arts   The capabilities found in graphic-arts programs can also be found in some of the other categories; as mentioned, it's difficult to make nice neat distinctions. Some GA applications make use of compression schemes (discussed briefly in a later section), others use full color, some deliberately create randomness, and still others are used to create ads, books, and t-shirts. The most frequently found GA applications are:

- ❑ Graphic design and paint programs
- ❑ Graphic arts and prepress
- ❑ Presentation or slide-making
- ❑ Desktop presentation
- ❑ Animation
- ❑ CAD rendering
- ❑ Photorealism

Paint-system basics   Paint or graphic-arts programs were one of the first nonCAD applications developed in computer graphics. Known by many names (rendering, paint and sketch, true-color image processing, etc.) it's an area loaded with specialized terms and concepts, many carried over from the darkroom and conventional graphic arts, and many concerning how computers deal with color information. The following is a brief primer to get you conversant with the basics.

Tools & attributes   One of the most important traits of a good GA or color image-processing program is a wide range of tool-selection capabilities. Options for selecting irregular areas, adding to or subtracting from the borders of existing selections, numerically specifying selection size, and moving a selection boundary around to choose another area of the image with the same shape are examples of its functionality. The ability to manipulate an image area or use it as a transparency mask is all part of GA controls and tools.

Another important feature is manipulation of a selected area, such as accurate scaling, rotation, skewing, perspective, and distortion. Selections can usually be pasted with variable transparency and a variety of attributes that govern the interaction of the pixels in the selection and background. An attribute such as Lighten Only, for example, would change only the pixels that are lighter in value than their underlying counterparts. The concepts of transparency and attributes are equally applicable to other functions, such as paint tools, fills, and gradients.

Selections can usually act as masks, protecting areas of an image from being altered during an operation like painting or pasting. In the simplest form, operations affect only an active selection. More complex implementations allow you to save the selection and load it as a grayscale image, with either solid black or white acting as a mask and different levels of gray determining levels of transparency.

Paint & fill tools   Paint tools usually include items such as pencil, brush, and airbrush; their measure is in the control the user has over the application of paint. Some are particularly enhanced by the ability to accept pressure from pen-input tablets, and apply specific parameters such as brush size and opacity.

Fill tools often come with the ability to apply patterns rather than solid colors. Gradient fill tools can include various spread patterns, control over the linearity or ramp curve of the transition, smoothness, and choice of the color space through which the transition occurs. Tools are usually available for sharpening, blurring, and blending pixels by hand.

Filter & special effects   Filters are functions applicable to selected areas or entire images. Simple filters perform tasks such as sharpening, blurring, and diffusing images. More spatial filters such as wave, spherize, twirl, and motion blur manipulate images in 2-D and 3-D space to create special effects. These effects can also be obtained through calculation functions that combine images or channels according to mathematics operations such as addition and multiplication. Many programs allow splitting and recombining channels of a given color space for individual manipulation. However, another source of special effects is available by recombining areas from more than one image or according to other color-space relationships.

File formats   Over a dozen file formats have been created over the years, all proposed to be a standard. Some of them have become de facto standards, by the nature and popularity of the application program that uses them. Most graphic-arts programs have filters and conversion routines that allow them to accept popular file formats. Some of the more sinister programs will accept a large variety of file format, but save files only in their format. Briefly, here's a list of the most popular file formats for graphic arts:

❏ BMP (Windows bit map): 24-bit RGB, 8-bit grayscale
❏ CGM (computer graphics metafile): 8-bit vector with easy scaling
❏ PCX: 8-bit color, 8-bit grayscale
❏ PostScript: vector-based page description
❏ TGA (TARGA): 16, 24, and 32 bits/pixel
❏ TIFF: 24-bit RGB, 8-bit color, 8-bit grayscale

It's beyond the scope of this chapter (and this book) to list and describe all the available file formats. It's unfortunate there really isn't any standard. Be wary of programs that don't offer a robust set of conversion utilities to change from one file format to another.

Converting from a bit-mapped format like TGA to a vector format like CGM is difficult, involving raster-to-vector conversion. Going the other way, vector to raster, is much easier.

Color space & models   Several different color spaces are used by most GA programs and image processors, including RGB (red, green, blue), CMYK (cyan, magenta, yellow, black—K is used for black because B represents blue), HSB (hue, saturation, brightness), and more (refer to chapter 2, *Color*, for more detail on color standards).

The RGB color space is used by the computer to display images on CRTs via additive light (all three colors produce white; absence of color yields black), as well as by most desktop scanners and video digitizers. The subtractive color process of CMYK is crucial in assuring that colors translate properly when creating separations for the professional printing process. (While monitors can't actually display in CMYK, the translations between RGB and CMYK values allow numeric specification at the least, and a display of equivalent colors at best.) While they also can't be displayed directly, the HSB color model and its relatives, HSL and HSV (which refer to level and value, parameters similar to brightness, as well as to hue and saturation), are often preferable for specifying color values and relationships, because they work in a manner much more akin to human color perception and intuition.

One of the primary functions of an image processor, or GA program, is to compensate for the way color translates between devices such as scanners, monitors, and printers. The ability to adjust the relationship of input values to output values, colors input from a scanner and output to a CRT, for example, is the key to maintaining or enhancing image fidelity. Simple controls include brightness, contrast, and shifting the entire color spectrum; more advanced versions include adjusting distribution of gray levels and the input/output curves of the individual color components.

While color correction and manipulation are best accomplished in 24-bit true-color mode, most images used for computer-based productions use indexed-color or pseudo-color of 8 bits for the sake of file size and display time. Virtually all image processors can reduce full-spectrum images to a standard system palette, or to an adaptive palette optimized for a given image.

Graphic arts & color theory   Creating sketches with a computer can provide information in the early phases of design to appeal to a designer's sensitivity to color. Such drawings use the computer's ability to generate seemingly endless colors and change them with impunity. They can capture not only the form—but also the emotional qualities that are the germ of architectural or product design thought.

Colors interact to form images of both spaces and form. Principles that explain the behavior of color have been surfacing for generations. The rules for rendering shading and shadow on drawings were formalized in the Beaux Arts workshops in the nineteenth century. But images created with conventional paint are static.

With computer graphics, color investigation and experimentation of an image can become dynamic. We're able to read black-and-white photos because they're made up of contrasting gray colors. When working in full color, many more contrasts exist that can be manipulated; hue, saturation, and color temperature all come into consideration. These contrasts are the substance of color drawing and, by their use, artists, designers, and illustrators can make their ideas more understandable to others and to themselves.

Colors themselves speak a reactive language. An image in red has an emotional content that can't be found in blue, and yellow suggests a mood that's different from green. Using these psychological clues, designers are able to express meaning and convey intent without detail in sketches.

True-color image processing   Image processors are considered by some as the digital equivalent of the photographer's darkroom. These programs are sophisticated graphic-arts tools that allow screen images to be retouched, combined, and manipulated for color balance, brightness, contrast, size, and resolution. They have become indispensable for electronic prepress operations and are also essential when creating on-screen visuals for multimedia productions, especially those that incorporate images acquired from scanners and video digitizers.

Once again there's a blurring of the lines, as true-color capabilities are brought to not only graphic arts but also document processing, making it possible to develop desktop prepress systems. Somewhere between color DTP and actual photographs lies the area of computer-generated photorealistic images—images so real it's almost impossible (in fact, many times it *is* impossible) to tell if it is or isn't computer-generated.

As mentioned previously, it's very difficult to draw nice sharp distinctions between various applications, so the best I can do is form some generalizations. I also don't want to get into an esoterical discussion about why one application or program belongs in one category rather than another. However, there are some reasonably distinct applications that have been employed in specific areas. Two of those areas are photo or image editing, and the generation of life-like or photorealistic images. In this section, I'll discuss a few of those techniques.

*Image editing
& photorealism*

Electronic photo retouching   In the past, most people who read a newspaper or a magazine took it for granted that the pictures they saw were exactly what the photographer's camera saw, whether it was a picture of a burning building or someone handing over a check to a charitable organization.

Before image processing and computer retouching, photographers took their pictures, they were printed, and then the press operators recreated those pictures on the pages of the publication. Now all that has changed. Pictures, even when taken with conventional cameras, can be put into computer form (digitized) and then altered. Want to remove that distracting telephone pole in the foreground of a house that's for sale, or the mole from a model's shoulder? Not a problem with today's systems.

That's the good news. The bad news is that computer manipulation of photographs might become so advanced that it will no longer be possible to use photographs routinely as evidence in court trials. The technology has already become so good that you can no longer tell an original photo from a manipulated one. Manipulation of photographs isn't new; the technology is just better. Photo technicians have long used airbrushes to remove scars or tone down bald spots, but graphics and photography experts were able to tell that the photo was altered.

The world of photojournalism is wrestling with this difficult subject. When is it okay, and when isn't it? The National Press Photographers Association (NPPA), a professional organization of newspaper and television photographers, has already made its position known. In a statement of principal drafted at the second annual Electronic Photojournalism Workshop and revised in July of 1991 by the NPPA board of directors, the association says: "We believe it is wrong to alter the content of a photograph in any way that deceives the public. Accurate representation is the benchmark of our profession." The statement ends with the following: "Altering the editorial content of a photograph, in any degree, is a breach of the ethical standards recognized by the NPPA."

Image sampling & texture mapping   Analogous to music sampling, in which sounds from the environment are recorded, distorted, and used in unique ways to create music, *image sampling* is the visual equivalent of a sound bite, and is used to create new visual forms, textures, patterns, and types of architecture. Through the use of image sampling, a designer, graphics artist, or simulation scene creator can accurately record and digitize images from the existing visual world for a new design, illustration, or imaginary world.

The digital scanning process makes graphic information (patterns, scenes, designs, etc.) equal and uniform, as it converts all images to dot patterns of varying color. As a result, the image can be transformed through numeric operations (even when the algorithms are transparent to the end user). Recorded images can be fragmented, combined, distorted, duplicated, or subjected to random automated operations.

Design activity no longer needs to be characterized as leading from abstract conceptual images to detailed realistic images. Diagrammatic images can include representation of activity, fragments of building elements, parts of cars, airplanes, or other products. These can be viewed in a photorealistic manner by then superimposing the image on three-dimensional models, or by directly "sketching" on scanned information with the computer.

Electronic brainstorming is possible by superimposing existing buildings, drawings, or any other available visual material onto real or constructed sites. The idea of an object in the landscape, tower in a park, pattern in a dress, or new car can be tested very quickly and then illustrated with detailed information that can go beyond that provided by a charcoal or pencil sketch for evaluation by the designer.

The ability to digitize any color or representation of texture and apply it to a proposed model permits discussion and evaluation of material selection for a building, shapes and textures of proposed appliances, or backgrounds for movies. In a traditional setting, issues of color and material are frequently settled at the end of the design process as they're applied to the final presentation drawings. When designing electronically, all images are potential presentation drawings and all images have material and color. The range of issues confronted by a designer or clients increase, and occur at an earlier stage of design.

Combining image samples into a new design or plan expands the scope of potential tools and techniques available to the architect and designer, but also raises fundamental questions about issues of originality, creativity, authenticity, and the nature of the design process itself. Photorealistic conceptual sketches could very well amplify the differences between what is and is not appropriate in design or architecture.

However, texture mapping of actual patterns or surfaces has been found to be extremely useful in creating simulation scenes that can be quickly rendered. This allows fast scene updates, which contributes immensely to the realism of the simulation.

Image sampling and texture mapping are an efficient way to generate a realistic, if not perfectly accurate, scan or model. However, if you want the ultimate in realism and the resources are available, then you should consider photorealism.

Photorealism   It has been estimated that we receive over 80% of our input through our eyes. Visual elements, shapes, textures, movement, and the interplay of light define most of our perception of reality. For workstations and PCs to simulate the reality we see, they must be able to display a visually accurate picture of reality—the display must look as real as a photograph. It was the desire to create such images that led to the development of the area of photorealism within computer graphics.

The movement toward photorealism started in the early 1970s. It began with the synthesization of images (pictures) that had smooth surfaces. Smooth-shading tricks developed by Gourad and Phong were used to make the eye see smooth objects modeled as polygonal surfaces. Improvements were made by Ed Catmull, who used mathematically smooth surfaces called *bicubic surface patches* to model objects that were supposed to be smooth, instead of trying to approximate them with a lot of polygons.

The visual complexity of the scenes we see arises from surface variations and the interplay of light rather than from the shapes of the objects alone. A typical room includes objects of relatively simple shape but with varying surface qualities and lighting. A wall, for example, is a simple rectangle, but the paint on the wall might vary from matte to glossy, the surface could be smooth, pebbly or anything in between, and it might be illuminated by the sun, several lamps, or a candle.

Computerized picture creation begins with the creation of a scene, or model, in software. Once the model is created, it's displayed or printed by a renderer. The model, which might be a representation of a room, contains geometric descriptions of the room's objects: polygons, lines, spheres, cylinders, patches, splines, and so forth. But surface geometry and texture mapping alone isn't enough visual accuracy to qualify as photorealistic.

Ray tracing   In the early 1980s, a rendering technique called *ray tracing* was developed. Prior rendering algorithms hadn't considered the refraction and reflection effects of basic geometrical optics. Ray tracing calculates a light ray's reflection from each surface it encounters on its way to the eye of the viewer. Each surface is used to determine the point of illumination. Ray tracing gave software developers and users new tools for lighting and modeling in a scene.

Fractals   A modeling method based on fractals was the next step in photorealism. In 1980, PIXAR developed an animated film depicting a mountain range that was continuously refined with more and more detail as a virtual camera approached the mountain and flew over it.

Radiosity   The principal issue in achieving photorealism is that most computer pictures lack visual attributes—the surface characteristics of the object. This step in the emergence of photorealism came in the mid 1980s from a group at Cornell University. Borrowing the radiosity algorithm from radiative heat-transfer engineering, they modeled the effects an environment has on lighting. For example, as light shines on a wall, the wall radiates its color, which contributes illumination to nearby objects.

A photorealistic picture must have surface textures, shading, and light sources in addition to geometry. The modeling software must be able to describe every detail of a scene that a camera would see, and the renderer must be able to create an accurate image from this information.

The equations used by ray tracing and common rendering software handle specular reflection, but don't account for one of the most important interactions: the interreflection of light between surfaces. Radiosity methods treat diffusely reflecting surfaces correctly—objects are illuminated not only by light bulbs, but also by light reflected from other objects.

Diffusely reflecting surfaces are difficult for ray tracing because they reflect light in a way that works against ray tracing's basic strategy. Ray tracing follows a ray's reflection from a surface to determine the point of illumination. This process is very efficient if the surface is a mirror. However, diffusely reflecting surfaces behave just the opposite; they reflect light in all directions with equal intensity.

Radiosity methods originated in the fields of radiant-heat transfer and illumination engineering. In analyses of problems in these fields, the surfaces of an environment are broken up into small pieces, or patches. The transfer of radiant energy between each patch and every other patch is then computed, typically by solving a matrix equation. In radiosity algorithms for computing light interreflection, each small patch is a potential source of light energy.

Radiosity doesn't render an image. The process simply adds shading information to the surfaces of the scene. You need not choose the view until after the process is complete, at which point a rendering algorithm performs the perspective transformation, determines the visible surfaces, and interpolates the precomputed shading data—producing the final image.

Radiosity alone does not provide highlights, reflections, or refraction, because it's limited to diffusely reflecting surfaces. These effects are important not only for realism but for providing visual cues about geometry and surface quality. Fortunately, it's possible to partly add these effects during the rendering phase with effective results. Even more striking results can be obtained by using a ray tracer as the final rendering engine. Some of the most dramatic images produced to date are the result of combining radiosity and ray tracing.

Modeling vs. rendering   Both modeling and rendering are very difficult problems, and software developers have had to deal with both. The developers of most CAD programs, for example, were forced to develop both a modeler and a renderer (another example of the merging of applications). However, they were generally unable to solve the entire problem of photorealistic picture creation. The lack of standards for file formats and device drivers created by the proliferation of incompatible products has further handicapped the industry's ability to make visual accuracy accessible to users.

Separation of the modeling and rendering domains is the key to making photorealistic computer pictures widely accessible: One way to separate modelers (e.g., wire frames) and renderers is the creation of a standard interface between them. With a standard interface, any compatible model can have immediate access to the full power of all the features of any interface-compliant renderer, without a file-conversion process. The user can choose a renderer on any basis that seems appropriate: cost, efficiency, speed, or image quality. This selection can even change during the development of a single model.

The success of PostScript demonstrates the advantages of a standard interface. The existence of PostScript, available with the Macintosh and Laserwriter, led directly to the breakthrough of desktop publishing in the mid 1980s. Developers created various page-layout systems (modelers) at that time to drive PostScript, confident that PostScript interpreters (renderers) would be available on faster, cheaper printing devices.

In the early days of photorealistic computer graphics (1974), shaded-picture algorithms used polygons to crudely model every object, smooth or not. In those days, because computers were very slow, the computations were focused primarily on solving the hidden-surface problem.

There are three major steps in rendering a photorealistic two-dimensional digital image from a three-dimensional scene. First, the content of the image is determined by a virtual camera that projects the scene into two dimensions. The two-dimensional area that goes into the rendered image is the screen window, analogous to the standard photographic frame.

After determining the content of the image via the camera definition, an array of pixels must be defined to represent the scene. The rectangle of pixels that represents the content of the screen window is called the *frame*. Finally, the image is produced by deriving a digital value at each pixel, which represents the part of the scene that projects to the neighborhood of that pixel. Figure C-6 shows the results of a multistep, multiapplication process to generate a photorealistic image.

While the camera model typically used in computer graphics is a simple pinhole, photorealism programs offer a camera with a lens and an adjustable aperture to calculate the passage of light through the scene, its interaction with surfaces, and its projection onto the viewing surface. This makes it possible to introduce depth of field and motion-blur effects.

Photorealism implies that the renderer's camera simulation doesn't introduce artifacts into the image from the computational process. A few of the most important features of a photorealistic rendering program are:

❏ Hidden-surface removal, so only visible objects appear in the image
❏ Spatial filtering, so aliasing artifacts aren't present
❏ Dithering, so quantization artifacts aren't noticeable
❏ Temporal filtering, so the opening and closing of the shutter causes moving objects to be blurred
❏ Depth of field, so only objects at the current focal distance are sharply in focus

Photorealism has been the quest of computer-graphics users and designers since raster displays became popular. One leader in that area is Pixar. The company has many credits from the movies and has developed a popular set of software known as RenderMan.

RenderMan   Photorealistic RenderMan is Pixar's rendering software, which can create images with the nap of velvet, the shine of polished gold, and the reflections of multiple light sources—all displayed realistically. It accepts curved geometric primitives so that geometry can be displayed accurately, and the basic shapes include a diversity of man-made and natural objects. This includes patches, quadric, and representations of solids. RenderMan also provides the ability to deal with complicated scenes containing from ten thousand to several million geometric primitives.

RenderMan is the same technology that was used to produce some of the most memorable scenes in *Terminator 2, The Abyss,* and *Beauty and the Beast.* It's available for the Macintosh as MacRenderMan, for PC and UNIX users as the RenderMan Toolkit, and for PC/DOS as an integral part of several third-party design packages. RenderMan has been endorsed by Apple, IBM, Digital, Hewlett-Packard, NeXT, Sun, Intel, Autodesk, Wavefront, the Walt Disney Company, and several other important companies.

RenderMan provides general shading operations in determining the color at each point on the screen. Because a shader is attached to each surface, the shader procedure can be computed at all visible surface points on the screen. In this way, the user retains powerful and precise control over surface and lighting characteristics.

This control includes the ability to employ scanned textures. Such texture mapping can be used to affect not only the color of the surface, but also its bumpiness, reflectivity, or transparency. Because the shader is programmable, multiple textures can be dropped into the shading calculation in an arbitrary fashion to achieve a variety of effects. The shader procedures are called in a parameterized fashion, allowing for simple and interactive user control without reprogramming.

RenderMan supports elements necessary to create images on a computer, including the difficult functions like motion blur, CSG (constructive solid geometry), displacement, texture mapping, and atmospheric effects like fog and fire.

Pixar, who developed RenderMan, worked with over twenty computer-graphics organizations to develop the 3-D graphics standard known as the RenderMan Interface. This format describes settings, objects, lighting, and the cameras and motion that create an image. Compatible modeling software, such as VIDI's Presenter Professional, use this format to create platform-independent files called RIB (RenderMan interface bytestream), which can then be rendered by software containing RenderMan on any supported computer. RIB is quite similar to PostScript in that it encapsulates a 3-D scene description, much like PostScript encapsulates a description of a 2-D scene. Therefore, users working in a RenderMan environment can make pictures on almost any kind of hardware. Only the rendering speed and the ease of use will vary.

RenderMan also has a shading language that makes it possible to give objects a highly realistic look, including full textural displacement (altering the surface geometry). This language can also be used to create special effects—including such things as glow and fire.

Because RenderMan is an open system, users can benefit from acceleration products that speed the creation of images (many times over a normal Macintosh or PC). The StarTech i860 RenderEdge board for the Macintosh, for example, speeds rendering on an individual Mac, giving near-workstation performance. Several ISVs have developed interfaces to RenderMan from within their programs, which allow the user to create models, arrange scenes, set lights, apply and alter shaders, and then output RIB files for rendering.

A modeler allows the user to create 3-D objects. To use RenderMan, the modeler must output RenderMan-format RIB files. This includes standard polygonal modelers, as well as more advanced spline and NURB-based modelers.

Most 3-D modeling programs today are polygon-based. 3-D modeling in polygons is like making a sphere out of folded-up cardboard. It's a crude representation, and doesn't really look like a sphere when examined closely. The greater the number of polygons, the closer the approximation is to the real object. More polygons, however, means much larger data files. A simple scene can easily consist of thousands of polygons in order to closely approximate the typical range of forms and surfaces in an image. Spline-based modelers, such as VIDI's PresenterProfessional for the Macintosh, RenderWare from PM Source, and FastCAD from Evolution Computing for PC/DOS platforms provide compact files and true round shapes.

After the model is created, it might need a surface, like plastic or wood, and colors to make it appear realistic. This is where the artistry comes into computer picture making and where shaders are needed.

Shaders create the surfaces and all the effects in a RenderMan scene. While other modeling programs typically wrap pictures or computed textures on an object to give it a life-like appearance, shaders are actually intelligent 3-D surfaces—small programs that literally endow an object with a complete appearance. Shaders are procedural (mathematically-based) descriptions of how light interacts with a particular surface, for example, and whether that surface is deformed in any way, such as the threads on a screw, stones in a wall, or veins in a leaf.

The power of shaders lies in their ability to completely simulate every aspect of light interaction, color, and surface displacement. This power is released through programs that include RenderMan, like those from VIDI, PM Source, Evolution Computing, as well as Pixar's own scene-layout program—Showplace. Similar to page-layout software, Showplace allows the user to lay out a 3-D scene by selecting existing objects from Showplace's object library or importing objects created by RIB modelers.

From within each of these programs, the user can assign shaders and looks to an object and access the key parameters that control a shader's characteristics. This includes the interaction of ambient and other forms of lighting, the color of specular highlights, and displacement of the environmental reflections that give an object a much more life-like appearance.

The RenderMan Interface   As mentioned earlier, Pixar worked with leading computer-graphics organizations for many months to define the RenderMan Interface, which specifies a comprehensive way for a software program to describe objects, scenes, lights, and cameras for the creation of photorealistic images. The interface has been endorsed by much of the computer-graphics industry, including Autodesk, Cadkey, Digital Arts, Digital Equipment Corporation, IBM, Intel, NeXT, and Sun Microsystems.

The RenderMan Interface is a collection of procedures to transfer the description of a scene to a rendering program. The rendering program takes this input and produces an image. This image can be immediately displayed, printed, or saved in an image file. The output image can contain color, as well as coverage and depth information for postprocessing.

The significant technical advances of the RenderMan Interface lie in the full generality of its shading language and its incorporation of texture mapping. A software developer using the RenderMan Interface writes, compiles, and runs a conventional computer program, calling a set of special procedures to describe the scene. Some procedures control the color, texture, and placement of objects, while others control the lights that illuminate the objects and the camera viewing the scene.

The RenderMan Interface is designed so that the information needed to specify a photorealistic image can be efficiently passed to different rendering programs. The interface is designed to be used by both batch-oriented and real-time interactive rendering systems. It can drive different hardware devices, software implementations, and rendering algorithms. In order to achieve this, the Interface doesn't specify how a picture is rendered, but instead specifies how the picture is to look.

RenderMan Interface Bytestream   The file format of the interface is known as the RenderMan Interface Bytestream, or RIB. RIB files permit modeling-system clients to communicate requests to a remote rendering service, and provide a way to save requests for later submission to a renderer. Utility programs for shader management, scene editing, and rendering-job dispatching can also use information in the file. For example, RIB files provide a mechanism for 3-D clip art by allowing programs to insert objects into preexisting scenes.

Iceman   Pixar has also introduced new technology for managing full-color continuous-tone images. Pixar describes the new technology, called Iceman (*ICE* stands for Image Computing Environment), as a full programming language for images that are resolution-, platform-, and ply- (number of color channels) independent, extensible, optimizable, and capable of implementing "image expressions." It supports image logistics, enhancements and correction, spatial transformations, painting, editing, and compositing functions. It uses the control structures of PostScript and can be implemented as an extension to PostScript.

Voxels   A *voxel* is a word derived from *pixel*. A *pixel* (or picture element) is a 2-D sample of a digital image. It has a specific location in the plane of a picture, and is defined by two coordinates (usually x and y). A *voxel*, or volume pixel, is a sample that exists in a 3-D grid, positioned at defined x, y, and z coordinates. Each voxel also possesses a value, but a voxel's value is rarely used to represent a simple color or other visibility property. Instead, a voxel's value represents a sample of volume data from the real world.

Voxels are generated by various instruments, particularly 3-D raster-scanning instruments. Perhaps the most familiar example of these instruments is the x-ray computerized tomography (CT) scan machine. A more recent voxel-generating instrument that has revolutionizing biological science is the laser-scan confocal microscope (LSCM).

The LSCM produces a voxel volume by scanning a highly focused laser beam across a microscopic plane inside a semi-transparent specimen, and recording the light reflected or produced by fluorescence with a very sensitive detector. To derive maximum information from voxel data, you need the relationships among the structures of the volume. This technique is known as volume rendering, or volume imaging. *Volume rendering* relies on two principal methods.

The first method, called *image ordering* (or *ray casting*), positions the volume behind the picture plane. A ray is projected perpendicularly from each pixel in the picture plane through the volume behind the pixel. As each ray penetrates the volume, it accumulates the properties of the voxels it passes through and adds them to the corresponding pixel.

The other method, called *object order* (or *compositing* or *splattering*) also combines the voxel values to produce image pixels. The image plane is positioned behind the volume, and each pixel is assigned an initial background value. A ray is projected perpendicularly from the image plane through the volume to the viewer. As the ray encounters each successive layer of voxels, the voxel values are blended into the background, forming the image according to each voxel's interpreted opacity. It's as if the volume were held up in front of the picture plane and pressed flat against it. Over the next few years, voxels, volume imaging, 3-D image processing, and volume-rendered animation might very well become an integral part of most scientific, engineering, and medical disciplines.

Texture mapping and photorealistic images represent the ultimate in image synthesization. These tools and techniques are used to create scenes or models that never existed or were too difficult to create or capture. For situations where real-world information must be used, often in real time, we use a different technology—industrial image processing and machine vision.

The idea of using a TV camera and computers to replace people in hazardous or boring jobs has been a long-sought-after and sometimes elusive goal. Early developers underestimated the complexity of the task and claims were made that have yet to be realized. That caused a backlash, resentment, and mistrust of the concept. However, there were enough successes, general commitment to the logic, and need for the concept that the industry was sustained and grew at a slow but steady rate.

Industrial image processing

Systems used in machine vision (also called *inspection*, *QC*, *process monitoring*, and *security*) employ a digitizer or frame grabber at the output of a photomultiplier or a camera. Some systems look at scene (for physical and/or color conformity) while others look at a strip across a production line. Some systems, once installed, use only a display for testing because the production line isn't manned.

Machine vision is used to replace human vision in complex dangerous, and/or high-throughput manufacturing situations. Seen in the early 1960s as the way of the future and an essential technology to increase productivity and quality, machine vision had great promise. However, as is the case with many technology forecasts and dreams, not too many systems lived up to the promise. In the late 1970s it became clear that duplicating a human's pattern- and color-recognition capabilities wasn't an easy task. However, at the same time it was realized there were several situations where a machine-vision system could indeed do as good, and in some cases a better job. By the mid to late 1980s the industry was applying machine vision to assemble and inspect products, guide robots, identify parts on an assembly line, and provide crucial information for statistical process control.

Simulation is the basis for most computer-graphics applications and many business applications. When a user develops a spreadsheet to forecast a market or business plan, that is a simulation. Some people might argue that a photorealistic image is also a simulation. Many others think of flight simulators when they think of a simulation, and it's true that that is one of the most popular applications. The problem of defining what simulation is can be avoided by adding the term *photorealistic* or *real-time* in front of the word *simulation*.

Simulation

Simulation applications represent real objects with algorithmically generated graphical objects, and create simulated movement of these objects for scientific test and analysis. The primary difference between simulation and animation is that in simulation, motion is used to approximate the behavior of a real object, with the express purpose of deriving useful information about how the object would behave under similar conditions. Animation, on the other hand, is more concerned with the aesthetics, or enjoyment values, derived from the simulation. Traditionally, simulation is an entire market segment in itself. However, for purposes of covering all imaging applications, I've included it in this category.

Photorealistic simulations focus on the realism of a computer-generated picture, with little concern for the time required to compute it. In real-time simulations, interaction and speed of rendering are the foremost concerns. The difference between static photorealistic graphics and dynamic real-time graphics is huge. Static images exist for their own sake—they're equivalent to photographs of synthetic worlds.

Real-time graphics, however, engage you in interaction with a computer that expands what you can do and how you do it. Your interaction with realistic images enables otherwise impossible applications, such as virtual-reality games and visual simulators for driving and flight training. Creating a realistic scene to train pilots or people learning to drive a car or a submarine without the dangers associated with making a mistake has been the goal of computer scientist for decades. To be considered real-time, the rendering speed must be at least 10 frames per second, and quality can be increased by adding hardware capability.

One of the basic assumptions most people in computer graphics make is that photorealism is the ultimate goal. Common sense tells us that the more realistic an image or a simulation is, the more useful it will be.

However, according to Gavin Lintern, a professor of aviation psychology at the University of Illinois at Urbana-Champaign, it might be time to question that assumption. Lintern has been involved in the field of flight simulation since 1975, training students on flight simulators and conducting experiments. The surprising conclusion of his experiments is that highly realistic flight simulators aren't always more effective for teaching students how to fly. In some cases, added realism can even be counterproductive.

In the beginning he tried to make the simulations as realistic as possible. In 1985, he began systematically removing visual cues—taxiways, corn fields, buildings— and found that for some things, lower fidelity or the schematic approach is better. For example, he found that schematic displays rather than higher-fidelity images reduce the amount of landing practice required by a student before soloing in a light aircraft by as much as 15%. He also discovered that a pilot's ability to fly in simulated crosswinds was better following simulator training without crosswinds.

Lintern speculates that increased detail in a simulation might actually cause students in certain situations to overcompensate in their reactions, and thus develop bad habits that then take time to correct. Lintern doesn't suggest that realistic simulators are useless. Indeed, he acknowledges that for some things realism might be crucial. But he does maintain that the rush to provide photorealism for everything might be premature. What vendors and users ought to do, he says, is take time to conduct behavioral studies to determine which type of characteristics are important for simulation training and which aren't.

Business visualization   Visual data analysis (VDA) is working its way from acceptance in the scientific and engineering industry into a position of increasing interest and use in the commercial arena. VDA, better known in business markets as business visualization or Biz Viz, can be used by corporate users interested in seeing graphical representations of their data. VDA is fanning out into other commercial areas including insurance, banking, and credit cards. This technology is popular not just on UNIX-based workstations or Silicon Graphics systems, but also on X terminals, PCs, and Macs.

VDA is highly interactive software that combines graphics displays and analytical techniques to quickly interpret large amounts of data. Examples are AVS's software package, the Application Visualization System (AVS), and Precision Visuals' VDA product, PV-Wave (Workstation Analysis Visualization Environment).

Business visualization software has been used to aid credit-card companies in decreasing financial risks by identifying cardholders most likely to default on their bill. Stockbrokers, statisticians, and people dealing with a lot of data, can tie that multivariant data into a 3-D model they can interact with. Rather than comparing variables individually, such as a sales representative's region, quarter, and sales results, a 3-D block model will provide much more insight.

Many analysts have predicted that this technology could revolutionize the way people view data. Visual data analysis will become to technical oriented jobs—financial analysts, decision support systems—what the spreadsheet has become to commercial computing. It will be, in essence, a way to do visually via graphics what the spreadsheet does via numbers.

However, it's taking time for Biz Viz to achieve widespread use in offices. And it has only just begun to creep into the commercial side. This has largely been due to the expense of high-end graphics workstations. However, with high-performance graphics now available for the PC and Macintosh and the new lower-cost workstations, price and performance will no longer be the barrier.

Visualization products combine tools for graphics, analysis, data management, and data input in a dynamic environment. Each of these pieces of technology has been available to users, but not in a single application covering the full scope. In some ways the progression of this particular technology is a bit analogous to the evolution we went through from electronic publishing to desktop publishing.

According to many in the industry, VDA allows users to consider increased amounts of data in a form more conducive to logical analysis. Most people look at maybe one or two percent of the data they have. They miss a tremendous number of trends and patterns that they would have seen if they had been able to look at the entire data set. The visual recognition system in the human brain can extract patterns out of all this. VDA provides more information to the brain, and lets it match patterns in order to extract relationships between the different kinds of data it's looking at.

Virtual reality   Virtual-reality (VR) systems are ones that place the user in a computer-generated or -enhanced environment so realistic as to cause the suspension of disbelief. The person experiencing the simulation actually believes that he or she is in the environment. VR systems promise to be the ultimate simulation systems, but there's still a lot of work to be done in their development.

To obtain that level of disbelief, users tend to be more critical of factors such as image quality, tracking-system lags, and the ergonomics of peripheral design. Yet in the arcade implementations of VR, there's an apparent enthusiasm (and absence of criticism) by users when they emerge from one of them.

No longer a novelty or dream, but not yet a part of everyday life (even in the computer field), the much-publicized, sensory-blending technology is slowly making progress. Initially confined to research labs, VR has become available to the general public in arcades and a few situations in medicine and architecture.

However, many of the serious demonstrations are boring, uncomfortable, inactive, visually impoverished, "safe" virtual worlds, where there's little more to do than move a virtual chess piece, observe flying fish and butterflies, or open a virtual door. Although such demonstrations might feature Gouraud shading, radiosity algorithms, and texture maps, it's impressive to only those who understand what the computing technology has to do to achieve such realism in anything approaching real time. But it doesn't have enough impact for the naive or uninformed user.

It's also true that the arcade systems are visually impoverished, but there's a major difference in the experiences they offer to users. In the arcade systems, the user is motivated both before and during the immersion period—before immersion by being part of an over-enthusiastic line of people desperate to "have a go," and during immersion, by the need to not be deprived of the experience of being shot, trampled upon, eaten, or crushed in a racing car. As a result of such motivation and despite an increased level of arousal, once immersed, arcade users simply have no additional resources available to do such mundane things as assess the quality of the technology itself.

The first steps toward virtual reality were begun by the U.S. Air Force. Projects were started to develop display helmets for flight simulators in a lab at NASA Ames Research Center (near San Jose). This simulator had two components: an electronic image and electronic manipulation. These early prototype systems allowed users to view 3-D images that moved relative to their head. In conjunction with the display helmet, the user wore a glove (since named a *data glove*) and could interact with the image.

The name *virtual reality* initially applied to such helmets (which were later reduced in size to a large pair of goggles) and glove systems. However, there were soon adaptations of the system using screens, joysticks, and other display and input devices. Thereafter, any system that provided 3-D multidirectional view with interactivity (sound for some reason was an option) became known as VR. In the early systems, and still today, there's a tradeoff between motion and high resolution. A more powerful computer is needed (will always be needed).

One of the first practical applications of VR was in the field of telepresence surgery. It was developed to enhance laparoscopic surgery (e.g., in the removal of the gall bladder). Recent innovations in video technology have allowed direct viewing of internal body cavities, such as the abdomen, through natural orifices or tiny incisions, instead of surgery, which involves large incisions and directly viewing and touching the internal organs and tissues. This type of surgery is less invasive, resulting in less serious side effects, faster recovery, and lower insurance costs.

A VR surgical simulator makes it possible to bring other methods of display into the system, such as CT or MRI scans to create sophisticated 3-D images. The VR surgical simulator offers one key advantage: The surgeon uses the same tools to practice with as to perform the surgery. No more joysticks, and the like, which aren't like the actual tools used in surgery.

In another example, VR has been used in a computer-assisted stereoactic neurosurgery system. A brain surgeon, wearing a special set of stereo viewers, has a superimposed 3-D view of a brain tumor (that was obtained from a CAT scanner) to look at while he probes a patient's head with a microscopic laser cutter/viewer.

Japanese consumers have already adopted VR systems and are quite happy to put on the goggles and gloves. They're used in stores to simulate how appliances can be located in a kitchen or a TV can be placed in a living room. So VR isn't just for games and medicine; more common practical uses are already with us and more are coming.

The next generation will employ contactless sensors. These sensors are known as "gesture sensors." A user's actions are monitored by two or three cameras. The user's hand actions are then encoded and assigned to various functions. In addition to freeing the user from clumsy equipment, these developmental systems offer great promise for the handicapped.

Also under development are special glasses with small lasers in the side. The laser's beams are reflected off the back of the lens into the wearer's eyes. The lasers generate a scanning pattern the same as a CRT. The pattern, which represents a stereo pair, is then used to stimulate the cells on the retina. The result is a truly virtual image that isn't seen on the lens (because they're too close to focus on) but rather in the brain, due to direct retinal stimulation. Sound farfetched? So did TV when it was first described.

Bit-map & raster operations

In the past, the distinction between the two major technology and application segments was vector and image processing. Image-processing techniques became too pervasive in too many applications to provide the simple segmentation it once did. Trying to define what is or isn't image processing is beyond the scope of this book (and most certainly its author). Basically, any manipulation of a raster image can be considered image processing. That definition can be conveniently used to exclude vector-based systems and applications (CAD, ATC, GIS, etc.). However, any rasterized image that's manipulated in a window could fall under such a broad heading.

The manipulation of images at the pixel level (as opposed to the manipulation of a line or vector) requires the use of a bit-map and raster operations.

Bit maps

A bit map is an array of pixels. Each pixel in the array has an x and a y coordinate, and a depth or z value (also called the *pixel value*). It's possible to direct an action at or read the value of any individual pixel, hence the word *map*. IBM prefers the term *all points addressable* (APA), but the concepts and results are the same.

Bit maps were differentiated from earlier vector or stroke displays and character- or cell-organized displays. The vector displays were found in high-performance, high-resolution CAD and air-traffic-control (ATC) systems. Character-based displays were found in dumb ASCII terminals and early PC displays. Bit-mapped displays used more memory (which was very expensive) and required more sophisticated control techniques.

Raster operations

Raster operations refer to the techniques used to manipulate the individual pixels and their bits in a raster display. It's an older expression that related to the differentiation of display technology, because the operations in raster operations are based on Boolean mathematics and really aren't limited to a scanning system.

As mentioned, early displays used a vector drawing technique (also called a *stroke writer*). When raster techniques, the scanning techniques developed for TV, were adopted to computer graphics, opportunities (and some necessities) were presented to operate on individual pixel values. Using Boolean logic, the bits of a pixel could be combined in AND, OR, and exclusive OR fashions. This allowed interesting combinations of color mixing, invisibility, and other effects. Raster operations (commonly known as raster ops, or ROPS) are an integral part of all graphical user interface systems.

Graphical user interfaces

Graphical user interfaces are environments that are completely bit-mapped. They rely heavily on raster operations and offer little or no vector operations. The three most popular GUIs are the X Windows System for workstations (usually with a MOTIF front end), the built-in Macintosh GUI, and Microsoft's Windows for the PC. Within window environments, image mapping, color mapping, and bitBLT operations are the most crucial.

GUIs present some basic challenges to a system. In a DOS system, for example, a character is represented by 2 bytes. In Windows, it requires 72 bytes because Windows, like any other bit-mapped GUI, deals with each pixel in the character. Because a GUI must be able to move blocks of pixels, overlay them, and store them for later use, huge amounts of data travel around the system. That means, with a simple frame buffer, a lot of CPU time and enormous demands on the system's bandwidth are required. Anything that can be done by the display controller to off-load the host will help.

BitBLT   Bit boundary block transfers (bitBLT) is an important feature for applications in graphic arts, image processing, windowing, and text location. A bitBLT is the movement of a defined area within the display from one location to another. For example, imagine a block in the upper left corner that contains some image (a menu, icon, or picture). The user or the application program might require that the block be moved to the lower right. For operator convenience, it should be moved as quickly as possible. It must also leave the area where it was originally located unblemished. This is also useful for copying icons or special symbols from off-screen memory to on-screen space.

BitBLT speed is how quickly each pixel within a defined area can be moved to another location, and is measured in pixels per second. The speed specification might not take the time needed to select the function and set up the conditions needed to move into consideration; therefore, raw pixel/second speed could be misleading.

Color look-up tables   Display memory (the frame buffer), contains a certain number of bits (usually 8) for each pixel displayed on the screen. The values of these bits are called *pixel values*. The output of the frame buffer is fed to a color look-up table (LUT), also known as a color map. An LUT is a small table with entries specifying the RGB values of the currently available colors; the entries can also be called *color cells*. The pixel values are interpreted as indices to the color cells, thus to refresh the screen, the display hardware uses the RGB values in the color cells indexed by the pixel values. The size of the LUT is less than or equal to $2n$ color cells, where n is the number of bits in a pixel value. A device with an 8 bits-per-pixel value, for example, will have a color map with up to 256 color cells, indexed through pixel values ranging from 0 to 255.

In many cases, similar graphic effects can be generated by either changing the pixel values (raster manipulation) or changing the RGB values stored in the color cells (LUT manipulation). Why change the color cells instead of the pixel values? The main reasons are memory, speed, and graphical interfaces.

Off-screen pixel maps   Many applications use off-screen pixel maps to generate some graphics. These pixel maps use a lot of memory and might not be necessary with LUT manipulation techniques. Also, because only a few (or few dozen) color cells are changed with LUT manipulation, as opposed to hundreds or thousands of pixel values, you usually get much better performance by changing the color cells. Finally, LUT manipulation can avoid some of the flickering effects usually seen in graphics-based raster manipulation (especially animation). The disadvantage of LUT manipulation techniques is that they use at least twice as many color cells as raster manipulation techniques. As color cells tend to be a valuable resource, this is undesirable.

Overlay planes   Another very useful LUT manipulation technique is the overlay plane. It's often necessary to add some other image (usually something simple like labels) to a complex drawing. Using a simple raster-manipulation drawing tool like a paint program, the overlay graphics will corrupt the base drawing. If the overlay is erased, the base drawing will have to be redrawn, which can be very expensive and often very ugly.

A typical example of the use of an overlay plane is a TV image that has labels announcing the channel or next show on top of the image. Another is an air-traffic-control system, with a static map display and moving aircraft icons drawn over the map. You can probably think of many other examples.

Overlay-plane applications usually divide 8-bit pixel values into 7 bits for the base drawing and 1 bit for the overlay plane. In more expensive systems there are separate overlay planes. The key to this technique is giving all pixels in the overlay plane (i.e., pixels with the overlay-plane bit set to one) the same color. Thus, drawing or erasing in the overlay plane is simply a matter of setting or clearing one bit.

Double-buffer animation   Double (or multi-) buffering is used by most high-quality animation applications. The technique is similar to the overlay-plane technique described previously. In low-cost double buffering, the frame buffer is split into two 4-bit frames. The application draws two pictures in the viewable window (which could be full screen), and then manipulates the LUT to make only one of them visible. Each picture can have several colors (up to the limit of the pixel depth per frame), usually the same set of colors in each picture. To get the animated effect, the application modifies the second, hidden picture and quickly changes the LUT, displaying the second picture and hiding the first. Then it repeats the process.

Because the technique works very quickly and the drawing process is hidden from the user, the animation is very fast and smooth. The alternative raster-manipulation technique using bitBLTs is sometimes slower and usually generates undesirable flickering or other graphical side effects as the drawing is created.

More expensive display controllers designed for animation or simulation will offer two (or more) 8-bit (or larger) frame buffers. Double buffering works only if the application is set up to take advantage of the hardware's capabilities.

Color cycle & alternate-color animation   While overlay planes and double buffering are the two most important LUT-manipulation graphics techniques, others can be useful for some applications. Following is a brief discussion of color-cycle animation and alternate-color animation. Their implementation is much simpler than the earlier examples and, as promised, I won't present any code examples.

Both techniques are pure LUT manipulations. The raster graphics are drawn once, and all other graphical effects come solely from manipulating the LUT. They have the advantage of being very fast, but the disadvantage of being very inflexible.

Color cycle   Color-cycle animation is one of the simplest LUT-manipulation techniques. It's frequently used in video games and simulations where a flashy effect is needed. One application of color cycling is a sparkling or fluid effect where pixels in a window are drawn with random pixel values, and the colors associated with the color cells are rapidly cycled. The colors are typically cycled simply by shifting them by one pixel value per iteration and storing them. Some simple object-motion effects can also be generated by assigning the same pixel values to larger areas, such as lines or rectangles.

Alternate color   Alternate-color animation is similar to color cycling. With this technique, only two unique colors are used: foreground and background. The background color is set to be the same as the window background color. Several instances of a single object are drawn in different locations, with each location representing different positions along the path of the object's animation. Each instance is drawn with a different pixel value. As the foreground color is remapped to different instances' pixel values, the object will appear to move.

Both cycling and alternate color animation can be extended to handle many objects, overlapping objects, etc. with some restrictions. The major restriction is that you can't change the path of the animation once the object instances have been drawn. If you want a dynamic path, you'll need to use an overlay plane or double-buffer technique, described previously.

Multimedia   Volumes have been written about what is and isn't multimedia. It's not the purpose of this book to enter into that discussion and, therefore, I'll provide a suitable definition for display and capture systems, and the merging of applications.

Multimedia involves the generation of information for later presentation. The process of generation can include the mixing of video information (with or without sound), digitally generated information (from paint and rendering, word-processing, or CAD programs) and specialized authoring programs. Tremendous image-manipulation and processing can take place (e.g., Lucas Film to Animator from Autodesk). Compression techniques can take 24-bit color and make it reproducible at 8 bits in order to save storage space or transmission time.

Multimedia is a somewhat new area that was created in the early 1990s and overlaps, in some cases, the image and video segment of the computer-graphics industry. It covers video capture, video output, recorder control, display overlay, sound, and other related items. The two main types of programs found in this segment are authoring and indexing.

Multimedia is another application area that contributes to the blurring of lines between applications. GTE Imagitrek and Philips Interactive Media Systems have developed a new type of interactive television that will allow television programs to interact with material printed on compact discs (CDs). The television/CD combination would take advantage of Philips' existing Compact Disc Interactive (CD-I) system that already uses a television for its display screen.

Philips is not the only company producing a television-based CD system. Commodore has a system called CD-TV, based on a different format. Both systems are primarily entertainment-geared, though there have been some serious applications in factory training and educational titles available for the CD-I systems.

The management of Philips Interactive Media Systems has stated that as TV enters into the digital domain, we'll see the worlds of television, computer, and communication coming closer to each other. This will create an important platform for growth in interactive multimedia.

GTE has been experimenting with applications for digital media for several years. The company has home users with digital television, interactive telephones, pay-by-view digital TV, and interactive services over optical cable, broadcast, telephone lines, and combinations of all the delivery methods.

Yet with all the developments and promises of great new worlds, we still have the same old problems of getting manufacturers to agree on standards.

Multiple standards

The multimedia market is no different than any other computer-graphics market and suffers from a bewildering array of "standards," none of which are followed strictly enough to provide stability. To be safe, applications developers have had to support more than one, which results in doing their work several times over. Consumers have also had too many choices, any of which can lock them into some applications and out of others.

Nearly every important vendor in the industry has proposed a different decompression technology for digital video, and there seems to be no hope of a single standard for storing video data files. Not even MPEG (Motion Picture Experts Group), a standard developed by the International Standards Organization (ISO) is immune—MPEG expanded first into three, then four, and then back again to two groups.

Vendors offering digital-video compression technology in some form include Apple (QuickTime), Microsoft (Audio Video Interactive—AVI through DV-MCI), IBM (PhotoMotion or DVI), Intel (DVI through DV-MCI), and Philips (CD-I with MPEG); other vendors offering similar technologies include CoSA, Fluent Systems, Icom Simulations, Iterated Systems, Media Vision, UCV Corp., and Xing Technology.

The Multimedia PC (MPC), promoted by the MPC Marketing Council, a subsidiary of the Software Publishers Association (SPA) and Microsoft, CompuAdd, Tandy, Zenith, and others, is an example of the current fragmentation of standards. Despite its powerful backing, the Windows-based MPC might be ignored by consumers and professionals, as well as by vendors.

IBM's efforts   In late 1992, IBM formed a marketing relationship with MediaSourcery and third-party multimedia software vendors. The purpose of the union was twofold: to coordinate marketing of Ultimedia-Compatible Tools Series (UTS) software products and to define standards that enable all UTS tools to work smoothly with all other UTS tools. There are five major tools categories:

❑ Authoring tools
❑ Video tools
❑ Audio tools
❑ Graphics tools
❑ Animation tools

The standards being developed cover file formats for exchanging media, object-oriented techniques for manipulating data, CUA rules to provide a common look and feel to the tools, and a standard system interface for media data and devices to protect both the tools and the applications created with them from differences in file formats and media devices. For all practical purposes this is an ISV standards committee. Products range across DOS, OS/2, and Windows 3.x platforms. The committee will not devise new proprietary formats, but instead define methods for working within existing standards.

Companies participating in this union include Network Technology Corp., MEDIAscript Multimedia Architecture, Mammoth Micro Productions, Mammoth StudioXA (authoring software), HumanCAD 1.1, Mannequin (human-design CAD software), Allen Communications, Autodesk, Multimedia Explorer, Animator Pro, Time Arts, Lumena, ColorTools, Quest Multimedia (authoring system), Vision Imaging, and Multimedia Studio (presentation software).

This effort incorporates a number of phases. Phase 1 is to standardize drag-and-drop techniques, CLP format, and file interchange. Phase 2 adds control protocols, including OLE and DDE. The program is targeted squarely at training and Mar/Com departments in Fortune 1000 companies. Based on IBM's marketing strength—enterprise computing—the goal of the union is to bring order to the world of multimedia and ensure that products will work together seamlessly.

Video   The production and display of video, both captured and live, in a computer is now well known. Video is used with a computer for communications (e-mail and teleconferencing), training, clip-art generation, entertainment, advertising, and dozens of other applications. The most common usage is in production, communication, and multimedia.

Production   There are various application programs used for video production. These programs use both vector and bit-mapped graphics techniques and are known as:

❑ Titling
❑ Story boarding
❑ Special effects (i.e., "Toasters")
❑ Keying and framing

Using video with a computer for communications is becoming more popular every day. Teleconferencing is one area that has been in development for almost two decades. Attaching video clips (still images or small segments of live motion) to e-mail was popularized with the Macintosh and can now be found on all platforms.

Ask almost any multimedia producer (or "wannabe") to name the first item on his or her wish list, and most will ask for video. For less than $500, a producer can buy a digitizing board to grab frames or small clips of video from a VCR or camcorder. However, digitized video can create too much data, which will eat up a computer's storage and slow throughput. At standard display rates, a 150Mb disk holds less than five seconds of full-screen video. That's why efficient hardware-based digital compression and decompression is a must for full-screen video work.

Many desktop-video products are primarily concerned with controlling analog video signals and manipulating and displaying the video stream as it passes through on its way to mastering or distribution. Here's a brief survey of desktop components. Keep in mind, however, that many products support more than one type of application.

Frame grabbers   The original desktop-video board is the frame grabber or digitizer. A frame grabber captures and stores individual video frames for use as stills in graphic design, desktop publishing, or multimedia. Since the basic frame grabber boards lack compression, very little of the digitized video is actually saved.

Samplers   Samplers are low-cost slow-scan digitizers that can capture only a still image.

Overlay boards   An overlay board is a frame grabber that mixes computer-generated images and either displays them or sends them to a video recorder.

Video in a window   A video in a window board displays full-motion digital video on screen for presentations. Some can overlay text and graphics, but the lower-cost versions don't offer that feature.

Codec digitizers   Built around chipsets that perform compression and decompression algorithms in hardware, these boards can digitize, compress, and store entire video sequences to a hard disk or CD ROM, permitting video editing and real-time playback.

A single frame of uncompressed NTSC video (640×480, 8 bits deep) represents over 350K of data. Two hours of uncompressed video is nearly 80 gigabytes. For data rates, an uncompressed NTSC 30-frame/second signal represents 22Mb/second.

As a result of real-time data compression and decompression (codec) chipsets found on some digitizing boards, a new level of desktop-video integration is now available. These new generation codecs, using JPEG, MPEG, or DVI techniques, as either stand-alone add-in boards, optional daughterboards for digitizer/frame grabbers, or chips on the motherboard of the computer, bring near-broadcast-quality video to the desktop. They are supplying the compression muscle to digitize, record, and play back full-screen video at 30 frames per second.

Moving beyond first-generation technology, which lets users grab frames, overlay titles, and generate special effects, these boards can orchestrate fully digital documents, including video, animation, and sound, completely within the computer, and record the results to disk. Together with bundled or third-party video-editing software, the boards provide a capable editing environment for relatively modest applications, such as those for adding video clips to presentations or interactive multimedia applications.

Some, such as the DVI boards, offer enough real-time compression for video-conferencing and video-mail applications. Professional producers still can't perform entire broadcast-quality professional productions on desktop computers, but they can save time and money by performing rough "off-line" edits on the desktop before sending videos to sophisticated editing equipment for the final master.

Compression standards

Application developers and board designers attempting to interface ordinary audio and video into the digital world of computers have learned very quickly about the issues of bandwidth, storage, and throughput. Compression is the key to overcoming such obstacles. As a result, the digital-compression domain is a boiling cauldron of invention, out of which increasingly efficient chipsets and algorithms have (and continue to) emerge. Standardization suffers accordingly. For example, although JPEG is a firm standard as a still-image compressor, its motion varieties wander off on their own. Motion JPEG documents produced on one brand usually don't play on another.

The software-based compression built into Apple Computer's QuickTime is one variation of JPEG. QuickTime is rapidly emerging as a low-end standard, supported by popular noncompressing boards such as SuperMac's VideoSpigot. But the lack of standardization among higher-end JPEG products and the fact that JPEG wasn't initially designed for motion video has led developers to consider other standards. For most, the choice comes down to DVI or MPEG, a sophisticated motion technique formulated by the same International Standards Organization that developed JPEG.

DVI might be a proprietary standard, yet it's platform independent and upwardly compatible, offering a programmable codec chipset that's flexible enough to run new standards. Theoretically, standards such as JPEG, MPEG, or the H.261 standard for video conferencing could all be implemented with DVI technology because of its programmability.

DVI is only one of a bevy of competing video-compression standards. Here are the leading contenders:

JPEG (Joint Photographic Experts Group)   Designed to encode still images. Most motion JPEG versions compress with good quality at about a 20-to-1 ratio, with some products claiming up to 40:1 compression. (A lossless mode is also available, with an absolute resolution of about 5 to 1.) A symmetrical standard (compressing and decompressing at the same rate), it encodes redundant data occurring within each frame. It's most efficient for image areas of smooth transition, and provides good quality at maximum compression, but it can be slow.

MPEG (Motion Pictures Experts Group)   MPEG is also referred to as MPEG-1 to differentiate it from the subsequently defined MPEG-2 (and former MPEG-3) video and HDTV standards. MPEG-1 is intended for high-quality full-motion video images and audio. It delivers decompressed data up to the 1.5-Mbits/second range, and can play back full-motion video at 30 frames per second. MPEG-1, commonly referred to just as MPEG, uses different hardware to encode and decode. It uses a compression technique based on motion estimation and interpolative frames, also referred to as interframe compression, to eliminate redundant data occurring in sequential frames. Compression is fast in real time and quality is good at a 50:1 ratio, but only fair at its maximum 200:1 compression.

MPEG-2 is designed to provide compression in the 3- to 15-Mbits/second range (also known as MPEG++). MPEG-4 is for data rates in the 30-Kbits/second and below range for the ISDN and public-switched telephone networks.

Px64   Also known as CCITT Recommendation H.261, Px64 is a standard for motion video compression in video-phone and teleconferencing applications. Px64 transmits over digital copper or fiberoptic lines at 30 frames per second, and is designed to make use of 64-Kbits/second transmission channels.

QuickTime   Apple's media-integration architecture provides for video, audio, animation, and device control through four software-based compression algorithms: video, animation, stills, and graphics. Its Video Compressor permits fast decompression of movies or 24-bit still images while maintaining good picture quality. It yields compression ratios from 5:1 with good quality, and when bolstered with hardware-based compression, the range can extend from 5:1 to 25:1. As mentioned previously, it's based on JPEG.

In 1992, Silicon Graphics and Apple Computer announced that Silicon Graphics would support QuickTime, Apple's multimedia software architecture. SGI licensed the QuickTime compression algorithms from Apple and supports the QuickTime Movie file format in its software applications. This enabled IRIS users to create, edit, and play QuickTime movies from either IRIS or Macintosh computers.

SGI believes the QuickTime movie file format is becoming an industry standard for synchronized time-based media. At the same time, digital media is becoming a core technology in SGI systems. Through this agreement, SGI will be able to offer their customers digital-media compatibility with access to standard file formats such as QuickTime. This agreement is an important step in Apple's strategy to unify the industry around QuickTime in a single multimedia content format. It also gives SGI another multimedia vehicle with which to compete against Sun's SMCC.

Silicon Graphics has developed and is distributing value-added QuickTime compression/decompression algorithms (CODECs) for the IRIS-product family of MIPS R3000- and R4000-based computers, and Apple has rights to distribute the Silicon Graphics-compatible CODECs with its products. The CODECs were available with all of SGI's systems by the end of 1992.

QuickTime for Windows   QuickTime for Windows will play unmodified QT files, while AVI files require conversion to QT format. Apple also claims that the QuickTime format is "too rich" for AVI, given that QT has a built-in time base and can be composed of multiple video and audio streams. What Apple doesn't stress is that QuickTime for Windows is play-only. Only media created on the Macintosh platform will be available and can be played only by application software that has been written to use the QuickTime DLL. One measure of QuickTimes success, though, is Apple's claim that over 500 QuickTime applications have been announced.

Apple and WordPerfect have developed an OLE server for QuickTime, and 19 vendors—including Adobe, Corel, Creative Labs, Intel, Lotus, Media Vision, SuperMac, and WordPerfect—support it.

Apple and Microsoft have integrated Indeo video-compression technology into QuickTime on both Macs and PCs. This allows Macs to play unmodified Indeo files on both Macs and PCs, an advantage over AVI because no file conversion is required.

DVI   One of the most promising hardware-based compression technologies is DVI (Digital Video Interactive). A joint development of IBM and Intel Corp., DVI is both a chipset and a standard that covers everything from a software interface specification to compression. DVI compresses full-screen, full-motion video, animation, and still images into small files. At its 100-to-1 compression mode, users can play back one hour of full-screen video and high-quality audio from a single compact disc. DVI is available on PCs with IBM's ActionMedia II board and now on Macintosh IIs with New Video's EyeQ board.

Like JPEG and MPEG, DVI is a *lossy* technique, meaning that as it digitizes, it encodes data and throws away redundant (similar and adjacent) pixels, thus reducing file size. It also exploits weaknesses of human vision (such as the inability to perceive edges precisely) and throws away data that won't be missed by the human eye. (There are other *lossless* compression standards, favored in archiving and medical imaging, in which, to ensure accuracy, no information is discarded.)

DVI products support two modes of video compression: Real-Time Video (RTV) and Production-Level Video (PLV). The RTV mode achieves near-VCR-quality video with up to 128×120 display resolution at 30 frames per second. Like motion JPEG, it's used for editing and final production of partial screen displays, where the smaller image's lower resolution is less noticeable. It's also used for off-line editing and prototyping of full-screen video before delivery to a more advanced video-mastering system (such as PLV).

RTV is to JPEG as PLV is to MPEG. When digitizing video to a disk file for later playback or editing, RTV offers the same relatively low 20:1 compression ratio as JPEG. But RTV also offers an efficient real-time mode that digitizes video into a data stream for direct playback of full-motion video at a variable rate of from 100:1 to 150:1. The video stream can even travel smoothly over local- and wide-area networks for near-VCR-quality interactive playback on other computers, making it ideal for networked teleconferencing.

Like MPEG, DVI's more advanced PLV mode offers near-broadcast-quality video, with up to 512×480 display resolution at 30 frames per second. Designed for multimedia publishing, PLV makes it possible to digitize video at high resolutions with professional-level digital audio, and then play it back interactively at that same high resolution. Although MPEG can compress files at a rate of 200:1, the quality usually begins to diminish at rates greater than 50:1. Because the DVI chipset offers greater speed and better algorithmic efficiency of signal, PLV can achieve very high-quality images at 100:1, twice that of MPEG, and three to five times that of the various JPEG implementations.

Neither DVI/PLV or MPEG, however, are ideal if the application is video editing because they can't isolate single frames precisely, a must for professional off-line video editing. JPEG and DVI/RTV both provide easier editing environments because they use intraframe-compression algorithms, also called *spatial compression*. In this approach, each frame is examined and compressed separately, with no regard to the contents of surrounding frames. Both MPEG and DVI/PLV, however, use interframe (also called *predictive* or *temporal*) compression, which examines and stores a sequence of frames (an intrapicture). These interframe techniques identify the data that remains the same from frame to frame, and record only the data that changes, thus reducing redundant data and increasing compression rates. But because interframe compression doesn't save discrete frames, it makes it difficult to isolate a single frame. DVI/PLV has a slight edge over MPEG here, however, letting frames be flagged for later reconstruction as discrete entities.

The drawback with PLV—and it's a big one—is that users have to send their tape masters or compact discs to Intel or an authorized service bureau for mastering on a mainframe computer at a cost of up to $200 per minute. In addition, they might have to wait up to a month for results. In fact, some MPEG enthusiasts argue that DVI really isn't a desktop technology at all. The RTV component can be used to edit video but it's essentially the same as plain-vanilla motion JPEG, which means that playback is generally limited to smaller windows and lower frame rates. To get the full benefits, users need to compress the video as PLV and then wait.

Because of Intel's commitment to DVI, the company added DVI capability to a special version of the 486 processor, enabling users to take advantage of it without needing an add-in board. The company also developed a software version of it, dubbed SoftRTV, to work with Windows AVI (audio video interactive). This allows users to have multimedia on a laptop. Microsoft and Intel have also made SoftRTV a part of Video for Windows (VFW).

Video for Windows   Video for Windows is a software compression/decompression standard for the PC that's similar to Apple's QuickTime. Compression rates are 15 frames a second of 160×120 pixel windows, without hardware assist (from an add- in-board). With a hardware assist from a board, VFW can display 640×480 pixel windows at 30 frames per second.

VFW supports various compression algorithms, including DVI PLV, RTV, MediaVision's algorithm, and Microsoft's RLE (run-length encoder), formally called the Crunch coder/decoder but now known as MS Video. VFW is also flexible enough to use other manufacturers' proprietary compression/decompression algorithms, such as SuperMac's Compact Video Compressor, which comes with the Spigot for Windows multimedia board. SuperMac's CODEC allows asymmetrical compression of 230×240 pixels.

JPEG for AVI   C-Cube, in conjunction with Intel, Microsoft, and others, has defined a file format for bit-mapped images and video data that is compressed using the JPEG algorithm. JPEG still-image files are supported under Windows as Device-Independent Bitmap (DIB) files, and JPEG video files will be supported under Video for Windows as AVI files. The JPEG-DIB format allows still-image compression up to 15:1 with no loss of image quality. A number of vendors— including LSI Logic, Truevision, VideoLogic, New Media Graphics, Xing Technology, Fluent, and Creative Labs—have endorsed the file format. C-Cube also worked with Creative Labs to jointly develop video capture, compression, and display products for Video for Windows.

MPEG for VFW   Microsoft developed Video for Windows (VFW) to be as open as possible and to have various compression modules added to it. Over 15 hardware and software companies got together with Microsoft to define the MPEG VFW standard.

DVC (Digital Video Computing)   Digital Video Computing, or DVC, is an effective real-time communication-methodology collaboration between Intel and Microsoft. Captured video can be forwarded, stored, and edited for later use. Any 32-bit PC is capable of playing back DVC video without any special hardware. DVC also fits into existing infrastructures of businesses that have Intel-based PCs running Microsoft Windows.

DVC video playback uses software-only decompression in Video for Windows. The ability to modify the resolution, playback rate, and image quality is Intel's contribution to the collaboration. This technology, named Indeo, offers scalable playback, real-time capture via an i750-based board, and AVI-file compatibility. Based on subsampling methods, Indeo uses what Intel terms a 9-bit pixel. Each 4×4 pixel block is represented by 128 bits for Y, and eight bits each for U and V. Adding those together and dividing by 16 (bus width) gives the result of 9 words per 4×4 block. Compression is obtained by subsampling, filtering (reducing the image from 512×480 to 256×240), and compressing, ending with a 50:1 compression ratio. The compression method can change within an AVI file, allowing optimal compression to be actively chosen.

Video for Windows introduces the AVI file format, digital video capture, and an installable codec interface. Three codecs are provided with VFW: Microsoft RLE, Microsoft Video 1 (licensed from MediaVision), and Intel Indeo for 286, 386+ and 486 (with or without an i750 board) systems. Microsoft also provides a conversion program to convert QuickTime movies into AVI-compliant files. The specific components of VFW are:

❑ An enhanced Media Player that enables users to cut, paste, and play back digital-video sequences under Windows 3.1.
❑ VidEdit, a video editor that enables users to combine, edit, and compress digital-video clips.
❑ VidCap, a simple tool for capturing digital video.
❑ Three codec algorithms.
❑ A CD-ROM containing 70 minutes of video clips (not all of which are redistributable).
❑ The VFW Converter to convert QuickTime video for playback in the Windows environment.

VFW extends the Windows 3.1 architecture by establishing new architectural components, including:

❑ The Audio Visual Interleaved, or AVI, file format.
❑ An installable codec interface, a standard interface for installing additional software and hardware codecs.
❑ The Video Capture Interface, a standard interface for video-capture hardware.

OLE is also an important component of VFW. By using OLE, application software can accept compound documents composed of text and video.

As noted previously, VFW provides for installable codecs. This opens a new opportunity for hardware and software vendors to differentiate their product by offering a superior codec. SuperMac, for example, use their CompactVideo codec to offer a 2× improvement in video-playback rates under VFW.

One of the major drawbacks of AVI is, unlike QuickTime, there's no inherent time base to maintain synchronization between the video and audio tracks. It's possible, therefore, to lose sync during long playbacks. Intel and Microsoft claim to have achieved good synchronization in AVI and that it *shouldn't* be a problem. You might observe a loss of synchronization, however, especially when video is played back in a large window.

In any segmentation there's a small group of items that just don't fit well in the main categories. Computer graphics is no exception. For those situations, there's the "other" category. Process control, CBI (Command, Control, and Communication), robotics, industrial (ship loading, railroad yard, control, etc.), and all other applications that haven't yet been defined fall into this segment.

One of the reasons these applications aren't otherwise categorized is that they're either very uncommon, or they use such a mix of functions that they defy categorization. By this point, however, you've been exposed to the main ideas in computer graphics, image systems, and TV. These "other" applications will be no surprise to you if you look into them or they happen to be your main interest.

Monitoring & process control   Monitoring and process-control applications visually represent to the user data feedback in real time from continuous processes that are essential to equipment and facility operation. Graphically formatted summaries or representations of discrete data in progress during these processes act as the basis of an alarm system that immediately informs the operator as to the status of the processes.

Command, Control, Communications, & Intelligence   Command, Control, Communications, and Intelligence (C3I) applications monitor the ongoing status of tactical or strategic operations in dynamic scenarios for rapid decision making. This application addresses both military and commercial applications. Surveillance and radar data provide vast amounts of information and make extensive use of graphic display systems. You might also see these applications listed as C4I (Command, Control, Countermeasures, Communications and Intelligence), or as C5I, with the fifth *C* being *Computers.*

Technical data analysis   Technical data-analysis applications are used to analyze technical or experimental data in the most expedient and accurate way possible. This data might have been generated from radar, satellites, instruments, or captured from other electronic measuring devices such as thermocouples or strain gauges, or generated by engineering-analysis programs. Although the original data can be generated by a sensor, technical data analysis is not considered an imaging application. Typically, the original data is processed not for display but rather for statistical content. Computer algorithms are then used to produce visualizations, graphics, charts, histograms, and/or plots to represent the results of the analysis (scientific visualization).

The "other" imaging-applications category includes microscopy, forensic science, and currently experimental activities such as automated beef grading. However,

Other applications

these new applications will tend to be linked to cost-sensitive industries. Were they not cost sensitive, they most probably would have previously adopted image processing.

Summary   The purpose of this chapter was to acquaint you with the major application segments, their general characteristics, and the fundamental functions needed to realize the applications. It should also have shown you that the three main segments— computer graphics, image processing, and TV—are indeed merging and in many cases are already merged. You should have learned that no application uses a single function, but takes advantage of a combination of line-drawing and bit-mapped raster operations.

If you got all that, enjoyed some of the stories associated with the applications and their evolution, and were able to tolerate my little diatribes—and got this far—then the mission of this chapter has been a success. I hope the rest of the book will be as informative and enjoyable.

Color

Color is an essential component of most display systems. Color information comes from TV digitizers, scanners, files from other parties, and applications you're using. You then mix, blend, combine, change, delete, and add new colors to the process. In the process of editing and creating, the colors are displayed on your monitor, saved to files, and sent to various types of printers. Thus, color literally runs through your computer system, network, and organization and most likely none of it (or very little of it) is compatible. Why? Because color is a very complex science (some say it isn't science, but rather art), and it's difficult to agree on, reproduce, and standardize—difficult, but not impossible.

This chapter will introduce you to the various color models, the attributes of color (I could have said *physics* but that usually puts people off), various standards, and some calibration systems.

The subject of color, like so many other topics touched on in this book, has filled volumes. The physics, chemistry, processing, reproduction, and general use of color is a very complex subject. All I'm going to attempt here, in just one small chapter, is to give you an overview of the subject and make you aware of the issues, terms, and interrelationships. Although you won't become a color scientist, you will see some lovely pictures.

Color is everywhere in our lives. It was only due to technical limitations and cost that our first books, TVs, and computers were either monochrome or black and white. Today we don't have such limitations and can enjoy color in our newspapers, computer displays, and, of course, TV. This chapter offers a gentle introduction into the nature of color: how color is perceived by the eye, the

What is color?

differences between additive and subtractive color, and the organizations of various color schemes or models.

Pure (unfiltered) sunlight is the primary source of all colors, and is known as *white light* or *pure white light*. The fact that white light contains all colors was first demonstrated in 1666 by Isaac Newton, who experimented with passing a beam of sunlight through a glass prism. The light that came out of the prism was divided into the rainbow array of the colors that make up sunlight, and is commonly referred to as the *color spectrum*. Of course, the effect of a prism had been noted long before Newton's time, but it had always been attributed to some sort of latent color embedded in the glass of the prism. The scientists and philosophers of the time spent untold hours discussing and trying to explain what color was, how it was seen, and how to reproduce it reliably.

Newton's breakthrough came as a result of an unusual experiment—he passed the resulting rainbow of light through a second prism, and found that the rainbow was reassembled into white light, as shown in the illustration in FIG. 2-1.

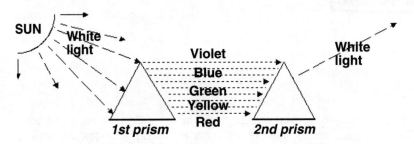

2-1
Newton discovered the nature of light by passing the color spectrum from a prism into a second prism and producing white light.

After Sir Isaac Newton's discovery about the nature of color, scientists, printers, mathematicians, and chemists set about defining color so it could be faithfully reproduced. This wasn't easy and dye experts for the clothing industry went one way, paint producers for artists and others (houses, signs, etc.) went another way, and printers found still another direction. Over the centuries as the world shrank and these divergent disciplines grudgingly learned about each other, a movement was established for developing a universal color description. It took decades of debate, testing, and parliamentary negotiations, but finally in France in 1931 the Commission International de'Eclairange (CIE) established a system that defined and measured color mathematically—it took only 265 years.

Newton's original model of a barrage of emissive particles propagated by wave motion has served us well over the years. It has made lens design, color spectrum, and all sorts of other problems manageable. However, quantum theory expresses light in terms of energies and to some this is a basic contradiction. Interesting experiments have been conducted to prove that light is an energy wave, which results in proving that it's composed of particles. Experiments to prove that it's composed of particles result in proving it's a wave.

I'm not here to debate quantum physics vs. traditional concepts (nor do I know if I could). The wave-motion model works quite well for the descriptions of color I'm trying to present here, and with due apologies to my readers who favor the mysterious world of quantum physics, that's the only model I'll use.

A *wave* is any form of disturbance that exhibits a periodic pattern. All waves have a definable period (denoted as capital T), which is usually expressed in time units (seconds). All waves have a specific physical length that depends on two factors: the frequency of the wave and the speed of its travel (known as *propagation speed*). Wavelength is denoted in equations by the lowercase Greek letter lambda (λ). Propagation speed of light, for most cases, is assumed to be at the speed of light, which is denoted as lowercase c. Frequency or period of a wave is denoted in equations as lowercase f, and measured in hertz (Hz), or cycles per second.

All of these items are related to each other and can be expressed as a simple equation:

$$\lambda = \frac{9.84 \times 10^8}{f}$$

Where:

λ = wavelength
f = frequency
9.84×10 = speed of light in meters per second (c)

What this equation illustrates is that as the frequency goes up, the wavelength goes down or gets smaller. Because the constant c is in meters, the wavelength will be in meters.

The visual spectrum is between 770nm (nanometers) to 380nm. The longest wavelengths appear as red to the human eye, and the colors change as the wavelength gets shorter, progressing through orange, yellow, green, blue, indigo, and violet. An illustration of the entire electromagnetic spectrum is shown in FIG. C-7.

The point is that all colors have a different wavelength or frequency and that the frequency is very high with a correspondingly small wavelength.

Perception

One of the earliest works on human perception is credited to Dr. Tatsuji Inouye, a Japanese ophthalmologist. After the 1905 Russo-Japanese war, Dr. Inouye studied the vision loss of soldiers who had suffered shrapnel and bullet wounds to their heads. He found a specific region in the back of the skull that is the major center for visual perception. The area, which is commonly known today as the visual cortex, is very exact.

Visual cortex

Researchers over the years have found that parts of images are projected onto exactly similar positions within the visual cortex. The projections are so exact that it is common to refer to that part of the brain as a *map*.

In the late 1960s, neurobiologists at the University of Wisconsin discovered that the visual cortex was only one of several maps within the brain. In fact, they mapped over a dozen locations where images are contained. While at Wisconsin, John Allman and Jon Kaas discovered that the back half of most primate brains contain more than a dozen postage-stamp sized image areas of the same scene. It has been likened to a wall of TVs all tuned to the same channel.

Although each one of these image areas contains the same scene, the brain uses each one for a different purpose. One area is used to detect motion, others shapes (geometry), and a third to respond to color and contrast. Within the color image areas, there are what the researchers call "blobs." The blobs are found in other image areas and there is some overlap of function. What color-sensitive blobs do is to respond to differences in light wavelengths (colors) and intensities between an object and its background (contrast). Different cells within the blobs react to different light wavelengths and the brain compares the responses to get a sense of an object's color.

Color vision is trichromatic, so only three parameters are needed to describe a color or the relationship between any two colors for a given set of viewing conditions. It has been estimated that the human eye can discriminate over 50,000 shades.

Rods & cones   Physiologists and other scientists have studied human (as well as primate) color perception and discovered the eye is composed of a lens through which light passes to the inside back wall of the eye, which is known as the *retina* (see FIG. 2-2). The construction of the retina is somewhat complicated, but understandable. It is primarily composed of two types of nerve endings, or *sensors*, which have been identified as *rods* and *cones*—so named because of their conical and cylindrical tips. The nerve fibers of the rods and cones from all parts of the retina are collected and leave the back of the eye in a bundle known as the *optic nerve*. That part of the eye is called the *second cranial* and forms a blind spot in human vision because there are no nerve endings or sensors there. The rods and cones are not randomly located across the retina. Cones are located at the center of the retina, the *fovea centralis*, to about a 20-degree subtended arc from the lens. From there, they diminish in quantity and rods become more concentrated to the edges of the visual area, about 100 degrees.

Much of this information is taught in high school and freshman college classes, so it should come as no surprise. These rods (which respond to intensity and are used in night vision) and cones (which react to color and fine detail) have been studied in

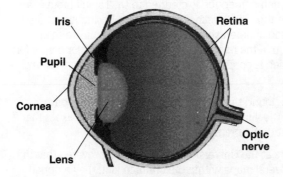

2-2
A diagram of the human eye, which contains a lens that focuses light onto the back wall of the eye, called the retina.

detail for decades. Rods contain a substance known as *rhodopsin*, or *visual purple*, which is found to be sensitive to all wavelengths except, long-wave red. It has been further discovered that there are three sets of cones, each one responding to a different primary color. The cones are actually thought to be the same and they just have different levels of photopigments. The photopigments are red, green, and blue (RGB).

The blue cones respond to light that has a wavelength of 445nm, the green cones have a maximum sensitivity of 535nm, and the red cones fire when light has a wavelength of 575nm (which is actually yellow). The distribution of the cones is 64% red, 32% green, and only 2% blue (remember this when you are reading the section on *Perceiving color* later in the chapter).

The cones are not binary switches but more like a Gaussian filter with a high sensitivity in its center (the wavelength it reacts most strongly to) and a tapering off on either side. Therefore, red cones will see some green, and vice versa. However, the center wavelength of the blue cones are far enough away from the red and green that they don't react very much at all to other colors or wavelengths. This too is an important point to remember.

Regardless of the structural and chemical arrangement of the nerve endings that form the retina, this is the place where the sensitive photopigments reside. It is here that light triggers a complex set of events that leads ultimately to the firing of optic-nerve fibers and makes it possible for us to see and perceive color.

Harmony, balance, & psychology

Graphic artists are taught color harmony less scientifically than a mathematician or computer scientist. That's too bad on both accounts. First, that artists spend a lot of time in trial-and-error approaches to obtaining the desired results (yes, I know, that's what makes it "art") and, second, that scientists aren't taught anything about art or the use of color. Artists are taught to select color according to color harmony, or how colors interact. They learn that more effective results are obtained that way than through random selection (you can see this any time you are confronted with a headline or banner that's constructed with letters each of a different color). Colors are said to be harmonious when they have something in common (a little red in the yellow, a little yellow in the green, etc.). In general, neighboring colors are harmonious.

GUI borders

The scientific method of achieving harmony is to vary the values along only one or two of the axes in a given color space. Those colors exactly opposite each other on the color wheel, which are known as direct complements, provide vibrant disharmonious colors. Although this can be stimulating, looking at vibrant or complementary colors for a long period of time can induce eye fatigue—something that the developers of GUIs like Apple's Macintosh and Microsoft's Windows spent a lot of time working on. Users who play around with the color-selection controls of their GUI usually muck up their color schemes trying to get a unique look or exciting arrangement. After a day or two of striking, bright, contrasting colors for their borders, they usually revert back to more subtle harmonious colors and never quite know why.

Harmony & balance

If a saturated color is used over an extended period of time, it should be contrasted with an unsaturated tone if possible. Triadic complements, those colors that are 120 degrees apart on the color wheel, are less vibrant than direct compliments. Triadics still have a somewhat disharmonious effect, however, when highly saturated colors are used. Colors that are only 30 degrees apart from the direct complement on the color wheel are known as split complements. Split complements are more harmonious than direct or triadics, and produce interesting effects.

The human eye, as has been pointed out throughout this book and especially in this chapter, operates in very specific and sometimes confusing ways. Without going into the evolutionary propositions for this behavior, you should still understand it. One of the characteristics is the way the eye perceives foreground colors depending on the background color (as you might suspect, it's different among various people, but interestingly, it doesn't seem to have a cultural bias). A yellow spot or patch, for example, appears warm when on a white background, but harsh when on a black background (refer to the examples in FIG. C-8).

A blue spot stands out on a white background, but on a black background it's difficult to see. For me, a blue spot on a red background on a CRT appears to be floating in front of the screen. That is due to a process called *chromostereopsis*, in which the brain interprets the wavelength differences as a variation in depth.

Psychology & imagination

Every color in the spectrum has an effect on you. The reasons aren't quantified but the theories abound and are beyond the scope of a book like this. Nonetheless, many of the effects are well documented and useful to know. Green is said to be calming and has been used in hospitals and institutions for years for that reason. Red is stimulating and often said to cause anger, and yet more people say it is their favorite color than any other. Blue is considered to connote loyalty, deity, justice, sincerity, regality, as well as depression and discouragement, and of course is the color of the sky and ocean. According to leading ink suppliers, blue is America's most popular color. Purple makes people think of royalty, dignity, mysticism, magic, the law, martyrdom and suffering. White is associated with purity, chastity, innocence, faith, oneness, perfection, and day. And black symbolizes mystery, night, evil, sorcery and death. As I'm sure you're aware, the selection of colors for flags, company logos, and advertisements is a major consideration.

Gradients, the blending of one color into another is also interesting. A green background that fades or blends into gray makes a person think of depth. That's logical enough because if you look from a high point at grass covered hills they do fade to gray or a grayish brown as they approach the distant horizon. So the model is part of our basic consciousness and, when replicated on a monitor or printed page, there's an autonomous reaction. You can be sure that advertisers make great use of these cues to deliver subtle almost subliminal messages or implications.

Color has also been used to enhance memory. It has been successfully used in experiments studying the effect of isolating a word with a color. When a word is placed within a sentence in which the rest of the words are its complementary color, it not only stands out but is remembered better. For example, envision all the words in this sentence to be in the color blue and the word *one* in red. Recall of the one isolated word is reliably higher when that word is isolated with color. If you look for this technique when you look at advertisements, you'll notice that it has been used for a while.

Color perception and appreciation are also functions of age. Infants and young children give the best responses to single and multiple use of bright primary subtractive colors, and poor response to blended colors. However, with age, social conditioning, and cultural influences, we develop a more sophisticated use and appreciation for color. In a recent study on video-text information systems, it was learned that younger subjects found multiple-color information more appealing, whereas older people tended to prefer two-color combinations (possibly what they were taught over the years to expect for text displays).

All of the previous sections on color describe how colors are created, sensed, and how they affect our emotions. But there is another element of color perception—the nature or color of the light source. Suppose an apple were illuminated by a pure blue light, as shown in FIG. 2-3.

In this case, the red skin of the apple would absorb all the blue light, making the apple appear to be black or very dark. Conversely, if the apple were illuminated

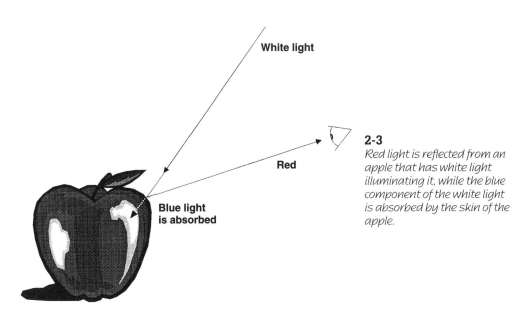

White light

Red

Blue light is absorbed

2-3
Red light is reflected from an apple that has white light illuminating it, while the blue component of the white light is absorbed by the skin of the apple.

with a pure red light, all the light would be reflected—making the apple appear bright red.

With the exception of unfiltered sunlight, we seldom encounter pure white light. Sunlight, candlelight, incandescent light bulbs, and fluorescent lights put out distinctly different colors, and characteristics of light. While these light sources look white, they're actually made up of slightly different mixes of colored light. Even though the human eye is sensitive to these differences, the brain is responsible for processing the input from the eye—and it's the brain's perception that allows us to perceive both candlelight and fluorescent light as being like white light.

On an absolute scientific scale of color, candlelight is very red, incandescent light bulbs are slightly red, sunlight is neutral, and fluorescent lights are blue-green (although the phosphors of fluorescent lights can be mixed, and there are sunlight models available). Film is very sensitive to the different qualities of light. This is why professional photographers carry a variety of color filters to compensate for lighting conditions.

Just as lighting conditions can vary, color perception varies from person to person. For example, some people are color blind—perceiving limited color, and in some cases no colors whatsoever. Others might be particularly sensitive to blue or some other color. To compound the problem of color perception, some people are more sensitive to particular colors at low levels of illumination and less sensitive to the same colors when brightly illuminated.

There is an interesting theory that humans have just recently developed the ability to perceive the higher frequencies of blue and green. The data (anecdotal, I'm afraid) is from the earliest of Greek and Egyptian literature. Their stories are consistent in describing the sea and sky as red. Reference to blues and greens don't show up in literature I'm told until Roman times—interesting, isn't it?

The following sections will deal with the practical issues of using color, and list some of the standards, tools, and issues in getting color from one place to another.

Color components

Color is a three-dimensional manifestation of light. It has been studied, measured, philosophized, and argued about for centuries. However, in the last couple of decades, the various systems, opinions, and special interests are at last agreeing on the components and relationships of color. They might use different names and offer different mathematical models for their methods, but at least they all agree that it's a three-dimensional model. The components that go into the description of color are as follows:

Hue

Hue is defined as the actual color we see. It's the wavelength of light of a color in its purest state with no bias or influence by white or black. The continuum of the color hues creates a color wheel.

Brightness

Brightness, which is also referred to as *value*, *amplitude*, or *lightness*, determines how light or dark a color (hue) is or how close it seems to black or white. Colors can be separated into light or dark when compared.

Saturation

Saturation, also called *intensity*, *chroma*, *purity*, or *vividness*, measures the clarity of color. As other colors (hues or wavelengths) are mixed or added, the color becomes less distinct, approaching gray.

Gamut

The CIE model is based on centuries of empirical work done in various laboratories throughout the world. It represents the full range of colors, referred to as the *gamut*, that the human eye can see or will respond to. As FIG. C-9 shows, the range of RGB phosphors available for a monitor, as well as the range of process (printing) inks only covers a portion of the gamut a human can perceive.

That means that as good as they are, no mechanical means devised by man can yet duplicate or imitate the full spectrum of colors. Keep this in mind as you read about, consider, and perhaps witness the wonders of 24-bit true color. True color will never match the gamut of the human eye's perception. Furthermore, be careful of using the word *gamut*. Marketers, in their never-ending quest for product differentiation, which includes the discovery of new words (or new uses for existing words), have taken to use the word *gamut* to describe various color models. Thus, you'll probably encounter the expressions CMYK gamut and RGB gamut, etc.

Over the centuries, people developed various names to describe the almost infinite range of color. The CIE model offers the best solution. However, because of the three-dimensional nature of the model, it's sometimes difficult to use. A two-dimensional slice of the model, which uses brightness vs. saturation, has been developed, known as the *color triangle*. As FIG. 2-4 shows, the triangle consists of seven positions within one hue or color. The top or peak of the triangle represents maximum brightness and purity or saturation. The left base of the triangle represents black (no color) and the right side of the base represents white (all colors).

Although this by itself is not a unique representation, it is the intermediate points that are interesting. You've no doubt heard over the years people making references to aspects of color known as tint, tone, and shade. The triangle shows how these

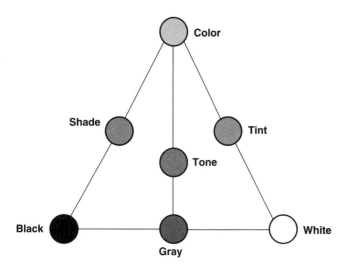

2-4
A color triangle is just one of several color models used to show the relationship between hues, tints, brightness, and saturation.

terms fit within a color or hue. Shade is the quality a color takes on as it loses brightness and approaches black. Tint is the quality it gets when it approaches blending with other colors. The tone of a color is its quality as it moves from saturation toward gray.

One other two-dimensional color representation that's popular is the color wheel. It is a minor modification of the hue vs. saturation view. The main difference is the center is left blank and the colors are blocked around the circle or restricted to discrete steps, as shown in FIG. C-10. This model is useful for illustrating the primary colors of RGB and CMY, which will be discussed in the next section.

The main point or idea to grasp here is that what appears to be white light is actually a blending of millions of shades of colored light. When white light is passed through a prism, it spreads out. That is because the waves or frequencies of the various colors are bent by different amounts. In addition to the wavelength or color involved, there's also the issue of how the colors reach our eyes—either directly from a light source like a monitor, or reflected off a sheet of paper.

Transmitted light (additive colors)

In color theory, the process of blending colored light is referred to as additive color. In additive color, it's been found that the primary three colors—red, green, and blue—are used to create white light. By using equal amounts of red light, green light, and blue light, they will blend together to make pure white. Therefore, the colors red, green, and blue are referred to as the *primary additive colors*, and commonly referred to as RGB.

All the colors of the spectrum can be generated by varying the intensity of the three primary additive colors. For example, equal amounts of blue and red light make magenta (a deep purplish red). Equal amounts of red and green light make yellow light. The diagram in FIG. C-11 shows how red, green, and blue light can be added together to create other colors.

Notice that the center of the diagram, where all three colors overlap in equal amounts, is white. When all three primaries are absent, you get black.

Color monitors, like those used for TV and computers, create color using the three primary additive colors. The color monitor is, itself, a light source and produces transmitted light. If your color images are to be presented directly on the monitor screen, understanding and controlling the three primary additive colors will enable you to very precisely control the colors that appear on the screen—within the limits of the display controller's capabilities.

Film recorders create images on photographic film by exposing the film to very fine beams of red, green, and blue light—the primary additive colors. With the right software, you can make very fine adjustments to the red, green, and blue output and control the overall color balance of the finished image.

Reflected light (subtractive colors)

Most objects that we perceive, however, don't generate light; they reflect light from various sources. In subtractive or reflective color, the colors you perceive are produced when white light falls on a surface and is partially reflected.

To understand how light is reflected off objects requires a little explanation. In terms of physics, light is made up of waves of energy—just like the waves that are used to broadcast radio and television signals. Each color of light has its own wavelength or frequency; the colors towards the red end of the spectrum are made up of relatively long waves of energy, whereas the colors toward the blue end of the spectrum are made of relatively short waves of energy.

What makes objects appear in certain colors depends on how light waves reflect off the surface of the object and are absorbed by the surface. If an object appears to be pure white, it appears that way because its surface reflects all colors of light waves equally. Likewise, if an object appears to be pure black, it looks that way because its surface absorbs all colors of light waves. In the case of a white light source, objects appear to be certain colors because they reflect the waves of energy that correspond to those colors (refer back to FIG. 2-3). Colored light sources change the perceived color, but the principle (and physics) are the same.

An apple appears red because the surface of the apple absorbs the blue and green light waves while reflecting the red light waves. Likewise, a blueberry appears blue because it absorbs red and green light, and reflects blue light.

Unlike transmitted light, which is an additive process, reflected light is a subtractive process. When light is reflected off an object, colors are subtracted—and the colors we perceive are the result of the colors that aren't absorbed by the object. Therefore, objects that don't generate their own light are described by a different set of primary colors: the *subtractive primaries* —cyan (a turquoise blue), yellow, and magenta, commonly referred to as CYM or CMY. CMY are the secondaries of the additive primaries RGB, and RGB are the secondary colors of CYM.

The diagram in FIG. C-12 shows how the three subtractive primaries can work together to create intermediate colors.

Note that the center of this diagram, where all three colors overlap, result in black. In other words, the three subtractive primaries work together to subtract all colors of light — and the result is the absence of light. Pure black.

Since a printed sheet of paper doesn't generate its own light, printed images are created using the subtractive primary colors. If printing inks absorbed and reflected light perfectly, then just three colors of ink—cyan, yellow, and magenta—could create all the colors of the rainbow.

However, due to current ink technology, when cyan, yellow, and magenta inks are combined, they produce a muddy-brown color, so a fourth color, black, is used to print full-color images. This is why commercial printers refer to full-color printing as the four-color process. Black is given the letter designation of K (B might get confused with blue), and thus you get CMYK, as shown in FIG. C-13.

There has been a recent development of 6-, 7-, and even 8-color separation models in the printing industry. This is referred to as *high-fidelity color printing*, and its proponents claim it can achieve more intense and brilliant colors through the use of the extra screens. In reality, it's just a method to reduce the hue errors associated with impure inks. The printing industry is still confronted with the problem of getting a yellow, for example, that doesn't have some percentage of magenta or cyan in it.

There are several color systems that are used for various applications. They all have a drawback in applications other than the one they were intended for. Due to the differences between additive and subtractive color, the methods of reproduction (phosphors, inks, nature) and the subjective interpretation of color, it has been a daunting task to come up with a single universal color system.

Color systems

Color has been described by various models or systems. There are three basic color systems, also known as color-space coordinate systems: rectangular, opponent, and polar, as shown in FIG. 2-5.

Although colors can be thought of as forming the coordinates of a cube, the systems or models are not visually linear. Human perception of lightness or darkness doesn't vary uniformly with the amount of CRT brightness or ink applied, nor is it the same along each axis. Color-system coordinates are difficult to use because they don't correspond to the mechanism of human color perception.

A few of the better-known color systems are described in this section. This is not meant to be a course in color science so there won't be any matrix tables for converting from one model to another or algorithms to explain the construction of nonlinear color-space systems.

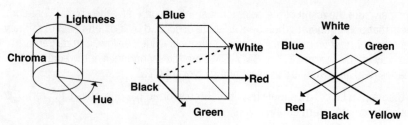

2-5
There are three basic color-space models for describing various systems. They can all be related to each other mathematically.

Polar color-space model   Rectangular color-space   Opponent color-space model

The CIE color system

In the 1931 CIE color system (CIE publication no. 15.2, 2nd ed., Commission Internationale de' Eclairange, Vienna, 1986: 19–20, 56-58), color is described by three variables or axes: hue, brightness, and saturation, and is often referred to as the CIE XYZ. These three properties allow any color imaginable to be precisely determined and assigned a coordinate or mathematical value. With that, it can be reproduced by anyone at any time, and transformed into almost any other color-space model.

The CIE model is elegant and you can examine any portion of it—inside, outside, top, bottom, or surface—and find a color definition, as shown in FIG. C-14. Because the CIE model is a three-dimensional description of color, it also can be represented as x, y, and z, and is often referred to in that form by the TV industry. The x axis is usually defined as the saturation and the z axis as the hue; however, they often get reversed. Everyone seems to agree that the y axis is luminance or brightness.

The CIE model can be represented by three two-dimensional representations: hue vs. saturation, saturation vs. brightness, and brightness vs. hue. In 1931, the CIE developed a two-dimensional chromaticity chart, as illustrated in FIGS. 2-6 and C-15, primarily for color specification.

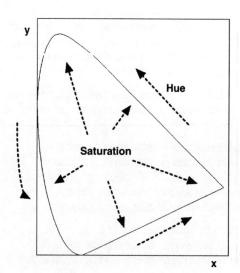

2-6
The CIE color chart is a two-dimensional representation of color, established in 1931 (refer to the color version in Fig. C-15A and B.

The 1931 diagram does not completely describe a color because the x and y values don't provide any information on the brightness or lightness of a color. The third, or z, axis is perpendicular and referred to as a tristimulus Y value, and represents the luminance factor.

There is a general consensus that all color models should have a traceability to the CIE tristimulus values. The color spaces defined in terms of these values include XYZ, CIRLAB, CIELUV, RGB, HSV, HSL, and HVC. The CIE tristimulus values don't by themselves constitute a complete color specification.

In 1978, the CIE formally approved the CIE u',v' uniform chromaticity scales diagram (which was proposed in 1976). The goal was to produce a color model or diagram that had a more uniform (at least perceptually) distribution of colors. The 1976 CIE u',v' diagram is shown in FIG. 2-7. Like the 1931 model, the 1978 diagram does not provide any information on brightness.

The CIE u',v' model

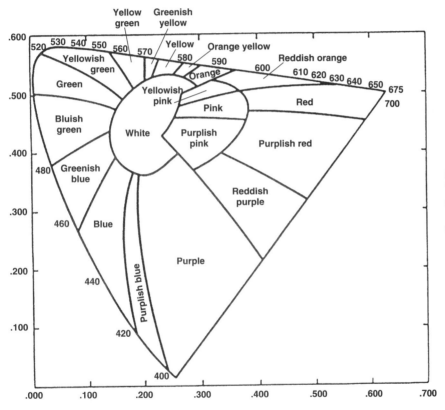

2-7
The CIE adopted the u',v' uniform chromaticity scale in 1979, but it too was only a two-dimensional color model.

In 1976, the CIE u',v' model was combined with a metric-for-lightness function, L*, and was used as the basis for developing the 1976 CIE L*,u*, v* (known more commonly as CIELUV) color-space system (CIE publication no. 15.2, 2nd ed., Commission Internationale de' Eclairange, Vienna, 1986. 29–30). The CIELUV system, shown in FIG. 2-8, is an opponent-type color system. The theory of an opponent-type model is that all colors are coded by the eye and brain into light-

The CIE LUV color-space model

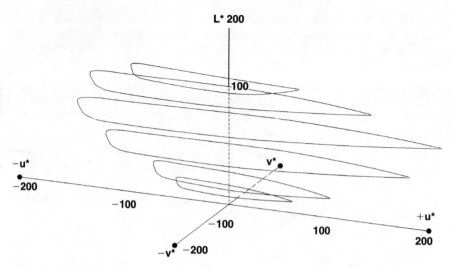

2-8

The CIELUV color-space model (also known as CIE L*,u*,v*) established a unique location for black by making each of the opponent coordinates a function of metric lightness.

dark, red-green and yellow-blue impulse or values, as described in the beginning section on *Color perception*. In the CIELUV model, it's assumed that colors perceived by the eye and brain are coded as light-dark (rods), red-green, and yellow-blue. It also assumes that colors are mutually exclusive and cannot be red and green at the same time or yellow and blue at the same time. However, a color can be described as red and blue (purple).

In the CIELUV system, there are two opponent coordinates axes, represented by u* and v*. The u* axis is for the red-green values and the v* axis is for the yellow-blue values. Furthermore, there is a polarity, whereby positive numbers in the red-green axis represent red colors and negative numbers represent green colors. Likewise, a negative yellow-blue value would be a blue color. As before, the L* axis is for brightness. CILUV is used in the computer and television area.

The CIE LAB color system

Another color-space model based on the CIE system is the CIELAB system, which was also established in 1976 (CIE publication no. 15.2, 2nd ed., Commission Internationale de' Eclairange, Vienna, 1986: 30–31). Expressed as CIE L*a*b*, the CIELAB system uses polar coordinates to describe its colors, and can be envisioned by examining FIG. C-16. CIELAB is used in the printing and photography area.

The CIELAB system, like the CIELUV, allows precise numbers to be assigned to any color located within the model. The skin of an apple, for example, might have quantities of L* = 42.83, a* = 45.04, and b* = 9.52.

Summary of CIE models

Although not perfect, CIE comes the closest due to its mathematical approach to colorimetry. There are several CIE color models:

- ❑ CIE XYZ, used primarily by the computer industry
- ❑ CIE LUV, preferred by the TV (video) industry
- ❑ CIE xyY
- ❑ CIE LAB
- ❑ CIE Yu'v' model 1964
- ❑ CIE lightness, model 1976

Other color-space models, such as RGB, HLS, HSV, HVC, and CMYK, can be calibrated to a CIE specification.

CMYK is the color system used for printing, and is a subtractive or reflective color system. Based on the three primary subtractive colors (cyan, magenta, and yellow) black is added to enhance the color printing and provide a true black. The color range or gamut of the CMYK system is even more limited in the number of colors that it can produce than the RGB system.

Worse still, inks are not additive, which makes it difficult to predict what color will be produced when two or more inks are overprinted. Specialists in the trade, such as color assessors and retouchers, do learn how to use ink-percentage dot values to predict color, but only after many years of experience and with the assistance of sample charts and proofs.

The best-known device that uses the RGB system is the color monitor. It is an additive color system in which the user selects a color by specifying the intensity of each primary (R, G, or B). The range of possible colors with the RGB system is a function of the intensity levels (resolution or range) of each primary. The general organization of the three-dimensional RGB model is shown in FIG. 2-9.

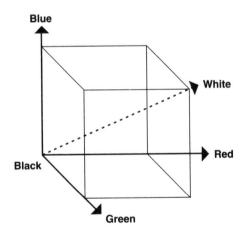

2-9
The RGB color-space model is used primarily for monitors and scanners. However, it is a single-quadrant (positive) model because no negative values are permitted. As the cube illustrates, the addition of all three primaries produces white.

In a typical 24-bit display system, each primary has 256 levels, which yields a spectrum of 16.7 million possible color designations. However, it's possible to specify colors that are indistinguishable on a monitor and totally unreproducible with any type of printing device. Also, the user interface of selecting three primary values is a bit awkward and unnatural.

Because neither the RGB or CMYK systems adequately define color, several other systems have been developed to define color space that can include both the luminous, transmitted colors of a monitor and the reflective colors from a printed page. Most color systems are based on three-dimensional models that are used to make mathematical transformations into colors.

In 1978, Tektronix developed the HLS system. In the HLS system, H stands for hue, L stands for lightness or luminance, and S stands for saturation. Rather than using a model based directly on display hardware, the HLS system uses descriptive parameters that describe color in a more perceptual sense. HLS was designed to be similar to the Ostwald color system developed in 1931 that represents full color, black, white, and the resulting tints, shades, and tones that result from mixing colors. The HLS system can be represented with a double-cone model like the CIE color model.

While the HLS system has some clear advantages over an RGB model, there are some deficiencies in HLS that limit its effectiveness as a user interface to color. Despite efforts to overcome it, the HLS system doesn't take into account the perceptual nonlinearity of human color vision. The actual model allows only for the specification of 3.5 million color designations and, as is the case of the RGB model, many of the colors are indistinguishable. As a result, numerous unique color designations will result in the same perceived color. Also, equal step sizes over the available color range don't produce equally perceived color changes. Last but not least, the HLS system is not related directly to a color standard. As a result, definition and control of color appearance are extremely difficult. The specification of colors between two or more devices is meaningless. An RGB or an HLS value on one display will not produce the same color on another display.

The HSI & HSV systems

The HSI (hue-saturation-intensity) and HSV (hue-saturation-value) systems are similar and, in both models, the brightness of the image (I in HIS, V in HSV) is separated from the chromatic components of hue and saturation. The HSI and HSV color models can be thought of as a hexagonal cone, as shown in FIG. 2-10.

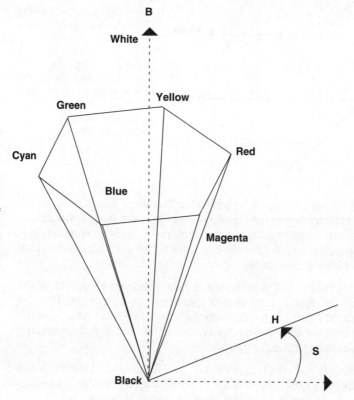

2-10
The HSI or HSV color model is like a hexagonal cone, with the brightness value of a given point inside the cone. In reality, the cone isn't very symmetrical as the range of saturation values available for a given brightness vary according to the hue.

The HSI/HSV model is very similar to the CIE cone. Brightness is the vertical value from the base (black) point, hue is the angle around the circumference, and saturation is the perpendicular value from the centerline toward the circumference. Because it isn't a true cone and has flat edges between the primary and complementary colors, saturation will vary for different hues.

The difference between HIS and HSV is the computation of the brightness component. The following expression shows the brightness model for HSI:

$$I = \frac{(R + G + B)}{3}$$

The HSV color system expresses brightness as shown in the following equation:

$$V = \max(R,G,B)$$

Saturation for either color system is as follows:

$$D = 1 - \min \frac{(R,G,B)}{Br}$$

The brightness component for V will tend to be larger (from one to three times larger) than the brightness component for I.

The HVC system

In 1989, Tektronix introduced the HVC system, known as the TekHVC model, for video-based implementation. In the HVC system, H stands for hue, V for value (variations in lightness), and C for chroma. The HVC system uses the conventions for color locations in a three-dimensional model established by the Munsell system, the Swedish Natural Color (NCS) system, and most importantly the 1976 CIE UCS (Uniform Chromaticity Scales) diagram. The visualization of this color model is shown in FIG. 2- 11.

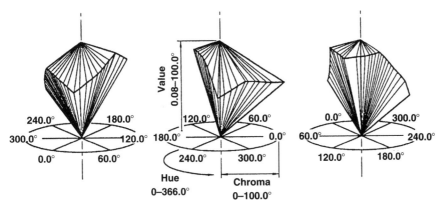

2-11
The HVC color model was developed by Tektronix in 1989. It's based on a three-dimensional color space, where H = hue, V = value or brightness, and C = chroma.
Tektronix

The XCMS system

The HVC color system has been incorporated into the X Windows system's color-management system, XCMS.

The XCMS (X color-management system) uses CIEXYZ as the hub for device-independent to device-dependent color-space conversions, and vice versa. The requirement for use of the systems is that each color space (device-dependent or device-independent) must have the ability to convert to and from CIEXYZ. This information is then stored as a set of functions that are used for the color conversions.

The YIQ/YUV color system

The NTSC system of color TV uses the YIQ/YUV color model, where the Y value is for the luminance or intensity (also commonly referred to as lumina), and the U and V or I and Q values are for the chroma or color components. NTSC was originally developed in 1953 to provide backward compatibility with black-and-white TV and fit within a limited transmission bandwidth, the system. The National Television Systems Committee (NTSC) standardized how color TV signals would be transmitted and the system has an almost infinite range of adjustments (i.e., hue and saturation). The relationship of NTSC color to CIE is shown in FIG. C-17.

Colors that can be displayed in RGB space can't be directly displayed in NTSC or PAL. Some type of color-space conversion technique is required. Because of this limitation, 15 bits of RGB color (5 red, 5 blue, and 5 green) is often all that's provided, which is less than the theoretical potential of viewed composite-color systems. The relationship of YIQ or YUV is expressed as a ratio format, and there are three popular modes: 4:1:1, 4:2:2, and 2:1:1.

The Munsell color chart

Over the years, people wrestled with the problem of creating a reproducible color-referencing system. One solution that was developed by an American artist, A.H. Munsell, was widely used for many years and is still used by some photographers. The Munsell system is a three-dimensional organization expressed as two two-dimensional charts, as shown in FIG. C-18.

If the cup shown in the illustration were described using the Munsell system, it would be 5G 5/10. The 5G indicates a green hue on the color wheel, and the 5/10 gives it value (brightness) and chroma (saturation). There are conversion tables and formulas for transcribing colors from CIE, CIE L*a*b*, and other systems.

When Munsell and Ostwald did their work in color theory at the turn of the century, their measurements were strictly perceptual, and their annotations were in what we now call JNDs, or *just noticeable differences*. Both men described a three-dimensional construction of color space. (What we're used to seeing on the computer screen as HSB—hue, saturation, and brightness—is the three-dimensional concept originally espoused by Munsell. He labeled his three-dimensional representation HVC, for hue, value, and chroma.)

Munsell started with a "pure" red, painted and displayed on a rotating disk, which acted to remove any preception of unevenness. In shifting that red color toward orange, Munsell counted 20 just noticeable differences, and labeled the new color a *hue*. In this manner, he produced a circle of hues with only ten colors, proceeding through ROYGBIV (red, orange, yellow, green, blue, indigo, and violet). Later, using an annotation system based on these JNDs, another set of ten half hues were added. Of course, the refinement can be carried further if desired.

The Munsell 3-D model is irregular in shape because weaker colors disappear faster than strong colors. Yellow, for instance, disappears faster in saturation steps. Ostwald depicted hues in a circle, but to make a color lighter he added white paint to a pure hue; to make it darker he added black. His resulting 3-D model takes the form of two cones joined at their bases. The importance of Ostwald's model to graphic arts is that printed colors are made lighter by tinting, allowing more white paper to show through. Likewise, printed colors are made darker by adding black (in an achromatic approach). Thus, you get the four-color CYMK system, where K stands for black.

Because of the color-range limitation of CMYK, the only way to get colors that can't be created with it is to mix an ink specifically for that color. This is done by combining pigments other than those of the process printing ink, as is shown in FIG. C-19. The PANTONE color-matching system for printing was established in 1963, by Lawrence Herbert, who joined the Pantone company in 1956 and purchased it in 1962.

The inks or colors of the PANTONE matching system (PMS) is one such approach. All the colors (inks) in the PMS are indexed and can be reproduced (theoretically) anywhere in the world. The main problem with the PMS or other special ink systems is the color purity of the inks to begin with. However, these are topics for a book on printing and not one on display system.

Pantone was initially a manufacturer of color cards for printing ink makers, cosmetic companies, textile manufacturers, and medical testing laboratories. The company branched out into other areas and specifically into the graphics arts area, which also encompassed the interior design, apparel, architectural, and industrial products. At the same time, the company realized that graphics designers were finding new ways to create artwork and colors with computers. It became clear to the managers of the company that they needed to address this new area. As a result, the company established the Color Systems Division in 1984, and in 1985 introduced the PANTONE electronic color system. Over the years, one company after the other signed licenses with Pantone to use its color systems (e.g., Adobe Systems, Aldus, Corel Systems, Crossfield Lightspeed, Genigraphics, Letraset, Micrografx, Radius, Quark, and SuperMac). Most computer and prepress printer companies have also signed up, as well as all color-matching-system suppliers.

Prior to Pantone's BCS, the only broadcast color standard was the eight color bars that are used when a station signs off or on the air. In early 1991, the company introduced its PANTONE broadcast color system (BCS). With BCS, a station can calibrate its equipment to reproduce the full range of colors offered in the PANTONE matching system. This aids advertisers in having their logos and commercials match their printed materials. Digital F/X was one of the first companies to adopt this new system for its Composium System. Composium has been a well-received system as an industry standard in component (D1) digital video productions.

The TruMatch system is based on a digital model of four-color space, described in even steps of hue, and arranged in the order of the visible spectrum. The system is rooted in the three-dimensional perceptual color theories of Munsell and Ostwald. The hues are illustrated in a circle.

Each hue is proportionally gradated in 15% saturation steps of hue toward white (zero dot density), and is based on the ability of imagesetters to produce 1% increments of yellow, magenta, cyan, and black, and hence its marketing claim of four-color space.

The system uses color-finder pages with eight saturation steps, which are presented as slices through the circle of hues, as shown in FIG. C-20. The vertical axis affects the brightness of a color by added black in 6% increments.

Other color models   There are several other color models, or *standards*, as some people like to refer to them. Most are private or vendor-supported systems, a few are de facto standards, and a couple are industry or formal standard color models—which one is which and why are not important to the issues of understanding color. However, you should be aware of their existence, which is why I'm presenting this list. Like all the lists in this book, I do not suggest it's exhaustive.

- ❏ Adobe color image model
- ❏ ANSI's Image Technology Committee (IT8), DDES (digital data exchange standard) for color
- ❏ ASTM's color metrology and standard practices
- ❏ CCIR 601-2 YCbCr, European TV encoder for nonlinear RGB signals (CCIR Recommendations 601-Z, International Radio Consultive Committee, 1990)
- ❏ ACAM - Alvey color-appearance model, which uses CIE XYZ and calculates the predicted color appearance in terms of lightness, colorfulness, and hue (LCH)
- ❏ Color curve system
- ❏ Colorid system
- ❏ Digital F/X - PANTONE broadcast color system
- ❏ DIN system
- ❏ EFI
- ❏ FSI Kolorist
- ❏ ISCC-NBS (533), based on the Munsell system
- ❏ ISO 8613 office document architecture, colour amendment 2: support for color
- ❏ Microsoft color management
- ❏ Munsell color system, a system of groups of sample colors whose hues change in horizontal and vertical planes
- ❏ OSA color scale
- ❏ PostScript level 1 and 2
- ❏ SMPTE-C RGB, specification of three phosphors and a reference white for studio monitors (SMPTE Recommended Practice RP 145, 1987, Society of Motion Picture and Television Engineers, White Plains, NY, June 1987)
- ❏ Swedish natural color system, NCS
- ❏ YES, Xerox's 1989 color-encoding standard to linearly transform XYZ or any RGB color space (Color Encoding Standard, Xerox Systems Institute, 475 Oakmead Pkwy., Sunnyvale, CA, March 1989)

Two-channel color   The use of rods and cones in the eye have prompted researchers over the years to create theories and in some cases systems based on this two-channel model. The obvious cost-reduction possibility of 33% in using two channels, sensors, or elements from the current three (or, in the case of printing, four) is an interesting area of investigation. Two-channel color displays have been tried before; early color photography and cinema was based on using just red and green.

The best known investigator of two-color systems was Dr. Edward Land (founder of Polaroid), who did research in the area in the 1950s and 1960s. In his experiments, he used only red and green color filters to create color images. He photographed a full-color image with a red filter in front of the camera and then photographed the same image with the same camera using a green filter. He then projected the film that was made with the red filter through the same red filter, and projected and superimposed the image made with the green filter, except he didn't use the green filter in the projection.

The result was an image that contained most, but not all, of the hues of the original image. Various researchers and college professors have reproduced Land's experiments and no one has really come up with a satisfactory explanation for the effect using conventional color-mixing theory. Land's original two-color technique produced many colors, but didn't reproduce blues. However, later researchers found ways to generate blues with two-color techniques.

Another early researcher in the two-channel theory is D. L. MacAdams. He developed mathematical models based on orthogonal functions, and calculated both doublet and triplet pairs using the CIE model. MacAdams' model required the orthogonal functions to have negative values as well as positive values, which can't be created using color filters. However, the researchers at RCA and Westinghouse had solved the problem (before they knew it existed) when they developed the two-channel color system used in the NTSC scheme. NTSC uses one channel for intensity and one for color or hues, the same as the human perception system, and it can reproduce all hues.

However, the method of TV encoding does have limits for the range of colors that can be reproduced. Brown hues are almost impossible to pass through the NTSC and PAL systems. Wood colors and skin tones, therefore, are about the hardest to reproduce, which can be easily seen in a store that has several large-screen TVs next to each other when a person's face is viewed. You'll notice in most cases each TV has a different color skin tone even though they're all receiving the same picture and were all set up by the same technician. Also, the TV color systems don't always produce the saturated colors you often see in the real world.

Various researchers have used LCD panels and CTS with a checkerboard pattern to implement Land's techniques. Commercially, a two-color super-twist LCD has been produced by In Focus using a subtractive color-mixing technique. Although the display obtains a good color range, it still isn't as much as you can get with a three-color CRT or LCD.

Experiments have been successfully conducted using an opponent-color technique. An opponent channel is one that switches between opposing colors, such as red and cyan. They're then constructed using a brightness (achromatic or white-black) channel and a color opposite (red-cyan, in this case) channel. Richard Young discovered in the mid 1980s that mixtures between these channels can create all the main varieties of chromatic red-green and yellow-blue, and the achromatic white-black color cell types found in the major subcortical visual pathway in the human visual system. He further discovered that at least 87% of the variance in the neural responses of the visual system to spectral lights can be explained by these two color channels.

Based on this research, it has been reasoned that it should be possible to build a display system based on these concepts. As you'll learn when you read chapter 4, *Flat-panel displays*, such displays have been built.

How color monitors create color

As mentioned throughout this book, the image on the monitor's screen is composed of pixels: the individual dots that create the image. For black-and-white or monochrome display systems, working with the individual pixels is a simple matter; the pixel is either turned on (white or a color) or turned off (black).

A note of definition is needed here. *Monochrome* means that there's just one color. A monochrome monitor can be green or amber, and vary in intensity or brightness from black (off) to maximum brightness. The color of a monochrome monitor is a function of its phosphor, but it will have only one phosphor—hence the *mono* in *monochrome*. The phosphor could be white (or white with a blue or yellow tint), which would produce various shades of gray between full brightness (white) and off (black). Whether or not it can display shades of gray is a function of the display controller's capability.

Many early display controllers were capable of only two states: on and off. If used with a monitor that had a white phosphor, they could generate black or white images. Over the years, the elementary black and white system got confused with monochrome systems and many people have been misusing the terms, and it's unlikely things will change.

Color, however, is another matter altogether. Since the monitor itself acts as a light source, it creates color using the primary additive colors, described earlier. For a color monitor, each pixel is comprised of a group of triads and each triad contains three small dots of color: red, green, and blue, as shown in the diagram in FIG. 2-12.

2-12
When a pixel is lit up on a color monitor screen, it consists of several RGB color phosphor dots, which use additive color to create individual colors on the screen.

Color phosphor dots ——→

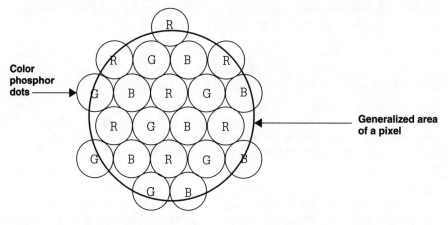

Generalized area of a pixel

Inside the monitor are three separate electron guns, which illuminate the red, green, and blue color dots on the screen of the monitor. Each gun fires electrons only at its corresponding color dots. These guns can vary in intensity; if more electrons are directed at a particular color dot in a pixel, that color dot will glow more brightly (for a detailed explanation of how a monitor works, refer to chapter 3, *Monitors*).

Colors are created by adjusting the intensity of the three guns on a single pixel. Obviously, if just one of the color dots of a pixel is illuminated, the pixel will glow in that single color. If all three guns hit the color dots of a single pixel at full intensity, the three RGB primaries blend to make the pixel appear white. If none of the color dots are hit, the pixel remains black. Colors are produced by varying the intensity of the three guns.

Since the intensity of the three electron guns can be so precisely tuned, color monitors have the ability to display millions of different colors. The important concept is that color monitors have the potential to produce any color of the rainbow; they must simply be instructed by the display controller as to which pixel of the screen is to display what color.

Since the monitor is capable of displaying such a wide range of color, it is the display controller that determines how many colors can be displayed on the screen at one time. The amount of displayable color is a function of how much display memory it has and the size of its LUT-DACs.

In an 8-bit display controller, there is an 8-bit frame buffer and three 8-bit DACs, one for each primary RGB color. Such a display controller has the potential of generating any one of 16.7 million colors. This potential is referred to as the *color palette*—and like an artist's palette, it represents the choice of colors that can be used. But the display controller can display only 256 colors at any one time. For this, the display controller brings into play what's known as its color look-up table, or LUT.

The LUT allows the selection of any 256 of 16.7 million colors for any pixel. Thus, to use the artist's palette example, the artist is restricted to using only a mixed combination of 256 of 16.7 million colors.

This is exactly how an 8-bit display controller works. Instead of applying paint to a canvas, the colors are defined electronically. From the 16.7 million color possibilities, 256 colors are chosen to be on the screen at any one time, and each pixel on the screen can be any of the 256 colors. This is stated as "256 displayable colors from a palette of 16.7 million." When the display controller calls for a specific color, for example, color number 112, the display controller goes to the look-up table to see which of the 16.7 million colors exactly corresponds to that color number.

Because only 256 colors at a time can be used, and even though that seems quite a lot, it's enough to only approximate the actual colors of real-life items and their surfaces. Therefore, 8-bit color is defined as *pseudo color*. Because a LUT is used to select the 256 colors from the palette, you'll also find 8-bit color referred to as *indexed color*.

The diagram in FIG. 2-13 shows how the display controller uses the look-up table with an 8-bit system. For this example, the user, via his or her applications program, has determined that a particular pixel must display color number 112 from the look-up table. As shown in the illustration, the LUT provides the binary numbers to describe the intensity for each of the three electron guns in the monitor. However, notice that the numbers that come from the LUT are three separate 8-bit numbers: $8 + 8 + 8 = 24$.

So even with an 8-bit system, the binary information coming from the LUT to the DACs is a 24-bit color number. Once the LUT has supplied the values, the display controller uses DACs which changes the binary numbers into the electrical signals that drive the monitor.

The term *pseudo color* is not limited to 8 bits; it's used to describe any artificial coloring of an image. For example, radiation that isn't visible, such as x-rays, gamma rays, temperature, etc., can be visualized using pseudo colors.

For 24-bit color, commonly known as *true color*, the process is much the same as 8-bit color. The only difference is that instead of being limited to 256 different colors on the screen at the same time, any of the 16.7 million colors can be displayed. The 24-bit binary number that defines the color for a particular pixel is actually made up

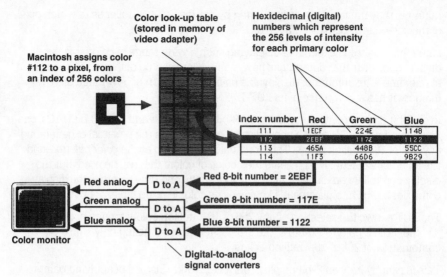

Color look-up table (stored in memory of video adapter)

Hexidecimal (digital) numbers which represent the 256 levels of intensity for each primary color

Macintosh assigns color #112 to a pixel, from an index of 256 colors

Index number	Red	Green	Blue
111	1ECF	224E	1148
112	2EBF	117E	1122
113	465A	448B	55CC
114	11F3	66D6	9B29

Red 8-bit number = 2EBF
Green 8-bit number = 117E
Blue 8-bit number = 1122

Red analog — D to A
Green analog — D to A
Blue analog — D to A

Color monitor

Digital-to-analog signal converters

Eight-bit color systems can display 256 simultaneous colors, typically from a palette of 16.7 million. Any of the 16.7 million colors can be displayed, but only 256 at a time. The colors are selected with a look-up table and digital-to-analog converter (LUT-DAC). In some systems, this is referred to as indexed color.
SuperMac Technology

of three 8-bit numbers (8 + 8 + 8 = 24). An 8-bit number can describe 256 levels of intensity for a color dot, so 256 × 256 × 256 = 16,777,216 different colors.

Since a 24-bit display controller has to deal with three 8-bit numbers at the same time, it requires three times the display memory of a standard 8-bit display controller. This is one of the reasons why a 24-bit display controller is more expensive than an 8-bit display controller.

The diagram in FIG. 2-14 represents a simplified view of how 24-bit color works in a display controller. With the 24-bit binary number, the intensities for the three electron guns of the monitor are directly defined by the application. Therefore, each of the pixels on the monitor screen can be any of the 16.7 million colors available.

2-14

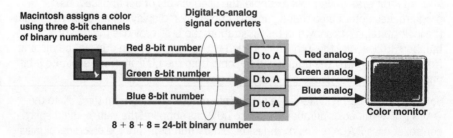

Macintosh assigns a color using three 8-bit channels of binary numbers

Digital-to-analog signal converters

Red 8-bit number — D to A — Red analog
Green 8-bit number — D to A — Green analog
Blue 8-bit number — D to A — Blue analog

Color monitor

8 + 8 + 8 = 24-bit binary number

In a 24-bit color system, the frame buffer's output goes directly to the digital-to-analog converters (DACs), which can generate any of the 16.7 million colors on the screen.
SuperMac Technology

Color ranges

As can be seen in the previous examples, there are various displayable color ranges that are a function of the bit depth of the display memory and the capacity of the LUT-DAC. The different bit depths of pixels and the resultant number of possible colors have been categorized and are shown in TABLE 2-1.

Table 2-1
The displayable colors for a controller, which are a function of its memory and LUT-DAC, have standard names. However, they can be referred to by either the number of bits or the number of displayable colors, or the name of the color range.

Name	Bits per pixel	# of colors
Low color	4	16
Pseudo color	8	256
High color	16	65,536
True color	24	16,777,216

Banding

The linear quantization of color data produces even increments or gradations between shades or colors. However, most devices and the human eye are nonlinear. Thus, a linear quantization at one end of the scale might produce steps that are indistinguishable but, at the other end, they would be too far apart. The result is that colors that should have a continuous tone appear to have steps, commonly known as *bands*, and the effect is called *banding* or *color banding*.

Limited palette & dithering

When a system has a limited palette (due to memory, LUT-DAC, or some other limitation) and a wider range of colors are needed than can be reproduced, a concept known as *dithering* is used. With dithering techniques, it's possible to increase the effective number of shades of gray or colors. Dithering uses a block or cell of pixels that can be (depending on the programmer or system designer) 3×3, 4×4, or as a large as 8×8.

Within these blocks, the available colors of the system are mixed in a predefined ratio. For example, to produce purple, an alternating mix of blue and red might be used. The ratio and the positioning of the pixels is a function of the desired resulting color. The cell size is kept as small as possible (to prevent graininess) and enlarged as the color range is expanded. Dithering was developed in the image-processing industry initially to enhance black-and-white images. As was discussed in chapter 1, *Applications*, there are several interesting dithering algorithms in use today.

If a system is limited to, say, 4096 colors, by using a 4×4 cell, the effective color range can theoretically be increased to 15 times 4096, or 61,440 colors. The operator of 15 is used because one of the original colors of the 4096 must be used in the cell. As the example shows, there's a great potential to increase colors with dithering. However, due to the way the eye works, it isn't possible to achieve the full range of possible colors with a dithering cell. Dithering was popular in early computer graphics systems as a way to provide a wide color range with limited hardware. Today, it's still found in low-cost paint programs and as part of the utilities of image-processing systems. It was never a part of the TV systems.

Color temperature

When all three RGB guns in a monitor are turned on to their maximum intensities, the monitor will display white. The particular white is measured in terms of its color temperature in degrees Kelvin, which is also referred to as the *white point*. This is the color that a black-body radiator (a heated cavity with an exit aperture) will emit when heated to that temperature. The surface temperature of a normal incandescent light bulb is slightly less than the color temperature of the light it gives off (around 4700°F for a 100-watt lamp). TABLE 2-2 lists some common sources of light and their respective color temperatures.

Table 2-2
Approximate color temperature,
in Kelvin, of common light sources.

Source	Temperature
North skylight	7500° K
Average daylight	6500° K
Xenon camera flash	6000° K
Cool white fluorescent	4300° K
Tungsten-halogen lamp	3300° K
Warm white fluorescent	3000° K
100W tungsten	2900° K
Sunset	2000° K
Candle flame	1900° K

Gamma correction

The explanation of 24-bit color in the previous section is very simplified. There are two other factors that enter into how 24-bit color is actually displayed on the monitor screen:

Color sensitivity of the human eye

The human eye is very good at determining subtle changes in color, but it doesn't register those changes in a mathematically linear fashion. In other words, for colors that are very dark, it might take a change of five units of color for the eye to detect the slightest change; with colors that are very bright, the eye might be able to detect a change of two units of color. This is known as the eye's *nonlinear response characteristic*, and is well documented in several books on optics, physiology, and medicine.

Nonlinearity is typical of most human senses and usually has the characteristic of a logarithmic curve. Nonlinearity is also a typical characteristic of most display devices. Human senses are continuous and most devices are discrete systems (some with very small increments between steps). However, in colorimetric or colorimeter-based systems, the color space is linear and continuous. Thus the task becomes one of matching the nonlinear and often discrete device to that of a continuous linear color space like the CIE model.

Nonlinear response of the monitor

The color dots that make up the monitor screen are a *phosphor compound*. The phosphor compound can be blended to glow either red, green, or blue when struck by the electrons—therefore, each of the different colors is actually a slightly different phosphor compound. As a result, each red, green, and blue color might glow slightly brighter, or dimmer, when struck with the same intensity by the monitor's electron guns.

The nonlinear curve of devices is commonly referred to as their gamma curve. Therefore, when a device is corrected to comply with some standard, it's said to have its gamma "adjusted." In the simplest description, all a color-matching or color-calibration system does is to correct the gamma curve of the device to a common standard. The gamma of a scanner's RGB sensors, or the file it produces, is adjusted so that final RGB output from it is set at known values. These known values are then matched or translated or corrected to the gamma curve of the desired output device, such as a monitor or a printer. The common denominator in the middle is the CIE color-space model, or some other mutually agreed-upon model.

A graph depicting the generalized response of the monitor and the sensitivity of the eye looks similar to the diagram in FIG. 2-15. To compensate for these two factors, display systems employ gamma correction to the exact binary numbers defined by the application. Gamma correction is an inverse curve that counteracts the actual response curve, as shown in FIG. 2-16.

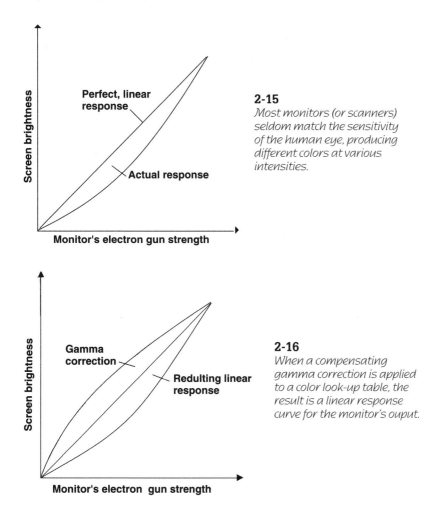

2-15
Most monitors (or scanners) seldom match the sensitivity of the human eye, producing different colors at various intensities.

2-16
When a compensating gamma correction is applied to a color look-up table, the result is a linear response curve for the monitor's ouput.

On a properly equipped display controller, each of the color dots (red, green, and blue) has its own gamma-correction table to correct for the sensitivity of the eye and the response of the color dots within the monitor.

It's important to note that the diagrams are simplifications—in real life, the gamma table is nonlinear. In other words, for any of the 16.7 million colors that can be defined, there might be more or less gamma correction applied to make the color display properly on the monitor screen. The diagram in FIG. 2-17 illustrates how gamma tables are used to create the image on the screen.

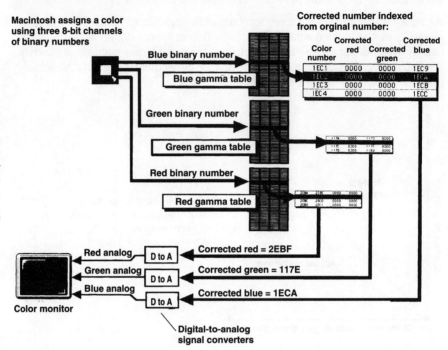

2-17
Gamma correction is accomplished by adjusting the color look-up table either by "eye-ball matching," via an application, or with a color-matching system.
SuperMac Technology

The gamma-correction table can be modified by the software application. With this in mind, it's the programmer and user who ultimately have control over the colors that appear on the monitor screen.

In addition to the intensity of characteristics of a monitor, every monitor will experience a color shift over time. Also, some monitors have or develop a bias toward one of the primary colors, tending to be more blue or more red than desired. All of this represents the gamma of a monitor. A monitor's *gamma* is the relationship of the source or input material, the monitor's portrayal of that information, and the expectations of the user. If the user expects apple-shaped things to look bright red, and they're only a muddy red or almost brown, then the user is going to be disappointed and will criticize the system.

For example, an image (with 85% cyan) can get distorted as it's processed so that it has 89% cyan (a 6% error or distortion) when it's printed (see FIG. C-21).

Display calibration & matching systems

Every computer display (monitor or flat panel) and printer produces different colors even though they're given the same data. The problem of color discrepancies between one device and another is magnified many times with output devices. Displays from different manufacturers can vary widely in the range of colors they produce, because each manufacturer uses different phosphor colors and sometimes even different electron-scanning technology. However, even on displays from the same manufacturer, or on the very same display, colors can vary because of:

❑ Variances in how the displays are adjusted at any given time
❑ Ambient environmental conditions such as temperature or humidity
❑ Where the display is located
❑ Time, because as the phosphor ages, its color-producing potential declines

For the graphics professional, display inconsistencies create a problem because the colors used in a design will look different, depending on which monitor is used to view them. To the user, it looks as if the colors themselves are different, but in reality, the color information in the graphic file is unchanged; it's simply being shown differently by different displays.

To remedy this problem, designers must have a way to adjust the colors on the display so they're consistent. While it isn't possible to make displays from different manufacturers' products produce the same color gamuts (because they might use different phosphors or scanning technologies), it is possible to adjust two displays from the same manufacturer so they produce the same colors. Even on displays from different manufacturers, it should be possible to determine all the common colors both displays can produce, and to adjust the displays so those colors appear the same.

For all of these reasons, monitors need to be calibrated from time to time. There are three basic ways to do it:

❑ Eyeball test—does it look right?
❑ Patch matching—compare the screen to a color patch
❑ Electronically—with a photometer

The eyeball test is what most people use. Seeing too much red in the image, they will adjust the color (assuming they have a control) much like they adjust their TV at home, until it looks right. This is very unscientific but surprisingly effective—the human eye is a very good photometer/comparitor.

Patch matching is when a standard color sample or two is held up against the screen and the monitor is adjusted to match it. This is done using one's eye as the comparitor and, when it looks right, the adjust is complete. However, if the color balance of the monitor is off, say biased toward blue, then, although the patch matching for single color or patch might look correct, all other colors or hues will be off.

Electronic color-calibration systems use a sensor (photometer) that attaches to the monitor.

To make such adjustments in a precise and fairly simple way also means finding a standard way to describe colors that can be implemented by any display technology. As described in previous sections, computer displays produce colors from three primary colors: red, green, and blue (or RGB). In contrast, color printers produce colors using four different colors: cyan, magenta, yellow, and black (or CYMK). Because a different group of basic colors is used to produce the gamut of colors available on a printer and because of the differences between transmitted and reflected light, some colors displayed on a monitor won't reproduce at all on a printer.

The source and destination of color in a system is shown schematically in FIG. 2-18. Each component can contribute a bias, have limitations, and use a different color model.

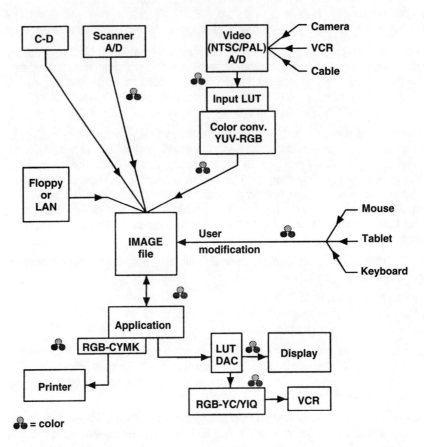

2-18
At almost every interface (hardware or software), color balance can be changed and biases introduced. The color symbol indicated the most likely points of bias.

To resolve the problem of display inconsistency, graphics professionals have adjusted their display colors to a specific standard. Since age and other variables will affect display colors, requiring periodic adjustments by the display's end user, the adjustment will have to be done more than once.

Calibration techniques

Various devices have been developed that can accurately read the brightness (or luminance) of each of the primary color channels, as well as software that adjusts the luminance levels to standard settings. These are known as *display-calibration systems*. There are now a few such products on the market. This section describes these devices and the differences between them.

Display-calibration technology involves using a hardware device known as a *photometer* to read the luminance of each primary color channel on a screen. The photometer is a small cylindrical sensor, sometimes built in the shape of a gun, that's placed against the face of the screen. The photometer has primary color filters and reports (typically on a small digital display) the intensities of each primary color for the area of the screen it can see, typically a few centimeters. The user can then adjust the color palette from within the application, which in turn modifies the graphics board's LUT to make the colors equal to what the user feels they should be. Adjusting or resetting the graphics board output (via its LUT) is known as "adjusting the gamma curve." It's actually a compensation for all the variables between what the application program called for and what the photometer actually sees at a given spot on the screen. It isn't very scientific, but it's widely used and sworn by.

Some calibration systems have the photometer's output connected to the computer, and its data is read by a software program that automatically adjusts the graphics board's output to standard or preset settings.

There are two versions of calibration systems: open loop and closed loop. An *open loop* system measures a spot on the screen, reports the results, and requires the user to make adjustments (either with a special program (that manipulates the LUTs) or via the monitor's color-adjustment controls. A *closed loop* system connects between the display controller and the monitor's RGB lines. Figure 2-19 shows a closed-loop system.

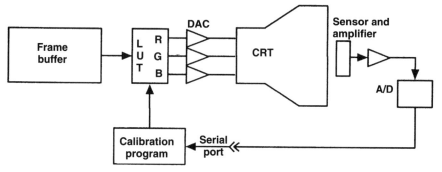

2-19
A closed-loop color-calibration system measures the screen color and then, via a calibration program, adjusts the LUT of the display controller to match a preset "standard" color.

A predetermined color is presented to the screen (via a special setup program) and is seen by the color sensor (i.e., photometer), which is attached to the face of the monitor the same as in an open-loop system. Then the system adjusts the color on the screen by manipulating the voltage levels of the RGB signals until the predetermined color matches what the photometer expected to see. The following is a brief list of some of the most popular color calibration systems:

❑ Barco
❑ Radius PrecisionColor Calibration
❑ RasterOps
❑ SuperMac

To have proper color fidelity, an increase in intensity from the graphics board should have a corresponding increase in brightness on the screen, called a *linear gamma curve* (refer to chapter 3, *Monitors*, for more on this). A display-calibration system runs the video board through its intensity settings and reads the display's brightness for each setting. If the brightness read by the display calibrator is too high or too low, the output for that setting on the graphics board is adjusted until the proper brightness is read on the display. But keep in mind that this is done only for one small spot on the screen. The assumption is the monitor has a perfect distribution of phosphors and intensity control across the entire face of the screen (it doesn't).

With a linear gamma curve, the distance (or difference in intensity) between any one setting and the next setting is always identical. A linear gamma curve ensures that the display will produce the correct luminance levels on each primary color channel. All monitors change over time. It's commonly referred to as a *drift* or *color shift*. Except for cases where a trained user (typically a graphic artist doing prepress work) is looking at the monitor, most people don't notice the drift. However, the color shift isn't linear and usually one color or gun will change more than another, giving all colors a blue or red tint.

Along with adjusting the gamma curve, most display-calibration software also has an option that allows the user to adjust the display's color temperature to match ambient lighting conditions, based on the temperature of the color displayed. However, if the software doesn't have such capability, all monitors can be adjusted, either internally or by front-panel controls.

Typically, a monitor has its RGB amplifiers and guns adjusted so that it produces a white screen (with full or maximum signals at the RGB inputs) that has a color temperature of 3,300 degrees Kelvin. The temperature of a typical color display is 9300° K, but, at this temperature, white has a distinct blue tint. The color temperature of daylight, in contrast, is about 5000° K (refer to TABLE 2-2). Some users prefer a white with a slightly bluer tint, often called *page white*, and set their monitors at 7800° K. By either manually adjusting the color of a display or letting the calibration software do it, the user can bring his display's white into conformity with whiter whites that occur naturally. This establishes the end point of the gamma curve, and it's typically assumed then that the curve is linear and fixed at the black point.

The best use for a color-calibration system is to keep the monitor stable and consistent at some white point over time. This allows the user to become accustomed to the way colors look and perform a mental calibration.

Display-calibration technology allows users to read and adjust the intensity of the primary colors on a display, so that different displays from the same manufacturer can be set with the same luminance levels. Obviously, a calibration device should be as accurate as possible and as compatible as possible.

Calibration can be achieved two ways, by building a sensor and the necessary hardware directly into the display, or by using an external calibration device that controls the signals going to the display from the display-controller board. Integral calibration has the advantage of directly controlling the output of the electron guns rather than modifying the output of the graphics board. External calibration has the advantage of supporting a wide variety of display types, and a single calibrator can be used for multiple displays.

These color-calibration systems are fascinating to watch and use, but should be kept in perspective. They're typically employed by people who develop prepress material for color ads, brochures, and other items. The idea is to create a color what-you-see-is-what-you-get (WYSIWYG) display; however, that is almost impossible to accomplish. In addition to the difference between reflected and transmitted color, the face of the monitor is highly reflective, curved, polished glass, whereas the printed back is a low reflective, unpolished, flat surface. Also, the purities of the phosphors used in the monitor have different error (impurity) factors than the impurities in the inks used for printing (known as SWOP specifications for Web offset printing and EURO hue errors). So color calibration or matching can provide, at best, only an approximation between displayed color and printed color.

Users and manufacturers often use the terms *image editing* and *color editing* synonymously, but they aren't the same thing. Image editing is the manipulation of pixels in the original image or bit map (from a file, digitizer, or scanner) to correct for color balance or to adjust the appearance of the image in some way. This often includes removing artifacts as unwanted portions of an image, or changing the tint of portions of the image. Color correction refers to adjustment of all or major portions of the image to restore the original color values or balance. The processing of an original image can induce changes in the original color balance, which, with the proper software, can be reset or color corrected.

There are two basic color-matching classifications: invariant and conditional. *Invariant* matches are identical and match all visual and photometric tests for all observers under all conditions. This type of color matching is accomplished only in exactly the same medium (such as matching paint or ink) and even then is very difficult to obtain. *Conditional* color matching is the one obtained in color- or device-dependent situations. Matches between a color display and a color printer are always conditional.

Color matching

To solve the problem of precisely matching the colors on a display with colors that can be reproduced on a display (flat panel or monitor), color printer, film printer, or other output device, there must be a common way of describing colors that can be accurately implemented on the display and on input or output devices. This technology is known as *color matching*.

The second issue related to color fidelity, that of matching a display's colors with those of an output device, is solved through color matching. Because different devices have different methods of creating colors (RGB on displays versus CYMK on printers, for example), color matching requires a universal method of describing colors that can be precisely implemented on both displays and output devices so the colors on each are the same. And not all colors on a display can be created on an output device, in any case, so a color-matching system should be able to match all the colors that are common to both types of devices.

Because it isn't completely possible for the same shade of red created on a monitor to be reproduced, say, on an ink-jet printer, a color-matching system has to be capable of finding a *best-fit* model. This is where the algorithms get tricky and the black arts enter the picture. Various manufacturers have different approaches for this problem. The most common method is to store a set of characteristics about the devices to be used.

Perhaps one of the major problems with specifying colors is that they're device dependent and nonlinear. Red on one monitor isn't the same as red on another monitor, a camera, a scanner, or a printer. Colors are inherently and intrinsically

Characterization of devices

different. A device's profile is the characterization of a given device, to either a color space (i.e., RGB, YUV, CMYK, etc.) or to a CIE colorimeter model. However, for a device's profile to be characterized and then translated into another color space or model also involves the gamut or palette of the devices involved. Going from a full-spectrum gamut like a 24-bit computer display to a limited-palette device like an ink-jet printer creates problems. Techniques like dithering (discussed earlier) are used to try and compensate for these discrepancies.

Most color spaces that can be represented with triplets, whether based on device-dependent colors, colorimeter, or some other empirical organization of colors, have important similarities. Color space can be linear or nonlinear with respect to visible radiation. Linear scales relate directly to measurement data, for example, the RGB values from a camera or a scanner. Such scales are usually referred to as *tristimulus values*. Common tristimulus-value scales are the CIE XYZ, RGB, the Xerox YES, and the linear versions of NTSC YIQ and PAL (CCIR 601) YUV. These are also called *luminance-chrominance spaces*. Another important type of linear space is luminance-chromaticity, which is based on the CIE xyY and Yu'v' models.

One thing to remember about color-matching and calibration systems is that they compensate for a three-dimensional color model, not a three-dimensional physical device. When you adjust the RGB guns in a monitor, that adjustment is for all points on the screen. The same is true for a scanner or a printer. If a scanner scans in a nonlinear manner for any reason, the color correction will be off. The same is true for a monitor or a printer. If the scanning beam of a monitor traces its path across the screen in a nonlinear fashion, the calibration will be incorrect. Typically, this isn't a big problem, but you should be aware of it.

Color-matching systems

Manufacturers of computers, software, printers, and inks have for years—decades—been trying to devise a way to get the inherently incompatible devices associated with color display and reproduction to be more compatible and consistent. The general model has been to reference a device to a neutral standard such as CIE, as depicted in FIG. 2-20.

Other intermediate standards have been used. For example, scanners are generally calibrated to the Kodak Q-60 RGB target for ektachrome-based transparencies.

The need for a color-matching standard is well understood and something users have longed for for many years. Various systems have been proposed and implemented, all with the hope of becoming the standard. In this section, I'll discuss a few of them, as follows:

❏ Apple ColorSync CMM (color-matching methods)
❏ Kodak Photo CD System, PhotoYCC-calibrated RGB model based on CIE
❏ PANTONE color-matching system (PMS)
❏ SuperMac SuperMatch professional color-matching system
❏ TekColor, AKA TekHVC, calibrated HVC based on the CIE LUV system

The follow sections contain a brief description of these systems.

Apple's ColorSync

In early 1993 Apple introduced its color-matching system, ColorSync. Designed to overcome the problems stated in the previous sections, ColorSync was also made as an extension to QuickDraw. The ColorSync architecture uses Apple's QuickTime multimedia standard, which allows it to be linked via the Components Manager to

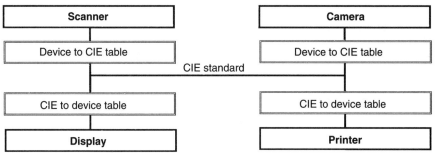

Apple third-party color-management resources and utilities. ColorSync provides three important features:

❑ System-level support for color matching
❑ Support for existing applications
❑ Opportunities for third parties to add value

The only way a color-matching system can be truly pervasive and not just a high-end add-on is when it's offered as a system resource where all applications can take advantage of it. By integrating ColorSync with the QuickDraw graphics model, Apple has made color matching a central part of the Macintosh. ColorSync provides support for several existing applications so users don't have to wait for applications to be revised before they can be used.

The system uses the Component Manager, which allows third parties to add value to the system. Apple provides base-level functionality to all users, but allows third-party systems to develop specific solutions. This enables companies like Kodak, EFI, and others to bring their expertise to the ColorSync architecture rather than having to offer replacement solutions.

ColorSync is founded on the device-independent color space of CIE XYZ. To create a device-independent color definition while maintaining compatibility with QuickDraw, which is based on RGB, Apple used their 13-inch RGB monitor as the default system profile. However, users can change the system profile to any other monitor. The source RGB data can be converted to CIE XYZ based on the source profile to provide a device-independent definition of color on the Macintosh. Device profiles are created for any device in the CIE XYZ color space.

Apple's ColorSync uses a color-matching method that provides the best possible match when the exact match from one color space to another is not possible. This allows one device to be matched as well as possible when it can't produce the right color. Colors are interpreted relative to the destination device's white point. This is especially good for scanned images. For spot color, the system uses colormetric options. And for fast matching, the system allows the user to select the saturation method.

ColorSync does not contain a color-calibration system and allows other third-party systems to be used. Companies like Radius and RasterOps, for example, have calibrators that support the ColorSync system.

Kodak's PhotoYCC color-management system

In late 1990, Kodak announced its proposed standard, PhotoYCC, for exchanging color pictures. Positioning themselves as "the world's expert in color," the company offered the first method for consistent high color across the photographic (including Kodak's Photo CD systems), broadcast, and computing industries.

PhotoCYY is a fast system and was designed using a minimum number of computations—far fewer than, say, CIE XYZ, LUV, or LAB color-space conversions. The Kodak precision color processor is a software processor designed to transform device-specific color information into a device-independent color space.

The Kodak color-management system is a set of products that precisely account for color-space differences, device calibration, and the impact of external conditions such as fluorescent lighting versus incandescent lighting. Kodak licenses and sells the system components to application and system developers, CPU manufacturers, peripheral manufacturers, and even end users. The Kodak color-management system uses device profiles. The Kodak precision device color profile (DCPs) characterizes the most popular input, output, and proofing components. Kodak's expertise lies in their ability to create the DCP for I/O devices based on the company's experience in color systems.

Designed to be device and operating-system independent, the system supports DOS, Windows, Macintosh, SunOS, and UNIX 5.*x*. It's compatible with Kodak's PhotoYCC as well as RGB-, CMYK-, and CIE-defined color-space models. Kodak's standard for exchanging color pictures among computers and output devices has been endorsed by Adobe Systems, Aldus Corporation, Autodesk, Sun Microsystems, and Truevision.

RasterOps' Correctcolor management systems (RCCMS) is based on the Kodak PhotoYCC and precision-device color profiles.

SuperMac's color-matching system

In the late 1990s, SuperMac Technology, in conjunction with several Macintosh color peripheral manufacturers, announced the SuperMatch professional color-matching system. It's a system, developed to improve the color fidelity between Macintosh-compatible color-graphics monitors, scanners, and output devices. The SuperMatch system allows Macintosh color-graphics users to precisely match spot color and continuous-tone color images on displays and input/output devices.

SuperMatch is based on TekColor technology and is licensed from Tektronix, Inc. It includes an open color-interface specification that supports color-fidelity matching across a broad range of color input and output devices. The SuperMatch system supports any device manufacturer using the TekColor color-fidelity system.

Rather than solving the problem by limiting a user to specific spot-color matching, the TekColor technology allows users to work with the full gamut of colors on a display and printer. Unreachable colors are also quickly identified, so that users know which colors can't be accurately reproduced.

SuperMatch is based on the CIE color-space standard. In this system, differences in color-creating technology between displays and output devices are accommodated by accurately reading each device's color gamut, translating the device's description of those colors into CIE color-space descriptions, and then converting the CIE color-space descriptions into device-specific descriptions of the same colors. Specifically, this approach:

❏ Compares color-capability descriptions from each display or output device to tell the user which colors each device can produce, and which colors the devices do or don't have in common
❏ Precisely matches the colors common to both devices, so the color the user sees is the color reproduced
❏ Makes as close an approximation as possible of the displayed color when it's outside the color gamut of the output device, if the user so desires

Each device's description is stored in a database that's automatically referred to when an application program needs to display or print a color. Each is individually characterized by a database entry supplied by its manufacturer, using an open specification.

Since the SuperMatch system recognizes all the colors of which any display or output device is capable and translates them into another device's native format, the system can easily support the most popular spot-color systems or any other specific color descriptions. As an example, SuperMatch supports Apple's ColorSync system.

Various Macintosh color-graphics peripheral manufacturers announced support for the SuperMatch system (e.g., Tektronix, Kodak, Color Imaging Systems, Howtek, Seiko Instruments USA, Sharp, Mitsubishi, QMS, Mirus, and Hitachi). Since the SuperMatch system is software independent, application software can take advantage of SuperMatch without modification.

TekColor color-management system

The Tektronix color-management system (TekCMS) is a device-independent color-matching system that uses the TekHVC color-space (which is based on the CIELUV model) and device-characterization tables. It employs calibration methodologies (using calibrators from the various suppliers) and has been accepted as a standard in the X Windows system as the Xcms. The main components of the TekCMS extensions are:

❏ An API library for color extensions
❏ A client-sever protocol (allows modification and query of the color map)
❏ X-server extensions
❏ TekCSC libraries to convert device-independent color specification to and from device-dependent RGB specifications

A TekColor interface specification is available to all color-peripheral vendors from Tektronix at no charge.

Other color-matching systems

There are other color-matching systems that are on the market and they all have interesting qualities and capabilities. This section was not meant to be an exhaustive review of color-matching systems, but only to provide an overall knowledge of the principles involved. Some of the other systems are:

❏ Adobe PostScript level 2
❏ Mincell
❏ PANTONE broadcast color system
❏ PANTONE matching system (PMS, aka PANTONE matching color, PMC)
❏ QuickDraw GX
❏ Radius PrecisionColor matching system
❏ RasterOps Correctcolor management systems
❏ Toyo

These are device-dependent systems that have been primarily used in the printing world in lieu of a color-matching system.

How to describe color

The words used to describe color vary from one person to another. "Not a news flash" you say. No, it isn't. The classic example is to ask three or more people to describe the color of something: a yellow car, an apple, a simple box. Of course they'll have a different description, but what is equally interesting is the conviction they have for their interpretation, even people who are color blind to some degree.

As I've pointed out several times in this chapter, color standardization, calibration, and references are a multifaceted science and art. Color can be precisely defined; that is the science. However, reproducing it on a monitor or a printed page is more difficult and there it takes on the aspect of art. You can find proponents in both camps who will argue these premises. Various companies with big investments in processes and business plans, who present themselves in altruistic roles, are trying to establish their version of color standards. My advise is don't take sides and use what works best for you on a project-by-project basis.

Jon Rice of Rice Communications (Yardley, PA) contrasts the popular notion (and ambition) of color WYSIWYG in computer graphics to WYGIWYFL (or "wiggywiffle") when it comes to video: What You Get Is Whatever You Feel Like. However, with the merger of computer graphics and TV, the development of the multimedia market and the increasing prevalence of marketing at all levels of our life, color compatibility is a must. The producer of a corporate marketing plan wants the videotape, magazine ads, promotional items (t-shirts, coffee cups, etc.) and most of all the product itself, to all have the same colors, especially for the company logo.

TV color

TV is merging with computer graphics, but it isn't just a simple matter of plugging in a TV signal—color is different in TV land. Referring to EIA RS-189A (part 73 of the FCC NTSC specification), the specified maximum values for color bars, which are used for camera and monitor color calibration and setup, are shown in TABLE 2-3. (For a complete RS-189A specification, contact the Electronic Industries Association, 1001 Eye St. NW, Washington, DC 20006.)

Table 2-3
The NTSC color system is based on a two-channel system of luminance (intensity) and chrominance (color ratios). To ensure receivers and cameras "see" and display the same colors, the FCC established the NTSC color bar specification.

Color	Luminance level (IRE)	Chrominance level (IRE p-p)	Chrominance phase*
Black	7.5	0	na
White	100.0	0	na
Gray	77.0	0	na
Yellow	69.0	62	167
Cyan	56.0	88	283
Green	48.0	82	241
Magenta	36.0	82	61
Red	28.0	88	103
Blue	15.0	62	347

* Relative to reference subcarrier

Any image or color that falls outside of these parameters, something that is easily accomplished with a 24-bit true-color computer-graphics system, is considered an illegal color. Such a color might not pass through the TV system. Technicians in TV studios use a vector scope to monitor the chrominance level and phase of the image signals to ensure compliance with the standard.

When grayscale flat-panel LCD displays were introduced to laptop and portable computers, it was necessary to convert color images into appropriate and balanced grayscales. After several tries, it was found that the NTSC color-bar system gave the best results.

The electronic device that transforms RGB signals into an NTSC color signal is known as an *encoder*, and its function is to perform the matrix transformation described above, limit each transmission primary to the appropriate bandwidth, modulate the subcarrier with the I and Q primaries, and combine the modulated subcarrier with the luminance carrier. For those readers unfamiliar with the concept of modulation, it's defined as the process of varying the amplitude, frequency, or phase of a signal in order to carry information on that signal. Refer back to FIG. 2-18, which gives a representation of how various color schemes or models are used and transformed in an integrated computer system.

Trapping is a process in color printing that eliminates gaps or outlines between color elements of a printed page. Called "light leaks," the gaps are considered unacceptable in a professionally produced publication. The gaps are usually caused by slight paper movement on the press, misaligned printing plates, the characteristics of certain inks, or humidity. These and other factors can cause text illustrations and photographs to shift position slightly.

Trapping

In traditional trapping, print-shop specialists photomechanically expand (*spread*) or contract (*choke*) an object's edges in minute increments to create a slight overlap of the inks for adjoining color elements of the film. The expansions and contractions compensate for misregistration that might occur on the press. Software programs like RipPrep from Graphics Edge are designed to apply those techniques through the use of computer software to EPS files originating on Macintosh, UNIX, and Windows-based systems.

Such programs operate by translating the source PostScript file into a proprietary graphical format that automatically analyzes each color interaction on a page. They then generate instructions that produce the spread or choke between each color.

High-speed processor-transformed colors

Maintaining color integrity during transformations among mixed media is a difficult problem. Among the difficulties engineers face are the accurate translations of color reproductions between a computer display and a fax machine, between a TV and a printer, or between a video camera and a color copier. Chances are that an image of van Gogh's *Sunflowers* passed electronically from CD-ROM to a color printer, for example, could easily come out green or brown.

Researchers at Matsushita Research Institute Tokyo have developed a high-speed color-transformation algorithm. Matsushita has developed a color-transformation LSI processor they call Prism, based on the algorithm that makes possible a device-independent color reproduction among different media. The chip provides a high-speed translation of an image's original color model into the output color, whether it produces a hard copy or an electronic display. It was first used in products such as color scanners, printers, color copiers, and fax machines developed by Matsushita group companies, then sold on the external market.

The standard set by CIE defines three characteristics of color: luminance (L), the color scale between red and yellow (a) and the color scale between green and blue (b). All colors can be expressed with the formula L*a*b, where the asterisks are numerical values for each characteristic. When L, a, and b values are plotted on x, y, and z axes, any specific color can be said to occupy a distinct point in three-dimensional *color space*.

The Prism color processor can convert color-image signals from device color space—where red, green, and blue (RGB) are the three axes—into L*a*b standard color space. The processor can also transform signals from standard color space into device color space: RGB for display, or CMYK for printed hard copies. Before this chip was introduced, the color-transformation process had been handled mostly by software installed in a frame memory. Such a frame memory must often contain a color look-up table as big as 50Mb, because the color transformation requires a complex, nonlinear computation, especially when involving a transformation between RGB and L*a*b, or L*a*b* and CMYK.

With the Prism color processor, a video-rate color transformation is possible. The Prism color processor based on the algorithm consists of a small, three-dimensional look-up table and a three-dimensional interpolator. Each color description would require 24 bits, or 8 bits for each of its three component characteristics. The processor divides that into *upper* 9-bit signals—or 3 bits each for R, G, and B (or L, a, and b)—and a *lower* 15 bits, or 5 bits each for RGB.

The upper bits are processed through a small look-up table, which can be represented as a 9×9×9 cubic lattice. The upper bits point to a specific cube in the lattice, and the output is six points defining that cube. An interpolator takes that output and combines it with the lower-bit data to calculate an output color value that would correspond with the input color value. In color space, the value of the output color is located in half of the designated lattice cube, hence the name *prism*.

Because of the way the new algorithm works, the memory required for the look-up table is reduced roughly from the conventional 50Mb to less than 50K. This architecture has also made possible a high-speed color transformation with fewer interpolation errors. More important, Matsushita's color processor is a general-purpose color-space converter, allowing users to define applications. Simply by changing the color definitions of the look-up table, the processor can carry out any color transformation.

3 Monitors

Everything discussed in this book so far has been about the computer side of display systems, the digital generation of images. This chapter will take you into the analog and physiological side of a display system. An old expression from the automotive industry to signify the ultimate test of a car's success (performance, price, style, quality, etc.) has been, "It's where the rubber meets the road." Adapting that expression to the computer graphics industry, you can say, "It's where the eyeball meets the image."

A lot goes on inside a monitor. It's the final step in a complex system that includes image generation on screen and how the user's brain, via the eye, perceives the image. This chapter will explain how a monitor is constructed, its important features and specifications, and the external influences on the eye and brain.

Physiologists estimate that the total capacity of the visual channel (the eyes, optic nerves, and visual centers of the brain) is between 30 and 40 million bits of information per second. Based on an average of 7 bits per character and 5 characters per word, the theoretical capacity is the equivalent of 48 to 72 million words per minute. But most humans read at only 600 to 1,200 words per minute. Given this, it's easy to see why graphics is so much more efficient than alphanumeric printouts. However, generating a reliable, comfortable, and usable image with a monitor is not an easy task. In addition to managing very fast signals and controlling very high voltages at high speeds, you also have to deal with the safety factors of radiation, fatigue factors of focus and reflection, and the management of color control, contrast, and brightness.

The first part of this chapter will discuss the construction of monitors and define a few terms. Then we'll look at some of the physiological elements that influence the selection and use of a computer display. A monitor can be described two ways: *physically* and *electrically*. Although the parts can be separated that way, they're so interlaced you can't really understand how a monitor works or what's important if you don't show the relationships. The elements that make up a monitor are shown in TABLE 3-1.

Table 3-1
The elements that make up a monitor can be split into two major categories: its physical characteristics and its electrical features.

Physical	Electrical
Aspect ratio	Barkhousen
Colors and phosphors	Brightness and contrast ratio
Curvature	Color purity
Diagonal sizes	Convergence
Dot pitch, triads, and trios	Flicker
Strips and stripes	Focus and dynamic focusing
Face	Geometric distortions
In-line and Delta gun	Image position
Persistence	Interlaced and noninterlaced
Rotation	Jitter
Shadow mask (aperture mask)	Linearity
The CRT	Auto-sync
Yoke	Position
Reflection	Raster scan
Spot size and dots per inch	Viewable area and overscan
	Refresh rate
	Resolution
	Square pixels

I won't, however, be describing these elements in exactly the order listed. That would make this an encyclopedia. The discussion will be, as much as possible, as it has been in previous chapters, in the form of data flow. However, monitors have so many interrelated parts that it won't be exactly a straight path. Although the form is important, it isn't the purpose of this chapter. The goal is to make display systems easier to understand. Part of that will come from knowing a little of the history of monitors.

History   The heart of a monitor is the cathode ray tube, CRT. The idea for it was started in 1878 when Sir William Crooks invented a tube that produced cathode rays. The concept was developed further in 1897 by Karl F. Braun. Used in various experiments at the end of the century, mostly by the Army Signal Corps, it wasn't really turned into a commercial product until after World War I, during the 1920s. Allen B. Du Mont started a company, Du Mont Laboratories, and in it produced the first oscilloscope. At the same time, AT&T, RCA, and Westinghouse were doing the original research on TV. In 1923, Valdimr Zworykin of Westinghouse developed the photoelectric tube, called an *iconoscope*, which could convert images to electrical signals. (Today the pickup device or image-capture tube is commonly referred to as an *image orthicon* or *vidicon*.) At the same time, working independently, Philo T. Farnsworth was working on a scanning system with a tube which he called the Kinescope.

Once such signals were generated, they could be transmitted. The first long-distance telecast was on April 7, 1927 between Washington D.C. and New York. In Japan in 1926, Kenjiro Takayanagi succeeded in getting the first flickering images to appear on the CRT screen he developed. In 1927, he helped found JVC, the Victor company of Japan. Within a few years, Du Mont and Zenith produced the first commercial TV sets. World War II interrupted the commercial development of TV, and the resources of the industrialized countries of the world were put into the development of RADAR and various types of scopes. During the war, experiments with color television began, and in 1948 CBS announced it had developed a system for color TV. In 1953, the National Television Standard for Color, NTSC, was adopted. So the foundations for computer displays have been around for a long time.

Various types of display techniques were developed over the years as the search for a fast, economical, and high-resolution display was sought. Graphics displays on computers are as old as oscilloscopes, which is exactly what the first displays were. The early systems used analog voltage signals to directly position or steer the beam on the face of the tube. These displays, referred to as *direct write*, were enhanced due primarily to military developments. Used for RADAR displays, they grew to 24 inches in diameter and became faster, but not much less expensive due to their limited production. The direct-write tubes were adapted to scientific and computer usage and became known as *vector-refreshed* displays. Unlike their inexpensive cousin, the TV CRT, vector-refreshed CRTs had flat faces. This eliminated annoying reflections and contributed to the overall quality of the display. Vector-refreshed (also known as *stroke* or *calligraphic*) displays are capable of producing very high quality and bright, sharp lines, but they were never inexpensive (relative to a TV monitor).

Vector-refreshed displays

When digital computers appeared, the first graphics monitors attached to them, vector-refreshed displays, still looked a lot like oscilloscopes. The vector-refreshed displays work by moving a focused stream or beam of electrons across the phosphor-coated face of a CRT to draw lines and arcs. The computer feeds digital x and y coordinate values to a pair of digital-to-analog converters (DACs), and the output of these converters drives the horizontal and vertical deflection amplifiers in the display to control the position of the beam. A third DAC controls the beam itself, thus the vector-refreshed tube requires the computer to generate three voltages (x, y, and beam intensity, or z).

However, the CPU in early computers was busy with other tasks and it was a drain on its resources to perform the time-consuming manipulations of electron beams in real time. To unburden the main CPU, separate display processors were developed to take care of beam-control details. The main CPU was used to build a series of drawing commands a display list that the display processor repeatedly executes When the main CPU wants to make a minor change in the image being displayed, it modifies the relevant command in the display list, and the change appears when the display processor first executes the modified command. If the changes in the on-screen image are major, the main CPU must turn off the display processor, massage the display list, then restart the display processor.

In the early years of computer graphics, various companies developed display systems based on the vector-refreshed tube design. Information Displays, Inc. (IDI), introduced one of the first commercial interactive display systems (the IDIOM I) in 1964, shown in FIG. 3-1. It was followed in 1967 by Adage (which was founded in 1957 and built systems to link analog and digital computers together) and in 1968 by Evans & Sutherland (the LDS-1). Ivan Sutherland is known as the "father of computer graphics" as a result of his work at Harvard in the early '60s (which influenced IDI's early designs). IDI pursued specialized military display systems, while Adage went into the embryonic CAD market and E&S established the simulation market.

3-1
One of the first commercial interactive display systems, the IDIOM I.

Beam-penetration tubes

Vector-refreshed tubes, although monochromatic, could be green, white, or blue, but users wanted many colors at once. One approach was the *beam-penetration tube*, which used the gun from a color TV tube to produce a slightly different beam current. The face of the CRT was coated with two phosphors (red and green), one on top of the other. Depending upon the current (or velocity) of the beam, different layers of the phosphor would be hit and activated. Then by simple color mixing, various color combinations could be obtained. Beam-penetration tubes were difficult to control and they offered a limited color range. As a result, they were too expensive and too awkward for widespread commercial use.

Storage-tube displays

Like the first TV tubes, vector-refreshed displays used oscilloscope technology. When a standard oscilloscope (aka a *scope*) writes a trace on the phosphor of the tube, the trace will fade in milliseconds. To overcome the fading, the screen was redrawn or *refreshed* 30 to 80 times a second. The number of times it was refreshed was a function of how many lines were on the screen. While display-list-based vector-refreshed displays are good for images that change frequently, they don't work well for graphic analyses of data. Large complex scatter charts, for example, would almost certainly flicker. Also, as CAD drawings became more complex with hundreds of lines, vector-refreshed screens began to flicker annoyingly. Computer scientists of the '50s and '60s combated flickering in such applications by using storage-vector displays. Like vector-refreshed displays, this method used oscilloscope technology.

One derivative of the concept was the direct-view storage tube (DVST) developed by Tektronix in 1967. A storage tube has a phosphor face that is embedded with microscopic conductive particles. Inside the tube there are several flood guns that constantly cover the phosphor with electrons. When an electron beam writes an image on the phosphor, charging it, secondary emissions occur. The flood gun's electrons are attracted to the charge given off by the secondary emission, and continuously regenerate it.

Storage scopes can hold a trace's image for as long as the power is on, and additional traces can be written on top of it. Like the vector-refreshed tube, the storage tube requires the computer driving it to supply x, y, and z voltages. The storage tube reduced the expense of high-speed refresh circuitry and was popular between 1979 to 1988. Storage tubes, like vector-refreshed displays, are monochromatic—one color. In the case of storage tubes, the color was green.

For both refreshed and storage-tube displays, the display-generation hardware must generate three voltages (x, y, and beam intensity, or z). The advantage of both of these display methods is that they don't need much memory—an important consideration in the early days of slow, expensive memory.

In 1973, Intelligent Systems Corporation pioneered the introduction of low-cost raster displays (the model 8000 for $7,000). The raster display relies on digital memory to store and refresh the image. Therefore, although TV tubes were less expensive due to their mass production, the expensive vector-refreshed tubes provided a higher-quality image. At the time, inferior supporting electronics and the resultant poor quality of the displays limited their market acceptance. However, technology development was on their side and everyone in the industry knew it was just a matter of time until raster displays displaced vector-refreshed displays. The same situation might exist today between CRTs and flat-panel displays.

The early raster displays

In the early days (late '70s), we had big, bulky, stationary monitors with big, awkward, attached keyboards called *terminals*. They were fixed in place because only bodybuilders could move them. The early '80s saw the introduction of workstations and PCs. They were smaller, lighter, had detached keyboards, and—in an attempt to differentiate them from terminals, by appearance if nothing else—they had various *gimbals* (tilt-and-swivel and cantilevered contraptions). Later, as more companies entered the market, cost cutting became the call of the day and one of the first things to go were the monitor-movement features. Slowly, tilt and swivel came back, first on the premium monitors and later on many of the more popular monitors.

Unlike TV displays, technical, industrial, and business displays must present legible and rock-solid alphanumerics, linear images, good contrast, and sharp focus over the entire screen with various brightness levels. They must also maintain color purity and white balance. Furthermore, as resolution and screen size go up, even more is demanded of technology to deliver the required attributes. So far, the technology gets mixed reviews. Some say it's delivering; others think things could be better.

As TABLE 3-2 indicates, the CRT has major problems in the rugged computing arena. It has a large-movement arm within which the electron gun and control circuitry sit. Furthermore, the glass will resonate at certain frequencies and eventually break, and the tube structure isn't flexible enough to absorb shock and vibration pulses.

Table 3-2
The strengths of CRTs have been compared to their weaknesses for years, yet they still are the best choice for the largest majority of applications.

CRT strengths	CRT weaknesses
Cost effective	Large volume and weight
High brightness	Distortion and repeatability
Wide color and gray spectrum	Light scattering on face and halo
High luminous efficiency	Longevity
High bandwidth	Spot size
Large screen area	Jitter
Large choice of suppliers	Need for high voltage
New black flat-faced designs	Radiation
Longer life expectancies	Ruggedizing

It can be done, but there's quite a bit of work involved in "ruggedizing" a CRT. Newer CRT technologies, such as the flat tension mask (FTM) from Zenith Electronics Corp., simplify the problem. The glass on the FTM is very thick up front and the yoke is relatively short. Both make the tube itself very tough. The FTM is discussed in a later section.

The other main areas in which a CRT receives criticism are its large size and ratios. Flat-panel displays find success in space-sensitive applications, laptop computers being the most prominent, followed by medical instrumentation, industrial controllers, and test and measurement equipment, as well as areas where radiation from a CRT is a concern. Size is almost always the issue when they're selected. Generally, a flat panel is used to replace a CRT unless there's a *footprint* problem (how much of the desk is occupied) or a need to conserve space. Although the only time they can beat out a CRT is in applications that absolutely require the profile of a flat panel and the area of CRT radiation; those applications are rising. By many accounts, flat-panel displays are being extremely well received in the industrial environment.

CRTs, although once forecasted to be obsolete by the '90s, are as healthy as ever. One of the reasons is because there can be continued improvement with little capital expense and the other is their inherent dynamic range in so many parameters. Sizes cover a range of 100:1, and they're scalable from 0.5 inches to 56 inches. Their luminance has a range of 10,000:1 and the resolution ranges from 100 to 1. They're reliable, have a color-display range of over 16 million to one, and have contrast ranges from 2:1 to 256:1. Not bad for a technology that's over seventy years old. As Jerry Pearlman, CEO of Zenith said, "The Japanese built six $100 million CRT manufacturing plants in the U.S. in the last few years. They didn't do it because the technology would soon be obsolete."

CRTs are used in applications ranging from virtual-reality systems to cockpits, TVs, and computers, as illustrated in FIG. 3-2.

Although it's true that flat-panel displays will replace CRTs in some applications and create new applications that weren't possible before, the future of CRTs will be strong for many years.

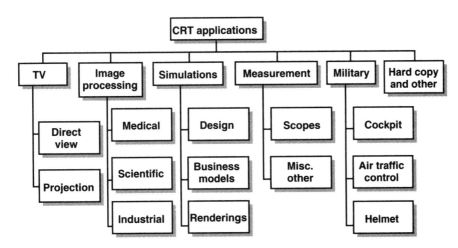

3-2
CRTs are used in hundreds of applications, from image processing and CAD/CAM to entertainment, test equipment, and military.

The monitor's screen is the most visible part of a display. However, there are several places along the path from the source of the image to the screen that can impact the quality of the display, as illustrated in FIG. 3-3. We've looked at some of the elements in the chain in the previous chapter. Although this chapter will concentrate on the monitor's components, it cannot be divorced from the controller.

What is a monitor?

These components also include the representation of the image or data to be displayed, the effect of the displaying device (and its associated components), and the observer. The monitor is just the next-to-last element in a long chain and, like any chain, it will be only as good as its poorest link or element. The components that make up a monitor are illustrated schematically in FIG. 3-4A, and their physical locations are shown in FIG. 3-4B.

The image you see on a monitor is actually displayed on the face of the CRT. Good monitor design begins with the CRT because electronics cannot compensate adequately for a poor-quality CRT. Therefore, to describe a monitor you first have to describe a CRT.

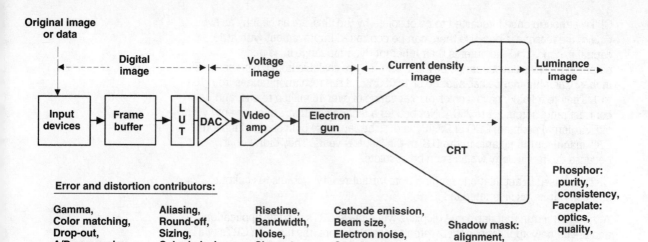

Error and distortion contributors:

Gamma,	Aliasing,	Risetime,	Cathode emission,
Color matching,	Round-off,	Bandwidth,	Beam size,
Drop-out,	Sizing,	Noise,	Electron noise,
A/D conversion,	Color indexing,	Slew rate,	Convergence,

Shadow mask: alignment, spacing & geometries,

Phosphor: purity, consistency, Faceplate: optics, quality,

3-3 *Image quality is affected by several components in a pipeline or chain of components, which starts at the source and includes everything in between the source and the viewer's eyes (and perception).*

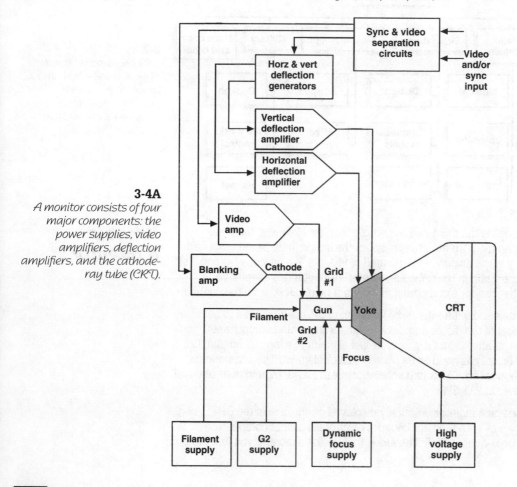

3-4A
A monitor consists of four major components: the power supplies, video amplifiers, deflection amplifiers, and the cathode-ray tube (CRT).

3-4B
The amplifiers are mounted on a circuit board that's attached to the end of the tube near the gun, the power supplies and deflection amplifiers are at the bottom, and the yoke wraps around the neck where the tube starts to expand to the screen.

The CRT

I like to start at the front, the screen of the CRT, and work my way back to where it all begins. The screen is where the final transformation takes place and the image shows up. The image is created by making the phosphor coating on the inside of the face of the CRT glow. Certain types of phosphors will emit light if they get bombarded (excited) by electrons, in other words, they *fluoresce*. That's how a fluorescent light works. It's coated inside with phosphor, and when it's excited by electrons it lights up. The quantum-mechanics description is the electron that strikes the phosphor molecule, imparts its energy to the phosphor, and causes it to emit a photon, as shown in FIG. 3-5. The photons are what we see when we look at an image on a CRT's screen.

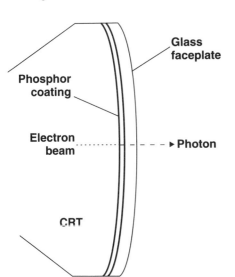

Glass faceplate

Phosphor coating

Electron beam ▶ **Photon**

CRT

3-5
When the high-energy electrons from the cathode hit the phosphor on the faceplate, the energy state is raised to the point that photons are released, which generates the image.

An incredible amount of study and experimentation has gone into the development of phosphors. They can be chosen for color, persistence, and granularity. Common phosphor materials include zinc, silicon, and potassium compounds.

Colors & phosphors The color a phosphor gives off is monochromatic—a singular color. In the case of monitors and CRTs, white (which contains all colors) is considered a single color. It's the white phosphor that gives a black-and-white or shades-of-gray monitor its white component. The black component is what you get when no phosphor is excited or lit up.

There are dozens of white phosphors available to CRT manufacturers and monitor builders. Some black-and-white CRTs have a phosphor that has a slight blue tint to it. These are said to be *page white*. Others have a pink or yellow tint and are gentler on the eye. As discussed in previous chapter, the eye is most sensitive to blue, so to prevent fatigue some monitor manufacturers have made their black-and-white CRTs with a warmer color white. The Electronics Industry Association (EIA) has a set of registered standard phosphors, the most popular ones of which are listed in TABLE 3-3.

Table 3-3
There are hundreds of different phosphor types available that generate every imaginable color and at various persistences. These are the most popular ones used in computer systems.

EIA, phosphor	Fluorescence	Persistence
P-4	White	Medium to short
P-22	Tricolor	Medium short
P-22LP (L9)	Tricolor	Long
P-45	White\Gray	Medium
P-40	Paper white	Medium short
P-192	Paper white	Medium

If you have a preference to a tint or color white, you can select a monitor on that basis. All monitor manufacturers know what type phosphor they're using. I've encountered a couple of companies over the years who refused to tell me what they were using, as if they had some secret sauce to protect. In one case, where I was really determined, I simply asked the CRT manufacturer. Refusal on the part of the monitor supplier to divulge a phosphor type is unacceptable. A user has every right in the world to know what colors he or she is getting bombarded with when sitting in front of a monitor.

The phosphor is applied to the inside face of the monitor in a liquid form and is poured in at the top or neck of the tube. Because of the appearance of the CRT when resting on its face while the phosphor is applied, they are also known as *bottles*. People who like jargon or who want to be cool can be heard asking monitor suppliers, "whose bottle are you using?" I've used the term myself a few times. However, a more correct or traditional term is *bulb*, as in light bulb. Figure 3-6 shows a modern flat-faced CRT.

3-6
Modern CRTs have very high deflection angles and display areas. The stem protruding from the end is the CRT's gun. Clinton Electronics Corp.

Persistence   Also known as the phosphor's efficiency, persistence is nonlinear. The phosphor can be excited rapidly and it will continue to glow after the excitement (electron beam) has been removed. The glow will decay and the rate of its decay is called its *persistence*. The human eye has a persistence too, as shown in FIG. 3-7. If a bright image is seen and then removed, the image will be retained for a while.

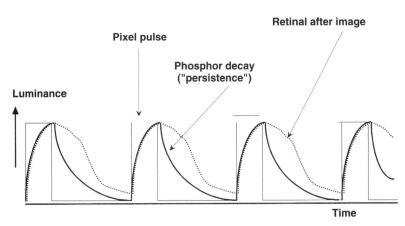

3-7
Given the same level of excitation, various phosphors will decay at different rates. The eye, too, has a persistence characteristic. The combination of these two physical characteristics was the basis for low refresh rate interlaced displays.

When TV was first developed back in the late '20s, electrical circuits and components weren't very fast. The cost of faster components was exponentially more expensive than more common slower ones (primarily due to the fact that only the military bought the fast ones; they didn't buy very many and they were willing to pay for them). Therefore, AT&T, RCA, and Westinghouse looked for every compromise they could and came up with a very clever, low-cost system. It relied on two principles: the persistence of the eye and the nonlinear persistence of certain screen phosphors (see FIG. 3-7). By using those two principles, the developers of TV were able to make use of an overlapping scanning technique to provide a picture with relatively slow, inexpensive parts.

The gun

The electrons that strike a screen's phosphors are generated in a single gun or multiple electron guns located at the narrow end or neck of the tube (or bottle). The source of the electrons is from a small piece of metal called the *cathode*. The cathode, when heated, produces a stream or ray of electrons that are attracted to the screen, and hence the name *cathode ray tube*. The electrons are generated when the cathode is heated, and are said to be *boiled off*. This, however, isn't what actually happens. When the electron gun is placed in the tube, the tube is evacuated of any air and sealed.

Electron guns, like ordinary light bulbs, require a vacuum to work, hence the name *vacuum tubes*. Vacuums are measured in terms of negative pressure, and pressure is calibrated in terms of atmospheres. The vacuum in a typical CRT is –14 pounds per inch, about 5000 lbs. That's a lot of pressure being exerted on the tube from the outside so they have to be made of thick, strong glass. This is also one of the reasons they weigh so much. Over 60% of the weight of a monitor is the glass of the CRT, which weighs between 50 and 120 lbs.

If you've ever looked inside a monitor or the back of your TV, you might have noticed an orange glow at the neck of the tube when it's turned on. That glow is the *filament*, and the source of the heat for the cathode. A CRT is a very large electron tube, similar in design to the big, antique, hot tubes that used to be in your father's or grandfather's old radio. Electron tubes work by creating a stream, or cloud, of electrons (with the heated cathode) and manipulating them with control elements. Electrons are negatively charged and will be attracted to a positive charge wherever they can find one.

Near the face of the CRT is the *anode*, which is given a very high, between 10,000 and 30,000+ volts, positive charge. That very high voltage is like a huge magnet to the low-current electrons and they strike the phosphor face at just under the speed of light. The higher the anode voltage, the brighter the phosphor will glow. So the gun in a CRT consists of a heated cathode in a vacuum that shoots electrons at the highly charged phosphor-coated screen.

As discussed earlier, Sir William Crooks developed the electron gun based on experiments he conducted in 1978 with the Geisler discharge tube. However, it was Valdimr Zworykin who added the necessary components for the modern-day version of the electron gun. The construction of a CRT's gun is shown in FIG. 3-8.

The CRT's gun consists of two primary sections, the triode and the lens. The *triode* is formed by the cathode (K), its filament heater (H), and two control elements: the control grid (G1) and the acceleration grid (G2). The video signal is applied to the cathode. The first grid, G1, is always a negative voltage relative to the cathode and acts as a valve, controlling the flow of electrons. (In the early days of electron tubes, primarily in Great Britain, the term *valve* was used to describe an electron tube.) Grid two (G2) however, is biased with a positive voltage relative to the cathode, and it acts as an accelerator. The physical relationship of these two elements, along with the cathode, influence the lower beam angle and center the voltage focus and, most importantly, the spot size. As the electrons exit G2, they're focused by the *lens*. Figure 3-9 shows a typical CRT gun for a monochrome tube.

When the electrons come off the cathode, they're like the spray from a water hose. To be useful they have to be narrowed, focused, and directed. In the early CRT and oscilloscope designs, that was accomplished by placing plates along the path and applying voltages to the plates at just the right time. Newer designs modified the plates into tubes. There are three to four elements to the focusing lens. This is a

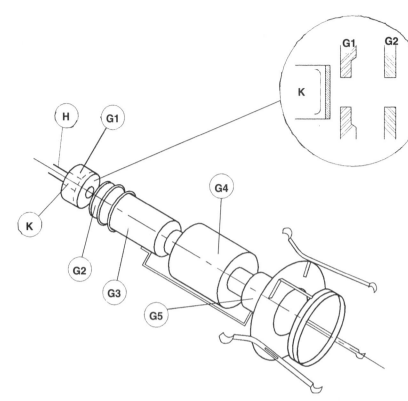

3-8
The CRT's gun has two main components: the triode and the lens. The cathode and its heater (filament) are in the triode along with the control grids (G1 and G2). The lens is an electrostatic focusing section, which contains the grids G3 to G5. Shown here is a monochrome unipotential gun. Clinton Electronics Corp.

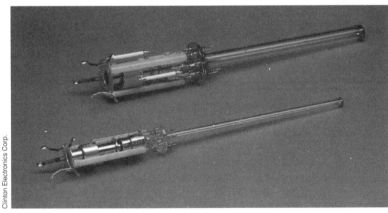

Clinton Electronics Corp.

3-9
Electron guns used in CRTs have a long, thin, glass tube at one end, which contains the heater or filament. The rest of the assembly consists of the control grids and focusing lenses. The guns are made as small as possible to allow higher deflection angles. Illustrated here are a 29mm and a 20mm CRT gun. Through advances in the metallurgy and design tolerances, modern-day guns offer greatly improved performance over past designs.

basic configuration, known as the Einzel lens (from the German word for *one*). A special version of this lens design, known as the *unipotential gun*, has been used extensively in monochrome monitors.

The electron stream is squeezed by the potential of the focusing elements of the lens into a beam. In the earlier oscilloscopes, the deflection or steering of the beam was done entirely by controlling the voltage on the plates at the end of the gun inside the tube.

The electrostatic lens is comprised of grids G3 to G5 (refer back to FIG. 3-8) and are mechanically connected within the gun structure, which is in turn connected to the high-voltage anode. Grid four (G4) is the variable element, operates within a typical range of –200 V to +400 V, and is used to maintain center focus.

As will be discussed later, high-performance monitors with large viewing areas and square corners require dynamic focus to maintain image quality in the corners; this becomes even more crucial with flat-profile CRTs. CRT guns can be optimized for either dynamic-focus or flat-focus requirements. A flat-focus gun will provide a compromise of focus quality from center to edge, and is generally suitable only for medium-resolution and text-based displays. Displays used in CAD, DTP, DIPS, and medical imaging require dynamic focus.

Spot size   The tightness of the focusing influences the spot size of the beam on the screen. The spot size, also known as the *electron-beam spot profile* or *electron spot size*, is the smallest area that can be illuminated on the screen. Spot sizes vary as a function of the screen size, the stability of the power supply, and the type of phosphor used. Spot size will be discussed throughout this chapter.

The spot size is primarily a function of the focusing elements and the intensity of the electron beam. When it strikes the phosphor, it typically has a Gaussian distribution, with the center being the most intense and the edges falling off gradually, as shown in FIG. 3-10.

3-10
When the electron beam strikes the phosphor, it creates a three-dimensional Guassian distribution of photonic emissions, brighter in the center and extending to a diameter larger than the declared spot size. When the beam has too much energy, the spot can create a secondary, unwanted image.

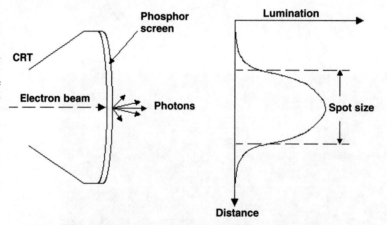

Depending on how the beam is formed, how it's handled by the focusing electrodes in the tube, and the type of phosphor used, the resultant spot on the face of the phosphor might exhibit the distribution pattern. If it does, it will be brighter in the center than at the edges. If the spot is very small, the difference probably won't be noticeable. However, when it can be seen (even if only with a magnifying glass), the less bright (or blurry) edges are often referred to as a *halo* or a *halo effect*. The effect is most easily seen at the corners of a CRT as the beam forms into an ellipse. Another type of halo effect that occurs due to reflections, known as *halation*, is discussed in the section on *Faces*, later in the chapter.

Dynamic focusing   Several monitors are specified as having dynamic focusing, also called *elliptical aperture dynamic focus* (EDAF) and *dynamic beam forming*

(DBF). These are techniques that vary the focusing voltages as a function of the beam's position on the screen. Since the length of the beam is longer at the edges, there's more probability that the beam will spread out as it travels. Dynamic focusing is accomplished by biasing the electronic focusing elements with the voltages of the defection amplifiers. This compensates the beam's focus as a function of where the beam is positioned. Dynamic focusing can reduce overall average spot size by as much as 30%, thereby giving a much sharper image.

CRT manufacturers have come up with novel ways of forming a tightly focused beam. Mitsubishi, for example, has developed the dynamic beam-forming technology and claims it improves focus in the corners by 30%. The company uses a quadrupolar electrode system. When the beam is passed through the focusing lens (see FIG. 3-11), it's modulated by the deflection voltage to maintain focus in the corners.

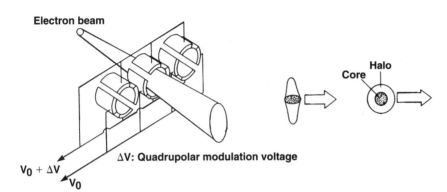

3-11
Mitsubishi's "dynamic beam-forming" lens sharpens the focus at the edges and corners. The beam is dynamically formed as it passes through the quadrupolar electrode. This lens arrangement reduces the halo effects.
Mitsubishi Electronic Corp.

Astigmatism   When the beam is moved to the edges and especially the corners, it can become distorted in shape, forming an ellipse or egg-shaped spot. This can distort the image, and is referred to as an *astigmatic distortion*. The distortion is caused primarily by the self-converging deflection yoke and the increase in distance from the main lens of the tube to the screen.

High-quality tubes control this distortion with dynamic and digitally controlled focusing techniques and with clever lens designs. Hitachi has developed the quadrupole lens to counter this problem. It uses a dynamic voltage that's derived from the deflection circuitry to control the electrodes that form the quadruple lens. This causes the beam to be slightly elongated vertically when at the edges, and thus compensates for the horizontal elongation of the beam by the deflection yoke.

These types of lens systems are not generally used in TV displays because the dynamic-voltage generation system is expensive. One of the factors that increases the cost is the high voltage needed by these systems, typically 1 KV or greater. However, the HDTV displays might require this capability due to their 16:9 aspect ratio.

Dual focusing   Designs using both electrostatic and magnetic focusing have been developed for CRTs used in high-cost projection systems. These projection tubes (PRTs) have evolved to where they can provide almost as good a picture quality as a direct-view TV. The beam in a projection tube leaves the cathode and is prefocused by the control grids. It's then focused by the main lens, which consists of large magnets around the midsection of the neck. The final stage is the electromagnetic yoke focusing.

Position

The electron stream can also be manipulated by magnetic forces, and that's the technique used by raster-scan CRTs. To create a magnetic force, a precision-wound coil of fine wire is placed at the neck of the tube just where it starts to expand out to the face. This coil is called the *yoke*, and it's one of the most difficult parts of a high-resolution monitor to construct. Some refer to it as "black magic" because it's so difficult to predict exactly how a yoke's construction will affect a CRT's behavior. Figure 3-12 shows the construction of a typical yoke assembly.

3-12
The yoke is located at the far end of the neck of the tub, as close as possible to where the bulb begins its expansion to the faceplate of the CRT.

There are two parts to the yoke: the top-bottom vertical (also called *NS, north-south*, or *line coil*) and the left-right horizontal (also called the *EW, east-west*, or *frame coil*). The beam (the stream of electrons) is deflected by the yoke's magnetic fields and can be placed anywhere on the screen with great precision.

The yoke is controlled by deflection amplifiers. The yoke and the deflection amplifiers have to operate at very high speeds, up to 100 KHz for a very high-resolution monitor. The amplifiers drive the yoke with voltage swings up to several hundred volts. Handling such high voltages at such high rates requires special components and very clever designs. These are major contributors to the cost of a high-resolution monitor.

The yoke serves as a very important component, but it also can defocus the beam. This isn't a desirable function, but all yokes have such an effect to some degree. It's most often noticeable in tubes with a large deflection angle.

Geometric distortions

Geometry comes into play when a beam is moved from the center of the screen to the corners or edges. The length of the beam from the gun to the screen increases (known as *time of flight*), and the shape of the beam changes from a circle to an ellipse, as illustrated in FIG. 3-13.

If the screen is flatter than the bending radius of the beam, a *pincushion* distortion will occur. Various problems prevail that prevent a perfect matching of the curve of the surface to that of the angles of the beam deflection. Therefore, magnets are applied to edges of the yoke. These magnets are carefully adjusted ("tweaked") to compensate for the distortions. Without the compensation, the screen's image can be distorted, as shown in FIG. 3-14.

"Fly-back hook"   **Squeezed edges**

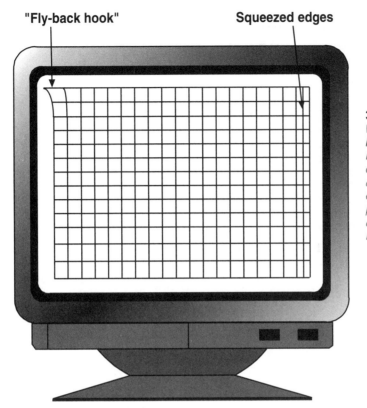

3-13
Without compensation, the beam gets distorted when it's deflected into the far corners. As elements in the deflection circuits and yoke components age or get physically jolted, various distortions can be introduced into the display.

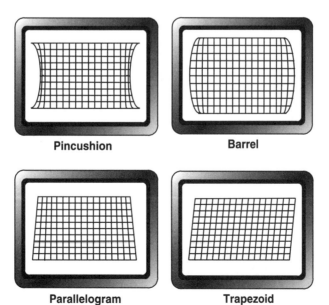

Pincushion   **Barrel**

Parallelogram   **Trapezoid**

3-14
Pincushion, barrel, parallelogram, and trapezoid effects can be seen on a CRT that has yoke-alignment or power-supply problems.

As another of the drawings in FIG. 3-14 shows, the distortion can move inward from the edges or bulge out toward the edges, called *barreling*. Pincushion and barrel distortion will exist in any monitor, no matter how well it's tweaked. The amount of distortion is seldom specified by the monitor manufacturer, but it's typically less than 1.5% of the raster height.

Figure 3-14 also shows an example of parallelogram distortion. This is when the edges of the raster scan should make a 90° angle, but are slanted one way or another. Like all other geometric distortions, it's due to misalignment of the yoke. Another form of distortion is *trapezoid* distortion. This is when one edge is a different size than the opposite edge. Examples of all these conditions (pincushioning, trapezoid, etc.) are shown in FIG. 3-14.

Like many other items associated with the yoke, geometric distortions can usually be corrected only by the manufacturer. Some monitors offer controls (usually inside the case) that allow for some compensation of pincushioning and other geometric adjustments.

Jitter & breathing   When a beam is positioned, it's done so by the deflection amplifiers applying control voltage to the yoke. If the image is stationary, as it is in CAD and other static images, the beam for a given line or point must be illuminated for several frames or even seconds. If the deflection amplifiers or their power supplies aren't stable, the illuminated spot or line will move with time. This movement can be apparent to the viewer as an annoying oscillation or shaking of a point or line, hence the name *jitter*. Jitter typically shows up on older equipment as parts age and change in their tolerance. Jitter can also be induced into the monitor by adjoining equipment. If the monitor is too close to a computer's power supply or another monitor, it can be affected. Apparent jitter can also be caused by improper selection of the refresh rate, as discussed later in this chapter.

Breathing is what has been used to describe a monitor's image when it shrinks a little and then expands. Usually it's a slow rate and reminds the observer of a breathing action. It's usually due to a poorly regulated power supply or the video amplifier running at saturation (full max color). In that mode, the amplifier suffers thermal overload and begins to shut itself off, at which time it cools just enough to allow it to come back on line. In the process, the color goes back to its saturated condition, which appears to be an enlargement. This might indicate a failure. If the monitor is being pushed to its limits driving the red gun (the one that most frequently shows the problem), it could simply be misuse. On the other hand, it could be exposing a weakness that will cause a failure later. If you have a choice and can test a monitor for this condition before you purchase it, do so.

Rotation   As discussed previously, the yoke determines the positioning of the beam on the screen. When controlled by the deflection amplifiers, it can be used to generate the raster pattern used for a scanning display. However, the positioning and alignment of the yoke on the neck of the CRT is crucial. If not done properly or disturbed due to movement or rough treatment, the yoke can slip and cause the image to be rotated. This is one of the tests that CRT manufacturers conduct before shipping a CRT assembly to the monitor builder.

As might be expected, the manufacturers' test equipment is quite accurate and sophisticated. However, as discussed in the *Linearity* section, a user can spot a rotation problem almost immediately—the lines on the screen are not parallel or don't line up with those of the bezel around the CRT. If a CRT's yoke is misaligned and shows a rotated image, there's no choice but to return the monitor to the manufacturer. Yoke alignment is very difficult and can't be performed by local service centers without specialized equipment.

Lines & hooks   In the early days of yoke design and development, the horizontal scan voltage, as described in the *Display and blanking time* section, frequently encountered problems. The manifestation was a vertical line or fold-over, which would appear in the image known as *Barkhousen* (which is actually a term that comes from unhomogeneous magnet construction; who knows how these terms get selected). This problem is hardly ever seen anymore, but ringing vertical bars on the left of the screen are commonly seen in today's display systems. These are caused by a combination of problems with the bandwidth of the controller and the monitor's deflection amplifier or yoke.

Hooks at the top of the screen are usually caused by the power supply's inability to provide enough current to the yoke when both the horizontal and vertical amplifiers are retracing back to the upper left-hand corner, zero. It's a common problem with low-cost flyback transformers, improper sync settings, and a measure of the monitor's quality.

Another specification used to measure the correctness of the beam's positioning is called *linearity*. Linearity is how well or how evenly the deflection circuitry moves the beam across the screen's face. However, it's impractical to measure each scan line for its linearity. Typically, monitor and CRT manufacturers will either add up or average (or take the root mean square, RMS) of all of the effects of linearity, pincushioning, glass impurities, casting, and other influencing items and provide a tolerance number for how close the beam's dot is to where it should be.

Linearity

Monitor and CRT manufacturers have been working at these measurements for decades and have found the practical solutions. Linearity-distortion measurements are often expressed by manufacturers in terms of percentage, and range from 2% to 10%. As good as the eye is, a 2% linearity is better than most humans can perceive.

Linearity is the ability of the monitor to smoothly or evenly move the beam across the screen. As information is displayed on the screen with the beam's movement, it can become quite apparent if it's a linear display. When displaying text (or a screen full of icons or a spreadsheet), for example, if some of the characters or icons are closer to some than others or are of a different width than others, then that monitor doesn't have a linear display. Linearity is also measured vertically. Characters or icons that vary in height also reveal a lack of linearity.

CRT and monitor manufacturers use a test pattern for checking the horizontal and vertical linearity of their products. Typically, it's a grid pattern, like a sheet of graph paper. Figure C-22 shows some typical test patterns that are used to check a monitor's linearity. A rigid X-Y frame is placed against the front of the screen and measurements are taken between the indices of the grid to determine linearity. Typically, this is done only on a sampling basis or in an engineering lab. Not all tubes are checked this way. However, with good quality-control procedures in component selection and assembly, most of the monitors produced today meet their published specifications on linearity (once you understand what the specifications mean).

Users and system builders can make their own empirical test of a monitor's linearity. The most popular is the H pattern test. A screen is filled with the capital letter H. All lines have an H in them, forming a quasi-grid pattern. With a little examination, any nonlinearity can be spotted. The human eye is amazingly good at spotting differentials or anomalies. You can't make a quantified measurement this way because that requires specialized equipment, but you can qualify or disqualify a monitor with this simple test. After all, who cares what the test number is? If the monitor doesn't look any good no one is going to use it.

Tube sizes & shapes

There are over a hundred different tube (CRT or bulb) sizes and shapes available to the monitor manufacturer. The four most important size parameters are the diagonal measurement, the aspect ratio, the curvature of the face, and the deflection angle. The first TV tubes were round, like their cousins in the RADAR and test areas. They grew in size, but there was always a wasted amount of the screen's face because only the box area in the center contained the image. In 1956, Zenith developed the first 21-inch rectangular color picture tube. It had "rounded corners" and a hemispherical face. The design was used up until the late eighties when tubes with sharper corners and flatter faces were introduced.

Diagonal sizes   There are currently monitor sizes being offered in one-inch increments from 9 to 37 inches, and there are also 45-inch models available. The early monochrome text-based displays used the 9-, 11- and occasionally 13-inch tubes. The Classic Macintosh used a 9-inch tube for its GUI. Today, 15-inch monitors are about the smallest you can find for a GUI. The 16- and 17-inch monitors have become very popular for most office GUI displays, with the 19-inch being preferred by professional DTP users and users of engineering applications like CAD. Some DTP users have gone to 24-inch monitors and some CAD users have gone to 27- and 29-inch displays. The 16- and 21-inch monitors are favored by casual users of desktop publishing and presentation applications. The larger monitors like the 36- and 49-inch and HDTV sizes are most often used for displays for large groups of people.

The diagonal size of a monitor can be confusing because manufacturers have various ways of expressing the size. Some use the outside dimensions of the tube, others use the maximum area of the phosphor coating. Therefore, the same-sized monitor might be listed as 20 inches by one manufacturer and 19 inches by another. Others list their monitors as 20 (19 v). That means the CRT or bulb has 20 inches diagonally and the maximum diagonal of the face's phosphor area (the viewable area, or v) is 19 inches. What is actually usable is yet another number. Figure 3-15 shows the generally accepted method of measuring a CRT's dimensions.

Active screen area   The active area of a CRT's face or screen is a function of the manufacturing process used, the type of deflection used, and the construction of the tube. The active area is not the same as the usable area. That is a function of the yoke construction and the focusing electronics. The range of the active area for popular CRTs or monitors is shown in TABLE 3-4.

Screen dimensions

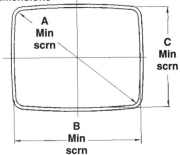

Bulb dimensions

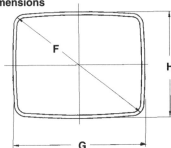

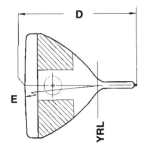

3-15
There are various measurements used in the specification of a CRT's bulb. Some monitor manufacturers use the outside bulb measurement (J), some use the inside (A), and others use the viewable or phosphor area. In the '50s, the Federal Trade Commission in the United States required TV manufacturers to standardize; the outside (J) dimension was chosen.

Table 3-4
The active or viewable area of CRTs varies from manufacturer to manufacturer and in some cases a manufacturer does not make all of the viewable area available.

Standard 3:4 aspect-ratio CRTs

CRT max. (view)	Horizontal view min	Horizontal view max	Vertical view min	Vertical view max	Actual area max	Actual area min	Diagonal max
12 (11)	6.30	6.69	8.27	8.66	57.97	10.39	10.95
14 (13)	9.45	10.24	6.93	7.48	76.57	11.72	12.68
15 (14)	9.84	10.63	7.28	8.11	86.21	12.24	13.37
16 (15)	10.91	11.42	8.19	8.54	97.54	13.64	14.26
17 (16)	11.61	13.39	8.46	10.63	142.29	14.37	17.09
20 (19)	13.39	15.35	10.24	11.22	172.28	16.85	19.02
21 (20)	14.57	18.11	10.98	11.97	216.75	18.24	21.71
26 (25)	17.32	17.52	13.78	14.02	245.55	22.13	22.44

Other size CRTs

CRT	Horizontal	Vertical	Area
23 (22)	Round 22 dia	(22)	380.0
29 (28)	19.68	19.68	387.3
32 (31)	HDTV 14.99	8.42	126.2
36 (35)	HDTV 17.63	11.61	204.6

CRT form or aspect ratio   Most monitors generally use a 4:3 aspect ratio, where one side is 1.33 times longer than the height. Monitors are offered in two configurations: landscape and portrait. Landscape is wider than tall and portrait is taller than wide. Some monitors, like the Radius Pivot, can be rotated to be either landscape or portrait. The ratio of the width to the height is the monitor's *aspect ratio*. For all monitors except HDTV and a few specialized square ones, the aspect ratio is 4:3. Knowing the aspect ratio can help you approximate the active area of a CRT. Consider the following calculations:

$$W = \sqrt{\frac{D^2}{1.56}}$$

$$H = 0.75 \times W$$
$$A = H \times W$$

Where:

D = the active area of the screen
W = the width of the monitor's active area
H = the height of the monitor's active area
A = the active area of the monitor

In 1980, monitor manufacturers in the U.S. and Japan were approached by workstation and government system builders and asked if they could build a large, 20×20-inch color monitor capable of displaying a 2048×2048 resolution image. The monitors were needed for an upgrade to the U.S. air-traffic-control system (ATC) that is administered by the Federal Aviation Administration (FAA). The square form was selected to replace the round 20- and 24-inch stroke refresh tubes that had been used in CAD and air-traffic-control systems. It was also logical to assume that other nations and the military would be interested in such a monitor. In 1982, Sony's Precision Graphics Systems division demonstrated a prototype of such a monitor at various trade shows, an example of which is shown in FIG. C-23.

Later in the middle '80s, interest began to develop in high-definition TV (HDTV). The French and Japanese pioneered the early systems, but the Japanese quickly took the lead. As they did, they also defined a new tube aspect ratio, 16:9, as shown in FIG. 3-16.

Curvature & deflection angle   The angle of deflection is the subtended arc from the edges of the face to the last element of the gun, as shown in FIG. 3-17.

90° tubes   Most hemispherical-type color tubes have a 90° deflection, with a face-plate curvature that logically depends on the radius of the tube. A 15-inch 90° tube has a 653-mm radius. Twenty-inch tubes have between a 819.7- and 827.5-mm radius, whereas a 25-inch has a 1,070-mm radius.

110°+ tubes   Monochrome tubes (most often used for DTP applications) have 110° to 114° deflection angles. Monochrome tubes have near flat faces and square corners.

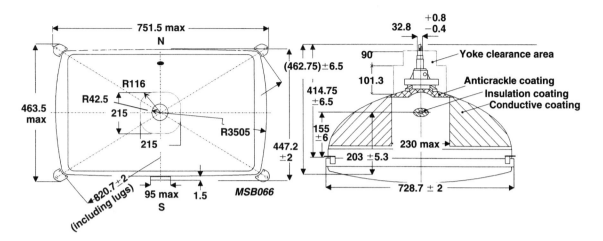

3-16 *The new HDTV class displays are wider than conventional displays, having a 16:9 aspect ratio (as compared to the traditional 3:4. This is more like the wide-screen aspect ratio of cinematic movies.*

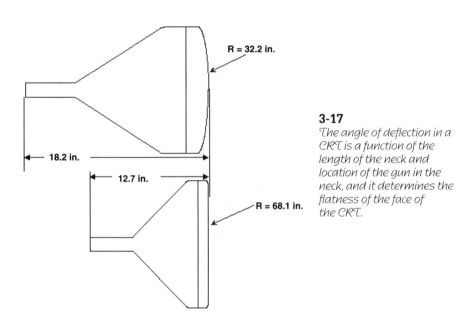

3-17
The angle of deflection in a CRT is a function of the length of the neck and location of the gun in the neck, and it determines the flatness of the face of the CRT.

Flat square The flat-square, or *2R*, tube, with a 90° deflection, has a radius that's two times as long as a conventional tube, hence the 2R designation. A 16-inch flat-square tube has a 1,370-mm radius, and the 21-inch has a 1,730-mm radius. The 2R flat surface also contributes to the development of square-corner tubes. They generally have a radius of 50 or more inches and square corners.

Cylindrical The Sony Trinitron (which is discussed in more detail later in this chapter) uses a cylindrical, vertically flat, 90° deflection tube.

Flat tension mask   The only truly flat-faced color tube is the Zenith flat tension mask (FTM). This too is covered later in the chapter when color CRTs are discussed.

Faces   CRTs are made of glass, and glass can have a variety of surface qualities. The face of a CRT has to be smooth (no bumps, pits, uneven thickness, or other aberrations), distortion free (no bubbles or waviness) on both surfaces (inside and out), perfectly transparent, and linear across the face according to its curvature (the radius can't change). After a CRT's face has been cast, it's polished to ensure its smoothness. Once that has been accomplished, the image quality can be assessed.

However, as will be discussed in various parts of this chapter, there are environmental considerations as well. The reflections given off of such a perfect piece of glass can cause eye fatigue, reduce contrast, and, if bright enough, blot out the image. *Halation* is the name given to the effect from internal surface reflections of an image or ambient lights. To overcome that, various techniques have been developed to make the face of the tube antireflective.

Antireflection   Reflection of ambient light on the face of the CRT has been a problem since the beginning. As a result, several techniques and solutions have been developed to mitigate the problem. Manufacturers use faces with gray-tint glass, silica (black) or silica coating, chemical etching, bonded thin-film filters, dark bulb, and antireflective (AR) bonded panels. Some of the more popular techniques are:

Chemically etched faceplate   This process reduces glare by diffusing reflected images, and provides some attenuation of intensity. There is also some defocusing of the image due to the multiple paths for light transmittance created by the etching. Chemical etching makes the image soft in appearance and can cause a slight enlargement of the spot size.

Dark-tinted glass faceplates   Tubes with 31% to 57% transmission glass have been used by various manufacturers to reduce reflections and increase contrast. Going from 51% to 36%, for example, improves the contrast ratio of a 27-inch tube from 12:1 to 17:1 (when measured in a 215-lux ambient).

Silica & other coatings   Several monitor manufacturers use an electrostatic film (ESF) coating of SIO2, commonly referred to as *silica*. Silica is used to provide an antireflection coating for the air-glass surface, and is reported to decrease the specular reflectivity from the 4.6% of bare glass to 0.2%. The coating also has 5 to 6 orders of magnitude less resistivity than bare glass, which prevents the buildup of static charge on the air-glass surface during CRT operation. This reduces the degradation of contrast from accumulating dust.

Narrow-band optical coating   Bonding thin-film optical filters that pass a narrow, monochromatic frequency (color) are a popular solution for monitors used in environments with high ambient light.

Polarized filters   Polarized filters consist of a circular polarizer, which in turn consists of a conventional linear polarizer and an optical retarder. The image from the screen through the filter is polarized and attenuated 60%. Ambient light first passes through the linear polarizing filter and is polarized or aligned horizontally. It then passes through a quarterwave retarder, which gives it a right circular orientation. Next, the light strikes the face of the CRT and then starts the path back toward the viewer's eye. However, its orientation is now left (since it's a reflection) and the reflected light gets blocked by the quarterwave retarder. Any remaining light, which will be primarily vertically polarized, is blocked by the horizontal linear polar filter.

Geometry   Sony's cylindrical Trinitron tube reduces reflections from the top. Since most offices have ceiling lighting, this can offer a big improvement. Flattening the face of the tube helps in general. The 2R and FTM tubes offer improved antireflectance.

Because of the use of a darker glass and other antireflection techniques, an increased-beam current is required to compensate for the decrease in brightness. New gun designs have been developed that have impregnated cathodes, multiprefocusing lens, and aberration-reducing construction.

Antistatic   Large size CRTs require high-anode voltages. In some cases, the presence of such high-voltage electrostatic charges are built up on the face of the CRT, which can give an annoying shock when touched or wiped. The electrostatic charges cause dust to adhere to the CRT's face, which can reduce the brightness and contrast. Therefore, various methods to prevent light reflections and electrostatic buildup have been developed. Tubes are coated with thin films of silicon oxide bound with ethyl silicate on the face and connected to the ground potential. The transparent silicon oxide acts as a conductor and shunts the buildup of any charge to ground. This keeps the face of the tube from collecting dust and removes the annoying static charge that zaps users.

As mentioned in the *History* section, Philo T. Farnsworth developed the idea for a scanning system in the early '20s. The scanning system was needed more for the vidicon or pickup device than the display device. But the display device had to be in synchronization with the pickup device to faithfully present the image. And so was born the notion of the raster-scan approach.

Deflection amplifiers & raster scan

The beam is started at the upper left corner of the screen and scanned across to the right by the horizontal deflection amplifier and its associated yoke elements. While it's scanning from left to right, it's simultaneously being scanned down from the top by the vertical deflection amplifier and associated yoke elements, but at a much slower rate. When the beam gets to the right edge, it's turned off and sent back to the left edge as fast as possible, where a new scan line is started. The result is a pattern that looks like that shown in FIG. 3-18.

When the beam gets to the lower right-hand corner, the vertical deflection amplifier sends it back to the top as fast as possible.

The voltage used to drive the deflection yoke is generated by the deflection amplifiers. It's a waveform that rises from zero volts to a higher voltage (between 50 and 200, depending on the monitor). There are two such waveforms: one for the vertical deflection and one for the horizontal. After the waveform reaches its peak value, it is quickly forced back to the zero voltage level.

Display & blanking time

The waveform is called a *sawtooth* because of its shape. It stays at the zero voltage point for a short while, which is known as the *retrace*, *blanking*, or *flyback time*. The flyback time is the time it takes the amplifier and its high-voltage power supply to

Monitor

TV

3-18

The raster-scanning pattern is the same in a computer display as in a TV; however, TVs use an interlaced technique and most computer displays use a noninterlaced method.

Vertical retrace

Scan line

Horizontal retrace
(flyback)

discharge the peak voltage that was generated. (The name also dates back to early high-voltage power-supply designs.) Figure 3-19 shows the generalized appearance of the sawtooth waveform. It's also a synchronization time.

The zero voltage point for both the horizontal and vertical deflection amplifiers is the position of the beam at the far left and top of the screen. As the voltage increases, the beam is deflected to the right and down, as shown in FIG. 3-19.

3-19

The waveform used to generate a raster-scanning pattern is commonly known as a sawtooth wave.

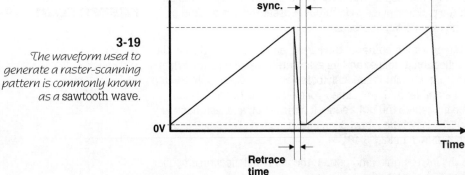

When the deflection voltage is at the zero voltage level, for the time it's there, the electron beam is turned off or blanked, hence the term *blanking time*. The blanking time is used for two display-timing purposes: reloading the display controller's output-shift register with data from the video RAM, and synchronizing the various signals needed by the monitor.

The synchronization signals are discussed later in the section on *Input signals*. The horizontal blanking or retrace times will vary from monitor to monitor and are typically between 2 and 20 S. The vertical blanking times also vary with the monitor. They're typically 200 to 300 times greater than the horizontal times, ranging from 250 to 800 S.

Recall the basic scanning pattern (shown in FIG. 3-18). When the entire screen is scanned, it's said to have completed one frame. However, it has to be done fast enough to avoid flicker. Flickering happens when the image decays faster than the eye's persistence will maintain it. For most humans, the flicker threshold at the center of the eye is between 20 and 50 Hz for a normally illuminated screen. It's much higher at the edges of the eye, our peripheral vision. The perception of flicker will be different from one person to the next. It's influenced by the environment of the user and monitor, the image being displayed, the refresh rate, persistence of the phosphor, contrast ratio, and the physiology of the eye and brain (which are also affected by age).

To provide a full frame of 525 lines, 60 times a second, the monitor would need a scan rate of 525×60, or 31.5 KHz. Although not exactly the speed of light, it was tough enough in 1920. That's when the mother of invention, necessity, came to the rescue. By scanning every other line and relying on the persistence of the eye and the CRT's phosphor, plus a little empirical engineering (they called it *tinkering* in those days), the problem was resolved (no pun). First the odd-numbered lines were scanned and then the even-numbered lines, as shown in FIG. 3-20.

Interlaced display & flicker

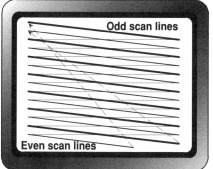

3-20
An interlaced scanning system has to run twice as fast as a noninterlaced system because twice as many lines are scanned in the same time, so interlaced display systems are more expensive.

Each half of the scan, or frame, is called a *field*. For NTSC, one field is scanned every 16.6 ms (1/60 of a second). That results in a full frame being scanned 30 times a second. With the human visual and electron persistence at work, plus the assumption that TV images change and that most objects cover more than one scan line, flicker isn't a problem. However, long-persistence phosphors cause a smearing effect when an image of the same color (especially red) is dragged across the screen. The field rate is related to the power line or main frequency. Therefore, PAL and SECAM fields are 20 ms (1/50 of a second).

Interlacing is often accompanied by jitter and interline motion when the screen is displaying characters rather than nonregular images or images with motion. The interline motion occurs when the image in one of the half-field frames appears to move into an adjacent display element in the other frame. This type of apparent or illusory motion will not occur if the display resolution is relatively high. For example, if the vertical pixel or raster line spacing is less than 0.05 mm, screen characters will appear to be jitter free at a distance of 500 mm. Thus, interlacing can reduce the probability of seeing flicker by doubling the effective frame frequency, but it will be effective only if interline motion can be eliminated by using a high-display resolution. However, even 1280×1024 resolution on an 11-inch monitor isn't enough. On an 11-inch monitor, you would need 4096 lines, which isn't very practical.

Noninterlaced displays

Long-persistence displays can cause smearing of a moving image, and the color intensity is not as brilliant as shorter-persistent phosphors. Therefore, manufacturers of computer monitors added faster parts and faster phosphors (both more expensive) and went to a noninterlaced scan. A noninterlaced scan simply scans all lines in numerical order (1, 2, 3, etc.). There are no fields, just a frame. This technique improved the quality of images and for many users eliminated the problem of flicker.

Noninterlaced displays were developed by the computer industry to improve color quality, and eliminate smear and flicker. In early computer displays, single-pixel flicker became an annoying and then serious problem. CAD drawings and graph presentations, with static (no motion) one-pixel-wide lines called attention to the issue of flicker in computer displays. This type of flicker gave vector-refreshed displays a longer life in the market.

Refresh rate

The number of times per second a screen is completely scanned is the monitor's refresh rate. Some people describe the scanning of one frame as *painting the screen*. Others refer to it as *updating the screen*. In this book. I'll use the term *refresh rate* for the description of how many frames a second a monitor is scanned.

Flicker, as has been mentioned, is influenced by many factors: center vs. peripheral vision, refresh rate, intensity, and contrast. If a person is looking straight ahead within a cone of vision that's 22° of his eye, he can see detail and, within an elliptically shaped cone of 173°, he'll be able to see motion.

Monitor manufacturers know this and try to offer the best compromise of high refresh rate and low-cost parts. In some cases, they're obliged by government standards to provide high refresh rates. In other cases, they use refresh rate for marketing differentiation. The general thinking is "the more the better." However, that isn't always the case because there's a point of diminishing returns on refresh rate, and a nonlinear cost curve. The diagram in FIG. 3-21 approximates the differences.

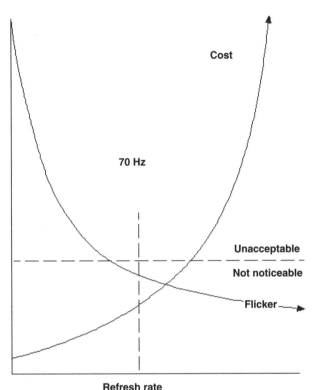

Cost

70 Hz

Unacceptable

Not noticeable

Flicker ⟶

Refresh rate

3-21
Cost vs. refresh rate vs. flicker. The curves show that as the refresh rate is increased to reduce flicker, the cost increases much more quickly. This is because of the more expensive high-speed parts that have to be used.

As the curve indicates, there's a point where an increase in refresh rate doesn't provide any further benefit, and the costs to obtain higher refresh rates gets prohibitive. I said the curve is approximate because it will vary due to the factors mentioned previously, and it will be influenced by lower-priced parts. Nonetheless, the basic relationship exists and users should keep it in mind when evaluating and comparing monitors.

For most situations and most eyes, a 72-Hz refreshed, noninterlaced display will be virtually flicker free. Higher or faster refresh rates won't, as the curve shows, contribute very much to the reduction of flicker perception. However, a higher refresh rate will provide a brighter display.

Eliminating flicker by increasing the refresh rate above the line frequency can, at certain frequencies, produce artifacts, such as *jitter*, that are perceived as flicker. This type of jitter, which is different than the type of jitter caused by problems with the monitor's internal power supply, often occurs when the refresh rate is close to the frequency of the main power lines. This jitter is not so noticeable on a screen that has most pixels illuminated, especially in a nonregular image. However, on a screen full of characters, even a slight amount of jitter can be disturbing.

For refresh rates within 0.4 Hz and 13 Hz of the main power-line frequency, jitter displacements in a character display as small as 0.0480 inch of visual angle are noticeable to observers. In such a situation, users tend to confuse jitter with flicker. In laboratory tests at the School of Optometry at the University of California, Berkeley, and Hewlett-Packard, observers who viewed a jittering display with a variable refresh frequency reported seeing flicker at refresh frequencies well above their thresholds.

Jitter can be interpreted as motion, flicker, character blur, or multiple images. As the difference between the power-line frequency and the refresh rate increases, jitter is seen more as motion than as flicker or character blur. Therefore, jitter adds noise to both the spatial and temporal resolution of a display and impacts productivity and fatigue.

Interlacing and refresh rate are just two (of several) specifications that require close matching between the display controller and the monitor.

Scan rates The vertical scan rate of a raster display is much slower than the horizontal rate, by a factor of the number of lines. For example, if the display is being driven with a 1024×768 controller, then the horizontal scan rate for a noninterlaced display will be 768 times faster than the vertical.

The number of times a second the screen is completely scanned is its refresh rate. If a display system has a 72-Hz refresh rate, that means the screen is completely scanned 72 times in one second. If the display has 768 lines, then the horizontal scan rate is, at a minimum, 55.3 KHz. An interlaced display with a 60-Hz refresh rate and 640×480 resolution will have 240 lines, 60 times a second, or a minimum horizontal scan rate of 14.4 KHz. The chart in TABLE 3-5 shows the relative horizontal scan rates for various resolutions, refresh rates, and interlaced or noninterlaced displays.

Table 3-5
Resolution vs. refresh rate vs. horizontal scan rate.
The table shows the scan rates needed for various refresh rates. Notice that resolution and refresh rate push up the horizontal scan rate (and therefore the cost).

Screen resolution Pixels	Lines	Refresh rate Hz	Horizontal scan rate KHz
640	480 NI	60	31.5
640	480 NI	72	38.0
800	600 NI	70	39.6
800	600 NI	72	47.5
1024	768 I	60	25.3
1024	768 I	75	31.5
1024	768 NI	60	50.6
1024	768 NI	70	59.1
1280	1024 I	56	31.5
1280	1024 NI	60	67.6
1280	1024 NI	75	84.5

The horizontal scan rate in the table is not just the product of the number of lines times the refresh rate; it's larger than that—which has to do with the time it takes the monitor to retrace the line back to the starting point. The retrace time is considerably faster (typically 10 times faster), but represents an important amount of time in the calculation of the horizontal scan rate. The following equation shows the relationship of the elements of a display system that influence the horizontal scan rate:

$$Hs = \frac{1}{\frac{PL}{B}} + HT$$

Where:

Hs = horizontal scan rate
PL = pixels/line
B = bandwidth
HT = horizontal retrace time

In the late '70s and early '80s, monitors offered by Conrac, Hitachi, Mitsubishi, and a few others had three possible settings for three different horizontal scan rates. A system integrator, or a brave user, could change a jumper inside the monitor and get it to run at a different rate. Often changing the scan rate resulted in the need to adjust the horizontal and vertical size of the raster area, as well as the position. However, it wasn't something that was done on a monthly, let alone a daily basis, so it didn't seem like a serious problem. In fact, it was a feature most monitor manufacturers were proud of.

As TABLE 3-5 shows, the range of horizontal scan rates can vary quite a bit, from 14 to 95 KHz. In the mid '80s when EGA and extended EGA were being introduced to the market, users were concerned about having their monitor made obsolete when they purchased a new display controller. Although there were monitors on the market that could be adjusted or jumpered, they weren't well understood by users. In a clever marketing move in late 1985, NEC introduced the MultiSync—a monitor that could automatically adjust its horizontal and vertical scan rates from the synchronization signals of the display controller. NEC's concept was quickly copied and soon every company offered an automatic synchronization monitor (*auto sync*). MultiSync is a registered trademark of NEC, yet the term is so descriptive that it has become common usage to describe any auto-sync monitor as a *multisync*.

Auto-sync monitors

Like any new technology, the first auto-sync monitors weren't perfect and required some adjustment from one resolution to another. As the horizontal scan rate is increased, the complexity and expense of the deflection amplifiers increases too, except in a nonlinear manner. Some monitors don't track all possible changes in resolution and refresh rate from CGA to VHR. They optimize their circuits directly to a standard (e.g., EGA, VGA, 8514A, or SuperVGA) by switching in a different timing capacitor for each mode. When a display-board manufacturer develops a model with a horizontal or vertical scan frequency somewhere between these modes, they have to hope the capture range of the horizontal and vertical synchronization circuits can lock on the signals. In those cases, the horizontal and vertical synchronization circuits will ignore picture linearity, which affects picture uniformity for uncommon ranges of display resolution.

Building a mass-produced monitor with very high-speed, high-voltage deflection amplifiers is a tricky proposition. As a result, some of the auto-sync monitors can't quite hit the high notes. The effect is that the screen isn't the same width at certain resolutions, particularly the ones that require the highest horizontal scan rate. The side effect of this is that the image isn't centered. The vertical amplifiers in the early auto-sync monitors were another limitation to the quality of the images at high scan rates.

To maintain picture uniformity at nonstandard resolution (V-H frequencies), monitor manufacturers have developed some very novel techniques. On the left side of the screen, special designs have been developed to control the frequency dependence of the linearity coil. In conventional monitor design, a *pin transformer*, which is frequency dependent, is used to control pin correction. New auto-sync monitors maintain straight edges of the raster because there's no pin transformer and this alignment is thus independent of frequency.

To compensate for the effects of different resolutions and synchronization signals on the right side of the display, designers have developed sampling circuits. The sampling circuits detect changes in the V-H frequencies and use S-shaping capacitors to provide small increments of linearity correction vs. frequency to adjust the image on the right side of the screen. This is called *S-shaping* because the normal sawtooth-shaped deflection current must be shaped to appear like an S, as shown in FIG. 3-22, in order to prevent characters at the end of the screen from appearing longer than ones in the middle of the screen.

3-22

Because of differences in the ratio of horizontal and vertical resolution and synchronization timings of various display resolutions, modern auto-synchronization monitors must adjust the sweep-voltage linearity to avoid distorting the image.

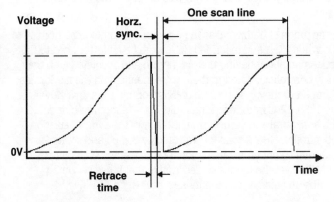

To control linearity, the S-shaping capacitors are switched in at certain points, thereby changing the timing characteristics of the horizontal sweep amplifier and slope of the waveform it produces. A very broad-frequency range is covered with just four capacitors by switching in different arrangements of the capacitors at different frequencies. The designers of such circuits pick 16 break points and switch in different value capacitors at those points to correct linearity. In other auto-sync monitors, there are three break points that cover from 15 to 55 KHz, providing much better linearity at frequencies near the break points.

To manage the problem of detecting the break points and switching in and out of the control capacitors, microprocessors were added that could store settings in a nonvolatile RAM. The RAM contains the width and centering settings for various resolutions and scan rates. Once microprocessors were introduced into monitors, new opportunities presented themselves, as will be illustrated throughout this chapter.

When IBM introduced VGA in 1987 and Apple started producing their own high-resolution display controllers, many people thought the auto-sync monitors had reached the end of their market life. But then Super VGA was introduced, quickly followed by Extended VGA and several other resolutions for the Macintosh and PC, so the need for a multirange, auto-sync monitor is still with us in PC and Macintosh land.

In modern auto-sync monitors, great care has been taken to provide the widest scan frequency possible, while providing correction for geometric distortion in the smallest possible increments of frequency. Correction is fine so that few if any resolutions exist that don't work with the newest auto-sync monitors. This ensures compatibility with all the standards and maximizes the quality and clarity the monitor displays no matter what standard is in use. The adaptability built into these new models anticipates future standards and also produces more flexibility, quality, and clarity for users who invest in various adapters along the way.

Stable power with adequate capacity is crucial to monitor performance. The power supply's stability and reserve affect picture jitter, width, brightness, and a dozen other subtle functions.

Power supply & image

Changes in horizontal size place demands on the high-voltage power supply. Monitor designers have developed linear switching-mode power supplies to improve regulation of the screen size and control the horizontal deflection voltage. The switching power supply used in some auto-sync monitors controls both the high voltage and provides power for the deflection amplifiers. By separating the power supplies that control high voltage (typically a switching-mode power supply) and the power for the deflection amplifiers (typically a linear supply), performance requirements are kept mutually exclusive. Separation of the two also allows removal of the pin transformer. The correction the pin transformer provided is accomplished by modulating the deflection amplifier's power-supply feedback voltage.

A common monitor high-voltage power supply has a stability or regulation between 1% and 3%, and some newer models achieve 0.1%. Tight regulation ensures a consistent screen size when the screen is changed from full white to full dark, or when switched from one resolution to another. The difference is noticeable when looking at a pattern, for example, of alternating white and black horizontal bars. Such a monitor exhibits smooth transitions and good control over the size changes.

In general, creating tighter specifications and optimizing design choices curtail a monitor's deviations in behavior. When manufacturers are confident a monitor is going to operate within specified parameters, they're able to give more capability to the user. For example, many manufacturers limit a user's ability to adjust screen brightness because it can significantly increase power requirements and can cause early product failure. If the design isn't tight and the range of power isn't controllable, it's very risky to give the user anything but minimal adjustability. To correct for a design that is not conservatively derated, manufacturers commonly offer a user limited adjustments.

As the beam is scanned across the face of the CRT, it's modulated to control the brightness of the image. The brightness of the image is controlled by the display controller and is sent via an amplifier in the monitor to the beam current control grid (grid 1) of the CRT. This amplifier is known as a *video amplifier* and it must

Brightness & image

operate at speeds up to 150 MHz in very high-resolution monitors. However, it has to operate only in relatively low voltage ranges. Brightness is also influenced by refresh rate and the quality of the video amplifier.

The largest influence on screen brightness is the high voltage applied to the screen's anode. If the control grid is wide open to the beam, as much beam current as possible will strike the screen. The actual brightness is measured in footlamberts (fL) or millilamberts (mL), and some monitor specifications will indicate these values. If only one value is given, it is the brightness at the center of the screen. Most monitors are less bright at the corners.

More brightness is generally required for images than for text. This is because images are primarily composed of shades and hues. Maximum brightness occurs only in the pure-white and saturated-color areas. Images are commonly considered to need 40 to 50 fL minimum, whereas a text display might require only 30 to 40 fL.

The page brightness for reading fine print is approximately 10 fL. The sun at its zenith illuminates the surface of the earth with approximately 5.2 108 fL, and a full moon provides approximately 1.5 10-3 fL. Radiologists look at x-rays with a light box that has a peak brightness of 500 fL. A monitor will produce between 20 and 60 fL. However, sometimes the fL specification given is difficult to interpret because it's specified as being "into the AR panel (or coating)." To use that number you have to also have the transmission percentage number n, which can vary from 45% to 85% from monitor to monitor and between manufacturers. Make sure to read the section *Contrast*, which often gets confused with brightness.

The video amplifier

Output signals from the display controller are low voltage with a reference level of zero volts (0 V) and a maximum level between 0.7 V and 1.0 V. The steps or gradations of the controller's output range from as few as 8 levels to as many as 1024, depending on the DAC chosen by the designer. The video amplifier in the monitor takes the low-voltage output of the controller and increases it to a higher voltage (between 10 and 60 volts, depending on the CRT) and directly drives the electron gun of the CRT.

Bandwidth

Amplification by itself isn't the difficult part. The big role for the video amplifier is to amplify the signals without degrading their bandwidth. A display controller that produces a 1280×1024 resolution with a refresh rate of 60 Hz typically operates at 110 MHz. However, the rise time of the amplifier is also very important; this is known as the amplifier's *slew rate*. Slew rate is a measurement of how fast the output signal of the amplifier reaches and maintains the desired voltage level.

As illustrated in FIG. 3-23, the slew rate of the video amplifier can have a dramatic effect on the clarity of the display. The photo on the left was taken with a display system that had a limited 0.1V/Msec rate, and the one on the right is from a display system with a nonlimited slew rate.

Referring back to FIG. 3-18, there are five factors to be considered in determining the required bandwidth: the number of pixels per line, the horizontal retrace time, the number of lines, the vertical retrace time, and the refresh rate. And those values along with the blanking times are what's needed to calculate the bandwidth. Refer

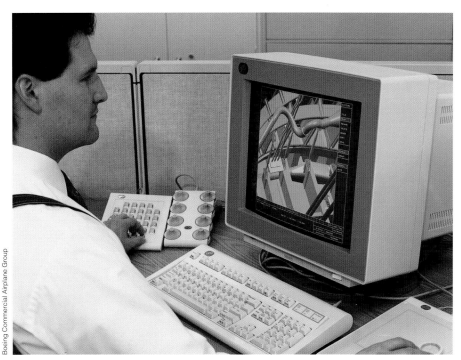

C-1 *Sophisticated computer workstations were used to design and preassemble (in a computer model) 100% of the Boeing 777 airplane. A Boeing engineer is shown here working on a fuselage section with system routings, all of which are depicted as full-color 3-D solid images.*

C-2 *Low-cost, powerful CAD programs like Autodesk's Generic CADD are being used to design houses. CAD allows architects to discover aspects of a design not possible with simple drafting techniques.*

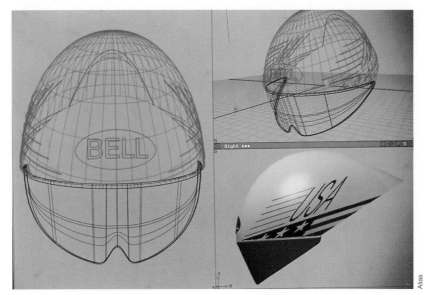

Alias

C-3 *Three-dimensional wire-frame models are used to develop and gain insight about designs quickly. After the model has been worked out as a wire frame, it can then be easily rendered for a realistic presentation of the design.*

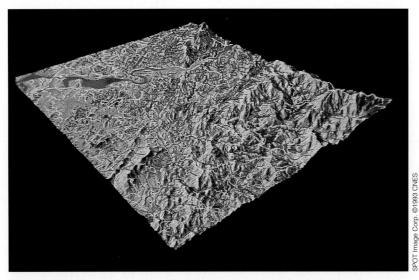

SPOT Image Corp. ©1993 CNES

C-4 *This image was created using ARC/INFO GIS software from ESRI to superimpose vector data (yellow and green lines) from the Tennessee Valley Authority (TVA) over a SPOT satellite image. High-resolution and large (19-inch) displays are necessary for applications like this.*

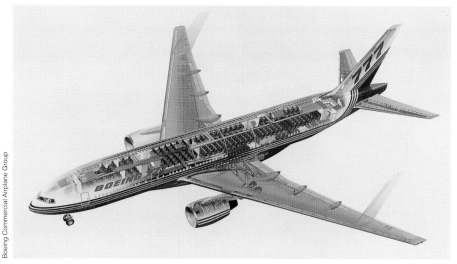

C-5 *The Boeing 777 is the first jetliner to be 100% digitally designed, using three-dimensional solid-modeling technology (refer back to Fig. C-1). Using very large displays, the airplane will be "preassembled" on the computer, eliminating much of the need for costly full-scale mock-ups.*

C-6 *Using a large, very high-resolution 1600 X 1200 monitor, the model for this picture was developed with Autodesk's CD Studio. Texture maps were designed on Photostyler from Aldus Corp., and additional textures came from the 3D Studio library. The picture has 11 light sources, both diffused and point, over 100,000 vertices, and took approximately 13 hours to render on a 33-MHz 486. The overall design took more than four months.*

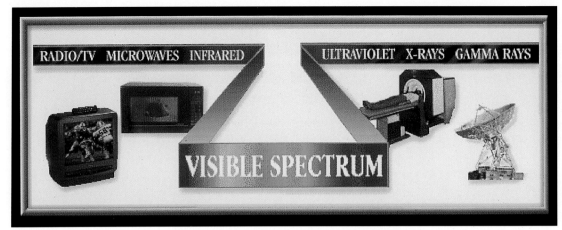

C-7 *The entire electomagnetic spectrum, only a small part of which comprises visible light.*

C-8 *Background and foreground colors are perceived differently, depending on their arrangement. Yellow on a white background is weak, but with a red background it becomes brilliant. This is known as the simultaneous color effect.*

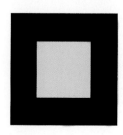

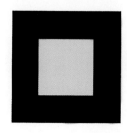

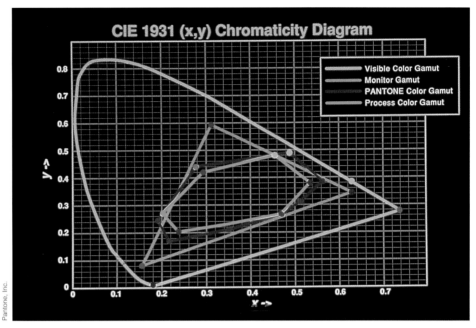

C-9 *The gamut of the human eye is much greater than any mechanical device (e.g., monitor or printer) that man has been able to devise.*

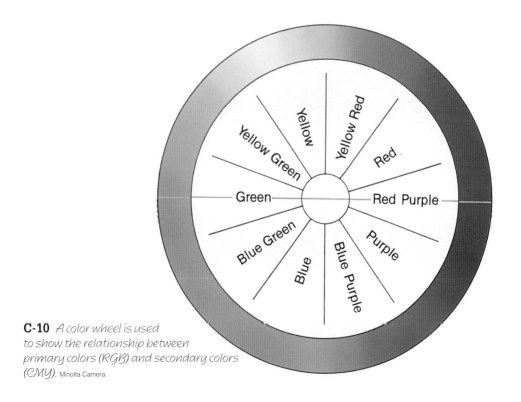

C-10 *A color wheel is used to show the relationship between primary colors (RGB) and secondary colors (CMY).* Minolta Camera

C-11 *Red, green, and blue are the additive primary colors of the color spectrum. Combining balanced amounts of red, green, and blue lights also produces pure white. By varying the amount of red, green, and blue light, you can produce all the colors in the visible spectrum.*

C-12 *Cyan, magenta, and yellow are the three subtractive primaries. Nearly any color can be produced with different combinations of these three colors. When you mix all three together in equal amounts, you get black. These three primaries are the basis of the subtractive color model, called CMY.*

C-13 *The three subtractive primaries (cyan, magenta, and yellow) don't produce a perfect black, so printers have added the black component, creating CMYK, where K represents black.*

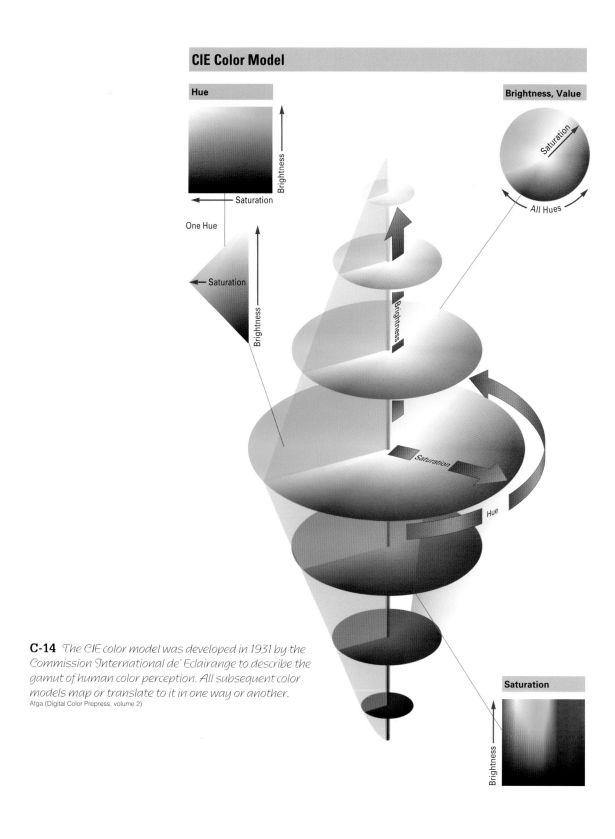

CIE Color Model

Hue

Brightness

Saturation

One Hue

Saturation

Brightness

Brightness, Value

Saturation

All Hues

Brightness

Saturation

Hue

Saturation

Brightness

C-14 *The CIE color model was developed in 1931 by the Commission International de' Eclairange to describe the gamut of human color perception. All subsequent color models map or translate to it in one way or another.*
Afga (Digital Color Prepress, volume 2)

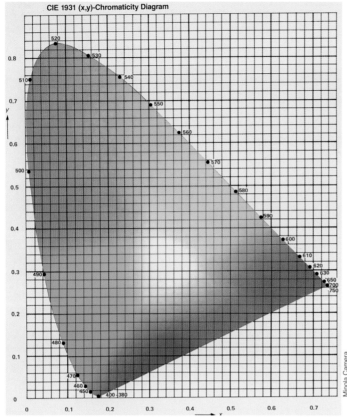

CIE 1931 (x,y)-Chromaticity Diagram

Minolta Camera

C-15 *The two-dimensional chromaticity chart of the CIE color model.*

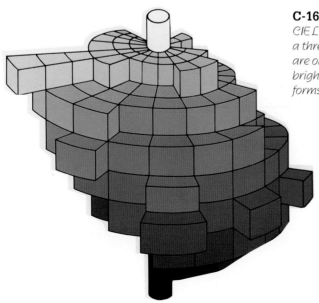

C-16 *The CIELAB system (also expressed as CIE L*,a*,b*) was established in 1973 to provide a three-dimensional color model. Color hues are on the outside around the center, value or brightness is the vertical axis, and chroma forms the horizontal axis.* Minolta Camera

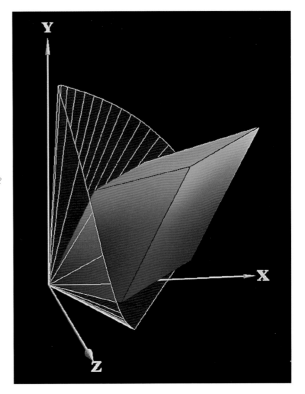

C-17 *The color gamut of NTSC TV doesn't fill the entire CIE gamut and has been given a special designation—CIE XYZ—to denote its difference.*
Gary Meyer and Linda Peting, Dept. of Computer and Information Science, University of Oregon

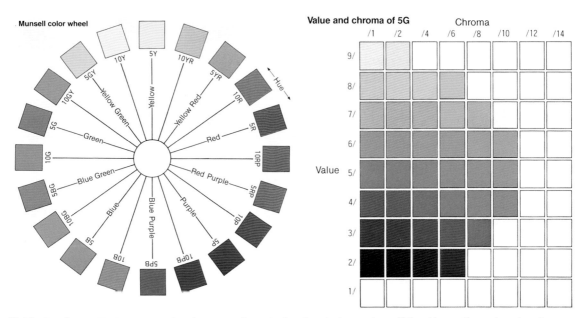

C-18 *The Munsell color system has been used most often by photographers. It's a three-dimensional system with specific notation that makes color reproduction and matching easier.* Minolta Camera

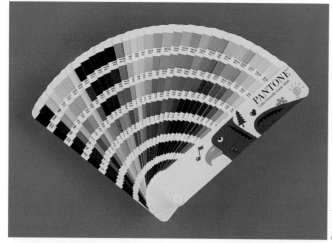

C-19 *The Pantone system was developed in 1963 by Lawrence Herbert as a method for consistent color matching for printers. It has since been adopted for use in color TV and color matching.*

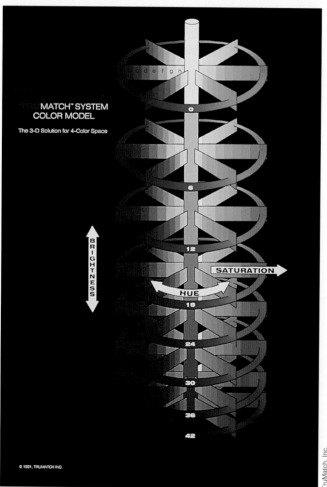

C-20 *The TruMatch system is based on the Munsell and Ostwald systems and is used to specify four-color CMKY for printing systems. It offers reproducible differences in brightness as small as 6%.*

Change in Data from Scan to Print

Original

Monitor

85% Cyan

70% Cyan

87% Cyan

CMYK Film Negatives

RGB Data

Laminate Proof

83% Cyan

84% Cyan

Printing Plates

87% Cyan

Printed Piece

89% Cyan

C-21 *An image with 85% cyan distorted during processing so that it has 89% cyan (a 6% error or distortion) when printed.*

Every step in the process of reproducing a photo as a printed piece can introduce color changes. Dot gain or loss in making the negative, outputting a color proof, and the printing plate as well as further gain on press, make it impossible, without a well-thought-out calibration process, to accurately predict the printed result.

Gamma Comparison

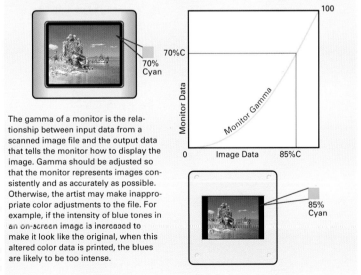

70%C

70% Cyan

100

Monitor Data

Monitor Gamma

0   Image Data   85%C

85% Cyan

The gamma of a monitor is the relationship between input data from a scanned image file and the output data that tells the monitor how to display the image. Gamma should be adjusted so that the monitor represents images consistently and as accurately as possible. Otherwise, the artist may make inappropriate color adjustments to the file. For example, if the intensity of blue tones in an on-screen image is increased to make it look like the original, when this altered color data is printed, the blues are likely to be too intense.

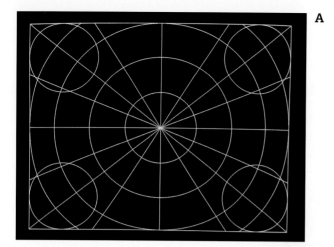

A

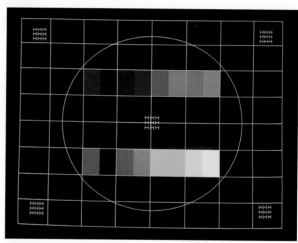

B

C-22 *Specialized test equipment is used as an input source for monitors to measure linearity (A), distortion (B), color calibration and brightness linearity (C), and other geometric and color components.* Team

C

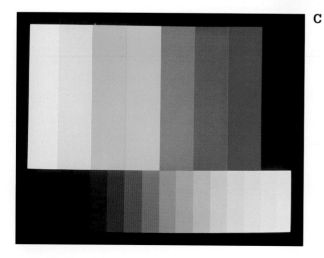

C-23 *The Sony DDM-2802C, commonly known as the "Sony 20/20," is a unique monitor with very high resolution (2048X2048), a square format (20X20 inches), very high brightness (23 fL), and super high bandwidth (358 MHz). Although criticized for its price, no one else has been able to produce a comparable display at any price.*

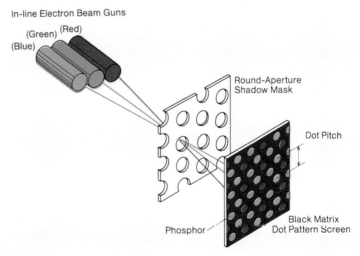

In-line Electron Beam Guns

(Green) (Red)
(Blue)

Round-Aperture
Shadow Mask

Dot Pitch

Phosphor

Black Matrix
Dot Pattern Screen

C-24 *The precision in-line (PIL) gun corrected the problem with horizontal convergence by putting the three color guns on the same horizontal level.* JVC

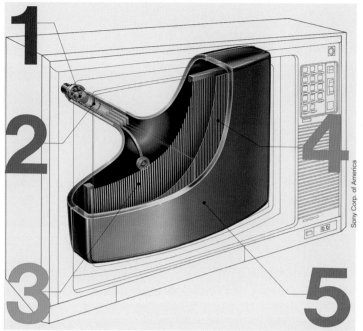

C-25 *A Trinitron tube uses a PIL-type gun (1 and 2), a mask made of very thin stripes (3), and a phosphor screen of even thinner stripes (4). As a result of that construction, the tube has a cylindrical shape (5), which helps reduce reflections.*

C-26 *A large, 20X20-inch monitor with 2048X2048 addressable resolution allows much more of an image to be seen at the same or greater resolution than on a conventional 14-inch 3:4 monitor.*

C-27 *Two examples of HDTV.* Zenith

C-28 *NEC has been successful in producing large, high-resolution, color TFT displays using active-matrix techniques.*

Tektronix

C-29 *Two examples of PALC flat-panel displays.*

Tektronix

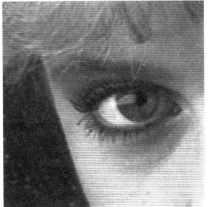

Eastman Kodak Co.

3-23
The photo on the left shows the effect of a slew rate limited amplifier. In the one on the right, the amplifier is nonlimited. Notice how much sharper and well defined the image is.

to the following equations:

$$PT = \frac{1}{X \times Y \times R} - \frac{VT}{X \times Y} - \frac{HT}{X}$$

Where:

X = pixels across one scan line
Y = number of lines
R = refresh rate, in Hz
HT = horizontal retrace, type in seconds
VT = vertical retrace, in seconds
PT = time for one pixel, in seconds

The minimum bandwidth for such a signal is:

$$B = \frac{1}{PT}$$

Where B = bandwidth in MHz. Using typical values for the popular resolutions, the chart in TABLE 3-6 shows how required bandwidth rises with resolution. As the chart shows, if a monitor has a bandwidth of 58 MHz, it won't do much good to drive it with a 1024×768 or 1280×1024 resolution image. What happens when the video bandwidth of the monitor is not sufficient for the signal being sent to it is a blurring and diminishing of luminance. This is relatively easy to understand. As the video amplifier is attempting to reach the desired voltage (its slew rate or bandwidth), the deflection amplifier is moving the beam across the screen. The result is the pixel (or, in the case of a really slow amplifier, *n* pixels) displayed in locations where it doesn't belong, and it gets dragged or streaked on the screen. The blurring or deformations are most noticeable at edges of high contrast, such as white letters on a black background (or vice versa) in the raster direction. Low-contrast edges show little blurring.

Table 3-6
Resolution vs. bandwidth. If a monitor doesn't have the necessary bandwidth, it doesn't matter what the display resolution is. Be wary of monitors that give a resolution specification and don't specify the bandwidth.

Pixels	Lines	R (Hz)	H (µS)	V (µS)	BW (MHz)
640	480	72	7.0	1036	32.4
800	600	72	6.0	800	50.6
1024	768	60	4.0	757	60.8
1024	768	70	3.8	757	74.6
1280	960	70	3.4	600	95.2
1280	1024	60	3.4	500	103.3
1600	1200	60	2.8	450	162.6
2048	1536	60	2.0	400	253.7

In many cases, if you try to drive an auto-sync monitor with a signal that's beyond its range, you'll get diagonal lines, one horizontal line, or no image at all. However, some monitor manufacturers offer monitors with less than a 70-MHz bandwidth as being capable of operating at 1024×768. Although they can produce an image, it will be slightly out of focus and that will cause eye fatigue after an hour or so. Monitors with limited bandwidth are less expensive than those with a high bandwidth, and high-frequency amplifiers are expensive to build and test.

Signal to noise

In amplifier design, the designer has to be careful to make sure that the amplifier not only doesn't generate any noise, but that it also doesn't allow any noise to pass through it from the source. When noise is present in an image it can have the appearance of reduced contrast, snow, blurring or secondary edges (shadows).

There is also a perceived noise that is due to the source. When a high quality monitor is used to directly display a computer generated image, viewers will often comment on its crispness or clarity. Similar comments can be heard when a live TV broadcast is observed. However, when movies or videotape are the source (even if from a TV studio) the image loses an observable crispness (some people refer to it as *depth*). This is due to the poorer signal-to-noise characteristics of such media.

Monitor-to-CRT interface

Most modern monitors have a small board mounted directly on the neck of the tube. The circuitry on this board amplifies the analog video signal from its 0.7-volt input level (from the display controller) to the 40 to 60 volts needed to drive the cathode of the tube. Because of the high bandwidth of the signals, printed-circuit layout line width, length, and spacing must be well designed to avoid any degradation of the video signal. Stray capacitance and inductance must be minimized (and well matched) to avoid undesirable overshoot and ringing at video frequencies exceeding 100 megapixels/sec. These are crucial interfaces, needed to provide images of consistent good quality.

Contrast

The *contrast ratio* of an image is the difference between the maximum and minimum brightness. Contrast is possibly the most crucial aspect of an image's quality. It's the value of the contrast ratio that determines the crispness or sharpness of an image or page of text. Contrast ratio gets expressed in a variety of ways: as a ratio (5:1), a percentage (50%), or an absolute value (5.0). The number doesn't mean much by itself and must be related to the screen or the viewer's eye. If related only to the screen, it can be misleading because the effect of the environment (i.e., ambient light and reflection) will impact it. However, it's difficult to measure it at the viewer's eye. Contrast is characterized by some on a pixel-to-pixel basis, and by others as the difference between the background and the foreground. The *background* is the nonactive area of the screen; the *foreground* is the area where images or text appears.

In the case of text, the background can be white, black, or some color or shade of gray in between. During part of the writing of this book I used my laptop, which has a monochrome VGA display with 32 shades of gray. I set my desktop word processor's screen colors so that the background is a few shades off white toward yellow, a sort of ivory. My normal text is a few shades off black toward blue, and I set bold as black. On my laptop, which is monochrome, I approximate the same settings. Assuming the off-white and off-black elements are each three shades off and the total range is 32, then the contrast ratio for normal text on my laptop is 26:1. Normalized to a scale of 10, that becomes 8:1, a very reasonable and comfortable ratio (for me).

Comfort is the operative word when considering contrast. Logically minded observers of my laptop have asked why I don't use full white for the background and full black for the text (and, in the case of character-based text processors, assign lesser-used functions like italics and bold to the grays). That would indeed produce the maximum contrast ratio. However, it would also be the hardest on my eyes. Extreme contrast, especially for a full screen of text, can be very fatiguing. In the days of ASCII-based text display, before WYSIWYG bit-mapped GUI displays, it used to be standard practice to defocus the screen a little so the characters would be "softer." However, with the artistic fonts like those found in all GUI-based word processor and spreadsheet programs, you want, some would say need, the greatest focus and maximal contrast.

Although contrast ratio is a personal-comfort item in my opinion, monitors have to be capable of delivering adequate contrast to meet various conditions and environments. The Human Factors Society has created a specification that has been adopted by ANSI (ANSI/HFS 100, 1988) for various monitor factors, including contrast. In a room that has an ambient light level of 250 candles/square meter (250 cd/m2), a contrast ratio of 10:1 is suggested for a 24-line text display.

For the analytically inclined, there are two basic formulas for expressing contrast. The first is one in which the ambient light is not taken into account. This measurement is also known as the *intrinsic contrast ratio*:

$$CRI = \frac{LP(on)}{LP(off)}$$

Where:

CRI – intrinsic contrast ratio
LP(on) = luminance of the on pixel
LP(off) = luminance of the off pixel

The second formula is one in which the effect of ambient light is taken into consideration. It's known as the *extrinsic contrast ratio*:

$$CRE = AL(ave) + \frac{IL(ave)}{AL(ave)}$$

Where:

CRE = extrinsic contrast ratio
AL(ave) = average ambient light
IL(ave) = average light of the image

The contrast ratio measures the difference between the brightest white and the darkest black. Although it's relatively easy to calculate the intrinsic contrast ratio, it's much more difficult to figure out the extrinsic contrast ratio. However, the black (background) is usually limited by reflections from ambient (room) light and the actual color of the screen (often gray when not illuminated). Making the CRT's screen black enhances the contrast ratio. Therefore, as mentioned in the preceding section, *Faces*, manufacturers increase contrast by using tubes with gray-tinted glass, silica (black) or silica coating, chemical etching, bonded thin-film filters, dark bulbs, and antireflective (AR) bonded panels. Polarized filters are also used to make blacks darker, but they can diminish the brightness of the whites.

In addition, some monitors use beam-current feedback techniques as a way of maintaining black levels. A beam-current feedback system works by sampling the beam current during the retrace time and then adjusting it so it's at the correct level for black.

Lowering the reflectivity of the phosphor and air-glass surfaces also increases contrast. Hitachi developed an antireflection coating for the inner surface that it claims to increase contrast by 90% to 120%. The company spin coats a thin layer of 250-nm diameter siO2 particles on the inner surface of the faceplate and bakes it with an infrared lamp before applying the conventional black-matrix and phosphor coatings.

Adding color

In the early '40s, experiments were being run with color CRTs. Of the many approaches and designs that were tried, the one that showed the most promise was the tri-gun shadow-mask model. Basically, it consisted of putting three guns in a tube, one for each primary transmission color: red, green, and blue (RGB). The phosphors and focusing, however, was more complicated. Instead of painting one monochrome phosphor on the screen, a pattern of three colors, RGB, had to be placed on it in a dot pattern called a *dot triad*. The arrangement of the three color dots physically matched the orientation of the three guns. However, getting the guns to hit just the right color dots was difficult. Therefore, a final focusing, or blocking element, was placed just in front of the phosphors. This focusing element consisted of a grill filled with small holes, called an *aperture mask* or *aperture grill*, which was developed by Harold Law at RCA Laboratories in 1949.

Along with focusing came other basic problems, such as color purity and control, astigmatism, and convergence. Added to that was the effect of color perception. Like flicker, color perception is a function of what part of the eye is being impinged. The fovea—the ellipse-shaped center portion of the retina—has the sharpest color-sensing region.

Monitors are controlled by electromagnetic forces. As mentioned in the following section, *Color purity*, even the earth's magnetic field can affect them. If the physical environment can be stabilized, the monitor can be corrected for color purity and other unwanted effects of external magnetism.

Degaussing

Correcting magnetic influences is called *degaussing*. It involves applying a steady but strong magnetic field around the face of the tube. Most monitors today have automatic degaussing, which consists of a coil of wire that's wrapped around the collar of the tube. It applies a magnetic field around the tube and forms a shield against stray fields. If a monitor is moved, the degausser will in most cases compensate for the change in environmental fields. Sometimes it takes a little time, typically 24 hours.

For monitors that don't have automatic degaussing, and even those that do but have been badly warped magnetically, you can perform a manual degaussing if you have the tools. A large-diameter (15 to 20 inches) coil that plugs into main power is used. It's held against the face of the tube, rotated, and pulled away (perpendicular to the face) slowly. It might take a couple of tries to get the hang of it.

Two factors can affect the quality of the colors displayed: the phosphors and magnetic influences. Long-persistence phosphors, the type used in noninterlaced monitors, have muted colors, even when run in saturation—it can't be helped, it's the trade-off. More controllable, and possibly more annoying, is color distortion due to magnetic influences on the monitor. Remember that the CRT positions its beam according to the magnetic fields created by the yoke. If, after the beam leaves the area of the yoke, it's influenced by a strong magnetic field, it won't hit the color triad in the spot it should. The result is a blob of color distortion. Typically, it looks like the desired color doesn't exist in the area you want it. This effect can be brought on sometimes by simply moving the monitor relative to its orientation with the earth's magnetic field. It can also be caused by the influence of a strong magnetic field generated by an adjacent power supply (from a computer, a speaker, or even another monitor).

Color purity

This final element has been called many things (especially by the people who had to build the first ones and those who had to make them work), with the printable names being the *aperture mask*, *dot mask*, and the *shadow mask*. It made mass production of a color tube possible.

The shadow mask

Over the years, considerable experimentation has been done on the aperture mask and the orientation of the guns. Four types have proven to be useful by various manufacturers: delta, in-line, slotted, and strip. The first successful design of a color tube used three color guns arranged in a triangular shape, and was called the *delta-delta color CRT*. The beams from the three guns are aimed at the screen through the aperture grill, as shown in FIG. 3-24. Each beam is aimed at the screen and aperture mask at slightly different angles. As a result of this angular relationship, the beam from the red gun will hit the red phosphor, the green the green phosphor, and the blue the blue phosphor.

The job of the aperture mask is to keep the electron beams from hitting too many dot triads. Only about 20 to 30% of the beam's electrons actually hit the screen. The rest of the beam is blocked from the screen and, therefore, the mask can be thought of as creating a shadow, hence the name *shadow mask*.

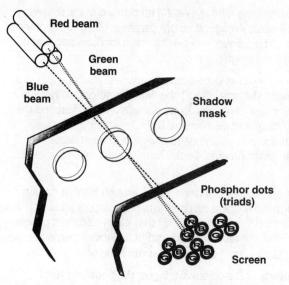

Red beam

Green beam

Blue beam

Shadow mask

Phosphor dots (triads)

Screen

3-24
The delta aperture grill (shadow mask) is designed to keep the gun's electron beam from hitting the wrong color dot triads on the screen.

The portion of the electron beam that hits the aperture mask flows though the mask to the anode connector and from there to the power supply. That current flow creates heat in the mask. The heat produced is a problem and can cause distortions in the mask due to thermal expansion. In a conventional CRT, the curved shadow mask is supported by a frame and suspended by small springs inside the tube. As the beam hits the mask, it heats up and moves due to temperature expansion. The springs allow that movement and return the mask to its position as it cools. The most severe problem is mask failure resulting in a short circuit or collapse into the phosphor screen. Heat-resistant masks composed of invar materials, sometimes referred to as *iron shadow masks*, have had a major impact on improving the reliability of high-resolution monitors.

Convergence   When the red, green, and blue beams leave the gun and go hurling toward the screen, it's very important that they hit the same triad dot at as close to the same spot as possible. If they do and if all three are at the same intensity, they'll form a white dot. If they're offset slightly, the dot will be white where they're superimposed, but it will have colored edges, as shown in FIG. 3-25.

When all the beams are completely superimposed on each other, they're *convergent*. If they aren't, therefore, the display is out of convergence. When a monitor has a misaligned convergence, it's easy to spot—all images will have a shadow of one color or more on the edges.

In the early days of color TV, it used to be a laborious task to get a tube converged or aligned. The screen was divided into nine sections and each section had three controls. Adjusting one influenced the others. Some sets had built-in test patterns to aid the service technician. The delta-gun array was used in TV sets into the early '70s.

Automatic convergence   CRT developers found that putting the three guns in line would eliminate a lot of the problem of convergence. This design came to be

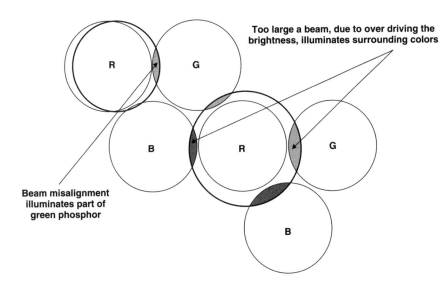

Too large a beam, due to over driving the brightness, illuminates surrounding colors

Beam misalignment illuminates part of green phosphor

3-25
If the beam hits the dot triad correctly, more of one color than another will be illuminated. This lack of convergence is made obvious by the presence of a color shadow on all edges or an inability to obtain the correct color in an image.

known as the *precision in-line*, or PIL, tube. It used a conventional aperture mask, but the dot triads were arranged differently, as shown in FIG. C-24.

Although this solved the convergence problem, it created a beam pattern problem; the three in-line beams now formed a slightly elongated shape. One solution was to change the design of the aperture mask from one full of holes to one constructed with slots, as shown in FIG. 3-26. Developed by RCA Laboratories in 1972, it quickly became the most popular type of tube for consumer products. The vertical strips eliminated the vertical-convergence requirements. From 1975 to 1990, considerable investigation was put into developing new alloys for the construction of the shadow mask. The invar mask, 36% nickel and 64% iron, has proven to be the best solution for thermal stability and flatter-faced tubes.

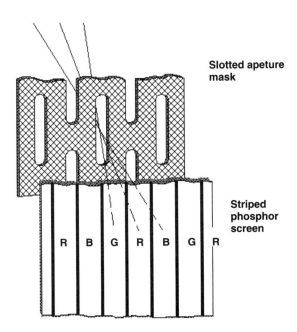

Slotted aperture mask

Striped phosphor screen

R B G R B G R

3-26
The slotted mask has improved convergence as well as brightness over the conventional aperture-hole mask.

Many of the newer monitor designs employ a self-converging yoke. As their name suggests, they perform both deflection and convergence functions. A self-converging yoke usually has small magnets on the outside of it, known as *helpers*. These types of yokes have to be designed, and sometimes hand-tuned, so that the red beam is deflected slightly more at the right side and slightly less at the left side. Computer-aided design techniques and modeling are used to create the designs for these yokes.

Self-converging monitors aren't perfect, although they're pretty good. Misconvergence in a typical 19-inch, 90° tube with 0.31-mm dot pitch is from 0.3 mm to 0.6 mm in the center and 0.5 to 0.8 mm in the corners. An 11-inch monitor has a 0.3-mm misconvergence in the center and a 0.45-mm misconvergence in the corner.

Modern-day monitors are better designed, with automatic convergence features. Tighter manufacturing tolerances and quality control have reduced the problem to that of the exception. Because of the success in "manufacturing out" the problem of convergence, user and technician controls for tweaking the convergence of a monitor have been eliminated. Therefore, if your monitor starts to show signs of a misconvergence (usually due to a physical shock or a degrading power supply), it will have to be sent back to the manufacturer to be corrected.

Beam forming

Color-CRT manufacturers like Panasonic, Philips, Rauland, RCA, and Sony have been redesigning the beam-forming region of the electron gun, between the cathode and grid 1 (G1), to provide more constant spot size as brightness is increased. They're using a technique know as *thick G1*, developed in the '70s for large monochrome displays by Hewlett-Packard from work by Hillary Moss.

With such a technique, the manufacturer can gain independent control of each beam—red, green, and blue—and obtain more sophisticated control of hue and brightness. In addition, Sony has introduced a method for separate control of the side beams of an in-line gun, greatly improving overall convergence and focus. Most of the major high-resolution CRT makers have added a prefocus lens at the electron gun's beam-forming region. This has improved the general performance of color raster displays and has made them the accepted technology for displaying computer graphics.

Focus has also been improved by beam-shaping techniques through the use of quadruple lenses. They optimize corner spot size and extend focus by using fields that mimic large lenses for minimum spherical aberration. Improved control of aperture and alignment keeps beams focused better when they're deflected, and dynamic focusing schemes are more widely used by most of the major manufacturers.

Panasonic uses an overlapping field lens (OLF). The gun's aperture lenses partially overlap, which Panasonic claims increases the effective diameter, reduces spherical aberration, and gives better focusing.

Gamma correction

After all the convergence, focus, and beam-control problems have been solved and the tube is about as perfect as it can get, the user is faced with the problem of color tracking, or gamma correction. All monitors have a certain amount of nonlinearity, which is due primarily to the cathode. It's usually a trial-and-error process to get a monitor's color balanced. Some monitors have a built-in processor that can be programmed to store several gamma settings.

Color tracking is how well the display system (monitor and controller) produce a linear change in color intensity on the screen from a linear color-change command to the controller. If, for example, the controller is commanded to produce red, green, and blue, which yields white at 50% of its maximum luminance, then the monitor should display that. The chart in FIG. 3-27 shows the ideal and a typical nonlinear curve.

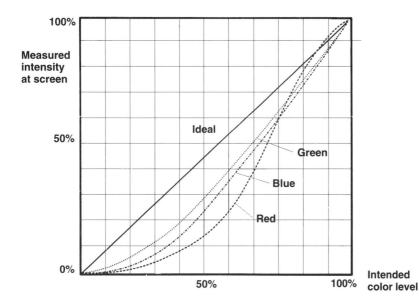

3-27
The ability of a display system to faithfully reproduce on the screen what was created by the source is known as color tracking.

As the curves show, an uncalibrated display system can be quite nonlinear. This is also known as being *nonmonotonic* and relates to, among other things, the quality of the digital-to-analog converter (DAC) of the LUT-DAC on the controller. If one DAC puts out more or less voltage than the other two, the system will have poor color tracking (some magazines call this *gray linearity*). In addition to the nonlinearity of a DAC, or lack of tracking linearity between DACs, the screen's phosphors and guns might also lack linearity between colors at different points on the screen.

Because the color range is a piece-wise or quantum-step process, it isn't possible to have a perfect, fully balanced display system. Therefore, display systems are typically calibrated in the center and at 50% luminance. Some systems have a 3×3 matrix that divides the screen into nine sections. Each section has a small memory associated with it, which stores the calibration data for balancing the system.

Triads, trios, & stripes

The three colors of red, green, and blue are phosphors that get painted on the inside face of the CRT and are known by several names: *dot triads, triads, trios, color dots,* and *trιdots.* For the purposes of this book, I'll use the term *dot triad.* The dot triad is the individual group of three phosphor dots on the screen of the CRT. Because there are three of them and they belong to a group, they form a triad. The term *triad* has nothing to do with shape.

The triads are printed on the face of the CRT. First (for in-line gun-based tubes), stripes of carbon are painted. This gives the tube a sharp black separation between triads. Then the phosphors are painted in between the carbon stripes.

Dot pitch
& dot triads

One of the most misused and often misunderstood elements of a color monitor is the dot pitch. *Dot pitch* (also referred to as *tridot pitch*) is a misnomer that we seem to be stuck with. The term *pitch* refers to the angle off center of the lines that run through the red phosphor dots in the dot triad. At some point, the measurement between the red dots of adjoining dot triads was referred to as the dot pitch. Dot pitch, however, is an angular measurement, not a diameter, distance, or resolution. There are over 45 definitions of the word *pitch* in a modern dictionary, and none of them can be associated with a distance measurement. However, the vernacular being what it is, we're probably stuck with this term. The red dots were used for the measurement because the brightness level of the red gun is adjusted (with the green and blue guns held constant at their maximum intensity) to produce a white dot on the screen during color calibration.

The distance between two immediate neighbor triad dots of the same color is the ultimate resolution of a monitor. It's a measurement that has attracted a great deal of interest as a means of qualifying a monitor's image-generating capabilities. However, due to the geometry of the dot pattern in a dot triad (see FIG. 3-28), some commonly held assumptions are not correct. The dots, for example, don't form an equilateral triangle, but an isosceles triangle pattern.

3-28
The term dot pitch *is often misunderstood and misused. As the diagram shows, there are several ways in which the measurement, and hence the specification, can be made. The dots don't form an equilateral triangle, but are in an isosceles triangle pattern, called a* triad.

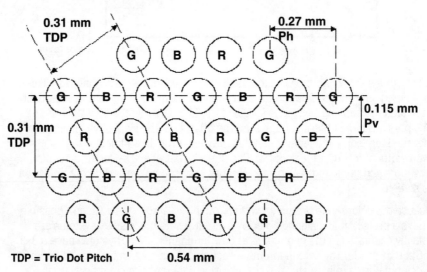

There's no clear agreement on the measurement between or of dot triads. Other ways of explaining the idea are that the dot pitch is the distance between the centers of adjacent or neighboring triads, the left edges of the green dots, or the red dots of neighboring triads. It doesn't matter; it all means basically the same thing. Common sense tells us that CRT manufacturers are going to try to paint the triads as close together as possible. Therefore, the distance from a green dot to a green dot or a blue dot to a blue dot will all be the same. If that's true, then the effective diameter of the dot triad should be the same as the dot pitch—but it isn't, because of the isosceles shape of the dot triad.

It's a geometric paradox about which way to measure dot-triad distance, as shown in the diagram in FIG. 3-28. There can be red dot pitch (measurements a, c, or d), green and blue dot pitch (measurements b, c, d, or e), or any one of 12 others. Because of the way the dots are oriented, a different number can be obtained for each one. Then, if red is used, as it customarily has been, and the angular measurement is made (c or d), you can argue that it's an off-horizontal-axis measurement and, when corrected using simple trigonometry, gives a smaller number—but is it realistic? No, it really isn't, and it almost becomes a metaphysical discussion, similar to how many pixies can you get on the head of pin. The discussion was started by marketing people trying to obtain product differentiation.

The main thing to keep in mind when someone discusses dot pitch is that it isn't the same as a pixel—pixels are typically 1.5 to 10 times larger than the dot pitch or the dot triad. The other thing to keep in mind is that it's the distance between adjoining or nearest-neighbor color dots, and which isn't the same thing as the aperture hole or slit of the shadow mask.

In the early '90s, the majority of the monitors in production had an average dot-triad size of 0.31 mm, and the newer models offered a 0.28-mm dot triad. All of the Japanese manufacturers had 0.26-mm tubes in production and 0.21-mm tubes in final development. In 1990, Hitachi demonstrated a developmental tube with 0.15-mm dot triad.

As the dot-triad size (also called *screen pitch* by some monitor companies) is decreased, the relative brightness is decreased, as shown in FIG. 3-29. This is logical because there's less phosphor area to be illuminated. It also becomes more difficult to get the phosphor to adhere to the screen. That problem was overcome by plating a titanium coating on top of the carbon stripes before applying the phosphors.

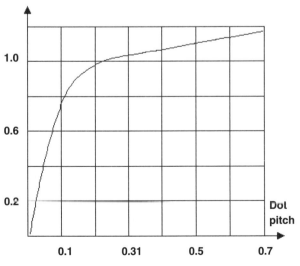

Brightness

3-29
As the size of dot triads gets smaller (finer), with all other parameters held constant, the brightness will decrease because there's less phosphor to be excited.

Mask aperture Most manufacturers don't specify the shadow mask's aperture (sometimes incorrectly called *mask pitch*, another misuse of the word *pitch*). When they do, it's always larger than the triad dot. That's only logical because it's in front of the phosphor dots—it should be larger to allow sufficient beam current to hit the triads. Since it's a larger number, might be confused with the dot triad, and has little or no meaning to a user, it isn't used. The size of the holes in the aperture mask (for a typical 19-inch tube) varies from 0.40 mm to 0.60 mm, and the distance between holes is typically 0.60 mm.

Another way of visualizing the alignment of the color gun's beams, the shadow mask, the dot triads, and the resultant spot size is shown in FIG. 3-30.

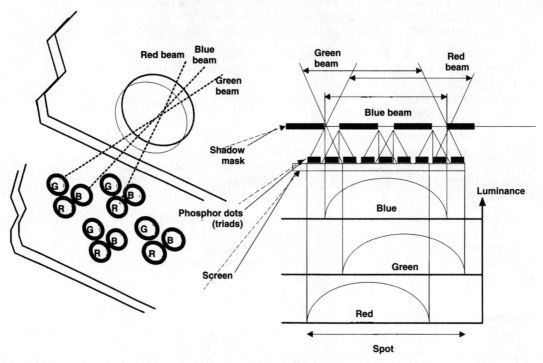

3-30 *The electron beams from each color gun pass through the shadow mask and strike the appropriate color dots on the screen. Several dots make up a spot.*

The Trinitron tube In 1968, Sony introduced a new CRT for TVs, and later for monitors, called the Trinitron. It used a different approach to CRT construction, relying on a horizontal-aperture grill instead of a traditional shadow mask, a different phosphor printing, and a new gun design, as shown in FIG. C-25.

The biggest difference between the Trinitron color system and the shadow-mask system is the number of electron guns used and the way they're arranged. The Trinitron uses one gun with three cathodes to fire three electron beams in a horizontal line. A shadow-mask system uses three guns in a delta arrangement, or PIL, as discussed earlier. Since the Sony gun is aligned vertically (they're all on the same horizontal axis), all that remains to be done to them is to align them horizontally. This is the reason the Trinitron uses a cylindrical tube. Furthermore, Sony contends that the Trinitron uses only one large electron lens, which offers a larger center point and allows the beams to be focused more accurately. The cylindrical shape of the tube gives it one more advantage—it reflects less ambient light.

The phosphors in a Trinitron are applied in vertical stripes instead of dots. Also, Sony was able to print very fine stripes so it could offer a distance between colors of only 0.25 mm in a 19-inch tube when conventional tubes were offering 0.31 mm. The finer phosphor distance (pitch) contributes to the image quality of the Trinitron tube and Sony earned a reputation for the best-quality display. Necessity, the mother of invention, visited Sony with a favor. Needing to keep the vertical RGB stripes from getting too close to each other (called *bleeding*), they put a very thin black barrier between them. This series of nonreflective stripes between the phosphors was another innovation to the design, which their marketing department dubbed the *guard grill*. These stripes absorb ambient light reflections and heighten the contrast.

The other difference in the Trinitron is its aperture grill, which is constructed of very thin vertical metal strips. The distance between the vertical strips is known as the *aperture grill pitch* (APT). The grill allows more electrons to hit the phosphor than a shadow mask, resulting in a brighter image. Also, the grill is less sensitive to the earth's magnetic field. The metal lines of the grill are very thin and, because they don't get hit with as many electrons, the tube runs cooler. However, Sony had to put an extra horizontal focus control and two thin horizontal support beams across the grill to help support it. If you look very carefully at the screen, you can see the shadow effect of these two beams; most users, however, don't notice it.

Strips & stripes   It can get confusing trying to figure out when something is a strip and when it's a stripe. The aperture grills found in most modern tubes and all Trinitrons are made of metal strips. The phosphors on the screen are stripes.

Flatness

As discussed in previous sections, the important factors of image quality are brightness, contrast, resolution, and color reproducibility. Recently, however, the flatness of a screen has been an important factor, especially for the larger-sized screens. The early TV tubes had a very spherical face, due to the technology of the time and the need to make the tubes as inexpensively as possible. When those tubes were used in more demanding situations for computers, however, several problems became apparent. That, coupled with the drive to make even better TV tubes has kept the CRT a dynamic and developing technology.

One of the areas of development has been in flattening the face of the tube. This is done by increasing the effective radius of the beam (also referred to as its *throw distance*). As scan rates and brightness levels were increased, a new problem with the aperture mask presented itself: the doming or bulging of the mask.

The first generation of flat-faced tubes were based on the use of an iron mask. The curvature-design tubes are restricted in flatness to some extent by the occurrence of local doming. The use of an invar mask (which became popular with increasing picture brightness) provides more freedom in flattening the face because of its substantial reduction of local doming.

The super-flat-faced monitors are about two times flatter than those of the conventional flat-faced monitor. With the development of the technology, 33-, 29-, and 27-inch color CRTs have been developed. To obtain the picture quality needed, various technologies, such as super-dark glass, invar mask, multi-prefocusing electron gun, and impregnated cathodes, have been used in combination with new face designs.

In addition to the control of the mask, gun designs, and contrast enhancement, subjective but important visual factors such as reality of the image have to be taken into consideration. As the size of the tube is increased, more of the image is visible by the peripheral-vision areas of the eyes. The inclusion of the periphery to obtain realism was one of the reasons behind the development of panoramic wide-screen movies. It's also one of the reasons for the 16:9 aspect ratio of HDTV tubes.

Although a large-screen monitor gives a wider viewing angle, it doesn't necessarily provide images that look *real*. This is because there's an incongruous impression created as the convex face is increased, because the viewing distance to the edges is not increased in proportion to the screen size, even though the height of the screen face increases in proportion to the screen size. The effect is illustrated in FIG. 3-31. Screen height is also referred to as the *sagittal height*.

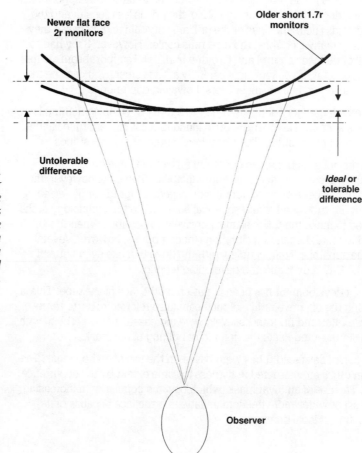

3-31
As the size of the monitor increases, the edges curve further away. This is especially noticeable to the peripheral vision and can cause a confusion between the up-down and left-right views.

The drawing in FIG. 3-31 shows the problem of using a highly exaggerated, curved screen to make the point. For the expression of the flatness, the term *effective radius* is used. The effective radius is the ratio to the screen curvature (1R) obtained from formerly used round-faced designs. The reference value is defined as the sagittal height at the edge of useful screen area, having a radius equal to 1.767 times the distance between the edges.

In 1983, a design concept of *flat square* (FS) was announced for large-screen CRTs, which used a spherical face with a maximum radius of 1.7R. After that, various tube or bulb designs were proposed that used aspheric surfaces. One was the SP (*square planar*) type, which had an effective radius of 1.8R on the diagonal axis and 3.9R on the periphery, achieving a remarkably flat face. The others were the HS (*high-performance square*) type and the NF (*new flat*). The effective radius of these types was 1.3R on the diagonal axis and 1.7R in the periphery. Figure 3-32 shows the relative difference between conventional and *super flat-faced* screens. The cylindrical shape of the Trinitron tube also provides a flat screen with square corners.

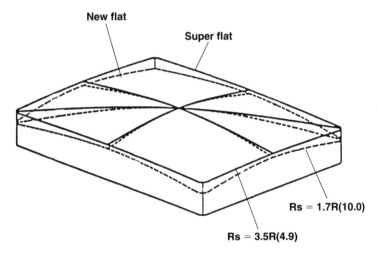

New flat

Super flat

Rs = 1.7R(10.0)

Rs = 3.5R(4.9)

3-32
There are three types of flat-faced monitors: Zenith's flat-tension mask, which is completely flat, the Sony Trinitron, and super-flat screens, which use the 2R technique.

Reflections from the face of the tube can be distracting, cause fatigue, and impact productivity. Therefore, monitor manufacturers have had additional incentive to flatten the face of the tube. The vector-refreshed and storage tubes are completely flat, large, with a very small spot size. These displays set the goal for all other displays and, whenever a new development is made in CRTs or flat-panel displays, a comparison to the vector-refreshed tubes is ultimately made.

Flat-faced color tubes are difficult to make primarily because of the shadow mask. Supporting it, manufacturing it (the holes have to change size and shape at the edges and corners), and compensating for temperature expansion due to the heating of the electron beam are complex problems. There are three approaches used to obtain a flat-faced CRT: the cylindrical, double radius (2R), and the flat-tension mask tubes.

The cylindrical tube In 1968 Sony introduced a new CRT for TVs, and later for monitors, called the Trinitron. It used a different approach to CRT construction, relying on a horizontal aperture grill instead of a traditional shadow mask, a different phosphor printing, and a new gun design.

The cylindrical tube, or Trinitron, reduces almost all reflections from overhead sources of light. Since there's only one curvature to the tube's face, a large proportion of other stray reflections are eliminated. However, it's still a polished piece of glass. The Trinitron, which is discussed in preceding sections, uses a 90° deflection tube.

The double radius tube Tubes with a hemispherically shaped front have a face-plate curvature that's a function of the radius of the tube. The longer the radius from the face of the tube to the gun, the flatter the face can be. That is the concept behind the 2R or flat-square tubes. As mentioned in the previous section on *Curvature and deflection angle*, the 90° deflection 2R tubes have a radius that's two times as long as a conventional tube, hence the 2R designation. The longer radius also contributes to the obtainment of a square corner, hence *flat square*.

The flat-tension mask tube Zenith began development of the flat-tension mask CRT in the mid '80s. In the flat-tension mask (FTM), the shadow mask is stretched flat and held tensioned in two dimensions directly behind the tube's flat glass faceplate, as illustrated in FIG. 3-33. The mask doesn't move under most display conditions, even at higher temperatures caused by high brightness levels. Because the FTM can run at very high voltage, and therefore produce high brightness levels, Zenith uses 31% transmission glass in their FTM monitors.

3-33
Flat-tension mask (FTM) technology is at the heart of Zenith Electronics' program to develop large-screen high-resolution color displays for computers and HDTV. A perfectly flat, glare-free faceplate and shadow mask are held under tension to form the front of the CRT.
Zenith

The Zenith FTM is 25 mm thick and has a variable dot pitch that's 0.2 mm in the center and gets larger toward the edges. The tensioned mask offers advantages similar to invar in that it can be heated to a greater extent than traditional masks before color purity is lost.

Often, when a person first looks at an FTM screen, they get the impression that the image has a pincushion problem. This is because our brains have been taught to compensate for the convex surface of traditional monitors and we've learned how to see an orthogonal image. When we see a correct image on an FTM, we have to retrain ourselves. It's subtle and doesn't take very long, but it can be disconcerting for a while and often amusing.

There are various techniques to improve contrast: light-absorbing glass (i.e., dark glass), antiglare or antireflection coatings, pigmented phosphors, and black-matrix screens. The antireflection techniques using low-transmission glass, reflective coatings, and other techniques are discussed in the previous section on *Faces*. Additional techniques are possible in a color CRT, and merit special mention.

Contrast enhancements in color tubes

Phosphor pigmentation   A technique that was developed by RCA in the mid '70s and is used by most CRT manufacturers today is phosphor pigmentation. Each phosphor color dot's grains are coated with a pigment that acts like a filter. It passes the color (i.e., spectral component) emitted by the phosphor, and absorbs any other colors or components. This greatly reduces light reflected from the phosphor layer and enhances the contrast without the penalty of brightness reduction that most of the antireflection techniques cause.

Black-matrix screens   Originally introduced by Zenith, black-matrix screens surround each phosphor dot, or each phosphor stripe, with a black light-absorbing outline or stencil. This makes the area between the phosphor dots or stripes unexcitable by the electron beam and reduces reflected light, increasing contrast without loss of brightness.

Sony's guard grill   As was mentioned in the previous section on the Trinitron, Sony needed to keep the vertical RGB stripes from bleeding into each other, and so a very thin black barrier was put between them. These nonreflective stripes absorb ambient light reflections and heighten the contrast.

The resolution of a monitor can also be measured in terms of spot size, although it's less common. The spot size is often incorrectly related to the dots-per-inch (dpi) resolution of a monitor. Spot size, also called *electron-beam spot profile*, can be affected by various factors, such as linearity and intensity. For example, if a 19-inch monitor is specified as having a spot size of 0.012 inches (0.305 mm), it will have approximately 85 dpi. If the brightness is turned up, the spot will be enlarged—and not in a linear manner, so it might become an ellipse or even egg shaped.

Spot size & dots per inch on the screen

When the brightness is increased, although there might be very accurate positioning of the beam, the adjacent spots will overlap. When this happens, the image takes on a blurry look. Also, the size and shape of a spot will increase and distort as it's moved to the edges of the line or monitor. Therefore, if spot size is being used as selection criterion for a monitor's resolution, you must determine if the spot size given by the manufacturer is in the center, as well as its brightness.

Monitors that have dynamic focusing will do a better job of holding the beam's spot size at the edges. However, for some applications, especially those with text, spot overlap might be required. Therefore, the spot size is usually larger than the addressable pixel size.

Spot sizes for 19-inch monitors will vary from 0.14 mm (0.0055 inches) to as large as 0.50 mm (0.0197 inches). However, don't be misled by this number—it doesn't necessarily represent what you can see. As mentioned previously (refer to FIG. 3-10), when the beam strikes the phosphor, it typically has a Gaussian distribution (or bell curve), with the center being the most intense and the edges falling off gradually. Although the effective diameter is only about 66%, in practice, spot size is measured at the diameter of 50% of maximum brightness or luminance. When the spot size is made smaller, approaching that of the aperture mask, beat frequencies known as *moiré interference* can occur.

Because of the difficulty of registering the aperture mask to the phosphor's dot triads, and the possibility that a particular dot triad might not produce the same brightness or luminance, it's necessary to make the spot size large enough to cover at least two dot triads. In some cases, it could be as large as three times the size of a single dot triad.

Color display systems with addressable pixel formats up to 2500×2000 aren't usually capable of displaying more than 1 to 2 million resolvable pixels. This difference is easily explained. The pixel width in color display systems needs to be between 1.2 and 1.7 times the dot triad (depending on the size and construction of the aperture mask) to avoid color *moiré* or *roping distortions.* Therefore, a screen that measures 20 inches horizontally and has approximately 1700 phosphor dots (0.3-mm dot triad) can accommodate only 1000 resolvable pixels at most.

The number of resolvable pixels is further reduced by beam misconvergence and spot distortions during deflection. Even a 16:9 HDTV system with an addressable interlaced format of 1920×1080 pixels will provide, at most, 1030×700 resolvable pixels. Since TVs using the NTSC format of 720×480 interlaced pixels display only about 350×330 resolvable pixels, HDTV CRTs represent an impressive advancement. However, they don't produce or provide pictures "as crisp as those in a movie theater," as often reported by the press, because they're limited by dot pitch.

Most monitor manufacturers give conservative spot-size specifications, when they give them. Also, not all monitor suppliers have the equipment to plot a spot-size profile. Therefore, it is sometimes difficult to get a spot-size specification from the manufacturer or supplier.

Monitor resolution   As has been mentioned throughout this book, the term *resolution* has several meanings. When used in a discussion about monitors, it's a complex image-quality metric and depends on many factors. Among them are electron-beam spot profile, distortions of the spot during deflection, video-amplifier characteristics, scattering of light in the phosphor layer and faceplate, sampling artifacts from raster scanning, the color-phosphor screen structure, and misconvergence of beams in color systems.

Spatial resolution is described as being measured in pixels on a line and lines on a screen. The total number of resolvable pixels in an image is the product of the numbers of resolvable pixels along the horizontal and vertical dimensions of the display. That's what the controller sends to the monitor. However, in practice what the monitor actually displays is usually less than the total number of pixels in the addressable pixel format—because of physical effects such as those listed in the previous paragraph.

There have been several proposals and numerous academic papers on how to measure or define the resolution of a monitor. The general consensus has been that measuring it in terms of line width is the most practical technique. Line width can be measured or predicted in a variety of ways, including MTF (modulation-transfer function); modulation index or depth; SQRI (square-root integral); line width at 5%, 50%, or 60% points; TVL (TV line limiting); visible line width; and shrinking raster. These techniques are well defined for monochrome displays, but less predictable for color displays. The subjective visual appearance still enters the evaluation.

Using line width as the basis for defining (although not specifying) a monitor's resolution has become one of the most popular and practical techniques. The *line* in the term *line-width measurement* is the maximum number of lines that can be displayed on a monitor. How wide a line is can be interpreted in one of three ways: from the 5%, 50%, or 60% point of a fully illuminated line. As FIG. 3-34 shows, a line is formed by a Gaussian distribution, the same as a spot.

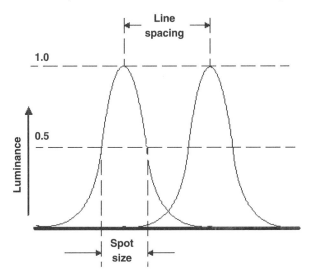

3-34
One of the more accurate ways to determine a monitor's maximum theoretical displayable resolution is to use line-width measurements.

As the figure illustrates, the actual percentage selected for the measurement of line width isn't that crucial because it's the same for every line. However, like so many things in the display system, the TVL technique, which uses the 50% point, is the most popular choice for most monitor manufacturers. As will be illustrated, the spot size is usually the limiting factor in line width.

Resolution   So what is the resolution of a monitor? The maximum possible displayable resolution of a monitor is equal to the width of the viewable area divided by spot size. That's the theoretical maximum resolution of a monitor, not a display system; however, that is all the resolution a user will realize.

If a 19-inch monitor has a maximum viewable width of 15 inches and a dot size of 0.011 inches, then it's theoretically capable of displaying a maximum of 1363 points per line. If it has a maximum viewable vertical height of 11 inches, then it's theoretically capable of displaying a maximum of 1000 lines. Why the emphasis on *theoretical*? Because few tubes are capable of reaching their maximum viewable area or their minimum dot size and, even if they're presented with an image that large, they might not have the video bandwidth or the focusing capabilities to display it. And, as pointed out earlier, the dot size will vary depending where it is on the screen. It's not as simple as the numbers on a data sheet might suggest, or as some publications have proposed.

Visualizing the resolution capabilities of a monitor can be difficult. Describing a screen as having so many pixels per line or so many lines is a bit abstract. Therefore, it might be easier to appreciate in terms of dots per inch (dpi) on the screen. Take an average 19-inch monitor, with a 15×11-inch viewing area, dot size of a 0.011-inch (0.28-mm) spot size, a 0.012-inch (0.31-mm) dot triad size, and a controller with 1280 pixels/line resolution for a model. Expressing resolution in dpi and comparing the three most easily quantifiable parameters—dot triad, spot size, and controller pixel resolution—while using the maximum (or minimum) theoretical sizes, you get the comparison shown in TABLE 3-7. Refer to the following equations:

$$DP(dpi) = \frac{1}{DP} = \frac{1}{0.012} = 83.1 \text{ dpi}$$

$$SS(dpi) = \frac{1}{SS} = \frac{1}{0.011} = 90.0 \text{ dpi}$$

$$P(dpi) = \frac{1}{HV} = \frac{1280}{15} = 85.3 \text{ dpi}$$

Where:

DP = dot pitch
SS = spot size
P = pixels
X = pixels/line
HV = viewable horizontal width (max) for a 19-inch monitor
dpi = dots per inch

The theoretical limit or the maximum possible resolution is the smallest dpi in the list. Why? Because it's like a series of pipes. The thinnest one is the one that restricts the water and it doesn't matter how many fat pipes you have on either side

Table 3-7
Typical specifications for color monitors. The three most common specifications for determining a monitor's maximum displayable resolution are dot size, dot triad size (dot pitch), and the number of pixels on a line. None of them taken alone are really a very good determination, yet pixels on a line is commonly used by manufacturers for a screen's dpi.

Monitor	Pixels	P_{dpi}
	640	65
14-inch	800	81
(9.9")	1024	103
	1280	130
	640	51
17-inch	800	64
(12.5")	1024	82
	1280	102
	640	44
(19-inch)	800	56
(14.4")	1024	71
	1280	89

of it. The pipelines in this case are the controller to the CRT, the CRT's electron beam to the phosphor, and the dot triad on the screen, as was illustrated in FIG. 3-3. Limit any one of them and that's the maximum you can get.

Spatial frequency As TABLE 3-7 shows, the limiting factor in the example is the dot triad. It's capable of displaying only 1229 pixels per line, or 82 dpi. However, if the controller was supplying only a 1024-pixel line, it would be more than adequate. There's more on this discussion of screen resolution later in the chapter, under *Important units of measurement.*

Although the dot triad and the addressable pixel resolution of the display controller are independent, they need to be considered together. If the addressable pixel resolution is substantially greater than the monitor's resolution, some of the pixels on the screen will be associated with two of the addressed pixels of the controller. The result will be an image that appears blurry or poorly defined and will limit the legibility of small parts of the image, such as small point-size fonts or features in an image. On the other hand, if the addressable pixels from the controller are less than the spatial resolution of the monitor, a coarseness in the raster lines will be evident.

In addition to affecting the quality and legibility of the image, it wastes the bandwidth or data capacity of the monitor. Line width is not synonymous with focus; a large spot can be just as well focused as a small one. For medium-resolution displays (300 to 600 lines) a larger spot would be better suited for meeting the needs of an application needing only low resolution by filling in the points or dots that comprise a character.

The calculated dpi is the theoretical limit or the maximum resolution. However, there's more to the actual visual image resolution than just the calculated physical characteristics of the monitor. The final determination is what the user can see on the screen. One technique that has been successful in finding that number is the modulation transfer function (MTF). It sounds complicated and some people try to make it seem more complex than it is, but it's really a straightforward concept.

In the previous section, we used the notion of line width and dpi to arrive at a measurement of resolution. To understand MTF and how it can help you find the maximum viewable dpi, let's begin with a monochrome display. Suppose the addressable resolution of a monitor's controller was 10 times greater than the monitor could reproduce. Further assume that every pair of pixels for every line consisted of one at maximum white and one at maximum black so that vertical stripes would be formed. What do you think would show up on the screen? If you said "gray," you're right. The monitor and your eye would average the signals from the controller.

Now assume you could adjust the width of the pixels being sent to the monitor with a knob. As you turned the knob, you would eventually hit a point where the pixel size matched the resolution of the monitor and your eye (for a given viewing distance). At that point, you would see discernible stripes of alternating black and white lines. That point would then represent the maximum resolution for the system (of you and all the hardware), and would have been found with an MTF.

The *modulation* in this case is the changing width of the white and black pixels. In all probability, the value, expressed in cycles per inch, which is the same as dpi, would be less than the calculated theoretical maximum value. That's because everything in the chain was involved and each element contributed some degrading factor to the final result. Figure 3-35 shows a typical MTF curve.

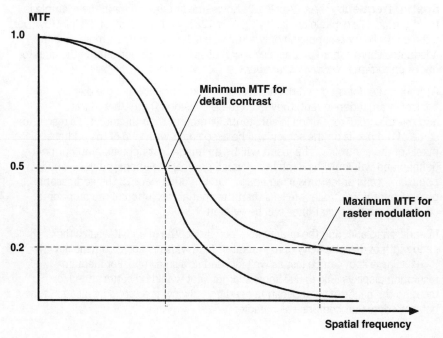

3-35
The most reliable measurement for a monitor's actual displayable resolution is the modulation-transfer function, but it's difficult to administer (requires special test equipment) and can be complicated to calculate. It's usually done by a manufacturer when a monitor is to be qualified.

The modulation value on the vertical axis is the contrast ratio, where the full-scale value (1.0) is equal to the maximum contrast ratio, and the base value (0.0) is where the display has "grayed out." Put another way, MTF is the luminance response to a sinusoidal waveform of constant amplitude and variable spatial frequency as an input to one direction of scan in a display device—MTF measures the capacity (or ability) of the display system to optically (or visually) respond to the input video (or data).

Spatial frequency is the viewer's ability to resolve the frequency of the pattern on the screen. In the above example, if, after finding the setting that allowed you to see the line, you moved away from the screen, you would find that the screen would again become gray. Conversely, if you could discern the lines and then reduce the contrast ratio, you would again reach a point where the screen appears gray. All of these items can be measured with the MTF.

As a general rule of thumb, an MTF of 0.3 at the highest displayable resolution and with the greatest contrast provides about the best image quality for a given display system. Beyond 0.3 MTF, the image will become blurred. This can perhaps be appreciated better if the MTF curve from FIG. 3-35 is superimposed on the contrast-sensitivity function (CSF) curve of the response of the human eye, as shown in FIG. 3-36. The area between the curves is the MTFA and it correlates well with picture quality. It can also be predictive even in situations with reflected ambient light on the screen.

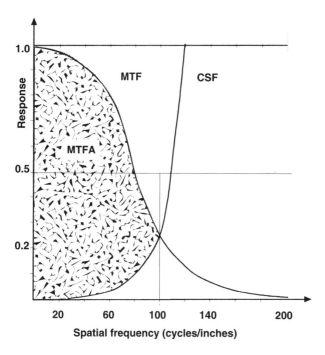

3-36
When the contrast-sensitivity function (CSF) of the human eye is superimposed on the modulation-transfer function (MTF) of the display system, the area between the curves (MTFA) correlates well with picture quality.
Carlo Infante

The use of the MTFA was adopted as part of the ANSI/HSI 100 1988 standard on human factors, based on work later published by Beaton (R. Beaton, "Display Measurements," SID Seminar Lecture Notes, Vol. 2, no. 9.4, 1989). The MTFA was then redefined by Carol Infante (C. Infante, "Numerical Methods for Computing Modulation Transfer-Function Area," *Displays*, April 1991: 80).

Overscan & why	A monitor that overscans has its raster adjusted to the very edges of the available phosphor area (see *Diagonal sizes* under the section *Tube sizes and shapes*). The concept was first used in European TVs. In Europe, TV tubes protrude from their cabinets, slightly exposing the edge of the CRT. In the U.S., TV tubes are encased with a bezel around them so the CRT is slightly inward. It's strictly a matter of taste and culture. The Europeans wanted to get the most display they could; the Americans wanted the tube to look as small as they could make it. (Some elaborate, almost Baroque, bezels within bezels were developed.)

When computer screens were introduced in Europe, users wanted a similar full screen. The first wave of U.S. suppliers ignored the request. However, when European companies like Philips, Siemens, and Thompson began offering such systems, the U.S. and Japanese manufacturers quickly adapted their systems. When they did, they found they needed a little more power from their deflection amplifiers and yokes. Also, issues of edge distortion (which aren't as crucial in a TV with lots of motion images) became more prevalent.

When NEC introduced their FG series monitors (in late 1991) as a replacement for the successful MultiSync, they employed overscanning, which they dubbed FullScan. With it, the monitors filled all the viewable area on the monitor's screen. By mid 1992, most other companies had similar capabilities.

High-performance high-resolution monochrome monitors

In the early to mid '80s, the argument between using color or monochrome displays used to occupy the pages of the leading journals. By 1987, the discussion ended and everyone used color except for DTP and a few image-processing users. Later, it was forecasted that X terminals would follow the PC and workstation evolution, first using monochrome displays and then gradually moving to color. However, instead of it being 90% monochrome and 10% color, it's been more like 60%/40% or 70%/30%. It appears that the time for the movement of color into the X-terminal market will be very much compressed. Does that mean that monochrome monitors are obsolete? Not at all.

Because of the aperture grill and the dot triad, color monitors have a limitation in resolution. Therefore, for very high-resolution, high-quality images, monochrome monitors generally offer a better choice. In applications such as reconnaissance image processing, medical diagnostics, photogrammetry, and document image processing, the monochrome monitor is often preferred. Therefore, users with the most demanding image-quality requirements typically use monochrome CRT systems because they're able to provide larger numbers of resolvable pixels and the smallest spot size. Commercial systems with formats up to 2500×2000 addressable pixels are capable of displaying up to 4 million pixels (allowing for a 25%–30% loss in resolution from deflection distortion and other effects). A 2048×2048 monitor is shown in FIG. 3-53.

Monochrome monitors are typically used in grayscale systems. The resolution of the grayscale can vary from 16 shades to 256 for most systems. Radiologists demand grayscales of 500+ and resolutions of 2048 ×536 (with 4500×4500 desired—see chapter 1, *Applications*). Grayscale systems are rated on their grayscale tracking and have characteristics similar to those illustrated back in FIG. 3-27 (color-tracking chart).

Monochrome monitors use a variety of phosphors, ranging from a white white to yellow white and blue white. The whiteness of a monitor's screen is calibrated in temperature units or Kelvin. The generally accepted standard for the white point has been 6500° Kelvin. Phosphor type P104 has proven to be very popular with monochrome monitors.

High-resolution monochrome monitors are available in a variety of sizes, the most popular being 19, 21, and 24 inches. The 19-inch versions have spot sizes smaller than 0.005 inches in the center, and 24-inch monitors with spot sizes of 0.01 inches (0.25 mm) and an active area of 17.5×12.5 inches can display 1750 pixels per line and 1275 lines×100 dpi. When the 24-inch monitors are used in a two-page display (one of the most popular applications for this type of monitor), they can quite adequately display an 8-point font, and even a 6-point nonserif font (without ascenders and descenders). That makes them ideal for typesetting and desktop publishing.

In the late '80s, a few companies developed ultra high-resolution (UHR) monochrome raster displays. Although these devices were technically successful, they didn't find a large market. Only a few applications, such as DIPS, medial imaging, and newspaper DTP, were able to justify the cost of these UHR displays. MegaScan (now a subsidiary of Advanced Video Products) developed the highest-resolution product, a 300-dpi display system using a 21-inch monochrome monitor. The system could support resolutions of 2560×2048 and 4096×3300. To get that level of resolution with a 72-Hz refresh rate, the display controller (also manufactured by MegaScan) had to have a video bandwidth of 1.5 GHz.

When the standards for TV were being developed, and various compromises were being made, it was concluded that the maximum resolution that could be economically obtained would be 500 scan lines, give or take a few lines. The final number was set at 525. That number provides sufficient quality and resolving power to allow reproduction of images from the studio to the home. Not great, but sufficient.

Why higher resolution?

With the advent of computer displays for photorealism, CAD, and GUIs, it became obvious that the number of lines needed to give good resolution had to be 1,000 or more. This was further supported when HDTV standards were being discussed and the 1100 line model was initially selected.

GUI users need all the resolution they can get to show as much of their workspace as possible. DTP users need to see as small a point-size font as possible. CAD users need to see as much of the drawing as possible at one time and they want the lines to be smooth and unconfusing. Anything that interferes with those goals reduces productivity.

High-resolution (HR) displays greatly increased resolution over the early systems. They also brought color to the display, which made layers and line separation easier to see—but the jaggies were still visible. They cause eye fatigue, make it difficult to see lines that are close or converging, and create strange-looking characters when the font size is small. The incentive for higher resolution has been great and many companies have offered products to satisfy this need.

Just how much resolution is enough is a simple question that has a complicated answer. It involves various parameters, such as application (productivity) requirements, technical obstacles, cost, and the eye's ability to even perceive higher resolution. Yesterday in the PC world, users were satisfied with running one text-based application at a time, which could be compared to the arrangement in FIG. 3-37.

As FIG. 3-37 shows, a user would typically type a letter, work on a spreadsheet, and possibly use a graphics application such as CAD, DTP, or presentation graphics.

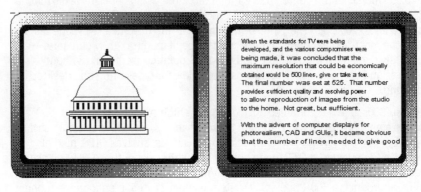

3-37
When just one application is being used, especially if it's a character-based one, a small screen with limited resolution will suffice.

CAD/CAM   **Word processing**

These single applications could be run on an 11-inch monochrome monitor with a Hercules controller quite well. The graphics applications were more demanding and if more than 50% of a user's time was spent on such work, a larger monitor and high-resolution controller were often required. Then GUIs became popular and multiple applications needed to be run on one computer and displayed on one monitor (see FIG. 3-38). This required higher-resolution display controllers and larger monitors. The monitors were typically 15 or 17 inches in diameter, with SuperVGA resolution. And that's the way it's been since the early '90s for PC users.

3-38
When GUIs are used and multiple applications are running, a higher-resolution screen is needed. However, as much screen area as possible is also needed in order to see the most amount of the various applications at the same time as possible.

Many CAD and graphic arts users, as well as workstation users, have opted for 19-inch displays with at least 1024×768 resolution. However, for 17-, 21- and 24-inch displays, 1024×768 is not necessarily the optimal choice.

Visual acuity, the capacity of the eye to resolve details, varies greatly in different regions of the retina. Peripheral regions of the retina have little power to discriminate particulars of form. The precise definition of acuity is given in terms of the reciprocal of the angular distance separating two contours when they are just distinguishable as two. A person with normal acuity would be able to discern two points separated by as little as 1 minute of arc (1') as being distinct. Actually, some eyes have a resolving power of as much as 2' or even 3'. Acuity, however measured, varies with illumination. For example, small print is difficult to discern in dim light and can be read with ease under higher illumination.

Contrast, luminance, and refresh are all related due to the physiology of the eye. As light intensity is increased, more and more rods have their thresholds passed, bringing a greater number into play and thus reducing the average distance between functioning receptors. At a certain point, the cones enter the picture. Vision is now best, and it improves steadily with continued increases in illumination, as is shown in FIG. 3-39.

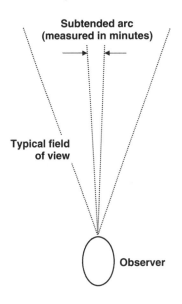

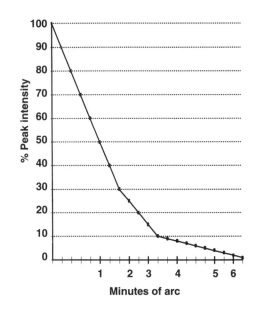

3-39
The ability to see fine detail (such as small print) is aided by brightness. As the chart shows, a person's acuity, which is measured in the ability to resolve two close points, increases with intensity.

Resolution is a term used in a number of specific cases in science to denote the process of separating closely-related forms or entities, or the degree to which they can be discriminated. The term is most frequently used in optics to denote the smallest extension which a magnifying instrument is able to separate or the smallest change in wavelength. It's defined as the ratio of the average wavelength of two spectral lines, which can barely be detected.

For the numerical measurement of resolving power, you must have a fixed statement of what is required for the separation of the two images to be observable. The statement generally accepted is Rayleigh's criterion for resolution: the images of two points are regarded as barely separated when the central maximum of intensity of one of the diffraction patterns falls on the first zero of intensity of the other. Resolving power is stated by giving the value of its minimum angle of resolution. This is the angular separation of two distant points that are barely resolved, according to Rayleigh's criterion (refer to the previous discussion on MTF).

Various researchers have measured the spatial visual acuity or resolving power of the eye. It has been found to range from 1' (one arc minute, sexagesimal measurement of an angle) to 4', depending on illumination level or contrast (refer to FIG. 3- 39). If you've ever squinted at the fine print in a newspaper or phone book, you know your ability to read it is improved when there's more light on the page. The additional light improves contrast and also brings into play the cones of the eye, which are denser and have better acuity than the rods.

This range describes a band of resolution that can be plotted against viewing distance. Such a plot can then be used to determine the necessary resolution for a raster graphics display, as shown in FIG. 3-40.

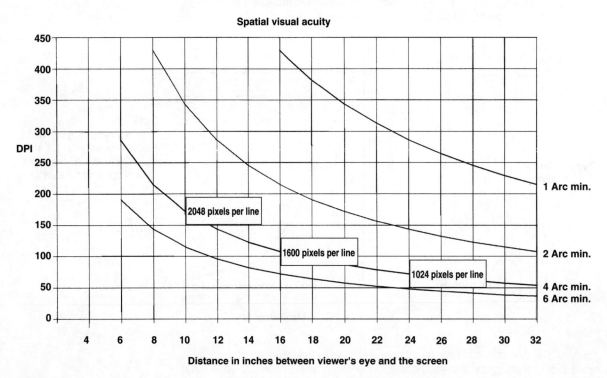

Spatial visual acuity

3-40 *At a normal viewing distance, the average person can see about 150 dpi. This suggests that there's a point where additional resolution won't bring much benefit. The test is easy. Hold a piece of paper up to your screen with 6pt., 8pt., and 10pt. letters and you'll realize what's useful and what isn't.*

As the chart shows, for an average contrast situation (2' to 3'), with a 19-inch monitor (14.25 inches horizontal viewing distance), at a viewing distance of 24 inches (about an arm's length), you can resolve a screen equivalence of between

135 and 170 dpi. Although that might be barely acceptable for desktop publishing using a sharp black-and-white display, it's more acceptable with a CAD drawing program using a color display. One of the reasons for this seemingly strange situation is the resolving power of a color display vs. a monochrome display. Due to the shadow mask in a color display, the dot size is larger and therefore the maximum number of dpi that a 1024, 19-inch color tube can display is 72.

The *stair-step* effect of a diagonal line, known as *aliasing*, is diminished as displayable resolution is increased, but there are limits. Very high-resolution (1600 pixels per line) color monitors typically have a 0.00827-inch (0.21-mm) triad dot size that yields 121 dpi. Working the other way, 121 dpi on a 19-inch screen yields a maximum of 1724 pixels, very close to the 1600 being offered by manufacturers today.

Jaggies

The net result of the shadow mask's dot size is that there's a bit of edge blurring that takes place in a color display. Although that sounds bad, it actually helps because it reduces the first-order effects of the transition from the background color (the screen) to the foreground color (the line)—a form of anti-aliasing. However, this effect does not begin to have a positive influence until the resolution of the color display reaches the theoretical resolution of the screen. It's still possible to see jaggies on a 1600 display, but they're so small that at normal viewing distance they aren't as offensive as they are on lower-resolution screens.

Various attempts have been made to develop an analytical measurement of the amount of operator confusion resulting from a jagged display. Although none have been universally satisfactory (several have been developed for very specific situations) it is well known that the problem exists. Therefore, no quantitative analysis can be made on how much improvement can be realized from higher resolution; it just is.

Eye fatigue   Greater resolution can improve a user's productivity in two ways: first, by showing more of the workspace, image, or drawing (as described previously) and, second, by providing a less fatiguing display. The sharp transitions produced by the jaggies cause the eye to actually over-scan. For example, when a sharply contrasted line is viewed, the eye tends to move (very minutely) back and forth across the edges of the line. This is a normal process; it's how the eye tells the brain that there's a line. However, if that line has noticeable jaggies, the eye scans even more, which can become fatiguing—without the operator really knowing why.

For optimal viewing with minimum eye fatigue, the common recommendation for luminance ratio (display brightness-to-background lighting) is between 1:2 and 1:3.

Eye focusing   Because the brain tries to compensate for illogical shapes and images, it sends focusing signals to the eye when a jagged line is encountered. This causes the eye to constantly (albeit subtly) adjust focus. This is obviously a fatiguing effort. It isn't known how much refocusing over what period of time causes what level of fatigue, but the net effect after a few hours is well known.

Reflections on the face of the monitor can have a similar effect. If a light, window, or some other bright object in the user's environment is reflected on the screen, in addition to impacting the contrast, it will cause eye fatigue. The eye will attempt to focus on the reflection and then the image and back and forth. The focusing and refocusing is subtle and the observer or user is usually not aware of it. However, after a while, the user will become tired and complain of eye strain.

Confusion   When jaggies are created on diagonal lines, an operator can still interpret them as lines (albeit if with annoyance) provided they aren't too close together, they don't cross at a shallow angle, and there aren't too many of them in the same area.

When the lines are close together, it's impossible to tell which line goes where. In the photograph, a radial line pattern is displayed on a VGA screen and a VHR 1600×1200 screen. As can be seen, the center is completely merged and indistinguishable on the VGA display. The VHR display suffers some of the same blending at the center, but is greatly reduced. In fact, even the finest vector display will blend vectors at the center.

Resolution is also a factor in the readability of text. Figure 3-41 illustrates the difference between a VGA screen and a two-page Super Desktop Publishing (SDTP) 1600×1200 screen.

3-41
High resolution helps applications like CAD and desktop publishing obtain greater productivity and less eye strain, as illustrated by this comparison between a SDPT 1600×1200 display (left) and a VGA 640×480 display (right) of the same text.

Anti-aliasing   In the early '80s, edge-filtering techniques were developed that made edges look smooth. This was done by making the intensity of the pixels next to vectors gradually darker the further away they got from the vector. Figure 3-42 shows pixels (black squares) with less intense pixels (gray squares) next to them.

Various techniques have been developed for this type of anti-aliasing that involve hardware and software solutions. In some cases, the technique uses subpixels, which is really just the lowering of the gain or brightness of a pixel (as brightness is lowered, the effective diameter of the pixel is reduced, and is therefore called a *subpixel*). The term implies that more pixels per inch on the screen are being generated, but that isn't correct.

Other techniques involve phase-shifting pixels. This is a time delay, or speedup of pixels, which results in one pixel being slightly superimposed over the edge of the next, or previous pixel. Once again, although these techniques and their nomenclature suggest additional spatial or pixel resolution is being obtained, it isn't. That doesn't diminish the effectiveness of the technique, but it is a criticism

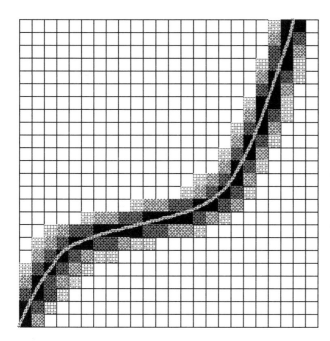

3-42
By shading the edges in an image between the color of the line or edge and the color of the area outside the edge, you can trick the eye into seeing a smoother edge. This anti-aliasing technique tends to make the edges a little wider, but in some situations it's an acceptable trade-off.

of the marketing tactics used to confuse the user (and possibly the competition). In any case, any anti-aliasing techniques used are independent of the monitor.

The next section is where everything will come together—all of the elements that affect visible resolution. So far, I've shown how a monitor's maximum theoretical displayable resolution in dpi is a function of its viewable area and its dot pitch. I've also explained that the displayable resolution is a function of the display controller's addressable range and the monitor's video bandwidth. We've examined the maximum theoretical limitations of the viewer's visual capabilities, as well as the modulation transfer function. And I've explained the importance of eliminating flicker and jaggies.

In that section, I'll develop a measurement and evaluation criterion, the dpi-to-screen size factor (DSF), for the best selection of a monitor with a displayable resolution. In order to tie all this together, however, I must first review a few items and integrate all of the information necessary to arrive at the final conclusion.

Addressable pixel resolution   As the resolution of the display controller increases, the number of pixels sent to the screen should also increase. However, remember, you don't always get what's being sent to the screen by the display controller on the screen because dot-pitch size and monitor size have an impact on the actual displayed resolution.

Viewable screen area   In the section on *Tube sizes and shapes*, I introduced the issue of actual visible area of a monitor. I pointed out that the usable portion of the monitor was about 90% of the advertised amount. TABLE 3-4 shows this relationship for the most popular sizes of monitors.

Displayable resolution   The resulting resolution displayed on the screen is a function of the relationship of the display controller's resolution expressed, in pixels

Important units of measurement

per line, the visible size of the monitor, and the monitor's dot pitch. These aren't linear, as illustrated in FIG. 3-43.

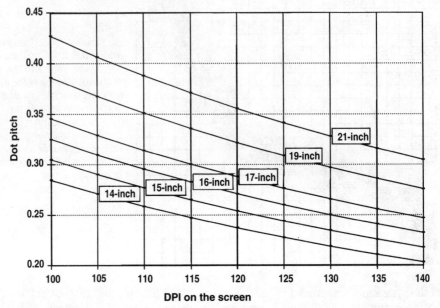

3-43
The dot pitch is the ultimate limit of the display resolution in dpi on the screen, but monitor size and display-controller resolution also impact the displayable resolution.

Application suitability

Although higher resolution makes displaying smaller characters possible, it won't ensure that those characters will be discernible. A SuperVGA display has 56% more resolution than a standard VGA display. The effect of that increase in resolution, when displayed on the same-sized monitor is a reduction of about 20% of the character size. That is equivalent to a two or three point-size reduction in your display, which can make things difficult to see. The only solution to this dilemma is to go to a larger-sized monitor or to sit uncomfortably close to a smaller one.

Using the area information from TABLE 3-4, changing from a 14-inch monitor to a 19-inch monitor is an increase of 125% of the viewable area, more than twice the gain of the resolution, thereby leaving you with a viewing improvement of almost 70% (125 – 56). Going from a 14-inch monitor to a 17-inch increases the viewable area by 65%, which is a net gain from VGA to SuperVGA of almost 10%—and remember, that 10% includes a gain of 56% in resolution. The result is that you'll get 56% more information on the screen and have a 10% enlargement in the size of characters.

Dpi-to-screen-size factor

As the previous information suggests, there are combinations of viewable area and pixel density that provide the best environment. Based on empirical and anecdotal data, you can select a range of factors from the data in TABLE 3-4 that indicates the best relationship between the number of pixels displayed and the viewable area of the monitor. The values are found by dividing the viewable width of the screen (from TABLE 3-4) by the number of pixels per line (from TABLES 8-5 and 8-6). Values between 50 and 80+ are the best dpi-to-screen-size factors, referred to as the DSF. See TABLE 3-8.

Table 3-8
**The DSF indicates the best relationship
between monitor size and displayable pixels.**

Pixels	Lines	Viewable diagonal monitor			Sizes in inches	
		14"	15"	16"	17"	19"
640	480	57	53	50	47	42
800	600	71	67	63	59	53
1024	768	91	85	80	75	67
1280	1024	114	107	100	94	84

On a 19-inch monitor, a display with 1280×1024 resolution produces characters that can be difficult to read. Furthermore, a 15-inch monitor with VGA resolution reaches the limit of "chunkiness" that can be tolerated. Therefore, there's an optimal DSF range for the best viewing conditions, which is between 55 and 80.

Generally speaking, productivity is directly related to an increase in display resolution, relative to the DS factor. The more information a user has on the screen, the less scrolling, zooming, and panning has to be done. The less time a user spends coping with the computer, the more time he or she can spend using it. Studies have proven that whenever a person is interrupted, it takes between 10 and 45 seconds for that person to regain his or her idea or thought process. Simply put, the more you can see comfortably, the more you can do.

Productivity

Productivity is as much related to physical and electronic characteristics as it is to the application and the characteristics of the user. As was discussed in chapter 1, *Applications*, there are three classes of users: casual (who spends four hours or less a day on a single application), professional (who spends five hours or more a day on a single application), and power (who spends eight or more hours a day on a single application). Each of these types of users can also be categorized as having a low budget or an adequate budget. There are also four basic types of applications: general-purpose GUIs (word processing, spreadsheets, and databases), DTP (desktop publishing and presentation, CAD (computer-aided design), and GAI (graphic arts and image processing). DTP, CAD, and GAI users might also use a GUI. Using the data from TABLE 3-9, you can see the best choice for each of these types of users.

Table 3-9
**The best combination of display controller and monitor
is a function of the application, the user type, and the budget.**

User/App	Casual low	Casual adequate	Professional low	Professional adequate	Power low	Power adequate
GUI	640 - 14"	800 - 15"	800 - 15"	1024 - 16"	800 - 17"	1024 - 19"
DTP	640 - 14"	800 - 15"	1024 - 16"	1024 - 17"	1024 - 19"	1280 - 19"
CAD	640 - 14"	800 - 16"	800 - 16"	1024 - 19"	1024 - 19"	1280 - 19"
GAI	640 - 14"	640 - 15"	640 - 15"	800 - 16"	1024 - 16"	1024 - 19"

The general rule might be, "more is better"—more tube resolution, more pixels, more visible area, and more refresh cycles. But as with all things in life, there have to be limits. Most of the "mores" are self-limiting by cost and available technology. The visible area, which relates to the physical size of the monitor, is limited by desk space or viewing distance.

The conclusion, then, is you want the largest DS factor you can get on your desk and in your budget. Figure 3-44 shows the average cost per pixel for a display system. From 1600×1200 to 2048×1536, the cost starts to increase, and from 2048×1536 to 2048×2048, the cost goes up rapidly and significantly.

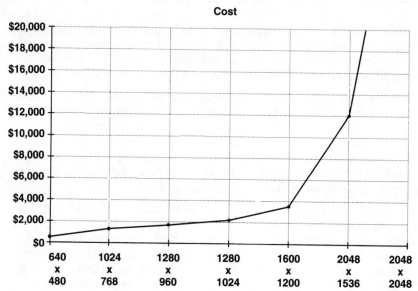

3-44
Since the numbers (pixels, memory, speed, etc.) increase by the product, resolution cost goes up exponentially with resolution. The added cost of faster components and often poorer yield rates also contributes to the price of very high-resolution monitors.

Visible resolution

The number of dots per inch (dpi) on the screen is influenced by monitor size and resolution, as stated earlier. However, even with a very high-resolution display controller, the limiting factor in a monitor's ability to display a high-resolution image can be the dot pitch.

The chart in FIG. 3-45 shows how addressable resolution influences the dpi on the screen for various sizes of monitors, and what the minimum dot pitch is necessary to support that resolution.

Most monitor manufacturers specify bandwidth on their data sheets (some call it *video dot rate* or *dot clock*). It's primarily influenced by the monitor's video amplifier, which takes the low-voltage output of the controller, increases it to a higher voltage, and directly drives the electron gun of the CRT.

The bandwidth of the monitor has to be equal to or greater than the display controller to ensure clarity. A display controller with a 1280×1024 addressable resolution and a refresh rate of 60 Hz typically operates at 110 MHz. Therefore, any monitor connected to it has to have 110 or greater bandwidth. As FIG. 3-46 shows, the bandwidth increases at a greater amount as the resolution increases.

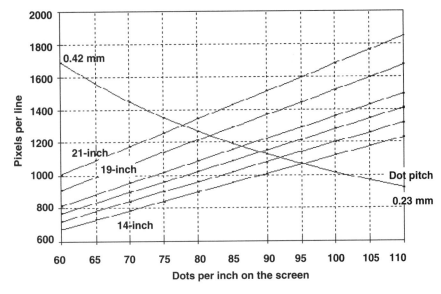

3-45
The dot pitch is the ultimate limit of dpi on the screen for a given monitor size. However, there is a nonlinear relationship between monitor size, dots per inch on the screen, and dot pitch.

Bandwidth vs. refresh rate per resolution

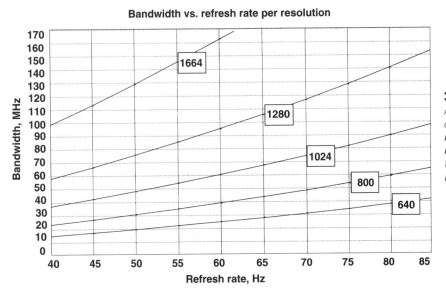

3-46
As resolution or refresh rate are increased, bandwidth must also increase. The relationship between the three parameters is not linear.

When the video bandwidth of the monitor is insufficient for the signal being sent to it, there's a blurring of the image and diminishing of luminance. The blurring or deformations are most noticeable at edges of high contrast, such as white letters on a black background (or vice versa) in the raster direction. Low-contrast edges show little blurring.

Monitors and controllers are available with 2048×1536 and higher resolution. They're still expensive, however, and not in full-volume production. The VHR and UHR monitors have 0.21-mm shadow masks, which limits the resolution that can actually be displayed. There have been developmental 0.17-mm (0.00669 of an inch)

What's coming

shadow masks. They would have a theoretical resolution limitation of 2159 pixel lines. Supporting a mask that fine in a 19-inch tube at the temperatures generated by such high voltages and sweep rates is not a trivial task. Since the world is just moving toward 1600, it will probably take two to three years of both market and technical development before you can have a 2000×1500 display on your desk.

Several years ago, a couple of companies (Metheus and Raytheon) developed a 2048×2048 (2K×2K) controller and a 24-inch square monitor in response to an FAA requirement. The project didn't get funded as quickly as originally anticipated and those products remained engineering prototypes. Today, more companies claim to have a 2K×2K controller, and there have been several more monitor announcements. However, these systems are rather expensive and won't be available for desktop systems for several years.

Emissive displays

The quest for the flat-panel CRT has been with us since the idea of a TV wall display was first suggested in the mid '50s. The current LCD technologies can't quite do the job, although they continue to improve. However, the attributes of the CRT such as full color, high luminance, and no off-angle loss of image are still highly desirable.

These emissive displays are also known as *microtip displays* or *microtip fluorescent displays* (MFDs). The idea for such devices, which use sharp, small, metal cones, was first proposed by C.A. Spindt in 1976, and even earlier versions were proposed by H. Kanter in 1962. In 1986, a flat-panel CRT with an array of metal field-emitter tips for cathodes was introduced by LETI-DOPT-SCMM of Grenoble, France. Although the concept isn't new, recent innovations have allowed field emitters to demonstrate impressive practical designs. Designs have been demonstrated using sharp-point cold cathodes and thin-film cold-cathode emitters. The thin-film technique consists of an array of closely spaced needles that are created on a semiconductor surface, as illustrated in FIG. 3-47.

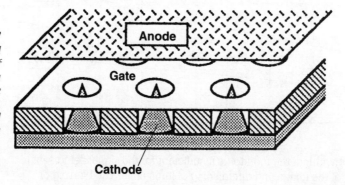

3-47
Field-emission flat-panel displays employ a matrix of micron-sized emitter tips in close proximity to an anode that, like a conventional CRT, holds a phosphor and is excited by an electron stream.

The use of cold cathodes offers advantages over hot cathodes in low-power applications and where geometry makes hot cathodes inconvenient. Large-area cold cathodes have been prepared using multiple field-emission devices. Because they're a cathode and generate an electron emission, they're packaged in thin vacuum packages. There's a phosphorus-coated screen that illuminates when the electrons strike it. Due to their size, they operate with relatively low voltages of 80 to 100 volts. Many descriptions have been made about the concept of such a display. Recent technological developments have made it possible to obtain reasonable yields and good reliability. However, addressing hundreds of thousands and even millions of cathodes is still in development. For more information on MFDs, see chapter 4, *Flat-panel displays*.

There are four large monitor sizes that have become popular in the last few years for CAD, DTP, and ATC applications: 21- and 24-inch monochrome, 20-inch square color, 25- to 27-inch color, and HDTV displays. The large, high-resolution monochrome monitors were discussed in the previous section on *High-performance high-resolution monochrome monitors*.

Large-screen display systems

Developed initially for air-traffic control (ATC) applications, Sony produced a 20-inch square monitor that has been adapted for other applications, including medical imaging, C3I (command, control, communications, and intelligence), and CAD, and is shown in FIG. C-26. Designated the *data display monitor*, the DDM 20/20 uses the Trinitron tube and offers a viewable area of 19.6×19.6 inches. The minimum resolvable screen line width (equivalent to spot size) is 0.046 inches (1.17 mm). As discussed in the section *Monitor resolution*, it yields a maximum displayable resolution of 426 points across the 19.6-inch screen. Assuming an average pixel-to-line-width ratio of 1.5:1, that yields a maximum addressable resolution of 724×724, yet the monitor is advertised as providing a 2048×2048 addressable resolution. As the photograph in FIG. 3-48 shows, much more of an image can be seen at the same or greater resolution than on a conventional 19-inch 3:4 monitor. There are several controllers for PCs and workstations that can drive a 2K×2K display.

Barco Chromatics

3-48
27-inch tubes offer a large viewing area of 21.25×15.98 inches for an actual visible diagonal of 26.5 inches. With a 0.29 dot pitch and a 300-MHz bandwidth capability, they're capable of being driven by 2560×2048, 2048×2048, and 2048×1536 display controllers. 27-inch monitors are offered in three aspect ratios: 5:4, 1:1, and 4:3.

Zenith has also developed a 22-inch version of the FTM monitor for the U.S. military. Its antiglare flat face, high luminance, and ruggedness makes it a useful display for field applications like oil rigs and land vehicles. The company has also announced the development of a 35-inch version of the FTM.

The 25- to 27-inch high-resolution color monitors

A few companies (Barco, Conrac, Intergraph, and Orwin) are offering 25- and 27-inch color monitors for applications that have been primarily for C3I, CAD, GIS, and ATC (see FIG. 3-48). Panasonic is the primary supplier of the 27-inch tubes with a 0.29 dot pitch, a 300-MHz bandwidth capability (just the tube) and a viewable area of 21.25×15.98 inches for an actual visible diagonal of 26.5 inches—a large viewing area. The monitors are offered in three aspect ratios (5:4, 1:1, and 4:3), and are capable of being driven by 2560×2048, 2048×2048, and 2048×1536 display controllers. Panasonic also makes a 0.37-mm version with 150-MHz bandwidth that can be driven by a 1280×1024 controller.

A 24-inch monitor can typically provide a 17.5×12.75-inch viewable area. That is large enough to display two full-size pages (either American 8.5×11, legal, or European A4). Super high-resolution monochrome monitors are extremely effective in this range.

HDTV monitors

As explained earlier in this chapter, HDTV tubes are much wider than they are tall, with an aspect ratio of 16:9 (refer back to FIG. 3-16). Designed for TV applications, they have a bandwidth of 30 to 50 MHz and a horizontal scan rate of 33.75 KHz. There are two basic models of HDTV monitors, which have been categorized as *broadcast* and *consumer*. The broadcast model is a 28-inch viewable, 90° deflection CRT with a 0.35 dot triad and 1.14-mm spot size, a 41-fL brightness and a 1000 line-resolution capability. The consumer model has a 34-inch viewable screen with a 110° deflection CRT, 0.48-mm dot triad, and 1.41-mm spot size, 160-fL brightness, and a resolution capability of 800 lines. Two examples of HDTV monitors are shown in FIG. C-27.

The first systems to use HDTV displays for nonTV applications were CAD systems and prepress systems, such as the Quantel Graphics Paintbox. The Paintbox uses a 28-inch monitor and has an enormous amount of RAM (200Mb), which allows an image to be stored with 5400×3700 pixels.

The larger, high-resolution monitors provide more screen real estate. The actual area of the large monitors goes up rapidly. When users run multiple applications on an average screen, they can have separate windows but have difficulty reading the contents of the windows.

The next stage of evolution was for users to acquire one of the larger monitors mentioned previously. With larger monitors, they can see multiple applications and read the contents of the windows, as illustrated in FIG. 3-49. However, although they provide more screen real estate, they're still rather expensive. Therefore, only power users and professional users with demanding applications have been able to justify larger monitors.

Smaller might be better

With the 15-inch flat-square monitor, you get the same viewing size as a 16-inch round-corner monitor. Furthermore, it has a footprint similar to and is priced pretty close to a 14-inch round-corner model. As a result, the 17-inch flat-square monitors offer serious competition to the large 19-inch round-corner monitors in the PC, workstation, and X-terminal markets.

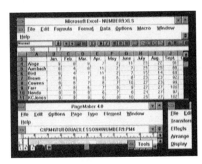

640 x 480 Monitor

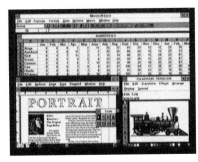

1,024 x 768 Monitor

1,280 x 1,024 Monitor

Number Nine Computer Corp.

3-49
The larger the monitor, the more of the application(s) can be seen. This is referred to as screen real estate, and is very important when multiple applications need to be viewed at the same time.

The answer will vary from user to user and application to application, meaning there will be no "best choice." The DS factor will help in most situations, but there will always be choices made for obscure or subjective reasons.

Signals sent to the monitor from the display controller can be quite varied. Although the connector arrangement might change, there are two basic types of signal configurations: composite and a separate horizontal and vertical sync. Some monitors have a small *personality board* mounted directly inside the back panel. It's typically the only board that must be changed to make a monitor compatible with different computers or interfaces. The external data connectors are mounted directly on the board and are attached to an individualized plate on the back panel—an approach similar to that used in the IBM PC and the Macintosh II. The personality board converts input signals, which vary widely from computer to computer, to a standard set of internal monitor signals.

Input signals

The primary standards, which apply to both computer and TV systems, were developed by the Electronic Industries Association (EIA), formerly the Radio-Electronic-Television Manufacturers' Association (RETMA). They were originally developed for monochrome systems and have been extended to the individual red, green, and blue signals used by color monitors. The basic video-signal standards are RS-170, RS-330, RS-343, RS-412, and RS-422. They differ in voltage levels and synchronization organization.

Composite   A composite signal contains all the video-luminance information, as well as synchronization information for the horizontal and vertical sweep. The components of a composite signal are listed in the following sections.

Display signal   The primary display or image signal, commonly referred to as the *video signal*, is the largest part (on a time-per-line basis) of the composite signal. It's measured (for TV purposes) in IRE units, based on a standard that was developed in 1958 by the IRE (which is now IEEE standard 205) and reaffirmed in 1972. This standard defines the levels as +100 IRE units for white, the blanking level at 0.0 IRE units, and the sync-tip level at −40 IRE units. Thus, the peak-to-peak level of a composite video signal, extending from sync-tip to white level, is 140 IRE units, as illustrated in FIG. 3-50.

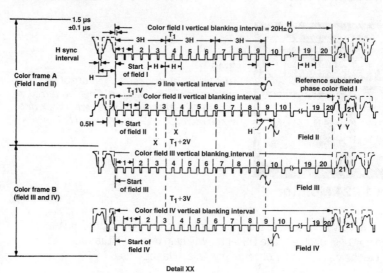

3-50
The composite video waveform is specified in IRE units and in voltage values between −0.268 and 0.714, ±0.1 V, where the 0.714 V is the reference white level and 0.34 V is the blanking level, but not the black level. One IRE unit is equal to 0.00714 volts.
EIA

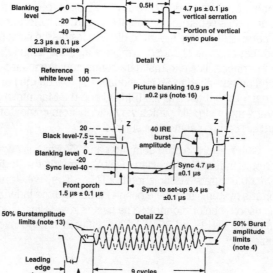

The range between the reference white and black levels, expressed in IRE units, is 92.5 IRE or 0.66 V. Some display-controller manufacturers don't follow this specification as rigorously as others. In order to get a slightly brighter display, they'll drive the monitor's input with a voltage that is 10% to 20% beyond EIA specifications. This won't hurt the input of the monitor's video amplifier but usually results in poor color tracking and smearing. This is due to the problem of driving the input amplifier into saturation.

Sync signal   The composite signal contains a vertical and a horizontal synchronization signal. As discussed in the section *Deflection amplifiers and the raster scan*, earlier in this chapter, there will be n times as many horizontal sync signals as there are vertical signals, where n depends on how many lines are being displayed and if the display is interlaced or noninterlaced. The horizontal-sync signal is a negative pulse that's –40 IRE units below the blanking-level signal. If the blanking-level signal is set to 0.0 V, then the horizontal-sync pulse will be at –0.284 V. Within the horizontal sync signal, there are three additional components (refer to FIG. 3-50): front porch, back porch, and the sync-tip pulse.

Front porch   When one scan line is completed, the video signal is blanked. The amount of time between the time it's blanked and the time the sync-tip pulse starts is the *front porch*. The front-porch timing will be different for various monitor types, but it's specified by EIA standards for various TV, closed-circuit TV, and high-performance monitors. Not all of these standards apply to computer monitors. The front porch is used by the monitor to stabilize the deflection amplifiers and flyback-voltage power supply.

Sync-tip pulse   A synchronization signal is needed to reset the sweep voltage and horizontal deflection amplifier and start the scan line again (at the right edge of the monitor). The *sync-tip pulse* is used for that signal.

Back porch   Before a scan line can be started, the monitor needs time to get amplifiers and power suppliers stabilized. That startup time is the time from when the sync-tip pulse ends and the video signal begins, and is known as the *back porch*.

There are various EIA specifications (e.g., RS-412, RS-343, and RS-170) that are used to define the voltage levels and timing for the composite sync signal. All of these specifications were for monochrome TV monitors. When color was introduced and decoded from the luminance and chroma values into red, blue, and green components, the green signal was chosen to carry the composite sync signal. This was referred to as "sync on green." Over the years, that distinction has been lost and it's common today, when dealing with composite color (RGB) signals, to find sync on all colors. If a monitor is expecting composite sync or separate sync, and doesn't receive it, typically the screen will be black. Some monitors will give a rolling or diagonally distorted image, indicating that sync is missing (see the following section on *Controls*).

When a monitor uses a video signal in composite format, sync stripping and dc black-level restore functions are performed. If the polarity of either sync is incorrect for the monitor, its polarity is inverted before further processing. This is extra work for a monitor and costs can be reduced if separate sync and video signal inputs are used.

Separate video & sync

It's more economical and logical to not use composite signals. There's also the possibility of a better-quality video signal when synchronization and video are separated. This is because the fast-rising signal, the edge of the sync-tip, can in some cases create harmonics that can be seen in the image.

Display signal   The display signal for a separate video-input signal is shown in FIG. 3-50, which looks very similar to the one shown FIG. 3-51, but with the synchronization removed. The basic difference in the blanking time (0.0 volts) is the combined time of the front and back porch plus the total time of the sync-tip. All three signals in a color system, RGB, will have the same characteristics.

3-51

The display signal for a separate video-input signal shown in Fig. 3-50, but with the synchronization removed.
Brooktree Corp.

Sync disabled		Sync enabled	
MA	V	MA	V
19.05	0.714	26.67	1.000
1.44	0.054	9.05	0.340
0.00	0.000	7.62	0.286
		0.00	0.000

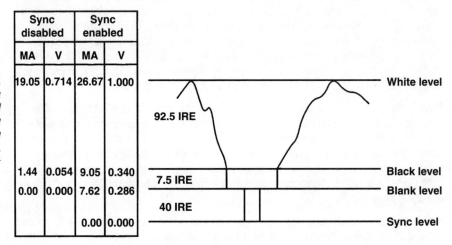

White level

92.5 IRE

Black level

7.5 IRE

Blank level

40 IRE

Sync level

Sync signal   When a separate sync signal is supplied to a monitor from the display controller, it doesn't have a front and back porch; it's just a TTL signal, usually negative going. The monitor then internally generates the necessary delays and setup times to stabilize the deflection amplifiers and flyback power supply. However, the TTL sync signal might not be as long as required for the monitor. Therefore, unless the monitor has a standard resolution and refresh frequency (e.g., a Macintosh or VGA), it will have horizontal and vertical blanking-time specifications. These timings influence the bandwidth and refresh time of the system (refer to the section on *Scan rates*, earlier in this chapter.

Controls & connectors

The early computer monitors had controls similar to TV sets and monitors. As technology improved and manufacturers gained experience with user needs, the strategy of control placement, access, and connector types changed. Although there are no standards, some of the most common approaches are described in this section.

Controls   Some monitors are equipped with no controls or only two controls: power and brightness. These are typically fixed-frequency monitors, often monochromatic, usually employed in specialized applications, and sold at very low cost. The controls on a monitor can be found on the front (typically under the display), the side (usually at the top and on the right side), on the rear (usually at the bottom, and in addition to other side- or front-mounted controls), or inside. Sometimes it can be a challenge just to find the power control. The next level of controls is contrast, and then position, geometry, and color controls. The following is a list of the more common controls and some of the newer microprocessor controls found on monitors.

Image position   Horizontal- and vertical-position controls are well known by most users, but are seldom used. When a monitor is capable of operating at various display resolutions and refresh rates (commonly known as a *mulitsync* or *auto-sync*), maintaining the image in the center of the screen and at full size is difficult. Therefore, two more controls are added: horizontal and vertical positioning (also called *horizontal* and *vertical centering*).

Geometry & stability control   In addition to positioning controls, it's usually necessary to control the geometry of the display. Therefore, there are two more controls: width and height (also called *horizontal* and *vertical sizing*). These controls allow the stretching (or shrinking) of the image area to fill the screen. However, in some systems, when the vertical or horizontal size is changed it doesn't change linearly. In the case of the vertical control, it results in a distortion that makes the top or bottom look squeezed. To compensate for that another control, vertical linearity, is added. Then the two are adjusted against each other with a test pattern on the screen to get the image balanced geometrically.

Monitors also have to have an adjustment for the oscillators that control the sync timing for horizontal and vertical scanning. When one of these oscillators shifts in frequency (also called *drifting*), the image will roll vertically, turn into a series of diagonal lines, or both. You can correct these conditions with the horizontal and vertical hold controls (just like your old TV used to have). However, in some cases, if the sync signal from the display controller isn't correct, you'll see such rolling or diagonal lines.

Modern monitors have a microprocessor that allows adjustment of all of these functions, and more. In *The CRT* section earlier in this chapter, effects such as pincushioning, parallelogram, and trapezoidal distortions are discussed. Modern auto-sync monitors can accept almost any signal produced by display controllers regardless of whether it's from a PC, Macintosh, or workstation. However, to do that they need very flexible and fine control over all the positioning and geometry controls. These microprocessor-based monitors allow adjustment of all the positioning, sizing, linearity, and geometry controls. They also have sufficient memory to store individual settings for 1, 2, or as many as 32 different display controllers, resolutions, and refresh rates.

Color & other controls   A common control found on many monitors is a degauss button. Although most modern monitors have automatic degaussing, some also offer a button. Color gain for the RGB amplifiers is almost always available only on the inside of the monitor; it isn't an end-user control. The same is true for the convergence, high-voltage adjustment, horizontal phasing, vertical trap, gain (white ref), and black-reference controls.

In the early '90s, companies like Mitsubishi, NANO, and NEC introduced color-adjustment capabilities for the end user through the monitor's microprocessor. This enabled the user to place a color against the screen and then adjust the red, green, and blue values so that the screen's rendition of a color matched the photo of a banana or a women's lipstick, for example. The color values could then be stored and recalled later. The next stage was to allow color points to be calibrated and stored. These techniques compete with but don't replace a true-color calibration system with feedback control. Refer to chapter 2 for more on color systems.

Connectors & input impedances   Monitors are offered with almost as many connector possibilities and combinations as controls. With only one or two exceptions, the connectors are on the back panel. The exceptions are connectors on the side or in the front. A few monitors are provided with an attached cable. The following is a list of the most popular choices of monitor connectors:

❑ BNC (1, 3, 4, or 5)
❑ 9-pin D type
❑ 15-pin Dsub (Macintosh)
❑ 15-pin miniDsub (IBM)
❑ BNC feed-through (daisy-chain connectors)
❑ Internal PC card edge
❑ RCA phono jack
❑ RG-59U or RG-6U coax connector

Some monitors have both a Dsub connector and BNC connectors. This allows the monitor to be used with whatever type of cable is supplied with the display controller. When a monitor has both types of input, a switch, usually on the front panel, is provided for selection. This also allows the monitor to be connected to two sources. In some PC systems where there's a VGA display controller and a coprocessor-based display controller, the monitor can be connected to both and switched back and forth.

The most common input impedance for a monitor is 75 ohms (75 Ω). Unless otherwise specified, that will be the monitor's input impedance. Some monitors have a small switch (usually a slide switch) that can be used to select either normal 75-Ω input, or a 3-kΩ.input. The 3-kΩ input is used when the signal going to the monitor is going to be daisy-chained to another monitor. Either a T-type connector is used or the monitor will have an input and an output BNC connector. The last monitor in the chain has to have its input set to 75 Ω.

The only other connector you might find on the rear of the monitor is the power connector. A few low-cost monitors have the power cable attached to the monitor.

Ergonomics, safety,& power

In addition to all the design considerations in getting a monitor to put an image on the screen, there are also health, comfort, and power-usage issues.

Ergonomics

In the previous sections of this chapter, I've discussed the importance of flicker reduction and focus, and how they can affect you. Prolonged exposure or viewing an image that has a fuzzy focus, poor contrast, or too much flicker will create eye fatigue and can, in extreme cases, cause headaches and even nausea. These are some of the ergonomic issues you have to consider when evaluating a monitor. Reflections from windows, lamps, desktops, and even other monitors can be equally distressing to the eyes, causing them to constantly refocus between the image and the reflections. When monitors are placed too close to each other, or too close to another power source, the image will beat or jitter, creating an apparent flicker. Even vibrations from cooling fans in nearby equipment can create minute physical vibrations or sympathetic resonances in the CRT neck, which will modulate the image. All of these factors can have a negative impact on your eyes and affect your comfort and concentration.

Monitor manufacturers try to minimize these effects through a variety of ways:

Flicker   This is primarily a function of the display controller. The monitor has to have an adequate vertical scan rate to accept the refresh rate or the image will flicker. If a display controller can refresh at 85 Hz, the monitor should have at least an 85-Hz (preferably 90) vertical scan-rate capability.

Focus   This is a function of power-supply stability, gun construction, sweep-signal geometry (i.e., s curve), and yoke design. Most of today's monitors offer good to excellent focus capabilities. However, with time, circuits can age and focus will deteriorate. In some monitors, you can make adjustments to restore the focus.

Contrast   Having a black screen and a powerful high-voltage system that can provide good brightness will provide the best contrast. Good contrast helps the eye focus and aids productivity.

Reflections   Highly polished glass and curved faces are the major contributors, from the monitor side, to reflections. Antireflective monitor screens are offered that have a diffused surface. They break down the reflected light and scatter it so the user doesn't see a clear image of the offending source. Some monitors are provided with a special optical filter that's bonded to the face of the tube to eliminate glare. The optical filters are better for high-resolution screens because diffused (etched) screens blur fine points and lines.

Jitter   Monitors use very sensitive circuitry to accomplish their tasks. They are, by design, magnetically sensitive devices. Therefore, if a strong magnetic field, such as the type produced by a computer or another monitor's power supply, is placed too close to your monitor, there's a good probability that it will jitter. Monitor manufacturers try to shield the monitor, but effective magnetic shields are very expensive and very few commercial monitors have them. Therefore, your best solution is to move either your monitor of the offending source.

Vibration   The primary solutions for this problem are to move the monitor, shock-mount it, or remove the source of the vibration.

Ergonomics were once thought to be trivial and a cause of unnecessary expense. However, organizations have found that improved productivity and reduced medical claims far outweigh any additional costs. Also, due to user demand, all monitor manufacturers provide such features (with a few exceptions) and so the cost arguments have all but disappeared.

Safety

In the mid 1980s, users in Europe and then the U.S. became concerned about the possibility of health hazards due to the various types of radiation produced by a monitor. This was partially due to two reasons. First, it was known that the CRT and its high-voltage power supply were capable of generating x-rays. Secondly, it became clear that there was a link between too much exposure to x-rays and the development of cancer. This was dealt with by U.S., European, and Japanese government agencies and, in 1971, the U.S. government passed the Radiation

Control for Health and Safety Act (21 CFR 1020.10). As a result, monitors are shielded using lead (in the CRT's glass and flashings on the case). The results are that x-rays from monitors are virtually undetectable from normal background radiation. So much for x-rays.

However, other types of electromagnetic radiation still emanated from monitors. X-rays are defined as ionizing radiation, whereas lower-frequency electromagnetic emissions are known as nonionizing radiation. Low-frequency nonionizing electromagnetic radiation, or LF-EMR, in the 30,000- to 40,000-Hz range is intrinsically generated by a monitor. This spectrum is subdivided into two segments: very low frequency (2,000 to 40,000 Hz), or VLF, and extremely low frequency (30 to 300 Hz), or ELF. The LF-EMR and VLF ranges are generated by the sweep horizontal circuits, and the ELF is generated by the power lines (mains) and the refresh rates of the monitor.

In the early 1980s, a lot of concern was expressed by residents of houses that were close to high-voltage power lines, and workers (or their representatives) who used monitors. It was widely suspected that LF-EMR could cause permanent damage to cell membranes, cause chromosomal defects, alter bone growth, and affect the endothelial cells of the eye. Studies were conducted throughout the 1980s at John Hopkins, Kaiser Permanente, the EPA, and other agencies and research centers. The studies and subsequent reports were often conflicting, resulting in a confused user base and regulatory agencies.

In 1987, the Swedish National Board for Metrology and Testing (MPR) established recommendations for maximum electromagnetic emissions from computer displays. The standards were updated in 1990 and designated as MRPII. MRPII recommends field-strength levels of no more than 50 nanoTeslas (nTs) per second at .3 m in front of the screen, and a maximum of 25 mTs/sec. at .5 m around the screen.

The MRPII standards also specify the electrostatic field strength generated from the surface static charge built up on the monitor's screen. In addition to causing annoying discharges when you touch the screen, the static charge also attracts dust and pollen. That concentration and attraction can aggravate conditions for people with allergies, as well as eye irritations. The maximum electrostatic charge allowed by the MRPII is 500 V. Most modern monitors meet or exceed the MRPII requirements.

Power In 1992, VESA established guidelines for power management in monitors. In the U.S., the EPA established certification of power-efficient devices. The desire to reduce power consumption, especially when a system isn't being used, has become an important issue.

VESA's general guidelines are to reduce the monitor's power consumption to 80% with the use of screen-saver programs. Typically, the user can set the period of inactivity (no mouse or keyboard input) for the initiation of the screen-saver utility. After three minutes of operation by the screen saver, stage one of the power-save mode goes into operation, which reduces the monitor's power consumption to 10%. Stage one's period can last up to 60 minutes (set by the user), and then the monitor switches into stage two, where the power consumption is only 7%.

Since most information workers leave their computer turned on while taking breaks, attending meetings, or going to lunch, power-saving functions, if installed on all monitors, could make a sizable contribution to energy conservation.

Monitors are far more complex than most people think. As bandwidth, refresh rate, and displayable-resolution requirements increase, their complexity grows. Because a monitor can be enhanced with ever higher resolution, brightness, size, and acuity, the life of the product is enhanced as well. Although flat-panel displays are also improving, it will be a long time, and some people believe it might be never, before a flat-panel display can replace a monitor.

Summary

It's true that, if you compare the way transistors replaced vacuum tubes and integrated circuits replaced discrete transistors, the death of the CRT is long overdue. Part of the reason it hasn't happened is because computer users want as large and bright a display as budget and space will permit. So far, CRT technology has been able to meet the demand. Probably the best candidate for the actual replacement of the CRT is the field-emission display. It offers the promise of a flat, thin profile, unlimited resolution, brightness, and producibility. Flat-panel displays, however, already hold an important place in the market and shouldn't be ignored. The next chapter covers these interesting devices.

Refer to TABLE 3-10 for conversions. I know we're all supposed to know this by now, but I still have to look some of these things up from time to time, so you might find this list helpful too.

Table 3-10
Monitor specifications are expressed in various units and not all conversions are well known. This table should help.

From	To get	Multiply by
1 mm	inches	0.03937
inches	centimeters	2.54
10 mm	inches	0.3937
inches	millimeters	25.40
10 mm	centimeters	0.1
cm	millimeters	10
lamberts	candela/sq in	2.054
lumens/sq ft	foot-candles	1
lux	lumens/sq ft	0.0929
lumens/sq ft	lux	10.764
meters	mm.	1000
meter	mm.	0.001
IRE units	volts	0.00714
Font points	inches	:72

4 *Flat-panel displays*

As you know, we now live in the information age. And if you've read some of the previous chapters, you also know that the easiest way you acquire information is with your eyes—which makes your computer's display a vital part of your system.

The simple readouts of original computers were replaced by alphanumeric CRT displays. Now many of the alphanumeric displays have been replaced by multiple windows of information containing graphics, video, and interactive menus and controls, as well as typical alphanumerics.

Because of the emphasis on multimedia, CAD, and HDTV, displays must be larger, provide better contrast and color, and have higher resolutions. It's also essential that they be ergonomically and aesthetically pleasing to the operator. Thus, the appropriate combination of features provides the best display image for your applications and, like everything else discussed in this book, one size does *not* fit all.

Displays are categorized as two types: light-source, or emissive displays, and light-valve displays. CRTs are light-source displays because they generate the light that forms an image by selectively lighting the display's pixels. LCDs are light-valve displays; their pixels selectively transmit or block ambient lighting or backlighting to form an image. (Please note that, in terms of color, both types are transmitive.)

Flat-panel displays (FPDs) are used for a number of applications, initially and primarily for laptop, notebook, and palmtop computer markets. Manufacturers are also using other kinds of FPDs (e.g., plasma, electroluminescent, and vacuum-fluorescent displays) in other applications.

This chapter will examine some of the most popular and interesting flat-panel displays. Some of the terminology might become confusing because of the acronyms. My first impulse was to avoid all use of them, but I decided against it because (unfortunately) that is the way these things are represented. There is a list of acronyms used in this chapter at the end of the chapter. These terms are also contained in a list of acronyms at the end of the main glossary, at the end of the book.

CRTs forever (maybe)

CRTs are still the most prevalent display technology and will continue to be so for the next decade. Millions of TV sets, computers, and workstations throughout the world have CRT displays. In 1991, 49.19 million CRTs were manufactured in Japan. Included in this figure are 16.7 million high-resolution tubes. TV tubes accounted for 54% and display tubes for 41%. Other kinds of tubes accounted for 5%.

A relatively large proportion of CRT production is for TV use. However, because the production base for TV CRTs has shifted to other countries, the ratio of Japanese-made products decreased until 1992, when the domestic production of CRTs for display began to grow in amount and value. CRTs are the standard that newer technologies are compared to. They offer brightness, contrast, colors, resolution, and reliability, as well as a wide viewing angle—all at a low cost. No other technology for workstation-sized displays is competitive in both price and performance.

The CRT has maintained its steady market position and renewed user interest through technological innovations such as high definition, a large screen, a flat face, superb display quality, and an excellent cost-to-performance ratio. Manufacturers will develop the technologies needed to enhance basic CRT performance, such as improvement of the electron gun and the deflection yoke and the use of the wide-band video circuit. Nonglare and antistatic technology will improve the working environments for CRT users.

The competition between CRTs and the flat LCDs and plasma display devices (PDPs) is keen. However, as a typical electronic display device, the CRT offers superior image quality and a better price, and displays more information than flat displays. Many users connect an external CRT to a notebook PC. CRT makers appear ready to cooperate with flat-display makers in expanding the demand.

Nevertheless, CRTs take up a lot of space. Their depth is roughly equal to their screens' diagonal dimension. They're also heavy and consume considerable power. They produce x-rays and low-frequency magnetic fields that are suspected of causing health hazards for computer operators. FPDs are thinner, lighter, use less power, and produce no x-rays or magnetic fields.

Unlike the CRT, the flat-panel display represented by the LCD will adapt to new applications. Applied products continuously emerge featuring thin designs, low weight, low-voltage drives, and low power consumption. The growing number of electronic household appliances using microcomputers has accelerated the demand for flat displays. Potential demand has been stimulated as new electronic appliances and a large number of portable appliances are being developed.

The quest for picture resolution on a flat-panel screen is an ongoing challenge. The technology has been changing from year to year, and what looks like the ultimate answer this year (in terms of speed, resolution, yield, etc.) could be replaced next year. It is, to say the least, a dynamic field.

There has been heightened activity among several candidate technologies that are vying for a crucial mass market. Some of the best known or most popular FPDs are:

- Liquid-crystal displays (LCD)
  Passive matrix (PM-LCD)
  Twisted nematic (TN-LCD)
  Supertwisted nematic (STN-LCD)
  Double supertwisted nematic (DSTN-LCD)
  Film-compensated supertwisted nematic (FSTN-LCD)
  Triple supertwisted nematic (TSTN-LCD)
- Active-addressed passive liquid-crystal displays
  Active matrix (AM-LCD)
  Thin-film transistor (TFT-LCD, or AM-TFT, and TFT-LC)
  Polymer-dispersed liquid crystal
  Metal-insulator metal (MIM)
  Double-diode active matrix (AM-LCDs)
  Plasma-addressed liquid crystal (PALC)
- Ferroelectric LCDs (FLCDs)
  Surface-stabilized ferroelectric liquid-crystal display (SSF-LCD)
- Electroluminescent
  AC thin-film electroluminescent (AC-TFEL)
  Active-matrix electroluminescent (AMEL)
  DC electroluminescent (DCEL)
  AC thin-film electroluminescent (AC-TFEL)
- Plasma displays (PDP)
  AC plasma-display panels (AC-PDPs)
- Field-emission displays (FEDs)
  Microtip fluorescent display (MFD)
- Light-emitting diodes (LEDs)
- Vacuum-fluorescent displays (VFDs)

We'll look at these main technologies as well as their predecessors in the following sections.

Flat-panel displays, or FDPs as they're commonly called, are generally composed of two glass plates pressed together, with the active display elements located between the plates. Simple flat panels form images by electrically selecting image segments to form alphanumeric characters or pixels.

High-resolution FPDs use a matrix-addressing scheme to electrically select pixels using transparent conductive electrode stripes on the front sheet of glass, and orthogonal (90° opposite alignment of the conductive stripes) electrode stripes on the back sheet of glass. The places where the front and back orthogonal electrodes intersect define the pixels and their electrical addresses by row and column.

Simple-matrix or passive-matrix flat-panel control involves applying pixel data (in the form of a voltage pulse), row by row sequentially. A row of pixels is activated when a common voltage is applied to the row electrode stripe while appropriate voltage is applied to each pixel on the column electrode stripes. Thus, each row of pixels is activated once per frame.

To provide the desired average brightness, passive-matrix displays depend on high pixel brightness during the short time the pixels are activated. Images on passive-matrix displays usually flicker at the frame rate because the pixels are on for a fraction of the frame time. But the response of the human eye is slow enough to filter out most of this effect.

The active-matrix addressing method increases a display's brightness and eliminates display flicker by keeping pixels activated a longer period of time. Active-matrix addressing uses an electronic switching device for each pixel—controlled by the row electrode-to-gate voltage, from the column electrode to the pixel. The capacitance of the pixel stores the voltage until it's refreshed or changed in the following frame. Functionally, the active-matrix panel is similar to a DRAM.

Pixels equal switches

A 640×480-pixel monochrome VGA display uses 640-column electrode stripes and 480-row electrode stripes. Adding color to the display triples the number of pixel elements and electrode stripes, with red, green, and blue subpixels required for each pixel.

A full-color VGA display must have 921,600 picture elements and switching devices for active-matrix addressing. Every pixel must be functional, because the human eye can perceive minute defects in a displayed image. The size and complexity of FPDs, as well as the necessity for 100% pixel yield, present tremendous problems in manufacturing high-resolution FPDs. The yield rate is typically only 20%, which means 8 out of 10 panels get rejected for one reason or another.

Pixels, pitch, & dots

Unlike a CRT where dot pitch or dot size is not equal to the pixel size, in FPDs the pixel size is exactly equal to the dot or pitch size (the one exception is the CRT-like field-emission display (FED), discussed later in the chapter). *Dot pitch* is a misnomer for FPDs, but it's used because of its alleged common meaning. *Dot size* is a better description.

The geometry is relatively simple. If a panel has an active area of 8 inches (203 mm) and there are 640 pixels, then the dot size should be 0.0125 inches or 0.31 mm. The actual dot size is something less than that, however, due to a variety of reasons. The electrodes of the rows and columns don't fill the entire pixel area, and in the case of active matrix LCDs they border the switch that drives the pixel. Also, most pixels have a Gaussian distribution of lumination. However, it's a close enough measurement that it can be used for general evaluations. A realistic example is a recently developed 15-inch (diagonal) LCD display with 1152×900 resolution. Its panel size is 301×235 mm (11.85×9.25 inches). The pixel *pitch* (to use the developer's terms) is 0.261 mm (0.0103 inches). Figure 4-1 gives a general idea of the dot size as a function of panel size and number of pixels.

LCD technology

The liquid-crystal display, or LCD, technology, became popular in the consumer market in the early 1970s as the familiar face of digital watches and calculators. They had a distinctive seven-segment display that used reflective light for illumination. If they hadn't been novel and inexpensive, it's doubtful they would have ever amounted to much because their display quality was poor at best.

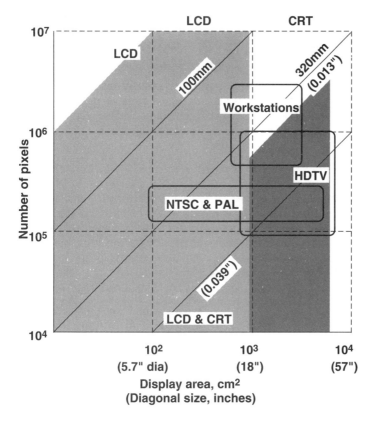

4-1
Different technologies yield different-sized displays, resolution ranges, and dot sizes. Some are better suited for TVs, workstations, and projection systems.

LCDs offer a thin design, light weight, space savings, and low power consumption. With these features, the LCD is well suited for portable use and has a growing number of applications. Industry attention has focused on the silicon thin-film transistors LCD (Si TFT-LCD) for technological development and promising products. The development of new drive systems will attract attention to the supertwisted nematic STN color LCD. New technologies for large screens and cost reduction will arise soon.

The pace of technological innovations in the LCD field is rapid. A number of leading manufacturers are making large investments in research and development (R & D) plants and equipment for active-matrix LCDs as an important part of their corporate strategies.

In the early 1960s, work on thin-film transistors (TFTs) was started in several labs in the U.S. The first liquid-crystal displays were described by Heilmeier in 1968, and were based on a phenomenon known as *dynamic scattering*. Engineers at RCA Labs and Westinghouse developed the idea of using TFTs for display addressing. During that time, Westinghouse fabricated a 6×6-inch active-matrix circuit; until then the largest being tried were 1.5-inch wafers. That work laid the conceptual foundations for today's active-matrix liquid-crystal display (AM-LCD) technology and established the general pixel-element design used to this day. In 1971, a new type of liquid-crystal display was described by Schadt and Helfrich: the twisted pneumatic display.

From 1972 to 1979, U.S. manufacturers, and especially Westinghouse, were the only suppliers in the field. For one reason or another all the U.S. suppliers walked away from the market, which in retrospect is puzzling because they were definitely on to something useful.

The LCD itself works essentially as a light shutter, and uses the matrix-addressing techniques described in the preceding section. Reflective varieties reflect ambient light, display modules using transmissive types incorporate their own lighting source, and transflective types can operate with either ambient or built-in light. The liquid crystal is sensitive to temperature, shock, and vibration—factors that must be satisfied before LCDs can be considered for use in rugged environmental conditions.

LCDs get their name for the liquid crystal used to construct them. It's an oily substance containing rod-like molecules (cyanobiphenyls) that respond to electrical fields by reorienting (polarizing) themselves along electrical-field lines—to pass or block the light used to create an image. The most popular flat panels are the 90° twisted-nematic field-effect LCDs (TN-LCDs). With no voltage (field) applied to a given pixel, the rod-like molecules of the crystal are aligned at 0°. As a voltage is applied, they gradually rotate through the liquid-crystal film until they are at 90°.

**Passing &
blocking light**

Light is polarized (for example, at 0°) by a polarizing filter and then passed through the liquid crystal. As the light travels through the crystal, it is rotated (*twisted*) 90° by the crystal, allowing it to pass through a second polarizing film panel on the other side that is aligned at 90°. When a voltage is applied, the liquid-crystal molecules align themselves perpendicularly to the second panel. No polarity rotation of the polarized light through the crystal takes place, and the 0° light is blocked by the second 90° polarizing film. Figure 4-2 shows the generalized construction of an LCD and how the light is manipulated through it.

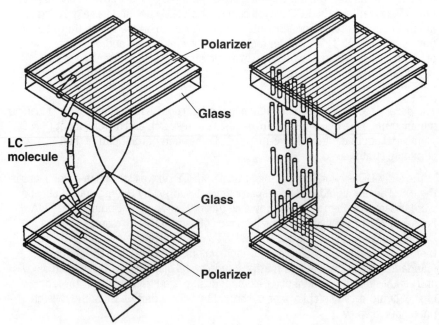

4-2
LCDs work by using polarized light that's twisted by voltage-sensitive crystals (left). When voltage is applied, the crystals don't twist or rate the light and it's blocked by the second polarized filter (right).

Polarizer

Glass

LC
molecule

Glass

Polarizer

LCDs require a light source to create a display. The first versions used reflected ambient light and weren't very bright due to scattering and polarization. Later versions used back-panel lighting and offered much greater brightness at the expense of power consumption.

LCDs that use reflected light require high ambient lighting for readability. However, the best way to view back-lit LCDs is in moderate to low ambient light. Thick-film electroluminescent (TFEL) lamps provide the thinnest backlight, while cold-cathode fluorescent tubes (CCFTs), in either a back-lit or side-lit configuration, provide a brighter, more efficient alternative. With a light source, modern LCD displays obtain a brightness between 3 to 10 foot-lamberts (fL).

Full-color LCDs use red, green, and blue filters on the subpixels to produce the primary additive RGB colors (see FIG. 4-3). Filter and pixel-area losses in the pixel subdivision reduce the light output to about 5% of the backlight illumination. Therefore, full-color LCDs require high-wattage backlighting to overcome the light loss.

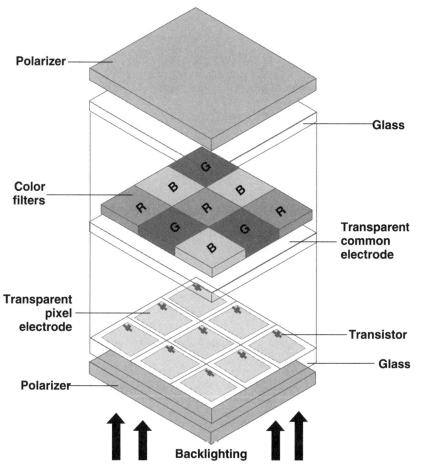

4-3
TFT color LCD displays use multiple or subpixels to produce color. Shown here is one visual pixel, which consists of a matrix of RGB filters. The output intensity of the pixel is the averaged amount of light through all the filters.
Sharp Corp.

Please note that the term *full color* does not mean *true color*. Full color in the case of LCDs simply means that all three primary colors (RGB) are generated. The range of intensities will vary depending on modulation techniques, frame rate, and the characteristics of the display controller.

A good contrast baseline for passive LCDs with a 1/200 duty cycle is roughly 3.5:1 for TN, 10:1 for STN, and 12:1 for DSTN, though the vendors don't use common methodologies to characterize their products.

A brief history of LCDs

Manufacturers have developed several types of LCD-FPDs, including passive-matrix LCDs (PM-LCDs), active-matrix display panels (AMDPs), and ferroelectric (FLCD).

By sheer prolonged research, the LCD has evolved to meet market circumstances at regular intervals. In portable computers, for instance, the twisted-nematic (TN-LCDs) displays that were prevalent from 1984 through 1986 quickly gave way to the supertwisted-nematic (TN-STN) displays of 1987 and 1988, with the double supertwisted-nematic (DSTN) displays coming in as a high-end alternative in 1989 and 1990, only to be superseded in quick fashion by the film-compensated DSTN (FSTN). TABLE 4-1 summarizes some of the developments in LCD technology.

Table 4-1
LCDs got started in the late
1960s and have evolved ever since.

Date	Type of LCD
1968	TFT LCD (thin-film transistor)
1971	TN-LCD (twisted nematic mode)
1986	FLCD (ferroelectric)
1984	STN (supertwisted bi-refringent effect)
1987	DSTN (double-layer STN mode)
1992	AAM (active-address method)

Over the years, the TN-LC molecule had the LCD market pretty much to itself, but other molecular structures have gotten a lot of workouts in the lab and some occasional unsuccessful market exercise. Researchers have been in especially hot pursuit of ferroelectric LCDs, but successful implementations have remained elusive.

The following sections will provide a brief description of the key characteristics of the various types of technologies.

Passive-matrix LCDs

Passive-matrix (PM) liquid-crystal displays, also known as twisted-nematic LCDs, are generally constructed using amorphous silicon (Si) technology, which was developed in the early 1960s.

PM-LCDs are slow because the liquid crystal used in them requires 100 to 200 milliseconds to respond to the fields applied to it. Slow response time minimizes flicker but results in ghosting and blurring of fast motion or changing images.

Passive-matrix LCDs have proven unsuitable for workstation and computer screens because of their poor contrast, limited viewing angle and slow response time.

In passive-matrix LCDs, each color pixel is activated less frequently than a pixel in an active-matrix display's brightness and contrast. Although an active-matrix display is clearer, it requires more electrical power.

Passive-matrix screens can be broken down further into subcategories. Three types used in color portable are supertwisted nematic (STN), film supertwisted nematic (FSTN), and triple supertwisted nematic (TSTN). The more lines there are to refresh in each frame of a passive twisted-nematic LCD, the more the display's image quality degenerates, severely limiting potential resolution.

Many of today's 640×480-pixel (i.e., pel) passive matrix displays are, in fact, driven as two separate panels, top and bottom, to prevent the multiplexing duty cycle from seriously degrading contrast. Different materials and addressing techniques have been employed to overcome the inherent drawbacks of conventional LCD materials. A few of the most common and promising materials and techniques are discussed here.

Supertwisted nematic Supertwisted-nematic LCDs (STN-LCDs) provide wider viewing angles and better contrast and resolution than TN-LCDs. STN refers to an increased amount of liquid-crystal molecule twist in the display material. STN-LCDs are used extensively in laptop computers and other portables.

Double supertwisted nematic Double supertwisted-nematic LCDs use two layers of liquid crystal to improve contrast and viewing angle. The tradeoff, however, is increased complexity, weight, and cost.

Triple supertwisted nematic The triple supertwisted nematic LCD (TSTN-LCD) was developed by In Focus Systems in late 1989. It uses three stacked liquid-crystal cells to provide a subtractive color system. Like color film, separate layers of cyan, magenta, and yellow control the spectral components of the white light. In practice, a color is turned off to subtract its component from white. Thus, to see red, the cyan would be turned off. Figure 4-4 illustrates the basic process.

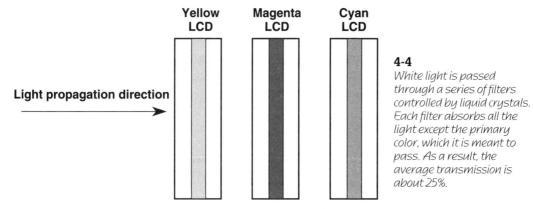

Yellow LCD   Magenta LCD   Cyan LCD

Light propagation direction

4-4
White light is passed through a series of filters controlled by liquid crystals. Each filter absorbs all the light except the primary color, which it is meant to pass. As a result, the average transmission is about 25%.

**Each LCD pixel
can be turned on to pass white light**

Optical-mode interference Compared with supertwisted-nematic LCDs, optical-mode interference LCDs (OMI-LCDs) offer a number of advantages. The OMI effect is about twice as fast as the STN and generally has a better black-and-white appearance and wider operating temperature range. The response times for STNs is in the range of 150 to 200 ms, while the OMI-LCDs can operate at less than 50 ms. New drive techniques have also been developed that eliminate side effects of frame modulation.

Active addressing In Focus, which is a spin-off of Planar Systems, Inc. (which is, in turn, a spin-off of Tektronix's display operations), is the largest U.S. supplier of LCDs, but it doesn't have its own fabrication facility. While the major Japanese manufacturers have staked their future on active-matrix displays, In Focus has put all its emphasis on unconventional approaches to passive LCDs. For its color panels, for example, it stacks three passive, monochrome LCD panels, custom built for the company by Kyocera, (a large Japanese electronics and ceramics manufacturer) in a unique subtractive generation scheme.

For speed improvements, it uses an active-addressing technique. The company's active-addressing scheme first emerged in 1992 and it represents a major departure from LCD tradition. Abandoning the conventional one-pulse-per-frame Alt-Pleshko-addressing scheme, active addressing drives each row of pixels more or less continuously and drives multiple rows at one time, achieving contrast and speed thought to be beyond the capabilities of passive LCDs.

Each frame is divided into 256 time intervals, and each row gets a signal at every interval. It changes in amplitude over that time, so it averages out to an RMS voltage, but at each time period it transitions to a new level, so there's effectively no time at which it's zero voltage.

While active-matrix LCDs integrate complex electronics into the display panel itself, active addressing uses conventional supertwisted-nematic (STN) LCDs and relegates complexity to external silicon, "where it belongs," according to In Focus.

There are a lot of ways to implement active addressing; the easiest is to use an ASIC as the mapping device. This makes it possible to use drivers and controllers already available on the market. In Focus uses an ASIC to map Alt-Pleshko into the more complex active-matrix scheme. The drivers are slightly different from passive displays. The column drivers are the same as from TFT-LCDs, but the row drivers are column drivers from STN displays. Two ASICs are used: one to drive the top half of a 640×480-pixel display, the other to drive the bottom half. The ASICs are not mounted onto glass and use conventional packaging.

In late 1992, Motorola and In Focus set up a joint venture to manufacture LCDs, with Motorola building the drive electronics. Motorola and In Focus did not seek or receive any government aid to set up the venture. Under the terms of the agreement, Motorola takes a 20% shareholder interest in In Focus. Motorola's backing of a U.S.-based display maker won high praise from observers, many of whom have long been lamenting the decline of the once-thriving U.S. computer-display business.

Other grayscale techniques Although STN-LCDs have been widely used in laptops, they've been criticized for their slow response and often poor-quality gray-scale. The demand for faster-response LCDs has been strong and has led several developers to abandon the PM technology. One solution to the problem of poor contrast and slow response has been the active-addressing technique described previously. This technique, however, is criticized because it requires a large number of circuits to perform arithmetic operations and to determine the amount of voltage to be applied to the LCD.

Two other methods have been proposed to simplify the solution: the multiline selection methods (S. Ihara, and T. N. Ruckmongathan), and the trilevel active-addressing method (B. Clifton). Frame-rate modulation (FRM), also known as frame-rate control (FRC), is the most commonly used technique to obtain 16 or more shades of gray with an STN-LCD. The criticism of FRM is that it can cause flicker when the refresh rate is increased. To overcome that problem, the number of grayscales has to be reduced to four levels. Other techniques that have been proposed have been the pulse-height modulation, or PHM (A. R. Connor), and amplitude modulation. These techniques have been criticized for the number of drive circuits needed to realize over eight gray shades.

In 1993, H. Mano described a technique called *partial dispersion driving*. It's a method where only several lines are driven simultaneously instead of all the lines. This technique results in a form of an interlaced display and has the benefit of fewer parts and less power usage.

Unlike PM-LCDs, active-matrix LCD (AM-LCD) pixels are energized all the time. This feature improves image brightness. AM-LCDs, some believe, can achieve contrast ratios of up to 100 to 1. The active-matrix drive, usually made up of TFTs (thin-film transistors) or diodes, allows the use of faster-response liquid crystal, which can effectively display video images without blurring.

Active-matrix LCDs

A passive-matrix LCD uses one transistor for each row and one for each column. Each row transistor is switched on in sequence and the column transistors are turned according to the image content. When the transistor is turned off, the element or pixel loses its charge and blocks the passage of light. Because the rows are scanned and the response time of LCDs isn't very fast, passive displays aren't very bright. In contrast, an active-matrix LCD uses a separate transistor for each pixel. This allows the pixel to stay on longer and thus produce a brighter display. However, building such displays is difficult and therefore expensive. A comparison of active-matrix and passive-matrix LCDs is shown in FIG. 4-5.

Because an active-matrix panel is essentially a giant IC with up to millions of TFT switches fabricated onto a glass plate, its manufacturing process is similar to IC fabrication on silicon wafers. But displays are much larger than wafers, making manufacturing more difficult and yields lower. Yields for small AM-LCDs are beginning to exceed 50%, but yields for larger sizes are still low—thought by some in the industry to be within the 10% range.

The visual acuity of the human eye is approximately one minute of an arc. At a typical viewing distance of 50 cm, a human observer can resolve a point defect of a 0.15-mm diameter. The size of the resolvable point defect is approximately one half size of a display pixel.

Active-matrix displays are more expensive to produce. With more transistors being used, there's a greater chance of transistor failure, which has driven manufacturing

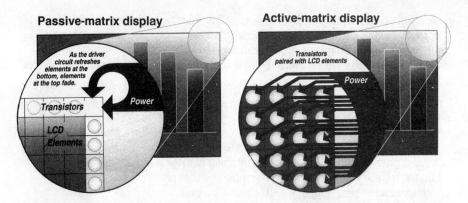

Passive-matrix display

As the driver circuit refreshes elements at the bottom, elements at the top fade.

Transistors

LCD Elements

Power

Active-matrix display

Transistors paired with LCD elements

Power

4-5 *A passive-matrix LCD uses one transistor for each row and each column. Each transistor is switched on in sequence and the column transistors are turned according to the image content. When the transistor is turned off, the element or pixel loses its charge and blocks the passage of light. Because of this scanning and the slow response time, passive displays aren't very bright. An active-matrix LCD uses a separate transistor for each pixel. This allows the pixel to stay on longer and thus produces a brighter display.* PC Week, 30 March 1992, p.30

costs up. Manufacturers, however, are announcing improved screen yields, which might help bring prices down.

The commercial development of active-matrix-addressed twisted-nematic LCDs has provided a flat-panel technology comparable in picture quality to color CRTs. The requirement for a thin-film transistor (TFT) at each pixel, however, imposes limitations on the resolution and aperture ratio. Research indicates that resolution in the hundreds of lines per inch (lpi) is possible, but aperture ratios will remain well below 50%.

Manufacturers use TFT redundancy as well as test-and-repair strategies to salvage faulty active-matrix panels. They repair faulty row and column interconnections and replace faulty TFTs with redundant TFTs. It's expected that AM-LCD manufacturing technology will mature over the next few years, with resulting price reductions.

Eight- to 10-inch TFT-LCDs are found in most notebook personal computers. However, technological advances in simple-matrix STN color LCDs are enabling these models. The STN color LCDs offer improved response speed, enhanced image quality, and greater brightness and gradation. New techniques are at work in their drive systems. Enhanced technologies combined with a lower price tag than TFT-LCDs make STN color LCDs attractive to many users.

It appears that the limit on TFT displays is about 19 or 20 inches. Above that, problems in production yields are a barrier; scanning and response speeds also deteriorate. The FPD manufacturers are searching for a breakthrough to solve these problems. Some of the most severe snags crop up in the sputtering and CVD processes, specifically maintaining uniformity and minimizing particle emission in the sputtering process.

NEC Corporation has started volume production of high-resolution, 13- and 15-inch color TFT displays. The displays, which are targeted at engineering workstations, offer a resolution of 1280×1024 dots. The panels contain 1.3 million pixels and about four million RGB dots, and can display 4096 colors, as shown in FIG. C-28.

The Centre National d'Etudes des Telecommunications (CNET), which is France's telecommunications research arm, and the French electronics group Sagem have developed a two- to three-mask thin-film transistor (TFT) process to make active-matrix liquid-crystal displays (LCDs). The process is less expensive than other TFT technology, with pilot-line yields more than 90% for the active-matrix plate. The team has produced a 10-inch color VGA display using the technology, putting it in the running for such applications as laptop and notebook computers.

Meanwhile, AM-LCD product prices are quite high. To make matters worse for Japanese manufacturers, in 1991 the ITC (International Trade Commission) levied a 63% duty on the importation of Japanese products into the U.S. The ITC ruled in favor of the Advanced Display Manufacturers of America, which claimed that to capture the U.S. market the Japanese were selling their panels for less than what it cost to produce them. In 1993, the tariff was rescinded.

The active-matrix LCD can be divided into two types of systems. One system uses an a-Si or polysilicon to form a TFT that controls on/off switchover. The other is a metal-insulator-metal (MIM) system that uses a diode for switchover.

AM-LCD types

Thin-film transistors   Thin-film transistors (TFTs), or more precisely, integrated-gate thin-film transistors, have a long history in electronics. In 1962, P. K. Warner described TFTs using CdS as the active material (and, according to W. E. Howard of IBM, the concept is even older, dating back to 1934). In a TFT, there's a gate electrode, a source, and a drain. When the gate is positive relative to the source, the source-drain impedance is very low, making the TFT look like a switch. This switching mechanism is the basis for turning on or off the rows and columns of a matrix-addressing system in an LCD.

Metal-insulator-metal systems   MIM screens are built with a diode-like device at each cell location. The metal-insulator-metal structure is sandwiched between two terminals, as opposed to three-terminal TFTs. The diode performs switching in place of the transistor. The metal-film layers used to create the diode are sputtered onto the CD glass in a relatively simple process. The relative ease of this manufacturing approach should result in cost savings. Other advantages include a thinner, more transmissive screen that requires less back-lighting than comparably sized TFT screens.

In mid 1992, Toshiba claimed to have made a color liquid-crystal display (LCD) that's as fast as a Braun tube-type CRT display used in desktop computers. Toshiba calls its original technology the *level-adjusted operation* (LAO) method and reports that it's based on TFT technology. Toshiba reports the speed of change from one screen image to another takes only 17 milliseconds. Existing color LCDs take around 40 to 60 milliseconds. This means Toshiba's LAO color LCD is two to three times faster than conventional color LCDs. Toshiba's LAO color LCD is expected to be applied eventually to high-definition color TVs as well as color LCD computers. It's also expected to find applications in multimedia computers. The faster response allows fast-moving objects to be viewed without smearing.

Faster TFT-LCD response

Toshiba found that the response time of LCDs is dependent on the last input voltage. By making the first pulse of a change in gray level slightly greater than the subsequent pulse, the response time can be speeded up by a factor of between 2 and 3 times. The adjustment of this first pulse is where the name *level adjusted* is derived.

Mega-pixel displays

Aiming for the 1990s two key market trends in consumer electronics—16:9 aspect-ratio wide-vision TVs and multimedia computer—in early 1992, Sharp developed a 6.5-inch high-resolution color TFT-LCD screen. The new design incorporates 1,228,320 pixels and a color palette of 16.7 million tones. Full color is reproduced by arranging RGB pixels in a triangular configuration. In the computer-display version, sharp contrast of graphics and characters is produced by using a stripe configuration of RGB pixels.

Making the LCD wider and larger required Sharp engineers to develop a new construction method for thin film that ensures even reproduction over a large area. The ultimate target is the coming high-definition TV market, which is why Sharp made the aspect ratio of this LCD screen 16:9 initially.

Plasma-addressed LCDs

Tektronix has developed the plasma-addressed liquid-crystal (PALC) display, an emerging AM-LCD technology. The plasma active-matrix panel functions like the TFT array, but with simpler, potentially higher-yield structures. Unlike solid-state LCDs, it uses channels containing an inert gas, as shown in FIG. 4-6. Under the trade name Tekvision, the PALC concept has been developed and supported in part by the Defense Advanced Research Projects Agency. Several examples of PALC displays are shown in FIG. C-29.

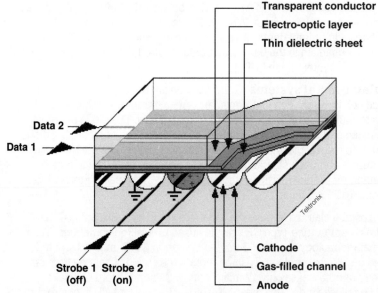

4-6
Tektronix uses a very fast ultra-thin liquid-crystal switch called a "pi cell," which sequentially displays RGB components in front of a monochrome CRT to produce a color display.

The design is based on a 1940s Columbia Broadcasting concept known as a *field-sequential color display*. This method produces color images by sequentially projecting the red, green, and blue components of each frame on a monochrome

CRT. Corresponding red, green, and blue filters, placed in front of the screen every 1/180 of a second, generate a full-color image at the normal frame rate of 60 Hz. In the original Columbia system, a mechanical *color wheel* spun in front of the screen.

To bring this concept into the '90s, Tektronix engineers applied some liquid-crystal technology. Two fast liquid-crystal optical switches combine with color and neutral polarizers to make up a Nu-COLOR *shutter*. Color is produced by sequentially displaying red, green, and blue field information on the monochrome CRT, while the shutter switches to transmit red, green, and blue.

The shutter relies on a high-speed, liquid-crystal technology based on a pi cell, developed at Tektronix. The *pi cell*, a very fast, ultra-thin, liquid-crystal switch, derives its name from the amount of twist it assumes (pi radians) in its undriven state. Unlike standard supertwisted-nematic cells, pi cells can switch at the 180 Hz needed to filter each color for a frame. This results in an ultra-high contrast, ultra-bright CRT picture.

Luminance exceeds 30 foot-lamberts (fL) and contrast reaches 100 to 1—two to three times that of conventional CRTs. As with monochrome monitors, resolution depends on electron-beam size, not showdown-mask dot pitch.

The PALC active-matrix approach eliminates the need for TFTs, replacing them with ionized gas to connect each pixel to its data line for application of the control voltage. Data-switching times are a short 5 microseconds per row, a speed that allows 30-Hz frame rates for large, high-resolution panels. The voltage is held by the pixel electrode capacitance until the voltage is updated in the following frame. Leakage currents, prevalent in TFTs, are virtually nonexistent in PALC displays, resulting in a reduction of the voltage decay to a negligible value.

Ferroelectric LCDs

The surface-stabilized ferroelectric liquid-crystal display (SSF-LCD), also known as a *ferroelectric liquid-crystal display* (FE-LCD), has demonstrated the capability to provide high resolution with very good brightness. The material in ferroelectric LCDs (FLCDs) is *bistable*, unlike the liquid crystal used in TN-LCDs and STN-LCDs. When an electric field is applied to it and then removed, a ferroelectric liquid crystal holds its polarization, much like ferrous materials hold magnetic fields after an applied magnetic field is removed (however, there's no magnetic material in an FLCD). Such a polarization, which can be electrically reoriented, is the defining characteristic of a ferroelectric material.

In contrast, twisted nematics (and, for that matter, CRTs) must be refreshed approximately every sixtieth of a second. The ability of the FE-LCD to hold its polarization until changed allows the changing of polarization much faster than the dielectric mechanism that switches conventional LCDs. FE-LCDs provide bright, flicker-free performance comparable to that of conventional TFT-LCDs. The response time of ferroelectric liquid crystal is about 100 nanoseconds, a feature that makes FLCDs especially well suited for video displays.

FLCD construction is similar to that of other LCDs, but the gap between the glass plates must be between 1 and 2 microns instead of between 5 and 7 microns. This spacing is difficult to achieve and maintain uniformly over large display areas. Part of the difficulties of fabricating such a small cell gap is that FE-LCD molecule alignment is more difficult in a thinner layer. As a result, any misalignments cause optical zigzag effects known as *chevrons*.

The conventional wisdom on FLCDs was that they're incapable of displaying grayscale and are, essentially, unmanufacturable. However, Canon has resolved FLCD fabrication problems. In late 1991, Canon showed off an impressive 960×1312-pixel, 15-inch monochrome FLCD and a pair of 1280×1024-pixel, 15-inch color FLCDs. The company claims a minimum 10:1 contrast ratio and a 50° side-to-side viewing angle. The company uses the monochrome display internally on a Japanese-language desktop-publishing system.

As a result of these developments, the vision of FLCDs as the display that will carry LCD technology into large sizes with the low cost of a passive LCD and the high quality of an AM-LCD might really come to fruition.

The first one at Canon to recognize the potential of FLCDs was Junichiro Kanbewas. He was also the prime mover in convincing top management to establish an ambitious company-wide FLCD project in 1986, abandoning all other flat-panel display development to focus exclusively on FLCDs. The cell gap issue is now no longer a problem because Canon developed machines that can reliably control cell thickness. The Canon FLCD cell gap is 1.25 microns, and its thickness must be kept to a tolerance of 0.05 micron.

Though Canon was the first to market with FLCDs, others are in hot pursuit. Major LCD companies such as Hitachi Ltd., Matsushita Electric Industrial Co. Ltd., Sanyo Electric Corp., Sharp Corp., and Toshiba Corp. have engineers and researchers working on FLCDs.

Work on a 12-inch, video-rate color FLCD was reported by Toshiba in 1988, and the 1991 Society for Information Display (SID) Conference included reports on FLCD work by Fujitsu Labs Ltd., a team from Hoechst A.G. (Hoechst Japan Ltd.) and the University of Stuttgart, a team from Japan's Semiconductor Energy Laboratory Co. and the Takasago Research Institute Inc., GEC Marconi Ltd. (Wembley, England), and Seiko Epson.

At SID in 1992, the bulk of the FLCD papers were from Europe. A team from GEC Marconi and Seleco S.p.A., with funding through the European Community's Esprit program, reported that it had developed a 12-inch monochrome video-rate FLCD measuring 1280×800 pixels. The ferroelectric LCD is now a serious contender for laptop-computer applications.

The commercial development of active-matrix-addressed twisted-nematic LCDs has provided a flat-panel technology comparable in picture quality to color CRTs. The requirement for a thin-film transistor (TFT) at each pixel, however, imposes limitations on the resolution and aperture ratio. Research indicates resolution in the hundreds of lines per inch (lpi) is possible, but aperture ratios will remain well below 50%.

Supertwisted nematic (STN) is a passively addressed technology that could achieve the high resolution and aperture ratio, but is constrained by a fundamental problem limiting its complexity.

FLCDs offer simplicity of construction with high complexity, high resolution, and a large aperture ratio. Resolution of over 1000 lpi have been obtained, and they don't need a memory element (a TFT) at each pixel due to their bistable nature.

The hallmark bistability that makes FLCDs so good has two unfortunate side effects: difficulty in generating grayscale and, therefore, a limited color palette and limited speed when redrawing large areas of a screen. However, an FLCD screen can rapidly redraw select portions of a screen, such as a cursor redraw. Canon's line-redraw time for its FLCDs is 70 microseconds. Current AM-LCDs respond in the 50-millisecond range; the fastest passive TN-LCDs draw at about 150 milliseconds.

Bistable side effects

To overcome grayscale limitations, researchers have developed two traditional pseudo-gray scaling techniques: temporal division and spatial division. The controller electronics is required to provide a 10-Hz minimum and 40-Hz maximum frame rate, but panels have been designed for rates as high as 80 MHz.

The color-palette limitation has been addressed by Canon. The Canon color FLCD pel (pixel) has the conventional red, green, and blue subpels used by color displays to generate eight colors, but Canon adds a fourth, unfiltered, subpel. The fourth subpel lends two levels of luminance to the pel's composite output, doubling the basic color palette to 16 hues. An intelligent control method called *error diffusion* can expand that to as many as 16.7 million hues by fooling the human eye.

First developed in 1966, the plasma display has a long technological history and has reached a high level of development. Manufacturing PDPs using printing technology has accelerated market expansion. Initially, the small- and medium-sized PDPs were used in electronic cash registers (ECRs), point-of-sale (POS) terminals, stock-quotation boards, and measuring instruments. In 1985, a large 640×400-dot PDP was marketed and used in the GRiD laptop computer. This application drew much attention at the time. Recently, LCDs have taken over as displays for laptop personal computers. Taking advantage of the features of high definition and large size, the plasma display is aiming to expand the market.

Plasma display panels

Alternating-current plasma display panels (AC-PDPs), also commonly referred to as simply *plasma display panels* or *gas discharge displays*, produce light by ionizing a gas. The construction of a typical plasma panel is shown in FIG. 4-7. Like most other FPDs, the AC-PDP uses a matrix-addressing technique of rows of electrodes on one glass panel and columns of electrodes on an opposing glass panel. Trapped between the two panels in an air-tight chamber is a low-pressure inert gas, typically neon or xenon. When sufficient voltage is applied between a pixel's row and column electrodes, the gas achieves a plasma state and discharges a monochromatic color. The type of gas used determines the color; neon typically produces a glowing amber-orange color.

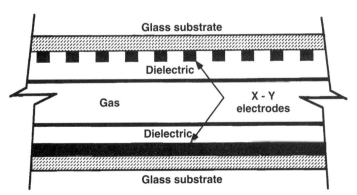

4-7
The plasma discharge display uses a conventional matrix-addressing technique and ionizes a gas between intersecting elements to create an emissive display. Photonics Systems

The PDP is attracting industry-wide attention because its screen size is easy to expand, self-emission offers excellent brightness and contrast, and the viewing angle is wide, helping to expand its application range. The PDP is extremely legible and offers a flicker-free image.

Electro Plasma, Photonics Systems, Plasmaco, and other manufacturers offer displays with an extensive range of pixel resolutions and panel sizes for various applications. AC-PDPs have been interfaced to many computer platforms—including PCs, Sun systems, Macs, and X Windows system machines, as well as ANSI terminals. For over 10 years, AC-PDPs have been widely used in military, medical, and industrial applications.

Types of plasma displays

Depending on the electrode structure, the discharge system is either dc or ac. The DC-PDP has the electrode exposed in the discharge space, and the AC-PDP covers the electrode with a dielectric material. The DC-PDP includes the pulse-memory model invented by Burroughs and perfected by NHK Technology Laboratory for TV use. The pulse-memory PDP continues discharge by providing a voltage-driven pulse train to display cells that have started discharge. This feature gives the memory function of the display an excellent brightness, ranging between 6 and 20 fL.

Characteristics of plasma displays

The AC plasma display panel (AC-PDP) was developed at the University of Illinois in 1963 by Professors Donald L. Bitzer and H. Gene Slottow. Somewhat similar to a ferroelectric LCD, once a pixel is illuminated in an AC-PDP, it remains so until extinguished. This inherent memory capability provides a display panel that's bright, flicker-free, and without the complexity of active-matrix pixel drivers. On the inside of their viewing screen, color AC-PDPs use RGB phosphors that are activated by ultraviolet light from the plasma glow—fluorescent lights use this efficient process.

AC-PDPs are as energy efficient as other types of displays due to the power-recovery circuits used to drive them. The AC-PDP electrodes form a high-capacitance load, which could result in the need for high-power display-driver circuits. Modern drivers, however, have power-recovery circuits. In each AC cycle, these circuits save the energy stored in the capacitance of the electrodes and use it in subsequent cycles.

Because AC-PDPs don't need to be continually refreshed and are therefore power efficient, they're attractive as large displays. Being thin and light makes them easily expandable in size. Photonics Systems offers a 60-inch diagonal AC-PDP. Large displays like these can provide real-size images for CAD/CAM and desktop-publishing applications without shrinking, approximating, or clipping the image.

AC-PDPs also have fast response times and can operate with update rates of from 25 to 60 frames per second. Other features include a wide viewing angle and excellent gradation characteristics. AC-PDPs are reliable, long lived, rugged, and have been popular for field display systems. Displays of 640×480 full dots and 1280×1024 full dots have been produced for applications requiring fast response, medium size, and a large information content, such as a workstation.

The criticisms of AC-PDPs include high cost, no grayscale, and no color. The advent of high-volume production should reduce the costs of this simple manufacturing process. Since the structure of a DC-PDP is generally simple, it offers advantages in fabrication of large panels.

Plasma displays are considered by many to be the most promising for very large flat-panel displays, and the best candidate for the "picture on a wall" HDTV solution. Both DC and AC versions of color PDP have been built and will be commercially available.

The development of coloring technology for PDPs is complete and a number of makers are marketing 20-inch color PDPs for workstations because the AC-PDP color display compares well to CRT monitors. Several manufacturers either are developing or have developed large, color PDP displays. Fujitsu Limited, Mitsubishi Electric, Oki Electric Industry, and Photonics Systems have all succeeded in the trial production of color PDPs and are improving their performance for practical applications.

Matsushita succeeded in trial production of a 26-inch full-color PDP with a 16:9 aspect ratio. The company plans to improve the display for practical use by enhancing its discharge efficiency, increasing its brightness, reducing its power consumption, and extending its lifespan.

Photonics Systems has a 30-inch AC-PDP with 64 levels of gray, a 024×768 resolution, and a 0.59-mm cell size. Fujitsu has demonstrated a 31-inch color panel using a reflective, three-electrode surface-discharge technique (RTSD). The initial display obtained 16 levels (colors) per pixel with 64 levels using dithering. The basic resolution is 640×480 and it can obtain a 2× subpixel resolution to achieve 1280×960. The Fujitsu design is different from other commercially available color AC-PDPs designs, with its opaque phosphor-covered display electrodes. Fujitsu has since expanded the design with new driver techniques to obtain 256 colors and a 1000-line resolution, clearly aimed at the HDTV market.

NHK (Japan Broadcasting Corp.) and other manufacturers are developing large plasma displays for HDTV. The Science and Technical Research Laboratories of NHK, in conjunction with Dai Nippon Printing, demonstrated a 40-inch color DC-PDP in early 1993. The display had 1344×800 resolution with 0.65mm cell size.

Photonics has produced some of the largest, highest-resolution displays, such as a 55-inch, 1920×1080, a 1.0-meter 1596×1212 (see FIG. 4-8), and a 1.5-meter 2048×2048-resolution model (see FIG. 4-9).

Photonics Systems

4-8
AC plasma-display panels (AC-PDP) use a row-column addressing technique. An illuminated pixel or element is produced when the gas between a row and an element is excited. Once switched on, the pixel will continue to glow until switched off.

4-9
Very large AC-PDPs have been built, like this one from Photonics, which is 1.5 meters in diameter with 2048×2048 resolution.

Photonics Systems

Electroluminescent displays

The first successful electroluminescent displays were built at Westinghouse in the mid 1960s where they developed drives for the demanding task of addressing electroluminescent (EL) displays. Each EL pixel required two TFTs and a storage capacitor, and the power TFT had to stand off 300 V. An active-matrix EL panel built to this design was displaying real-time video images in early 1975. However, the program at Westinghouse was canceled in 1979 because the company didn't want to go into the flat-panel business.

The thin-film electroluminescent display (TFEL) has become well known for its self-light emission, fully solid-state operation, long life, wide viewing angle, high contrast, excellent legibility, and rapid response. The electroluminescent (EL) display's high definition, large display capacity, low power consumption, and excellent visibility have won it favor for use with engineering workstations and progress is being made in improving gradation and coloring. Although most of the attention in the area of flat displays focuses on LCDs and PDPs, EL displays have strong potential in this field.

Characteristics of electroluminescent displays

Alternating-current thin-film electroluminescent (AC-TFEL) displays are solid-state devices that are constructed with thin-film phosphor deposits on one sheet of glass with a second sheet of glass acting as a protective cover, as shown in FIG. 4-10.

AC-TFEL display fabrication uses deposition processes, commonly used for IC chip fabrication. A thin-film luminescent layer is sandwiched between transparent dielectric layers using conventional matrix addressing of row and column electrodes. They produce or emit light when the phosphors are excited by an electric field. An AC-TFEL display is constructed as a capacitive device, with the

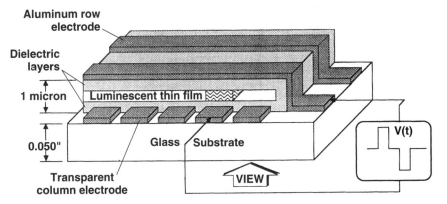

Aluminum row electrode

Dielectric layers

1 micron

Luminescent thin film

0.050"

Glass Substrate

Transparent column electrode

VIEW

V(t)

phosphors being activated or excited by the displacement current. These processes can be scaled up to produce larger display panels, and AC-TFEL displays lend themselves to automation and large-volume, low-cost production.

The luminance of an AC-TFEL can be raised by increasing the ac drive frequency or the capacitance of the panel. When used with power-recovery circuits, the high-capacitance AC-TFEL devices are used for low-power displays suitable for portable applications. The common rectangular plug-in night lights are also AC-TFEL devices.

Technological innovations in thin-film EL displays are advancing steadily. AC-TFEL display manufacturers produce displays in all standard display formats and sizes up to 19 inches diagonal. The leading displays are the large, high-definition models, such as 12- to 14-inch displays, with 0.20- to 0.25-mm-pixel pitches, with 1024×768, 1152×900, and 1280×1024 resolutions. This is the technological range in which the thin-film EL display is most efficient. Like the CRT, the AC-TFEL surpasses the LCD in contrast and viewing angle. They offer a typical contrast ratio of 150:1, a real brightness of more than 100 candelas per square meter (fL) at 80 Hz, and a 160° viewing angle.

For gradation displays, manufacturers are developing different systems of pulse-width modulation, amplitude modulation, and pulse-width modulation/amplitude modulation. The low power-consumption requirement is being met through developments in the drive systems, panel characteristics, and low electrode resistance. Some manufacturers market EL displays with a 9-inch, 16-gradation function that consumes 17 W of power. Development of units consuming 10 W or less continues.

Planar Systems and Sharp are the two major producers of AC-TFEL displays. Thin-film electroluminescent displays offer excellent brightness at low power (no back-lighting is required) and crisp high-resolution images, and have earned a reputation for ruggedness and sunlight readability. EL displays also shake off short-duration 100-g shocks without damage.

EL technology offers a high-contrast, crisp, light-emitting image. One reason for the contrast and brightness is due to the binary operation; each pixel is either completely on or completely off. As a result, AC-TFELs can create contrast ratios of

1:100. The perceived acuity is because the pixel, due to its solid-state nature, generates equal-intensity light in all directions with a nonGaussian distribution. Figure 4-11 shows the relative brightness and distribution for the four leading display technologies.

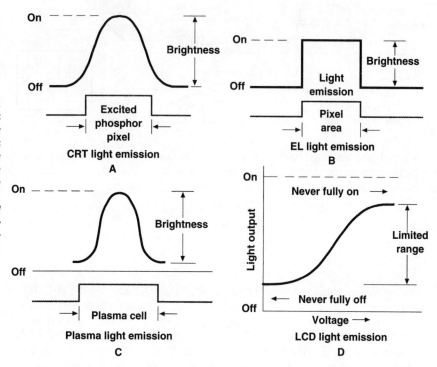

4-11
CRTs and plasma displays exhibit a Gaussian distribution of brightness when excited or activated. An LCD exhibits an S curve or a log curve (depending on materials) when switched. An electroluminescent panel operates like a solid-state device and switches full on or full off.

Color electroluminescent displays

Multicolor EL displays came out first. The practical use began with two-color displays combining green and red that reached the brightness levels of yellow-orange and green—the fundamental colors of thin-film electroluminescence. Developers must produce a bright blue phosphor to implement a full-color AC-TFEL display. Color-display brightness is determined by the weakest color for proper RGB balance.

Engineers use two approaches in developing EL color displays. One system uses an EL panel emitting white in addition to red, green, and blue filters. The other system uses a fine processing technology to form three light-emission layers of red, green, and blue. Red, green, and blue have different brightness ratios, so it will take time before a full-color EL display is ready for practical use.

Engineers at Planar Systems have produced a VGA-compatible, 640×480-resolution, grayscale display. Two years in development, the technology combines several levels of true brightness adjustment with dithering to produce 16 shades of gray. Planar has also shown a display with multiple colors—not to be confused with full color. Unfortunately for EL designers, Mother Nature hasn't yielded a blue phosphor to match the red and yellow, but Planar has a new approach to the problem.

There have been two main approaches to color EL, one taking its lead from the CRT and the other from the LCD. The CRT-like approach is to replace a monochrome phosphor with stripes of red, green, and yellow phosphors: the LCD-like approach is to overlay red, green, and blue filters on a white light source. The major problem with the striped-phosphor approach has been inadequate brightness, primarily in existing blue phosphors. The LCD-like approach suffers, like color LCDs, from light loss in the filters, as well as from relatively dim phosphors.

In early 1992, Planar had something of a breakthrough in conceptualizing multicolor and full-color EL. Developed in the labs at Planar International (Espoo, Finland), formerly the Finlux division of the Lohja Corp., the new color EL approach uses a single yellow phosphor and a pair of red and green filters, but the phosphor is the conventional ZnS:Mn used in monochrome displays—bright, mature, and readily available. Also, the new approach turns the traditional EL sandwich structure upside down, improving the display's optical characteristics. See FIG. 4-12 for a diagram of this type of display.

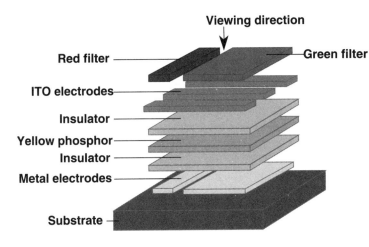

4-12
The Planar EL color display uses a single phosphor and a pair of red and green filters. Also, the substrate is located at the rear of the display and the filters at the front.
Planar

In the conventional EL display, the substrate lies at the front of the display; in the new Planar structure, it's in the back. With the filters at the front, they don't have to endure high-temperature processes. The single-phosphor approach also simplifies the manufacturing process over the striped-phosphor approach, which requires more etching steps and finer lithography.

The inverted structure of the new display eliminates the need for a circular polarizer and a rear reflector in the EL sandwich. Although the polarizer is an effective contrast enhancer, it absorbs about 63% of the light passing through it. In the new display structure, the filters at the front provide a contrast enhancement. Ambient light is absorbed on the way out, not reflected.

Microtip field-emission displays

The microtips display, also known as a *microtips fluorescent display* (MFD) and *field-emission display* (FED), is a relatively new technology. It was first proposed by H. Kanter in 1962 and then by C. A. Spindt in 1976. In 1986, a flat CRT with an array of metal field-emitter tips for cathodes was demonstrated by the French Atomic Energy Commission government laboratory, LETI-DOPT-SCMM, of Grenoble. There has been considerable reporting in the technical and business press about these field-emission displays. Much of the renewed interest in this CRT-type technology has been due to LETI CEA and IBM's laboratories in Greenock, Scotland. The LETI research facility has produced and shown operational 6-inch monochrome MFDs and a 6-inch RGB color-panel demonstration device. Work has also been done at the University of California at Davis and by Spindt at SRI International.

The excitement about MFDs stems from their similarity to CRTs. The CRT microtip fluorescent displays are based on cold electron emission from a matrix array of field-emitter cathodes—called *microtips*—and on low-voltage cathodoluminescent. It draws on some of the known principles of vacuum microelectronics. The process of forming arrays of tips between 1 and 5 microns was first described by Spindt and, in 1986, R. Meyer, also of LETI, coined the term *microtip*. An MFD is like a flat CRT, but with a major difference. A CRT has one gun and a complex deflection system to generate all its pixels; an MFD has an electron gun (actually just a microtip cathode) for every pixel. Whereas a CRT's beam scans each phosphor dot once per frame, the electron-beam impingement on each MFD pixel's phosphor dot is continuous.

The flat MFD-CRT is constructed from two glass plates that are put together with a peripheral glass FRIT seal, as illustrated in FIG. 4-13. The plates have a front-to-back gap spacing in the region of 200 microns, which results in a self-sustaining panel only 2 to 3 millimeters thick.

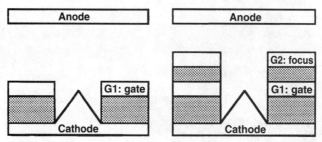

4-13 *Small, 1μm metal cones (cathodes) are used to create emissions with moderate acceleration from a low-voltage (<<≈l=>>80 V) transparent anode. The anode and cathode substrate are composed of a thin, 1 to 0.75μm, sandwich. Some versions have a second (G2) focus element.*

W.D. Kesling, et. al., Field Emission Display Resolution, SID '93 International Symposium, Seattle, May 1993, Society for Information Display.

The microtip fabrication process that creates the matrix of field-emitter cathodes uses techniques that are employed in IC fabrication. Photomasks, reactive ion etching, chemical etching, and vacuum deposition are all involved.

The microtip array is deposited on the backplate, and forms the cathodes, which are separated from the gate (the anode) by an insulator that's between 1 and 0.75 micrometers (depending who builds it). The gate is pierced by a series of holes, each with a diameter of 1.0 micrometers, as shown in FIG. 4-14.

The microtips themselves, each 1.2 micrometers or less high, are arranged every 10 microns (resulting in 10,000 per square millimeter) over the whole screen area. The pixel is defined, using conventional matrix addressing, by the intersection of a cathode column and a gate line. Because the array of tips is so dense, each pixel has many microguns—between 1,000 and 10,000 in a 0.1-per-square-mm pixel.

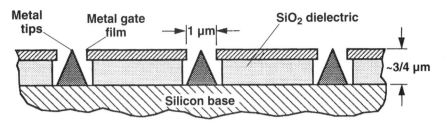

Metal tips   Metal gate film   ←|1 μm|←—   SiO₂ dielectric

Silicon base

~3/4 μm

4-14
This shows the basic structure of a microtip fluorescent display's cathodes. The tips are as small as 1 μm and there's one tip every 10 μm (see also Fig. 3-47 in chapter 3).
C. Spindt

This produces a high degree of redundancy, and several microtips can fail without any noticeable effect.

The display works by applying a voltage between the cathode and the gate, causing the microtips located at the point of intersection to emit electrons. Those electrons are accelerated toward the cathodoluminescent anode because of its voltage bias, thus turning on the corresponding pixel. Since the spacing between anode and cathode is so small, no electron-beam shaping or deflection is required, as in a conventional CRT, so there are no focus or deflector electrodes.

MFDs offer the potential for producing in a very bright, low-power, high-resolution, thin, flat-panel display with the same screen appearance as a CRT. It has a uniform focus and fast response time (2 seconds), doesn't produce any significant x-ray emissions, and emits no potentially hazardous magnetic fields.

Grayscale is an intrinsic property of MFDs, which means implementation is no more difficult than for any other matrix display. Grayscale is achieved by analog voltage or digital pulse-width methods. The use of amplitude modulation and pulse-width modulation avoids the flicker problems LCDs have with amplitude modulation and frame-rate modulation. Both monochrome and color displays have been demonstrated using this technology. Good color registration requires that the cathode and anode substrates be aligned to within a small fraction of a pixel dimension.

Addressing is done a line at a time so that each pixel in a line is on for a full scan time, thereby improving brightness. For this application, it's necessary to have a cold, efficient, intense cathode with good uniformity and long life.

The use of a cold cathode offers advantages over hot cathodes in low-power applications where geometry makes hot cathodes inconvenient. Large-area cold cathodes have been prepared using multiple field-emission devices. Because they're a cathode and generate an electron emission, they are packaged in thin vacuum packages. There's a phosphor-coated screen that illuminates when the electrons strike it. Due to the close anode spacing, anode voltage must be kept relatively low, with voltages of 80 to 100 volts. Many descriptions have been made about the concept of such a display. Recent technological developments have made it possible to obtain reasonable yields and good reliability.

Numerous research labs and companies in Japan and Europe are developing MFD technology. In the U.S., the MCC (Microelectronics and Computer Technology) organization solicited and has found sponsors to underwrite a vertically integrated MFD consortium project to speed the commercialization of this technology. The biggest challenges for FE microtip-array FPDs are in reliable and reproducible fabrication and characterization of these devices.

Vacuum fluorescent displays

Many vacuum fluorescent displays (VFDs) work in VCRs, audio equipment, microwave ovens, household electric appliances, automobile instrument panels, OA equipment, and amusement equipment. Many household appliances contain microcomputers and use VFDs as indication devices. This is a new application for the VFD and demand is rising.

The VFD is a triode consisting of the cathode, grid, and anode enclosed in a vacuum container. Thermions discharged from the cathode are accelerated by the positive voltage applied to the grid and anode. The accelerated thermions stimulate phosphors applied to the anode, and emit light. The vacuum fluorescent display provides the greatest degree of brightness of all the flat displays.

The VFD was developed and introduced by Ise Electronic Industry in 1967. Three manufacturers produce VFDs: Ise Electronic Industry (Noritake Company), Futaba Electronic Industry, and NEC. Applications in electronic calculators and clocks rapidly expanded the market volume for VFDs.

VFDs and LEDs are used for a great many applications, primarily as individual seven- and eleven-segment alphanumeric displays. Unfortunately, manufacturers have not found significant uses for them in computers except as CPU displays (to indicate clock speed or address).

Electrochromic display technology

Electrochromic displays have attracted interest because of their outstanding contrast at normal and wide viewing angles and their open-circuit memory. However, most electrochromic technologies have faced a number of technical drawbacks that have prevented them from being applied as displays. They've been primarily used in the area of *smart windows* (electronic window shades that can be made opaque), where computer display requirements don't apply.

The drawbacks of electrochromic displays are due to issues relating to structure and life—they're complex and costly structures often involving liquid electrolytes, poor resolution, poor cycle life, and lack of multicolor capability—and issues relating to display addressing and driving, such as the need to balance the writing and erasing charges and the lack of intrinsic matrix addressability.

However, a new electrochromic-display technology (tradename Polyvision) has been developed with addressing-driving features that overcome the previous hurdles. More specifically, it possesses intrinsic matrix addressability with a set of additional features, allowing the fast updating of a matrix. Therefore, there might be a new class of flat-panel displays on the near horizon.

Grayscale displays

Computers that use a monochrome LCD display must have a grayscale display capability. However, most applications written for CRT-based desktop PCs use color. Therefore, a means is needed to convert from color-based images and screens to grayscale representations, commonly referred to as *color emulation*. It isn't as easy as it sounds.

The current screen standard for PCs is the video graphics array (VGA), introduced in 1987 by IBM. It has a 640×480-pixel resolution and can display 16 colors simultaneously, from a palette of 262,000. With the 0.33-mm pixel spacing required by display standards, the 640×480-pixel pattern requires a rectangular area having at least a 10.4-inch diagonal.

Manufacturers of desktop LCD displays and portable computers use monochrome panels to display applications written in color. This is done by using gray shades to substitute for the colors. Conventionally, the 16 colors are mapped into 16 gray shades (levels of intensity) based on the relative intensities of the colors.

Even though color flat-panel technology has become available, monochrome panels will probably remain popular for portables because of their lower cost and the significantly lower power required for the backlight, which extends battery operation. Therefore, effective grayscale techniques have been developed in the past few years. I'll review a few of them in this section.

Basic grayscale display is accomplished by modulating the on/off time of the individual pixels in the LCD panel. This allows the eye to integrate the superimposed images to about 16 perceptible gray levels. However, due to the limited response time of the LCDs, flicker can occur. To overcome this problem, the LCD chip-controller manufacturers have developed various proprietary techniques involving distribution of time between on/off pixels, combined with frame modulation.

LCD chip-controller manufacturers using two-dimensional strippling logic can obtain 64 effective gray levels.

Amplitude modulation

In supertwisted-nematic liquid-crystal displays (STN-LCDs) and ac thin-film electroluminescent displays (AC-TFELs), the amplitude of the excitation is used to modulate the contrast ratio or the luminance.

One problem has been the STN characteristic of contrast degradation when the rms-drive voltage is reduced. Reducing the rms-drive voltage also reduces the viewing angle in a super-linear fashion. Nonuniform luminance-voltage characteristics have also been a problem in AC-TFELs. In addition, the effectiveness of their energy-recovery circuits is compromised by the very nature of amplitude-modulation driver circuits.

Halftones

One alternative to amplitude modulation is halftoning. Halftones vary the dot sizes in an image to change the effective or perceived contrast. When viewed at a distance, the eye integrates the dots (pels or pixels) into a smooth image of varying contrast.

There are at least two halftone schemes that vary the address-line geometry. The schemes use subpixels whose areas have ratios of 1, 2, 4, and 8, and produce 16 linear halftone gray levels. This is the strength of the schemes, but also their limitation because it doesn't allow any other meaningful variation in the gamma of the gray levels. Both approaches require high resolution for the subpixels, so they aren't applicable to the plasma-display technologies.

In one of the implementations, the number of X and Y address lines are doubled. This halves the duty cycle for the multiplexed X lines. (For LCDs, this might be the less desirable of the strongly nonlinear effect of lower duty cycle on contrast ratio and viewing angle.) The 4 bits for each pixel are distributed in two dimensions, which requires storage and reordering of the Y bits for each X line.

In the other implementation, the number of X lines remains unchanged, which keeps the duty cycle unchanged, but the number of Y lines is increased by a factor of 4 compared to the conventional amplitude-modulated scheme. Here, the data can be fed into the Y-driver registers without reordering the bits.

An opponent color LCD

In late 1990, Dr. Richard Young and J.A. Traxel (of GM research and development) proposed a way of implementing the Land effect (refer to *Two-channel color* in chapter 2, *Color*) in a modified LCD device. Instead of using three different, colored, parallel filter stripes, as found in standard color LCDs, they use two colors, which run diagonally. This method uses a composite color element formed by two elements (red and white); the conventional display requires three elements (red, green, and blue). For an equivalent total number of elements, the effective spatial resolution for this type of Land-type LCD is approximately 50% better in horizontal and vertical directions than for the standard RGB display. Both Young and Troxell emphasize that the total number of pixels can be reduced by 33%, thereby saving more than 33% on the cost of electronics and memory while maintaining a resolution equivalent to the RGB displays.

Opponent color liquid-crystal displays will have spatial resolution comparable to super VGA or TV monitors. In addition, the price of opponent-color units should be nearly the same as for conventional CRT monitors. The reason for the reduced cost is that opponent-color LCDs have to create fewer pixels and electrical connections.

Opponent colors can be generated by using a dichroic filter, according to Young's proposal. A polarized plate that incorporates selective dichroic dyes can serve as a dichroic filter. By controlling the degree of circular polarization, colors can be generated from white light passing through the cell. Liquid crystals (and dyes) can be compounded to give specific rotation to light coming through them. By selecting an LCD material that rotates white light by varying degrees and applying a voltage to the material, different colors can be made to appear.

This concept was originally proposed to Dr. Young by Nano V. Vax of the physics department at GM Research. Vax refers to early work on color displays by Dr. T. J. Sheffer of Brown Boveri Research Center at Baden, Switzerland. Quoting Dr. Vax: "The construction of an LCD panel utilizing the opponent-color method together with dichroic filter is nothing new. It is based upon standard techniques and methods the industry is using today."

Before any attempts were made to construct an opponent-color LCD panel, Young and his associates wanted to test their theories. A simulation of the opponent-type system for LCD was generated on a standard cathode-ray tube. The proposed diagonal checkerboard pattern was modified so it could simulate the opponent-color technique on a CRT.

In Young's opponent-CRT experiments, the average value of the red, green, and blue memory buffers at each spatial location was stored as the first channel. These values were normalized as the peak value was at 255, the maximum value of the display. This channel was sent equally to the three color guns in the odd diagonal pixels, producing the black-and-white image.

For example, if red had 50, green had 100, and blue had 150 at a given address, then a value of 100 would be stored as the first channel, and sent equally to the different drivers for the red, green, and blue guns. A specific value of white is produced at that pixel location when it is viewed in isolation. Likewise, the difference of the red and blue buffers (which was also normalized to a peak of 255) is stored as the opponent-color channel. The red gun is driven directly by this channel, and the blue gun by its negative; the green channel is completely turned off with a value of 0. If the final output signal to a gun is negative, it's clamped at 0.

In another example, if the red memory buffer had a value of 200 and the blue a value of 100, then a value of 100 would be stored in the opponent channel. The red gun would receive 100 and the blue gun would get 0. If the blue buffer had 200 and the red 100, then –100 would be stored in the opponent channel and 100 would be sent to the blue gun driver, with a value of 0 to the red gun driver. This takes a considerable amount of logic and electronic circuitry to operate correctly. Because there are no IC chipsets available for carrying out this type of operation, all of the experimental CRT displays are driven by discrete circuits.

Using conventional RGB cathode-ray tubes to simulate an LCD causes spatial resolution three times worse than it would be in an opponent-color LCD since six colors are employed with a CRT to create the two-color channel display. Simulated CRT displays were presented to a panel of people who were asked to judge what colors they observed. In the Land-type display, the results were encouraging. Hues other than red and white were seen, particularly greens, browns, and golds. Blues, however, were not observed, although this isn't unusual because the original Land-type displays exhibited the same characteristics. In the opponent-color display, the results were even more encouraging. In addition to the range of hues viewed in the Land display, blues could be readily observed. All observers comparing the two displays under simultaneous viewing conditions on two matched monitors saw a much wider range of colors in the opponent-type display than they did in the Land-type display.

The use of opponent-color display techniques have created new opportunities for LCDs. Using only two-color channels, they permit lower-cost and more rugged displays that can be used in field equipment and automobiles. Two-channel color displays have been tried before—refer to chapter 2, *Color*, for more information on the subject.

In a conventional RGB display, six pixels are used to obtain two spatial-resolution elements. With a two-channel opponent-color display composed of a white/black channel (W) and a red/cyan channel (Rc), the same six pixels now yield higher spatial resolution (three resolution elements for a 50% improvement). Figure 4-15 shows the comparison of the use of pixels between a three-color and two-color opponent system. Because of the way colors are created for LCDs, a mixture of blue and green is used to get cyan.

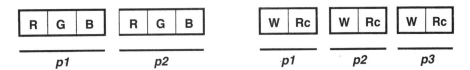

4-15 *A two-channel opponent-color display (W and Rc) offers greater spatial resolution in a given area. When two spatial elements are compared, the opponent color scheme is less expensive than a conventional three-channel RGB display.*

The opponent-color technique yields a lower-cost display (the number of pixels can be reduced from six to four for at least a 33% cost savings) without loss in spatial resolution. Lower costs are achieved because of reduced materials, fewer required drivers, and also smaller packaging costs for the reduced electronics.

Displays of this type have been built by Richard Young at General Motors. A conventional 640×480 RGB active-matrix liquid-crystal display, but without the RGB filters, was fabricated by Optical Imaging Systems. The display was column based. Because there were originally 640 color columns, each comprised of an R, G, and B color element, there were a total of 1920 driveable elements in the horizontal direction. Each of these elements was 110 microns wide. They were driven by 480 drivers operating in the vertical direction. Optical Devices Inc. fabricated an optical filter composed of alternating stripes of a gray linear polarizer and a red/cyan diachronic polarizer.

Images for map navigation, diagnostics, and emulation of conventional dashboard instrumentation were created and displayed in various voltage levels in the two channels of the display. The brightness signal was displayed in the odd stripes. It looks like a black-and-white photo if seen by itself. The opponent-color signal is displayed in the even stripes. This channel is the red/blue opponent signal at each location. If red is more intense than blue in the image, the pixel becomes more red. If blue is more intense than red, the pixel becomes more blue. An observer sees only red and blue combinations, therefore, when looking at this image by itself.

Flight displays

With the advent of the glass cockpit on modern flight decks, CRT technology has been used as the primary medium to display a wide array of information to flight crews. As the display industry has learned more about the capabilities and limitations of CRTs, basic guidelines for cockpit formats have evolved. The result has been wide pilot-community acceptance and high usability of complex integrated-display formats such as those seen on Boeing's 747-400.

With the Boeing 777 program, it became evident that LCD technology had matured to the point that it was considered as a replacement for the CRT. With lower energy and cooling requirements, higher projected reliability, and size and weight reductions, the LCD was chosen as the medium for all 777 format displays—using the 747-400 display formats as the baseline.

Prototype LCDs were used to evaluate the initial graphic-primitive characteristics in the 777. The evaluations showed that the established formatting guidelines for the 777 LCDs resulted in fidelity and quality equal to, and in some cases, better than the 747-400 CRTs.

FPDs for HDTV & large-area displays

The original emphasis for the development of HDTV was the famous "picture on the wall" concept that was so popular in the 1960s and 1970s. It was known then that the CRT wasn't well suited for the job. A 3×5-foot HDTV screen, based on a CRT, would be extremely large and deep, heavy, hot, and expensive—not really a practical consideration. Therefore, most of the effort for such large displays is being put on flat panels, either for large direct viewing or used as a project shutter.

Advanced TV or ATV (HDTV) was to be the market driver for flat-panel displays, with mass production of millions of sets creating the vast economies of scale for electronic components and subsystems. The notion of large picture-on-the-wall displays, in multiple rooms in the home of the future, is a concept that has been a part of our collective expectations for over three decades.

It now appears that the enthusiasm was unjustified. For the foreseeable future, flat-panel ATV sets will be limited to a much smaller quantity and will use projection systems. The higher price and margins of the large-screen flat-panel ATV systems will still make a nice profitable market. But the quantities won't be the mass-market driver for FPD electronics that has been envisioned. That role is now turned over to portable computers and someday to desktop systems.

But what flat-panel technology will prevail for ATV? Conventional wisdom says it should be active-matrix liquid-crystal displays. But brightness is an annoying problem—and the light source for projection systems has a noticeably shorter lifetime.

Monoliths

The scaling up of a technology, although not feasible in their case of the CRT, has been demonstrated in other technologies. Plasma flat panels, AC-PDPs, already produced in large sizes, might become an attractive choice for HDTV-FPDs. Color is obtainable, and they can be made in far larger sizes than AM-LCD can hope to achieve for years to come. But plasma detractors criticize the resolution and claim mass production of conventional TV-sized color plasma screens is still far down the road. FLCDs and FEDs, as well as AC-TFEL and PALC displays, are other possibilities.

Tiling

Tiling is another approach to large-area displays. This technique fits small, high-yield FPDs together (like floor tiles) to make a larger screen. Tiling was developed because of the low manufacturing yields expected for large FPDs. Magnascreen is one company exploring this particular approach. The major problem associated with tiling is that the human eye can discern errors in panel joints of less than one pixel in size when the panels are improperly fitted together. One solution to that problem has been to put a definite gap between the panels so they look like distinct panels. Interestingly, this is more acceptable to most viewers.

Projectors

Projectors have also been a popular approach to large-screen displays. Manufacturers in Japan have used three monochrome AM-LCD panels with respective red, green, and blue filters; a very bright backlight, and a projection lens to produce large full-color projected images. This approach is similar to the familiar technique of combining the images of three CRTs in a color projection system.

The possibility of using projection for large-area displays is intriguing because small high-resolution LCD panels are less expensive than large ones. One of the problems in this approach is the length of the projector's beam needed to produce a large image (think about the size of the projector at the movies and how far it is from the screen). The most popular solution is to fold the light path into a few inches of space behind the rear projection screen. This is the technique used for the 35- to 55-inch large-screen TV displays. However, this creates a new problem: correcting the image distortions and luminance nonuniformities produced by folding the beam.

CRTs (still)

Meanwhile, the old reliable conventional cathode-ray tube (CRT) is firmly entrenched in the market for sets with up to 35-inch screens, 95% of the world's market. This probably isn't bad for the U.S., which has a half-dozen plants in the country (but all foreign-owned) making large-sized CRTs and only a few producers of LCD screens. It will be interesting to see how the shifting technology battles shake up the North American TV market, the world's largest.

FPDs for all applications

For the most part, flat-panel display manufacturers have focused their technical energies on larger displays to serve an existing market, but their developments have found their way to the secondary display markets. This market, which includes pen computers, palmtops, personal digital assistants (PDAs), avionics, videophones, mobile-communications equipment, and all manner of data-collection terminals, will add to the production levels and help reduce cost.

New technologies are constantly being developed in pursuit of the picture-on-the-wall large-panel displays. A novel micromechanical light-value display has been demonstrated using conventional semiconductor-manufacturing techniques. The display uses a deformable-grating light-value (DGLV) technique. It's based on electrostatically controlling the amplitude of a micromachined reflection grating, and is capable of high-speed (20ns) color-selection operation.

Other systems are being developed for 3-D viewing without special glasses that will be employed in virtual reality, windowless flight decks of hypersonic aircraft, and entertainment centers. These and other novel and exciting developments will continue to be the hallmark of flat-panel display systems.

So are CRTs forever?

Despite the growing interest in flat-panel display technologies, the ubiquitous CRT stubbornly excels in certain characteristics. The CRT still rules in performance where you need better resolution and quality of image, and especially where you have to be sensitive to viewing angle. CRTs will continue to be the most popular and dominant display technology until flat-panel display image quality (brightness, contrast, and speed), prices, and yields become superior to that of CRTs.

Perhaps that isn't the most profound thing you've read in this book, but it does drive home the point. LCDs have been forecasted to win out in the marketplace because of the multibillion-dollar investments in R & D and manufacturing. This has been expected to rapidly mature the technology and drive down production costs. One of the most popular flat-panel displays is the AM-LCD using TFTs. The Japanese industry is solidly behind this technology, and demand greatly exceeds production capabilities. The manufacturing volumes of passive LCDs have narrowed the CRT's traditional cost advantage, according to several sources, and both are now at approximate cost parity. However, as popular as the AM-LCDs are, they continue to have manufacturing problems, and this could provide other display technologies the opportunity to leap ahead of AM-LCDs.

Passive-matrix LCDs offer the lowest-cost flat-panel display for most applications that don't require fast response. For applications that require fast response time, AM-LCDs, FLCDs, AC-TFEL displays, or AC-PDPs offer better solutions.

Other potentially successful flat-panel display technologies are FLCDs and PALC devices. Candidates such as FEDs, AC-PDPs, and AC-TFEL displays offer features such as wide viewing angles, high brightness, crisp images, and low-power consumption. With their already-demonstrated full-color capabilities, however, AC-PDPs and AC-TFEL displays will have to be produced at competitive prices.

To meet these challenges, nine U.S. display manufacturers (Cherry, Planar Systems, Plasmaco, Electro Plasma, OIS, Photonice Systems, Standish, Tektronix, and

Magnascreen) formed the ADC (American Display Consortium) in 1992 to do procompetitive research on flat-panel displays. The ADC companies offer all major display technologies. This is the kind of collaborative effort, with leveraging resources and building partnerships, that's an essential strategy for success in this highly competitive market.

But flat-panel displays are not the only contenders for the CRT's throne. In addition, there are other display technologies, such as three-dimensional and stroboscopic displays, that are being used for applications such as medical imaging, and military and commercial aircraft command and control. The demand for display devices and the imagination and resources being applied make it one of the most dynamic and exciting areas in computer graphics.

Controllers

Flat-panel controllers must support all display technologies including electroluminescent (EL), liquid crystal displays (LCDs), and plasma displays (PD). LCD panel interfaces are needed for both single-panel single-drive (SS), dual-panel single-drive (DS), and dual-panel dual-drive (DD) configurations. A single panel needs image data sent to it like a CRT (sequentially from an area of display memory). In a dual-panel image, data must be presented in alternation between the two panels. A dual-drive panel requires the image data for the two panels to be provided simultaneously.

In the past few years, LCD display-controller manufacturers have enhanced their devices to maximize and enhance the capabilities of LCDs. Some of the techniques and features used in these controllers are described in this section.

LCD display-enhancement features

Display quality is one of the most important features for the success of any flat-panel-based system. Because most application software is written for color CRT monitors, FPD controller manufacturers provide several proprietary features to maximize display quality on monochrome flat panels. Using extension registers, the chip suppliers can provide the flexibility to interface to a wide range of flat panels and offer full compatibility transparent to the application software.

RGB color to grayscale reduction

The 18 bits of color-palette data from the VGA standard color lookup table are reduced to 6 bits for 64 grayscales via one of three selectable RGB color to gray-scale reduction techniques:

NTSC weighting   59% red, 30% green, and 11% blue

Equal weighting   33.3% red,33.3% green, and 33.3% blue

Green only   6 bits of green only

NTSC is the most common weighting, and is used in television broadcasting. Equal weighting increases the weighting of blue, which is important for applications such as Microsoft Windows 3.x, which often uses blue for background colors. The use of green only is useful for replicating a flat-panel display of software optimized for monochrome monitors that use the six green bits of palette data.

Grayscale algorithms

Most chips have a proprietary polynomial-based frame-rate control (FRC) and dithering algorithm built into the hardware, which generates 64 gray levels on monochrome panels. The FRC technique simulates 16 gray levels on monochrome panels by turning the pixels on and off over a period of time. The dithering technique increases the number of grayscales from 16 to 64 by altering the pattern of grayscales in adjacent pixels. By programming a polynomial, the FRC algorithm of some chips can be adjusted to reduce flicker without increasing the panel's vertical refresh rate.

The persistence (response time) of the pixels varies among panel manufacturers and models. By reprogramming the polynomial using a trial-and-error method while viewing the display, the FRC algorithm can be adjusted to match the persistence of the particular panel. With this technique, chips produce 64 flicker-free grayscales on the latest fast-response mouse-quick film-compensated monochrome STN-LCDs. The alternate method of reducing flicker—increasing the panel's vertical refresh rate— has several drawbacks. As the vertical refresh rate increases, the panel's power consumption increases, ghosting (cross-talk) increases, and contrast decreases.

Vertical & horizontal compensation

Vertical and horizontal compensation are programmable features that adjust the display to completely fill the flat-panel display. Vertical compensation increases the usable display area when running lower-resolution software on a higher-resolution panel. Unlike CRT monitors, flat panels have a fixed number of scan lines (200, 400, 480, or 768 lines). Lower-resolution software run on a higher-resolution panel only partially fills the usable display area. For instance, 350-line EGA software displayed on a 480-line panel would leave 130 blank lines at the bottom of the display, and 400-line VGA text or mode-13 images would leave 80 blank lines at the bottom.

Vertical centering displays text or graphics images in the center of the flat panel with a border of unused area at the top and bottom of the display. Automatic vertical centering automatically adjusts the display's starting address so that the unused area at the top of the display equals the unused area at the bottom. Nonautomatic vertical centering enables you to set the display's starting address (via programming the extension registers) so that text or graphic images can be positioned anywhere on the display.

Line replication (referred to as *stretching*) duplicates every *n*th display line (where *n* is a programmable value in several controllers), thus stretching text characters and graphic images an adjustable amount. This feature allows the display to be stretched to completely fill the flat-panel area. Double scanning is a form of line replication where every line is repeated or copied. It's used to run 200-line software on a 400-line panel or 480-line software on a 1024-line panel.

Blank-line insertion inserts *n* blank lines (where *n* is programmable) between each line of text characters. Thus, text can be evenly spaced to fill the entire panel display area without altering the height and shape of the text characters. Blank-line insertion can be used in text mode only.

Special fonts are often available that use a nonVGA standard font, so that text fills almost all lines on the flat panel and all lines of text are the same size. For example, an 8×19 font would fill 475 lines on a 480-line panel, and an 8×30 font would fill 750 lines on a 768-line panel. These special fonts are sometimes known as "tall fonts," and can be used in text mode only.

You can control each of these vertical-compensation techniques by programming the extension registers. Each vertical-compensation feature can be individually disabled, enabled, and adjusted. You can use a combination of vertical-compensation features by adjusting their priority order. For example, text-mode vertical compensation consists of four priority-order options:

- ❑ Double scanning+line insertion, double scanning, line insertion
- ❑ Double scanning+line insertion, line insertion, double scanning
- ❑ Double scanning+special fonts, double scanning, special fonts
- ❑ Double scanning+special fonts, special fonts, double scanning

Text and graphics modes offer two line-replication priority-order options:

- ❑ Double scanning+line replication, double scanning, line replication
- ❑ Double scanning+line replication, line replication, double scanning

Horizontal-compensation techniques include horizontal compression, horizontal centering, and horizontal doubling. Horizontal compression will compress 9-dot text to 8 dots so that 720-dot text in Hercules mode will fit on a 640-dot panel. Automatic horizontal centering automatically centers the display on a larger-resolution panel so that the unused area is moved to the right. Nonautomatic horizontal centering allows you to set the left border (via programming the horizontal-centering extension register) so that the image can be positioned anywhere on the display. Automatic horizontal doubling will automatically double the display in the horizontal direction when the horizontal display width is equal to or less than half of the horizontal panel size.

Some controllers offer a proprietary feature that can be invoked to map colors to gray levels in text mode. Often such techniques improve the legibility of flat-panel displays by solving a common problem.

Color to grayscale mapping

Most application programs are optimized for color CRT monitors using multiple colors. For example, a word processor might use a blue background with white characters for normal text, green for underlined text, yellow for italicized text, and so on. This variety of colors, which is quite distinct on a color CRT monitor, can be illegible on a monochrome flat-panel display if the colors are mapped to adjacent grayscale values. For example, underlined and italicized text would be illegible if yellow is mapped to grayscale 4, green to grayscale 6, and the blue background to grayscale 5.

Mapping algorithms compare and adjust foreground and background grayscale values to produce adequate display contrast on flat-panel displays. The minimum contrast value and the foreground and background grayscale adjustment are programmed in the extension registers.

Text enhancement is another feature of the advanced controllers that improves image quality on flat-panel displays. Many applications, such as MS-DOS, use dim white for normal text characters, which results in nonoptimal contrast on flat panels. When activated, the text-enhancement feature displays dim white as bright white, thereby optimizing the contrast level.

Text enhancement

This feature inverts the functionality of the intensity bit for white only. Highlighted white, which is displayed as bright white when the text-enhancement function is turned off, is shown as dim white with the text-enhancement function turned on, thus maintaining a difference between normal and highlighted text. You can typically change text enhancement on and off by changing a bit in one of the extension registers. Access to the control of that bit can sometimes be found in the computer's setup and in other cases in an application.

Inverse video

Inverse video can be enabled in text modes only on the flat panel (normal video is displayed on the CRT and, in graphics modes, on the flat panel), in graphics modes only on the flat panel (normal video is displayed on the CRT and, in text modes, on the flat panel), or in both text and graphics modes on flat-panel displays.

Summary

Somewhere in the late 1980s and early 1990s, people at all levels in the U.S. began to realize that the continuous and large investments the Japanese had been making in LCD technology since the 1970s wasn't just for clocks and simple displays. Even though the Japanese were very open about their intentions to build an HDTV picture-on-the-wall system and computer displays, the "leaders" in the U.S. didn't get it. More interested in junk-bond refinancings, real estate speculation, 20-mile-wide cyclotrons, and a pathetic NASA, the U.S. chose politics and laissez-faire procrastination about building a cohesive, technological, industrial base.

When the national consciousness woke up to the developments in HDTV, LCDs, and semiconductors being made by the Japanese, panic and finger pointing began. After that, typical response proposals began to find receptive audiences. Slowly, a feeble LCD community of manufacturers became visible and new alliances were formed. HDTV came to life in the U.S. and new and exciting digital-compression schemes were announced. However, all that could be done in the LCD area was small consortiums, a couple of joint ventures, and a government tariff reaction—too little, too late. You can't compensate for hundreds of millions of dollars investment in R & D and manufacturing processes over two decades with an ineffective tariff and a couple of joint ventures. Like TVs, CRTs, and automobiles, the U.S. had lost another technology segment—a segment that, like the others, is extremely large: the consumer market.

What you should get from this chapter is an appreciation for the general construction and operation of flat-panel displays. Such displays are a part of your everyday life and an ever-increasingly important part of computer-graphics display, TV display, and image-processing display. You should also understand that the FPD technology, especially the LCD segment, is still evolving and, like most things, there is no best solution. Also, the good old CRT is far from dead, as sexy as some of the new FPDs might appear.

A summary of the basic characteristics of the leading display types is shown in TABLE 4-2. It isn't an absolute comparison and shouldn't be used for critical analysis—just for relative comparisons. TABLE 4-3 shows some of the absolute differences between some of the leading types of displays, and is subject to change each time a developer in one of the areas makes a breakthrough. However, the relative differences should in all likelihood remain the same.

Tables like this are interesting to look at for general comparisons, but they don't reveal enough about a display to make a definitive choice. For example, is weight, radiation, or lifetime the most important factor? I caution you not to jump to conclusions when encountering such information. Following is a glossary of FPD acronyms for use with this chapter:

AMEL active-matrix electroluminescent
AM-LCD active-matrix LCD

Table 4-2
Basic characteristics of the leading types of displays.

Feature	CRT	RED	PDP	EL	PM LCD	AM LCD	VFD
Size	M	E	G	G	E	G	G
Resolution	E	E	E	G	M	E	M
Brightness	E	E	E	G	M	G	G
Color	E	E	G	M	G	G	M
Grayscale	E	E	G	M	G	G	P
Display quality	E	E	G	G	G	E	M
Weight & thinness	P	G	G	G	E	E	E
Response	E	E	G	G	P	G	M
Cost	G	G	M	G	E	G	E

E=Excellent   G=Good   M=Marginal   P=Poor

Table 4-3
Differences between some display types.

Feature	CRT	EL	DC-PDP	PM-LCD
Brightness	30 fL	20 fL	6 fL	15 fL
Contrast	75:1	100:1	10:1	5:1
Viewing angle	160°	160°	100°	45°
Pixel spread	<1 ms	<1 ms	<200 ms	>200 ms

DCEL   direct-current electroluminescent
EL   electroluminescent
FED   field-emission display, *aka* MFD (microtip fluorescent display)
FLCD   ferroelectric LCD, *aka* FE-LCD
FSTN   compensated supertwisted nematic, *aka* DSTN (double STN)
MIM   metal-insulator-metal (MIM)
OMI   optical-mode interference
PDLC   polymer-dispersed liquid crystal
PDP   plasma display panel
PM-LCD   passive-matrix LCD
RTSD   reflective-type, three-electrode, surface-discharge technique
STN   supertwisted nematic
TFEL   thin-film electroluminescent, *aka* AC-TFEL
TFT   thin-film transistor, *aka* TFT-LCD, AM-TFT, and TFT-LC
TN   twisted nematic
TSTN   triple supertwisted nematic, *aka* stacked STN-LCD
VFD   vacuum-fluorescent display

Glossary & list of acronyms

2-D Two-dimensional graphics, expressed in either real-world units (miles, meters, etc.) or in device coordinates x and y.

3-D Three-dimensional graphics expressed in either real-world units (miles, meters, etc.) or in device coordinates x, y, and z.

adapter *See* display adapter.

application-binary interface (ABI) ABI is the general term for any application-binary interface. It allows executable versions of software to run directly on a platform without recompiling or modification. DOS is an example of an ABI.

additive color The process of blending colored light. It has been found that the three primary additive colors—red, green, and blue—are used to create white light. Also known as *transmitted color.*

address An address can be any of the following things: a unique digital code that identifies a register-memory location or add-on board within a microcomputer system where information is stored, that portion of a program instruction that includes a specific memory location, the act of storing or retrieving data from a specific memory location, the discrete unit by which an aggregate of data can be referenced (words in memory, sectors on a disk, and pixels on a screen are all located by an integer address), or a physical address of data, for example a register number or a track and sector. A logical address is a mnemonic address for the convenience of users and programmers, for example a variable or a filename.

add-in board A plug-in board that adds functionality and features to a system, i.e., a graphics board.

ADO Ampex Digital Optical is a special effect that bends or warps images. Named for the company that developed the effect.

algorithm A sequence of prescribed operations or rules used to solve a function or problem.

aliasing The undesirable distortion of a raster image by insufficient display resolution; it causes an effect commonly known as *staircasing* or *the jaggies.*

alignment   Text alignment defines how text is aligned within the left and right indented paragraphs: either flush left, flush right, centered, or justified. Graphic alignment defines how objects align: along their sides, centers, tops, or bottoms.

alphanumeric   A set of characters that contain both numbers and letters. An alphanumeric display is one that is incapable of producing a graphic image.

animation   Producing the illusion of movement in a film or video with photography, or otherwise recording a series of single frames, each showing incremental changes in the position of the subject images. When shown in sequence at high speed, this gives the illusion of movement. Individual frames can be produced by a variety of techniques, from computer-generated images to hand-drawn cells.

anti-aliasing   A technique to reduce or eliminate the effects of aliasing. In computer graphics, this frequently involves spatial frequency-filtering techniques to reduce the effects of staircasing or the jaggies. Done with software or hardware, it's a form of dithering the jagged edges that can appear in angled lines in a raster display. *See also* dithering.

applications   A computer program written for a specific purpose, such as word processing or page layout.

area fill   A graphics function that fills a bounded area with a solid color. Also known as a *flood fill*.

aspect ratio   The proportional measurement of image size in terms of horizontal and vertical size. For example, an image with an aspect ratio of 4:3 has a horizontal length that is 4/3 the vertical height.

assignment   In volume rendering, the means giving values for color, opacity, and refractive index to each volume element.

atto   prefix signifying 10^{-18}

attribute   Any description property that applies to an output primitive, including aspects that affect appearance, a modeling transformation, view definition, or name set. An attribute value stays in effect until another change specification supersedes it.

attributes   Qualities given to a particular primitive or segment. For example, the attributes of a point are its color and location, while the attributes of a line are its color, length, location, and orientation.

autosizing   The ability to adjust the screen automatically to compensate for a different display mode. For instance, when you switch from SuperVGA (800×600) to extended VGA or high resolution (1024×768), you usually need to adjust the horizontal and vertical size, and recenter the image. In theory, autosizing makes the adjustments automatically. *See also* image settings.

back porch   The portion of a composite display signal that lies between the trailing edges of a horizontal sync pulse and the corresponding blanking pulse.

backward compatibility   Compatibility with previous or older versions and standards. Also referred to as *downward compatibility*.

bandwidth   The maximum frequency a monitor can accept without degrading the video signal. It's measured in millions or cycles of a second, or megahertz (MHz). Bandwidth plays an important part in determining the overall resolution of the monitor. Also referred to as *video bandwidth*.

BΘzier curve   A curve used in illustration programs that provides control handles for manipulating the shape of the arc; named after cathedral shapes in BΘziers, France.

bilevel   Any image that contains one background color and one foreground color (e.g., black and white). *See also* halftone.

binary   Having two states, often complements of each other, as with male/female, black/white, negative/positive. In computers, binary is 0/1 (zero and one). Used to code data for computation.

bit   Stands for binary digit—the smallest unit of information in a binary computer. A bit will have a value of 0 or 1. Eight bits make up a byte of information. A bit is the indivisible quantum unit of information, a choice between two alternatives of logic: the value of either 0 or 1. *See* binary.

bit map   A matrix of dots all the same density that forms an image, a grid pattern of bits stored in memory and used to generate the image on a raster-scan display. In a bit-mapped display, each bit corresponds to a dot or pixel on the raster display. A bit map is a pixel map of a depth of one (i.e., one bit per pixel).

bit-mapped display   A method of display memory organization that uses a separate area of computer memory to specify locations of individual pixels. One pixel contains one bit on several or all the planes (just the opposite of packed pixel). *See also* planar.

bit plane   The RAM used for storage of a bit map. When a display memory is thought of as a stack of bit maps, each bit map is called a bit plane or plane. *See also* planar and bit-mapped display.

blanking signal   A sequence of recurring blanking pulses related in time to the scanning process.

body   The main text on a page.

bottle   A vernacular expression for the glass tube of a CRT.

buffer   A temporary storage area, often used to compensate for speed differences between system components, a portion of computer memory reserved for temporarily holding data that's being transferred between a CPU and a peripheral (such as disk, printer, or image display). Buffers are especially useful to compensate for differences in data-flow rates, for providing a place for data to reside when events are asynchronous (for example, data being written to a display controller might have to wait while the controller completes its current operation), and to hold data still (as in a video frame buffer). Some buffer memory is part of the addressable memory of the CPU; some buffer memory is part of the peripheral.

bulletin-board system (BBS)   a computer that has been set up to facilitate the exchange of information among other computers via modem. Often, a service bureau will set up a BBS so that its clients can submit files for output.

bump mapping   Similar to texture mapping. This technique creates rough surfaces that could be difficult to calculate by holding a 3-D texture consisting of a typical 3-D section in reference. During rendering, local points in the actual model are referred back to the bump map and deflected. *See also* texture mapping.

bug   A term coined by Dr. Admiral Grace Hopper to describe a malfunctioning (computer) system. Any mistake or malfunction.

bus   A communication line consisting of a parallel data path within the computer system that's shared by system components. Usually described by the width of the parallel data lines available, typical computer buses are 8-, 16-, or 32-bits wide.

business graphics   The use of graphic representations, such as pie and bar charts, to show, explain, and compare various aspects of business operations, historical performance, and projections, usually statistical in nature, and to graphically depict relevant or comparative data. They can be either printed or produced on various types of film and electronic media for projection.

byte   A unit of measurement used to rate storage capacity of display and system memories and disks. A byte is composed of 8 bits of information, and is processed as a unit. One thousand bytes (1K) is a kilobyte; one million bytes (1Mb) is a megabyte. When bytes are used to represent numbers, they're usually organized as a positive integer with a value of 0 to 255 or a signed integer with a value from –127 to +127.

CAD   Computer-aided design, or computer-aided drafting.

CAM   Computer-aided manufacturing.

CATV   Community Antenna Television, usually referred to as cable television.

CAV   Component analog video; unencoded video signals that can provide greater color resolution. An NTSC encoder must be used to read the signals so they can be recognized by a standard NTSC receiver.

cathode-ray tube (CRT)   A sealed glass vacuum tube that contains an electron-beam emitter, or gun, a deflection yoke that focuses the beam, and a phosphor-coated screen that glows for a fraction of a second when struck by the beam.

cache   Very fast memory used as a buffer for transferred information. Typically found on display controllers at the bus and between the controller and the display memory.

cel   An abbreviation for celluloid, used in cel animation.

central processing unit (CPU)   The primary processor in a computer.

character generator   A device that displays letters and numbers electronically on a video screen for use in video productions.

characters per second (cps)   A speed measurement for the rate at which characters are applied to the screen or a printer.

children   The children of a window are its first-level subwindows.

chip   An integrated circuit.

chroma   *See* chrominance.

chrominance   The values that represent the color components of an image, such as hue and saturation. Abbreviated as *chroma*.

chrominance   The hue and saturation of the color of an object as differentiated from the brightness value or luminance of that object.

clipping   The process of removing those parts of an image that lie outside a given boundary, usually a window, viewport, or view volume.

clipping region   In a graphics context, a bit map or list of rectangles can be specified to restrict output to a particular region of the window. The image defined by the bit map or rectangles is called a clipping region.

code   The contents of a program (noun) or to write a program (verb).

color   The individual components of white light as perceived by the human eye. Color monitors use the three basic components of color to which the human eye responds: red, green, and blue. The final color seen on the video screen is created by mixing these primaries.

color encoder   A device that produces an encoded-color signal (typical composite video) from separate red, green, and blue color inputs.

color look-up table   A memory table used in 8-, 12-, and 16-bit display systems, whose entries specify the values of the red, green, and blue intensities used to drive a color monitor. Commonly referred to as the LUT.

color matching   A generic term for methods used to adjust monitor colors to match printed colors. Color-matching monitors have front-panel controls for the red, green, and blue colors that are used to mix all the other colors on the screen. In a standard monitor, these color controls are inside the case and unavailable for user manipulation.

color monitors   Color monitors use the three primary additive colors: red, green, and blue. The final color seen on the video screen is created by the combination of these primaries. The strength of the beam as it strikes the phosphor causes it to illuminate with brightness to match. The combination of all three phosphors creates the color of the pixel. *See also* cathode-ray tube and RGB monitor.

color map   A color map consists of a set of entries defining color values. The color map associated with a window is used to display the contents of the window; each pixel value indexes the color map to produce RGB values that drive the guns of a monitor. Depending on hardware limitations, one or more color maps can be installed at one time so that windows associated with those maps display true colors.

color value   *See* pixel value.

color separation   The process of separating the colors in a colored image (e.g., a photograph or painting) into their primary colors (CYM or RGB) for the purpose of reproduction by graphic printing or other methods.

composite   In broadcasting, the three separate color signals (red, green, and blue), plus timing or sync (synchronization) signals are combined into one composite signal that can be delivered over the airwaves or through a single cable.

computer graphics The overall discipline of creating or manipulating graphic images and pictorial data with computers. These can be used for CAD, animation, design, architecture, scientific imaging, business graphics, etc. Computer-graphics systems are usually interactive, displaying images on a computer screen as they're being created or manipulated.

command An instruction.

component video A color-video signal that uses more than one signal to describe a color image. Typical component systems are RGB, YIQ, and YUV.

composite The combination of color and synchronization in a single video signal. The color decoder (in the tuner) strips out this information for the internal color circuits. This is the basic manner in which all standard color TVs work. *See also* composite video.

composite video A color-video system that contains all the color information in one signal or on one wire. NTSC, PAL, and SECAM are composite-video standards. *See also* composite.

composite color A color-display signal that includes blanking, synchronizing, and color-burst signals.

composite color sync A signal that includes all the sync signals, chromatic and luminance information, plus the color-burst reference signal in its proper time relationship.

composite display signal A blanked display signal combined with all of the appropriate synchronizing signals.

composite sync A blanked display signal combined with all the appropriate synchronizing signals. The vertical and horizontal sync are combined on one signal and the monitor circuits strip out the individual synchronization signals for proper use.

compression The process of reducing the length of a raster scan by substituting a logical count of color changes. Most compression algorithms are line oriented—if they continue from line to line, they're described as *wrapped*. Compression can be lossless or lossy.

contouring The appearance of patterns or bands due to the limitation of either the resolution of the digitizer or the bits per pixel in the display.

controller *See* display controller.

convergence The ability of the electron beams from the CRT's guns to strike the screen's triads accurately. Each beam must be adjusted so that all three strike the correct phosphor triad individually or the color will appear incorrect or exhibit a color shadow.

convergency The alignment of the red, green, and blue electron beams that create each pixel. If they're properly aligned, the three beams converge at the same point, creating a single dot image. If they're misaligned, the user will perceive color shadows or bleeding colors along the edges.

CRT A sealed glass enclosure similar to a television picture tube that displays computer-generated images written on its face with a controlled electron beam. *See* cathode-ray tube.

cursor   The indicator of the location of the execution point on the screen. In a GUI, it's a symbol that's moved by the mouse; in an alphanumeric (nongraphic) system, it specifies where the next character will be entered. Regardless of the type of system, the cursor is a visible marker moved by the user with some type of input device to indicate a position on a CRT screen.

CYM/(CMY)   The colors cyan, yellow, and magenta, which are the three primary subtractive colors used in color graphic printing.

data   The generic term for information; in a more specific sense, it's sometimes used to refer to information acted on by a program.

data bandwidth   The amount of data, defined in bits, transferred in a single cycle to and from the image-store memory. Typically expressed as *n* megabytes per second. *See also* bandwidth.

data compression   Various techniques that reduce the data content and storage needed to represent an image. Compression can be lossy or lossless. It also reduces the time it takes to display and manipulate files and images.

data field   *See* field.

data rate   The speed of a data-transfer process, normally expressed in bits per second or bytes per second.

dataset   Another term for a file.

decoder   Translation device that changes composite video into separate RGB signals. *See* encoder.

default   The settings initially assigned or an action taken automatically unless otherwise specified.

deflection yoke   Controls the position of the electron beam in a monitor. It's composed of two magnetic coils that are designed to deflect the beam horizontally.

density   The quantity of data that can be displayed or stored in a given area of storage medium. On a screen or printer, it's typically expressed as dots per inch (dpi). In magnetic tape, it's expressed as the number of bits per inch (bpi). On a disk, density is related to the number of bits per track and the track width; a double-density disk can hold twice as much data as the same sized single-density disk.

device   A peripheral system used for display, storage, and input.

device coordinates   The dimensions or coordinates of a device (such as a display) expressed in spatial or address resolution units (i.e., 1024×768).

device driver   The device-dependent interface software that operates between a host computer graphics software package and the display hardware. The device driver generates a hardware device-dependent output and handles all device-dependent interactions with the host-computer software and display hardware.

digital   Discrete values of a quantity, expressed as bits in a digital system.

digital-to-analog conversion (DAC or D/A)   The process whereby a digital input signal is changed into an analog voltage. The analog-voltage value corresponds to the binary weight of the digital word presented to it.

digital monitor   A two- or four-state display that allows for either two (on and off) or four basic colors. Black and white, CGA, EGA, and other early or low-cost monitors have a digital input.

digital image   An image composed of discrete pixels of digitally quantized brightness.

display adapter   The display board in a computer that creates the display and sends it to the monitor. The display adapter determines the resolution and colors that will be shown; the monitor must be compatible with the adapter for the image to be viewable. *See also* display controller.

display area   The portion of a screen that has an active raster scan.

display controller   A subsystem within a computer that contains the control circuitry, video frame buffer, and output circuitry necessary to drive a monitor. *See also* display adapter.

display device   A display device is a graphics device on which images can be represented (for example, refresh display, storage tube display, or plotter). In this book, the display device is always the monitor or flat-panel display of a system. *See also* monitor.

display signals   The location and intensity of each pixel along individual raster lines are established by modulating the display signals.

dithering   A display technique in which black-and-white pixels are intermixed with continuous-tone colors to get shading and highlighting on a solid-model image, in contrast to the commonly used approach of varying the color and intensity of each individual pixel. Also a technique using two colors to create the appearance of a third, giving a smooth appearance to otherwise abrupt transitions. A method of using patterns to simulate gradations of gray or color shades. A process of anti-aliasing.

dot matrix   Symbols and characters formed on the screen by an X,Y pattern of pixels.

dots per inch (dpi)   Dots per inch are a measure of a printer's or video monitor's resolution. A laser printer's resolution is 300 dpi. Most monitors are around 72 dpi.

dot pitch   The distance between the triads, measured in millimeters. Each set of triads in the monitor are separated from the next, which is called the *dot pitch*. The shorter the distance, the better the resolution and the crisper the image. Color monitors can never have the fine resolution of a monochrome monitor because monochrome monitors have only one phosphor coating, placed contiguously in the CRT.

double buffer   Display system that consists of two display memories or buffers. A block (image) of data is alternatively written to one of two buffers. The displayed image is fixed and viewable while the second buffer is being loaded by the program, giving an illusion of real-time displaying. One buffer stores the current display information, while the other creates the next view. Double buffers provide continuity and realism in animated sequences. Also known as *double buffering*.

dragging   Moving a symbol across the CRT screen interactively with a graphics input device.

driver   *See* device driver.

electron gun   The CRT's gun consists of two primary sections: the triode and the lens. The triode is formed by the cathode (K), its filament heater (H) and two control elements: the control grid (G1) and the acceleration grid (G2). The video signal is applied to the cathode.

emulation   One device mimicking the behavior of another.

encoder   A device that translates RGB signals into a single composite signal. Performs the opposite function of a decoder.

entity   Lines, circles, arcs, or other drawing elements in a CAD database.

exa   A prefix signifying 10^{18}; one quintillion.

expansion board   Another name for an add-in board.

expansion slot   The card connectors within a computer for add-in boards. Extra space in the computer for plugging in adapter cards to attach added memory devices, printer, graphics devices, and other peripherals.

extended VGA   A term used to describe a VGA board capable of providing high resolution (1024×768).

extrusion   The conversion of 2-D data into a 3-D representation by duplicating values at different locations.

femto   A prefix signifying 10^{-15}.

field   A component of a record, a field consists of one or more contiguous bits or bytes and defines one variable in the record; a single field stores a single number or code.

file   A collection of information referred to by a single filename and with related purpose. Files can contain programs or data (or both). They can be new or old, read and/or write protected, and be either random access (as on a disc) or sequential (as on a tape). Files can be either blocked or unblocked, but usually consist of one or more blocks. If they're blocked, they have a block size.

fill   A graphics function that fills the interior of a polygon or an entire screen with a solid color, pattern, or image; solid coloring or shading a specified area on the display screen.

finite-element analysis (FEA)   A computer-analysis technique in which a structure is represented by a network of tiny interconnected elements for determining characteristics such as stress in mechanical structures.

finite-element model (FEM)   The network of elements representing a structure to be processed through finite-element analysis.

firmware   A program that resides in EPROM or ROM. A graphics board's BIOS is usually stored in a ROM. Once placed into the EPROM or ROM, it cannot be modified, damaged, or discarded by the user. Firmware can include some portion of the device driver and the data that describes the characteristics of the supported monitors.

fixed function controller   A graphics controller with a specific set of nonprogrammable graphics functions.

flicker   Flicker occurs when the electron gun paints the screen too slowly, giving the phosphors on the screen time to fade. As a result, the phosphors pulse lighter and darker. Flicker can cause headaches and eye strain, even if it's so slight that it can't be noticed consciously. The larger the screen, the more noticeable the flicker. A large screen fills more of the user's field of vision, thereby involving peripheral vision. Eyes are more sensitive to movement at the edges of the vision field.

fluorescence   The reaction of a phosphor to the bombardment of an electron stream.

font   A complete set of characters in a particular typeface, size, and style.

formatted   Information that's structured according to a predefined, external definition. For example, in a formatted record, name and address data would always begin at the same column, like in a checkbook register, and all the records would be the same fixed length.

frame   The total amount of instantaneous information (as perceived by the viewer) presented by a display. In two-field interlaced raster scan, a frame is the time interval between the vertical retrace at the start of the first field and the end of the second field.

frame buffer   A dedicated memory area in a computer or in a separate dedicated board, for temporary storage of pixel data to be displayed in one frame on a CRT. The depth of the frame buffer is determined by the number of bits stored for each pixel, which determines the dynamic range or number of colors and intensities that can be displayed. If ordinary memory is used as a frame buffer, it requires a video circuit (LUT-DAC) to read and display it. Sometimes referred to as the data that determines the image that's stored in the form of a bit map in the segment of display memory.

frame rate   The number of frames displayed in one second. This number varies according to broadcast standard. The NTSC standard supports a frame rate of 30 frames per second. PAL and SECAM standards support 25 frames per second. Film has a frame rate of 24 frames per second. Digital video can support a wide range of frame rates, limited only by the performance of the underlying hardware.

front porch   The portion of a composite display signal that lies between the leading edges of a horizontal blanking pulse and the corresponding sync pulse.

file transfer protocol (FTP)   A standard defined in TCP/IP used for transferring binary files between computer systems.

full motion   Video that moves at 24 to 30 frames per second is described as full motion. With speeds of 12–18 frames per second, the human eye is also able to perceive relatively smooth movement.

GFLOPS   FLOPS stands for floating-point operations per second, and G stands for giga, the scientific prefix denoting one billion. Usually pronounced ``gigaflops.'' The fastest serial computers currently have peak performances near 1 GFLOPS. *See also* MFLOPs.

gamut   The full range of colors that the human eye can see or will respond to.

generation/generation loss   The number of times an analog video signal is copied. The original, unedited video source is known as first-generation material. Edited videotape is typically second generation. Analog video and audio degrade each time they lose a generation by being copied. By contrast, digital video and audio remain a mirror image of the original no matter how many times they're copied.

genlock   A circuit used to lock the frequency of an internal sync generator to an external source.

geometric model   A mathematical representation of an object's size and shape in computer memory. Includes wire frames, surfaces, and solid models.

giga   A prefix signifying 10^9.

gigabyte   A term signifying roughly one billion bytes, also shown as Gb.

graphics   The generation of an image by a computer.

graphics adapter   An add-in board designed for driving a graphic display (i.e., monitor or LCD).

graphic input device   Components such as a mouse or joystick used for graphic data entry.

graphical user interface (GUI)   The interface between a user and a software program, which determines the way in which the user accesses the program. A GUI is a method of presenting information and system resources to a user via graphics on a CRT. Microsoft Windows and X Windows are examples of GUIs. They are used to impart a visual and tactile (through mouse controls) look and feel to the program, which is an important element to the user's perceived satisfaction. GUI software specifies the look and feel of the display screen, including how windows, scroll bars, menus, icons, and other user-interface features should look and be used. X Windows does not specify a GUI, but treats a GUI as a client. As a result, users are free to choose among GUIs, with OSF/Motif and OpenLook the most frequently used. Some efforts are being made within the software industry to standardize various graphical-interface elements.

gray level   The brightness value assigned to a pixel. A value can range from black, through gray, to white.

grayscale   The brightness available as valid gray levels for a given image processing system. The grayscale represents the discrete gray levels defined in a system—for instance, an 8-bit system includes the values from 0 through 255.

gun   The electrons that strike the screen's phosphors are generated in an electron gun that's located at the narrow end or neck of the tube. The source of the electrons is from a small piece of metal called the *cathode*. The cathode, when heated, produces a stream or ray of electrons that are attracted to the screen. The gun also contains focusing elements.

halftone   A halftone is a bilevel that's used to create the appearance of shades of gray by grouping matrices or various dot sizes to form patterns to represent different shades. Used mostly in printing, it's also used in LCD displays. *See also* bilevel.

hatching   Filling a display area with a pattern of line segments.

header   The text or graphics that appear on the top of a page, such as the chapter or section title.

hertz (Hz)   A unit of frequency equal to 1 cycle per second, which measures the vertical refresh rate. A refresh rate of 70 Hz means the screen is refreshed (repainted) 70 times per second. *See also* kilohertz and refresh rate.

high-color   Color with a displayable range of either 15 bits (32,768 colors) or 16 bits (65,536 colors).

high-definition television (HDTV)   A proposed television system with nominally twice the number of image scan lines (NTSC) as current television, i.e., 1024 lines vs. 512, giving a much sharper, higher-resolution picture. However, it has yet to be standardized, and the industry is far from a consensus (for example, the Sony system has 1125 lines).

high resolution   A relative term used to describe any screen image produced with appreciably more than the NTSC standard of a 512-line video picture. Resolution is usually described in relative number of scan lines (e.g., 2000) or by pixel ratio (e.g., 768×512), and a high-resolution image generally refers to one with a minimum of 1125 lines.

horizontal resolution   The number of pixels in one scan line of a display or the number of pixels in a display system's x value. A 1024×768 display or frame buffer has a horizontal resolution of 1024. Horizontal resolution is related to the bandwidth.

horizontal scan frequency   The number of pixels horizontally across the screen times the number of times a second they're scanned. *See also* scan rate.

hue   A color value (red, green, blue, yellow) rather than intensity or brightness.

icon   A small image that graphically represents an object, concept, function, or message on the computer screen; a graphic representation of a program, file, or system resource.

image analysis (IA)   Any image operation intended to numerically tabulate some aspect of the image.

image settings   Also referred to as *factory presets*. Most monitors provide controls for the size, position, and (sometimes) the color of the image. Most units also allow storage of the adjustments eliminating the need to adjust size and position when switching between display modes. *See also* autosizing.

indexed color   The use of a LUT to select colors from a pallet.

information   The content, amount of order, and structure in a communications or message. Its unit of measurement is the bit. A message that's apparently random or completely predictable contains little or no information; the maximum amount of information in a message is equal to less than the number of symbols in the message times the logarithm of the number of different symbols.

input device   A physical input device (e.g., a mouse, keyboard, or digitizer) that is part of a computer system.

input/output   The communications between one device and another.

integrated circuit (IC)   Complex electronic circuits fabricated within a single semiconductor crystal (typically silicon).

interactive   Interactivity describes the behavior of an application program in which a user can act on the output of the application to immediately add to, change, or remove that output.

interactive graphics   Using a CRT terminal to communicate with a computer through pictures with virtually instantaneous response to user commands.

interface   The connection between two entities. An API is a software interface. A connector is a hardware interface. A GUI is a user interface.

interlaced   A display-scanning system that interleaves the scan lines from odd to even fields to produce an image. The image in each frame is created by painting the screen with every other scan line. On the first field, all the even lines are scanned. On the second field, all the odd lines are scanned. This is done by scanning the screen from left to right/top to bottom on alternate lines 60 or more times a second. Since the human eye has a persistence of vision equal to about $\frac{1}{60}$ of a second, each field displayed appears to be visible as the next is scanned. Because the phosphors must wait longer before they are refreshed, they have more time to fade, so long-persistence phosphors are used. Interlaced monitors often have noticeable flicker. Fairly common a few years ago, interlaced monitors are considered unacceptable today. *See also* noninterlaced.

interlaced scanning   A raster-scanning process in which the raster lines that compose two or more fields are interleaved to form a single frame.

interpolation   The mathematical technique used with geometric operations when the output pixel coordinates don't land exactly on a defined pixel grid point. Interpolation divides the transformed pixel's brightness and distributes portions to the four surrounding valid pixel locations.

inches per second (IPS)   A speed measurement for plotters.

jaggies   Unwanted edges produced by lower-resolution printers or images that can appear on lines, edges, and highlights in a raster display. *See also* aliasing.

kilo   A prefix signifying 10^3.

kilobyte   A term signifying roughly 1,000 bytes, also written as K.

kilohertz (KHz)   A prefix signifying 10^3 Hz, a unit of frequency equal to 1000 cycles per second. *See also* Hertz.

LCD panel   A liquid-crystal display device that allows text and graphics on a PC to be displayed on a large screen or wall using an overhead projector as the light source.

landscape   A horizontal printing orientation.

line frequency   The number of horizontal scan lines per second, including both the visible raster lines and those that occur during the vertical-retrace intervals.

liquid-crystal display (LCD)   LCD screens are made up of liquid crystals sandwiched between two glass plates. They're typically small and flat, requiring very little power for operation.

lines per minute (lpm)   A speed measurement for line printers.

load   The process of transferring data or programs from a source to a destination.

low-color   Color with a displayable range of four bits (16 colors).

mapping   A computer-graphics technique for taking a two-dimensional image and applying (mapping) it as a surface onto a three-dimensional object. There are five main kinds of maps: a texture map, which deals with colors and textures; a bump map, which deals with physical surfaces (normal perturbation); a reflection map (or environment map), which deals with reflections; a refraction map, which deals with refractions and transparencies; and a chrome map, for airbrush chrome simulation. Maps can be mixed on most systems.

mask   A technique used in graphics programs that makes use of an opaque image to block out an area of an illustration.

mega   A prefix signifying 10^6.

megabyte   A term signifying roughly one million bytes, also Mb.

memory   Electronic storage devices.

micro   A prefix signifying 10^{-6}.

microsecond   A prefix signifying 10^{-6} seconds, μs.

micron   A prefix signifying 10^{-6} meters, 1.0μ.

milli   A prefix signifying 10^{-3}.

millisecond   A prefix signifying 10^{-3} seconds, ms.

misconvergence   The inability of a CRT to focus and position the RGB guns correctly on the phosphor triads, creating a color shadow.

moiré   An undesirable pattern created when halftone screens are improperly aligned.

MPRII   Guidelines for the emission of low-frequency electric fields, magnetic fields, and static electricity. Although there's no conclusive proof about the health dangers of monitor emissions, the MPRII guidelines are generally accepted as the most stringent safety guidelines.

multifrequency monitor   A monitor that can synchronize within a range of scan rates. *See also* multiscanning.

multiscanning   A monitor that can automatically synchronize to the display frequencies of a display controller (within a given range). A monitor that can handle a variety of sync signals. *See also* multifrequency.

nano   A prefix signifying 10^{-9}.

nanosecond   A prefix signifying 10^{-9} second, ns.

National Television Standards Committee (NTSC)   The television transmission standard formulated by the U.S. FCC, and used in the U.S., Canada, Mexico, Japan, and Korea. One of the three standards used worldwide, it supports 30 frames per second and a 525-line field and is used to identify the color-encoding method adopted by the committee in 1953. The NTSC standard was the first monochrome-compatible, simultaneous color system used for public broadcasting.

noncomposite   The red, green, blue, and sync signals used to generate a color display are provided on separate inputs and outputs.

noninterlaced   A method of refreshing the screen where every line is painted on every pass down the screen. Scanning is accomplished by displaying the odd and even lines sequentially, one after another. This has become the preferred method today. *See also* interlaced.

oscillator   An electronic device that generates a precisely timed signal. Oscillators are categorized by the frequency or Hz (signals per second) at which they output their signal.

overscanned   The practice of scanning beyond the edges of the visible area of a screen; typically done in TV to hide distortions.

packed pixel   The contiguous organization of a bit-mapped memory's pixels (the opposite of planar).

pages per minute (PPM)   A speed measurement for printers.

palette   A collection of colors from which a single color or multiple colors can be chosen. The palette is the maximum number of colors or shades possible by all combinations of brightness levels of the three primary color (RGB) outputs. The palette size is found by taking the base-2 value of the total number of bits of the outputs. A device with 8-bit outputs will produce 16,777,216 million colors.

pan   The movement of an image across or up and down a screen; moving across the x,y axis on a display screen.

pel   See *pixel.*

peripheral   Any input/output device such as a display, printer, or modem that is not a part of the main computer. A device separate from but used with a computer. Displays, mice, digitizers, printers, plotters, external hard drives, tape-backup devices, modems, and so forth are all peripherals.

persistence   The time it takes an excited phosphor to stop glowing.

phosphor   A substance that emits light when activated by an electron beam. Color monitors have phosphors that emit red, green, and blue colors, which are collectively referred to as RGB.

pica   A standard unit of typographic measurement equaling 12 points.

PICT   A standard format used for object-oriented graphics on the Macintosh.

pixel   A combined term for picture element, the smallest unit of a video display. Also known as a *pel*. Pictures on the screen are made up of hundreds of thousands of pixels, combined to form images. A pixel is the smallest segment of a raster line that can be discretely controlled by the display system, and also the coordinate used for defining the horizontal spatial location of a pixel within an image. Pixels on the monitor are the illuminated dots of glowing phosphor, the smallest element of a digital image. A pixel size can be no smaller than the spot a monitor can create. In a color monitor, spots consist of a group of triads. Triads are composed of three different phosphors: red, green, and blue. The phosphors are laid along side each other. Pixels can vary in size and shape depending on the monitor and graphics mode. The number of dots on the screen are measured in width-by-height fashion.

pixmap   A three-dimensional array of bits. A pixmap is normally thought of as a two-dimensional array of pixels, where each pixel can be a value from 0 to $2n-1$, where n is the depth (z axis) of the pixmap. A pixmap can also be thought of as a stack of n bitmaps.

pixel value   The binary value of the color and luminance of a signal pixel. Also called *color value*.

planar   The organization of display memory in bit planes. The opposite of packed pixel. *See also* bit plane and bit-mapped display.

platform   Any computer (e.g., a PC, Macintosh, or workstation).

point   A standard unit of typographic measurement, used to measure both line spacing and type. There are approximately 72 points to an inch.

port   A point or connector for access to a system. Also, the movement or creation of software to or for a platform or device.

portrait   A vertical printing orientation.

primary color   In a tristimulus color video system, one of the three colors mixed to produce an image. *See also* additive and subtractive colors.

primitives   Basic elements of a graphics display, such as points, lines, curves, polygons, spheres, cones, and alphanumeric characters.

protocol   The standard way for X clients and servers to communicate with one another. The X protocol is invisible to users.

pseudo-color   Color with a displayable range of eight bits (256 colors).

quantized (quantizer)   The conversion of continuous data into discrete components or values. *See also* analog-to-digital conversion.

random access   A method of accessing specific data quickly and directly, without following a linear sequence of locations; data that can be accessed in any order; opposite of sequential. Sectors on a disk drive can be randomly accessed; files on a tape cannot. Random access is possible only with digital data and is necessary for nonlinear editing.

random-access memory (RAM)   The internal computer read/write memory for programs and data that can be altered.

raster   An image formed by individual dots, as opposed to a vector, which supplies the beginning and end point. Most technologies for getting an image onto paper (or the computer screen) must first rasterize the image, the exceptions being pen plotters and dot-matrix printers.

raster graphics   Computer graphics in which a display image is composed of an array of pixels arranged in rows and columns.

read-only memory (ROM)   A part of the computer's memory used to permanently store programs whose contents can be read but not altered. ROM is usually used to store low-level operating routines.

real time   A recording or playing speed that shows things as they occur, between 24–30 frames per second.

real-world coordinates   Measurements expressed in the engineering units of the application.

RGB   An additive color system in which the resultant color is a function of the intensity of each primary (red, green, and blue). The best-known device that uses the RGB system is the color monitor.

reflective colors   *See* subtractive colors.

refresh rate   Also called the *frame rate, vertical scan rate,* or *vertical synchronizing frequency.* This number measures how fast the electron gun paints the image from the top of the screen to the bottom. The refresh rate is measured in Hz (hertz, or cycles per second). A refresh rate of 70 Hz repaints the screen 70 times per second. If the refresh rate is too slow, the glowing phosphors will begin to fade before they're repainted again, causing a noticeable flicker. *See also* scan rate.

rendering   The process of creating life-like images on a screen using mathematical models and formulas. The adding of shading, color, and lumination to a 2-D or 3-D wire-frame model.

resolution   The accuracy at which a parameter is divided into discrete levels. Pertinent resolutions in a computer graphics system are those of brightness, spatial, color, and frame rate.

resolution (frame buffer)   The number of pixels, represented by bits in the display memory, also known as *addressable resolution.* A display memory can be organized by pixels (bits) in the x axis (pixels per line) by the number of pixels in the y axis (lines) and by the number of memory planes in the z axis. A standard VGA display memory is 640 pixels across by 480 pixels (or lines) down, and typically 8 bits deep. The higher the resolution, the greater the detail and the more information that can be stored. Not all stored information can be displayed. *See also* pixel.

resolution (monitors)   The combination of the number of vertical and horizontal lines or pixels in a raster display device. Also known as *spatial resolution,* this term refers to how sharply an image can be defined on the screen of the CRT. Generally, the higher the numbers, the finer the display.

resolution (printers)   A measure of image sharpness, frequently in dpi. The more dots per inch, the higher the resolution. Addressable resolution refers to the shortest intervals of plotter pen movements, while mechanical resolution refers to the thickness of the pen lines.

retrace interval   The time period during which the direction of sweep is reversed and no information is displayed. Also called *return interval*.

RGB monitor   Computer color monitors display images comprised of separately controllable red, green, and blue signals, as opposed to TV displays, which use composite video. In an RGB color monitor, each of the color components (red, green, and blue) are input on separate lines. This variety of color is a function of each color signal's intensity. *See also* color monitor.

sampling   The chopping of the analog video signal into discrete values (pixels).

scaling   A function that adjusts an image to within a window.

scan rate   Also called the *scan frequency*, *line rate*, or *horizontal synchronizing rate*. Measured in KHz (kilohertz), it defines how fast the electron gun can scan each line of the screen—*n* times a second, where *n* is the refresh rate. The faster the vertical refresh rate, the faster the horizontal scan rate must be to keep up. The vertical scan rate of a raster display is much slower than the horizontal rate, by a factor of the number of lines. *See also* refresh rate.

scroll   The movement of a window's image up or down within the window.

segment   A logical definition of a set of graphics elements that are displayed, transformed, erased, or manipulated as a unit.

shadow mask   Monitors use shadow masks to keep the electron beams from overlapping where they aren't needed. A mask is a piece of metal punched with holes, so the electron beam can strike only the intended pixel. (Trinitron monitors do the same thing with an aperture grill made up of stretched wires.) Without a mask (or grill), the beam might light up adjacent pixels as well. The distance between the holes (or the slots in the grill) is the aperture pitch.

software   A program that resides on a floppy disk or hard disk. Software can be modified, damaged, and discarded by the user.

solid model   A geometric model that completely and unambiguously describes the surface edges and interior mass of an object in the computer.

spatial resolution   *See* Resolution (monitors).

sprite   A small bit map that can be laid over an image. Similar to a cursor.

stairstepping   *See* aliasing.

subtractive color   Reflected light is a subtractive process. When light is reflected off an object, colors are subtracted. Objects that don't generate their own light are described by a different set of primary colors: the subtractive primaries: cyan, yellow, and magenta, commonly referred to as CYM or CMY.

superVGA   A VGA controller capable of providing medium resolution (800×600).

sync on green   Early computer systems combined the synchronization signals (horizontal and vertical) with the green color signal. Special circuitry inside the monitor is required to use this form of video sync.

sync signal   A signal that synchronizes the scanning operation of a raster-scan monitor. It might also include a phase reference for an encoded-color monitor.

synchronization signals   These horizontal and vertical signals determine, up to a point, the size and aspect ratio of the visible raster pattern, the number of raster-generated lines displayed.

system bus   The parallel data and address lines that connect the CPU, system memory, and I/O devices.

system memory   The memory primarily associated with the CPU.

tera   A prefix signifying 10^{12}.

texture mapping   The mapping of 2-D images of textures on to the surface of a 3-D object. The 2-D image is mapped onto a 3-D surface when it's rendered by the computer. Described as the computer graphics equivalent of contact paper. *See also* bump mapping.

transformation pipeline   A pipeline is a series of mathematical operations that act on output primitives and geometric attributes to convert them from modeling coordinates to device coordinates.

transition   Connections between one scene and another, including cuts, wipes, dissolves, and special optical effects.

transmitted color   *See* additive colors.

triad   A pattern of three phosphor colors, RGB, put on the screen in a dot pattern called a *dot triad*. The arrangement of the three color dots physically matches the orientation of the three guns in the CRT.

tristimulus   The method of color generation that uses three primary colors or three color signals for image transmission and reproduction.

true color   Color with a displayable range of either 24 bits (16.7 million colors). Also called *full color*.

turnkey system   A ready-to-use computer system in which the vendor is responsible for installation, testing, and servicing the entire hardware/software package.

typeface   A letter form specifically designed to be made into words and sentences by mechanical means. More than just an alphabet.

undersampling   The sampling of an analog video signal at a rate less than that required to resolve a given spatial frequency.

unwrapped   The compression of a single line of raster.

user interface   A system by which information is exchanged between the user and the computer.

vector graphics   The branch of computer graphics that deals with line drawings. Images are represented as line segments (vectors) rather than as shaded images.

vector mode   A vector, or stroke, mode of display used to generate line segments from pairs of specified endpoints. CAD drawings are usually displayed in this mode. Vector mode is usually implemented on raster systems through software that illuminates specified pixels lying along a prescribed line segment.

vector-to-raster converter   The VRC is the circuitry in any printer or plotter that converts vector plotter data into raster information for printing using a technique such as dot matrix, electrostatic, ink jet, or thermal transfer. Pen plotters plot vectors and don't require a VRC. However, many CAD packages have facilities for rasterizing the drawing for a variety of printers.

vertical resolution   The ability of the monitor to display horizontal lines from top to bottom.

vertical retrace   The return of the electron beam to the top of the CRT screen at the start of each field or frame interval.

video   The signals associated with a TV-generated image or transmission. Video is another name commonly used for TV. It is also incorrectly used to describe a computer-generated signal or image.

video bandwidth   *See* bandwidth.

video adapter board   A misnomer for a graphics-controller board, which can be confusing when video (TV) is part of a system. *See also* display controller.

video image   The electronic representation of an image created by a video camera. Not the same as a computer-generated image.

video sync   The video display must be synchronized with the input video signal. This assures that the input image (from camera or computer) will match the output seen by the viewer. Two separate signals are required.

wire-frame model   A geometric model that represents an object's bounding edges with interconnected line elements. Also called *edge-vertex* or *stick-figure model*.

window   A rectangular area on the display screen.

world coordinates   The coordinates used to describe objects and places, expressed in conventional units (e.g., meters and inches).

workstation   An assembled set of computer components that include (as a minimum) a CPU, system memory, a display controller, disk subsystems, and a LAN controller.

wrapped   When a compression algorithm continues the compression operation after reaching the end of a line, it is referred to as wrapped. A single-line compression is unwrapped.

yoke   *See* deflection yoke.

Z buffer   A technique used to provide hidden-surface removal. It calculates the depth of a pixel, as shading or other scan conversion is taking place, and paints it only if it covers an already painted pixel.

zoom   The enlargement of an image, this can be done by pixel replication or recalculation. Also, scaling a display screen area so it's magnified or reduced in size.

AAM   Active-address method

AC-TEL   Alternating-current thin-film electroluminescent

ADC   Analog-to-digital converter

AMDP   Active-matrix display panels

AMEL   Active-matrix electroluminescent

AM-LCD   Active-matrix LCD

AM-LCD-MIM   Metal-insulator-metal

AM-LCD-PDLC   Polymer-dispersed liquid crystal

AM-LCD-TFT   Thin-film transistor, *aka* TFT-LCD, AM-TFT, and TFT-LC

ANSI   American National Standards Institute

ASCII   American standard code for information interchange

ASIC   Application-specific integrated circuit

ATC   Air-traffic control

AVGA   Accelerated VGA

BBS   Bulletin-board system

BCS   Broadcast color system

bpp   Bits per pixel

bps   bits per second

CAD   Computer-aided design

CADD   CAD and drafting

CAE   Computer-aided engineering

CAM   Computer-aided manufacturing

CAS   Computer-aided software

CCD   Charge-coupled device

CCFT   Cold-cathode fluorescent tubes

CdS   cadmium sulfide

CdSe   cadmium selenide

CGA   Computer-graphics adapter

CGI   Computer-graphics interface

CGM   Computer-graphics metafile

CIE Commission International de'Eclairange

CLT Color lookup table

CMOS Complementary metal-oxide semiconductor

CMYK Cyan, magenta, yellow, and black

cpi Characters per inch

cps Characters per second

CPU Central processing unit

CRT Cathode-ray tube

CRTC CRT controller

CVP Chemical vapor deposition

DAC Digital-to-analog converter

DARPA Defense Advanced Research Projects Agency

DC Device coordinate

DCEL Direct-current electroluminescent

DCP Device-color profile

DOS Disk-operating system

dpi Dots per inch

DRAM Dynamic RAM

DSP Digital-signal processor

DSTN Double supertwist nematic

DTP Desktop publishing

EGA Enhanced graphic adapter

EISA Extended ISA

EL Electroluminescent

EL-TFEL Thin-film electroLuminescent, *aka* ACTFEL

EPROM Electronically programmable ROM

EVGA Extended VGA

FCC Federal Communications Agency

FEA Finite element analysis

FED Field-emission display, *aka* MFD (microtip fluorescent display)

FE-LCD Ferroelectric liquid-crystal display

FIFO First in, first out

FLCD Ferroelectric LCD

FSTN   Film-compensated supertwist nematic

FTP   File-transfer protocol (defined in TCP/IP)

GA   Graphic arts

GUI   Graphical user interface

HDTV   High-definition TV

HGC   Hercules graphics controller (adapter)

HLS   Hue, lightness, and saturation

HSI   Hue, saturation, and intensity

HSV   Hue, saturation, and value

HVC   Hue, value, and chroma

I/O   Input/output

IC   Integrated circuit

IEEE   International Electrical and Electronics Engineers

ips   inches per second

ISA   Industry-standard adapter (also, Instrument Society of America)

ISO   International Standards Organization

LCD   Liquid-crystal display

LCD-FLCD   Ferroelectric LCD, *aka* FELCD

LCD-FSTN   Film-compensated supertwisted nematic, *aka* DSTN and double STN

LCD-STN   Supertwisted nematic, *aka* STN-LCD and TN twisted nematic

LCD-TSTN   Triple supertwisted nematic, *aka* stacked STN-LCD

LED   Light-emitting diode

lpi   Lines per inch

lpm   Lines per minute

LR   Low resolution

LUT   Look-up table

MAC   Macintosh computer

MAC   multiplexed analogue components

MDA   Monochrome display adapter

MFD   Microtip fluorescent display

MIPS   Millions of instructions per second

MOSFET   Metal-oxide semiconductor field-effect transistor

MPC Multimedia PC

MPU   Main (or micro-) processing unit (same as CPU)

MR   Medium resolution

MTBF   Mean time between failure

MUSE   NHK's HDTV

NAB   National Association of Broadcasters

NBS   National Bureau of Standards

NCGA   National Computer Graphics Association

NHK   Japan Broadcasting Corp.

NIST   National Institute of Science and Technology (formally NBS)

NTSC   National Television Standards Committee

OLUT   Output LUT

OS   Operating system

PAL   Phase alternate-line method

PALC   Plasma-addressed liquid crystal

PC   Personal computer

PDP   Plasma display panel

PLV   Presentation-level video

PM-LCD   Passive-matrix LCD

PMS   Pantone matching system

R & D   research and development

RAM   Random-access memory

RAMDAC   Random-access memory digital-to-analog converter

RGB   Red, green, blue

RGBA   RGB, alpha

RLE   Run-length encoder

ROM   Read-only memory

ROPS   Raster operations

RTSD   Reflective-type, three-electrode surface-discharge technique

RTV   Real-time video

SECAM   Sequential couleur a memoire

SHR   Super high resolution

SIGGRAPH   Special Interest Group on Graphics (ACM)

Si   amorphous silicon

SiN   silicon nitride

SiO   silicon oxide

SIP   Scientific image processing

SSF   Surface-stabilized ferroelectric liquid-crystal display

STN   Super TN

SVGA   SuperVGA

SVHS   Super VHS

TFEL   Thick-film electroluminescent

TN   Twisted nematic

TSR   Terminate and stay resident

UV   ultraviolet

VDIG   Video digitizer

VESA   Video Electronics Standards Associations

VFD   Vacuum fluorescent

VFW   Video for windows

VGA   Video graphics array (also video graphics adapter)

VHR   Very high resolution

VLSI   Very large-scale integration

VRAM   Video RAM

VRC   Vector-to-raster converter

WYSIWYG   What you see is what you get

XCMS   X color-management system

XGA   Extended graphics adapter

YIQ   Luminance and chroma (TV)

YUV   Luminance and chroma

References

Anderson, Bruce. "Making the Video-Computer Connection." *Computer Graphics Review* (July 1990): 48.

Argiro, Vincent and Van Zandt, William. "Voxels: Data in 3-D." *Byte* (May 1992): 177.

Blinn, J. *Raster Graphics, Tutorial: Computer Graphics* (edited by Kellogg Booth). IEEE.

Blume, Hartwig. "Very-High Resolution Monochrome CRT Displays: How Good Are They Really?" *Society for Information Display International Symposium Digest of Technical Papers* XXII (May 6-10, 1991): 335.

Brown, Michael. *Desktop Video Production.* New York: Windcrest/McGraw-Hill, 1991.

Cavigioli, Chris. "Image Compression: Spelling out the Options." *Advanced Imaging* (October 1990): 64.

Chiyokura, Hiroaki. *Solid Modeling with Designbase.* New York: Addison-Wesley, 1988.

Clifford, Peter and Ward, Michael. "The End of Dedicated Prepress?" *Personal Workstation* (January 1991): 40.

Foley, J. and van Dam, A. *Computer Graphics: Principles and Practice, 2nd ed.* Reading, MA: Addison-Wesley, 1990.

"Getting Results with CADD," Autodesk, 1992.

Glassner, Andrew S. *3D Computer Graphics: A User's Guide for Artists and Designers.* New York: Design Press, 1989.

Hall, George M. *Image Processing.* New York: McGraw-Hill, 1991.

Johnson, Peter. "From Computer to Page." *Computer Graphics World* (January 1990): 28.

Jones, O. *Introduction to the X Window System.* Englewood Cliffs, NJ: Prentice Hall, 1989.

Khoury, Joseph and Ramm, Peter, "A New Generation of Bio Image Analysis Systems." *Advanced Imaging* (February 1991): 28.

Lemke, D. and Rosenthal, D. "Visualizing X11 Clients, Proceedings of the Summer." 1988 USENIX Conference.

Machover, Carl. *C4 Handbook: CAD, CAM, CAE, CIM.* New York: TAB/McGraw-Hill, 1989.

Meyers, Janet. "New Advancements Enhance Image Analysis." *Computer Graphics Review* (May 1990): 28.

Peddie, Jon. "Display List Processing in the PC." *ComputerWorld* (October, 1988).

Peddie, Jon. *Graphical User Interfaces and Graphics Standards.* New York: McGraw-Hill, 1992.

Chapter 1

Peddie, Jon. "Trends: The Very High Resolution Market." *Computer Graphics Today* (August 1988).

Pimentel, Ken and Kevin, Teixeira. *Virtual Reality*, New York: Windcrest/McGraw-Hill, 1992.

Scheifler, R. and Gettys, H. *X Window System, 3rd ed.* Burlington, MA: Digital Press, 1992.

Shoup, R. "Color Table Animation." SIGGRAPH '79 Conference Proceedings, ACM, New York.

Wallace, John, and Fujii, John. "Radiosity." *Byte* (May 1992): 173.

Weiss, Miles and Freiherr, Greg. "All Eyes on Planet Earth." *Computer Graphics World* (November 1989): 36.

Yarmolich, Paul. "Desktop Animation Becomes a Reality." *Computer Graphics Review* (July 1990): 10.

Chapter 2

Burger, Jeff. "Seven Steps to Color Sense." *New Media* (May 1992) 49.

DuFlon, Ray. "Color Display Systems Achieve Color Consistency." *Computer Technology Review* (Summer 1990): 113.

Geldard, Frank A. *The Human Senses*. New York: John Wiley & Sons, Inc., 1972.

Hubel, David H. *Eye, Brain, and Vision*. Scientific American Library, 1988.

Hunt, R. W. G. *The Reproduction of Color in Photography, Printing and Television*. Tolworth, UK: Fountain Press, 1987.

Kasson, James and Plouffe, Wil. "An Analysis of Selected Computer Interchange Color Spaces." *acm Transactions on Graphics* (October 1992): 373.

Land, Edwin H. "Color Vision and the Natural Image, parts I and II." *Proceedings of the National Academy of Sciences* 45 (1959): 115-129 and 639-644.

Montgomery, Geoffrey. "The Mind's Eye." *Discover* (May 1991): 50.

Motta, Ricardo J. "Color Encoding Computer Images." *Information Displays* (March 1991): 4.

Murch, Gerald M. "Standards for Color Displays and Output Devices: Background and Issues." *CAD & Engineering Workstations '92 and Business Graphics '92*. 13th Annual Conference & Exposition, National Computer Graphics Association (9-12 March, 1992): 658.

Murch, Gerald M. "Color Displays and Color Science." in John Durrent's *Color and the Computer*. Orlando, FL: Academic Press, 1987.

Norman, Richard B. "The Emotion of Color." *Plan & Print* (March 1991): 32.

Oliverio, Barbara. "The ABCs, RGBs, and CMYs of Color Image Processing." *MicroCAD News* (March 1990): 64.

Reis, Charles. 'Exact' Color Matching: What Who Sees? What Who Gets?" *Advanced Imaging* (October 1990): 8.

Reis, Charles. "Toward Real Two-Channel Color: New Approach to an Old Problem." *Advanced Imaging* (February 1991): 52.

Rice, John. "Show Me Your True Colors." *AV Video* (November 1991): 12.

Taylor, Joann M. and Tabayoyon, Al. "The TekHVC Color Space: A Device-Independent Color Model for Use In the X Window System." *Xhibtion 90* 21-24 (May 1990): 13.

Young, Richard A. "Principal-Component Analysis of Human Cone Spectra." Address, Optical Society of America, Rochester, NY (October 1987).

Chapter 3

Adachi, O., Wakasono, H., Kitagawa, O., Konosu, O., and Ashizaki, S. "Super-Flat-Face Large-Size-Screen Color CRT." *Society for Information Display International Symposium Digest of Technical Papers* XXII (May 6-10, 1991): 37.

"ANSI/HFS 100." Human Factors Society, Santa Monica, CA (1988).

Bechis, Dennis J. "CRT Technology Survey." *Information Display* (December 1991): 8.

Bedford, Bill. "High Resolution Monitors Emerge To Meet Advanced Graphics Needs." *Computer Technology Review* (Spring 1990): 95.

Compton, Ken. "Electron Guns for CRT Displays." *Information Display* (June 1989): 14.

Conrac Corporation's *Raster Graphics Handbook*. New York: Van Nostrand Reinhold Company, 1985.

Dasgupta, Bassab B. "Deflection and Convergence Technology." Society for Information Display seminar lecture notes (May 6-10, 1991): M-4.

Eccles, David and Sandoval, Gregory. "High Resolution CRT Monitors: Beyond High Definition." Stanford Resources Information Display Monitor Conference (March 26-27, 1991).

Farrell, Joyce E., Casson, Evanne J., Haynie, Carl R., and Benson, Brian L. "Designing Flicker-Free Video Display Terminals." *Displays Technology and Applications* (July 1988): 115.

Geldard, Frank A. *The Human Senses*. New York: John Wiley & Sons, 1972.

Infante, Carlo. "On the Resolution of Raster-Scanned CRT Displays." *Proceedings of the SID* 26, no. 1 (1985).

Infante, Carlo. "CRTs: Present and Future." *Information Display* (December 1988): 8.

Infante, Carlo. "Numerical Methods for Computing Modulation Transfer-Function Area." *Displays* (April 1991): 80.

Lehman, Fred. "CRT Monitors for the 1990s." *Information Display* (April 1990): 6.

Liberman, David. "The CRT: Still King of the Displays." *Electronic Engineering Times* (July 16, 1990): 40.

MacNaughton, Boyd. "What to Look for When Choosing Your High Res Display." *Advanced Imaging* (September 1991): 34.

Masterman, Hugh C. "Desiging Standards-Compliant Monitors: Where Are the Problems?" *Information Display* (August 1991): 13.

Maxwell, Conrad A. "Acceptable Image Quality for Color VGA." *Information Display* (June 1991): 8.

Moscony, John J., Matthies, Dennis L., and Nosker, Richard W. "The Evolution of the Shadow-Mask Tube." *Information Display* (January 1991): 6.

Peddie, Jon G. "High Resolution: How Much is Enough?" *MicroCAD News* (October 1989): 47.

"Resolution Specifications and Measurements for Color CRT Monitors." May 31, 1990: Sony Corporation of America, Precision Graphics Division.

Rosen, Brian. "Matching Specs to Pixels." *Electronic Engineering Times* (July 31, 1989): 44.

Seiter, Charles. "24-bit Monitors Fast and Functional." *Macworld* (January 1992): 124.

Smith, Bud. "How Exactly Do Pictures Get on Screen?" *Personal Workstation* (October 1990). 42.

Tyler, Christopher W. *The 120 Hz Interlace Option: A Flicker-Free Future for Video*

Displays. San Francisco, CA: Smith-Kettlewell Institute for Visual Sciences.

van Raalte, John A. "CRTs for High-Definition Television." *Information Display* (January 1992): 6.

Chapter 4   Brody, Peter T. "Active-Matrix TFTs Are in Trouble: Cadmium Selenide Is the Answer." *Information Display* (February 2, 1992): 5.

Buzak, Thomas S. "Switching Pixels with Gas." *Information Display* (October 1990): 7.

Conner, A.R. and Johnson, T.R. "Multicolor Display Using Two STN Layers" *SID 92 Digest* (May 1992): 236-238.

Connor, Arlie R. "Active Addressing for High-Performance Passive-Matrix LCDs." *Information Display* (October 10, 1992): 11.

Fujiwara, Okumura H. "A New Low-Image-Lag Drive Method for Large-Size LCTVs." *Society For Information Display International Symposium Digest of Technical Papers* XXIII (May 1992): 601.

Gottschalk, Mark A. "The Many Faces of Display Technology." *Design News* (March 8, 1992): 55.

Heilmeier, G. H., Zanoni, L. A., and Barton, L. A. "Dynamic Scattering: A New Electroptic Effect in Certain Classes of Neumatic Liquid Crystals." *Proceeding of the IEEE* No. 56 (1968): 1162.

Howard, W. E. "Thin-Film-Transistor/Liquid-Crystal-Display Technology: An Introduction." *IBM Journal of Research and Development* 36, no. 1 (January 1992): 3.

Leroux, T., Ghis, A., Meyer, R., and Sarrasin, D. "Microtips Displays Addressing." *Society For Information Display International Symposium Digest of Technical Papers* XXII (May 1991): 601.

Liberman, David. "Color EL Takes a New Tack." *Electronic Engineering Times* (April 20, 1992): 31.

Liberman, David. "Picture-Perfect Pixels." *Display Devices* no. 6 (Fall 1992): C20.

Lowe, A. C. and Pleshko, P. "Microtip field-Emission Display Performance Consideration." *Society For Information Display International Symposium Digest of Technical Papers* XXIII (May 1992): 523.

Patel, Jay S. and Werner, Ken. "Ferroelectrics: Ready for Prime Time?" *Information Display* (October 10, 1992): 14.

Pleshko, Peter. "Halftone Gray Scale for Matrix-Addressed Displays." *Information Display* (October 1990): 10.

Schadt, M. and Helfrich, W. "Voltage-Dependent Optical Activity of a Twisted Neumatic Liquid Crystal." *Applied Physics Letters* no. 18 (1971): 127.

Uchida, Tatsuo. "Flat-Panel Display Technology Meets Many Needs." *Display Devices* no. 6 (Fall 1992): 12.

Woodward Sr., Ollie C. and Long, Tom. "Display Technologies." *Byte* (July 1992): 159.

Woolnough, Roger. "Microtips Tech May Spawn a Flat CRT." *Electronic Engineering Times* (January 14, 1991): 35.

Young, Richard A. "Getting More for Less: A New Opponent Color Technique for Two-Channel Color Displays." SPIE Proceedings 1250: Perceiving, Measuring and Using Color (1990).

Young, Richard A., Traxel, John R., Smith, George W., and Vaz, Nuno. "New Techniques for Two-Channel Color Displays Using Liquid Crystals." Address, Optical Society of America, Orlando, FL (Oct. 15-20, 1989).

How to Speak Imaging. Unisys Corporation, 1990.

Microcad News, June 1990.

Multimedia: A Glossary Intel Corporation, 1991.

Pixel Handbook. Judson Rosenbush, Pixel Vision, 1989).

Raster Graphics Handbook. Conrac Corporation, 1980.

The Imaging Glossary, Telecom Library, 1991

Video Glossary, Presentation Products Magazine. November 1989.

Glossary

ergonomics, 184-185
future technology, 175-179
HDTV, 178
history, 108-113
IDIOM I, **110**
image, 139-140
image quality, **114**
input signals, 179-184
interlaced scanning system, **133**, 133-134
jagged displays, 169-170
large-screen displays, **177**, 177-178, **179**
monochrome, 87-88, 164-165
noninterlaced displays, 134
power consumption, 186-187
power supply, 139-140
productivity and, 173-174, **174**
raster scanning, **132**
refresh rate, 134, **135**, 135-136
resolution vs. refresh rate vs. scan rate, **136**
safety, 185-186
scan rates, 136-137
specifications, **161**, **187**
storage-tube display, 110-111
units of measurement, 171, **187**
vector-refreshed displays, 109-110
visible resolution, 174, **175**, 175
visual acuity, **167**, 167, **168**, 168-169
monochrome, 87-88, 164-165
monoliths, 219
Moss, Hillary, 148
motion picture experts group (MPEG), 57, 60-62
for VFW, 64
MTF (*see* modulation-transfer function)
multimedia, 1, 56-58
IBM and, 58
standards, 57-58
Munsell color chart, 84-85

N

National Press Photographers Association (NPPA), 41
National Television System Committee (NTSC), 84
color bar specification, **104**

Newton, Isaac, 68
nonlinear response characteristic, 92-94

O

object ordering, 49
object panning, 26
off-screen pixel map, 55
OLF (*see* overlapping field lens)
optical filters, 130
optical-mode interference LCDs, 198
oscilloscope, 110
overlapping field lens (OLF), 148
overlay boards, 59
overlay planes, 55
overscans, 164

P

PALC (*see* plasma-addressed liquid-crystal)
panning, 26-27
hardware control, 27
object, 26
software control, 27
view-port, 26
PANTONE color system, 85
passive-matrix (PM), 196-199, **200**
phosphor, **116**, 116-117, **117**
phosphor compound, 92
phosphor pigmentation, 157
photographic processing, resolution, 7
photorealism, 42-43
PhotoYCC, 102
picell, **202**
pixels, **88**, 171, 192
off-screen map, 55
replication, 22-23
value, 53
plasma discharge display, **205**, 205-206, **207**, 207
characteristics, 206
large color, 207, **208**
types, 206
plasma-addressed liquid-crystal (PALC), 202-203
PLV (*see* production-level video)
polarized filters, 130-131
power consumption, monitors, 186-187

prepress, 7, 37
price (*see* purchasing concerns)
production-level video (PLV), 62
projectors, 219
propagation speed, 69
pseudo color, 89
purchasing concerns, 5-6
brands, 5
discriminatory buyers, 5
price, 5, 6
specialist buyers, 5

Q

QuickTime, 61
QuickTime for windows, 61-62

R

radiosity, 43-44
raster operations, 28-56
ray casting, 48
ray tracing, 43
real-time video (RTV), 62
red green blue (RGB), 71, 144
color system, **81**, 81
phosphor dots, **88**
reflections, 185
rendering, vs. modeling, 44-48
resolution, 6-10
addressable, 9
bandwidth vs., **141**
color, **8**, 8-9
color monitor, 158, **159**, 159-161
desktop publishing, 7
displayable, 9-10, 171-172, **172**
graphic arts, 7
halftones, 7-10
high, 165, **166**, 166-167, **170**
image processing, 7
line-width measurement, **159**
most common, **10**
photographic processing, 7
pixel, 171
prepress, 7
productivity and, **21**
spatial, 9
vector operations and, 20-22
visible, 174, **175**, 175
rhodopsin, 71
RTV (*see* real-time video)
rubberbanding, 15

Look for These and Other Windcrest/McGraw-Hill Books at Your Local Bookstore

To Order Call Toll Free 1-800-822-8158
(24-hour telephone service available.)

or write to Windcrest/McGraw-Hill, Blue Ridge Summit, PA 17294-0840.

Title	Product No.	Quantity	Price

☐ Check or money order made payable to Windcrest/McGraw-Hill

Charge my ☐ VISA ☐ MasterCard ☐ American Express

Acct. No. _____ Exp. _____

Signature: _____

Name: _____

Address: _____

City: _____

State: _____ Zip: _____

Subtotal $ _____

Postage and Handling
($3.00 in U.S., $5.00 outside U.S.) $ _____

Add applicable state and local
sales tax $ _____

TOTAL $ _____

Windcrest/McGraw-Hill catalog free with purchase; otherwise send $1.00 in check or money order and receive $1.00 credit on your next purchase.

Orders outside U.S. must pay with international money in U.S. dollars drawn on a U.S. bank.

Windcrest/McGraw-Hill Guarantee: If for any reason you are not satisfied with the book(s) you order, simply return it (them) within 15 days and receive a full refund.